Journalism Today

ITS DEVELOPMENT

AND

PRACTICAL APPLICATIONS

Journalism Today

ITS DEVELOPMENT AND PRACTICAL APPLICATIONS

THOMAS ELLIOTT BERRY

Professor of English, State Teachers College
West Chester, Pennsylvania

CHILTON COMPANY—BOOK DIVISION

Publishers

Philadelphia and New York

Preface

This book is intended as a basic text for the survey course in journalism. Its purpose is to give the student a broad yet incisive picture of the most important phases of the newspaper world and of the essentials of journalism. Every attempt has been made to arrange the material in a clear, logical order so that the student can locate it readily. Thus the book should serve both as a text and as a handbook.

In writing this book the author has gone directly to the newspaper world. He has drawn on his own experiences as a full-time, professional newspaperman on one of America's largest dailies and on his free-lance work for several other large dailies and magazines. But, even more important, he has had the advice and the assistance of some of America's leading journalists. Added to this personal experience and professional assistance are the author's findings as a college teacher of journalism. As a result, he hopes that he has written a book that will satisfy the most critical of newspapermen and professors of journalism.

Although the student will probably gain most from a study of the chapters in their present order, such a procedure need not be followed. Individual class needs may well dictate another arrangement. The author strongly suggests, however, that the material on the news story be covered before any later chapter is studied.

For genuinely appreciated help in one or more of the major phases of this work, the author wishes to thank the following: his colleagues in the Department of English at West Chester; his brother, Sam Berry, Jr.; and the staff of the Chilton Book Division.

T. E. B.

Contents

Contents

The History of Journalism

Chapter **1** | Introduction

As we stand in the pressroom of the large metropolitan daily watching the 64-page paper roll smoothly off the big cylinders, we find ourselves wondering how society could ever exist without the newspaper. The newspaper, we say, is a necessity; it fills a great need. It keeps us informed on the leading questions of the day and it provides amusement, entertainment, and edification. How could we live comfortably without it? Yet the newspaper as we know it is a comparatively recent development, and the history of journalism is filled with struggles, dark days, and triumphs, presenting all in all a highly interesting study.

Although news sheets and news books were printed in England as early as 1621, printing did not begin in America until 1638, when the first press was set up in Cambridge, Massachusetts, under the watchful eyes of the Harvard College authorities. Under strict supervision, the printers turned out sermons, a catechism, a psalter, law books, almanacs, and broadsides. When a second press was established beside the first, a Bible was printed in one of the Indian dialects. One can almost see the diligent college authorities, filled with the importance of their mission, watching over the activity of this contraption which they felt could save or ruin the world. As other presses appeared in the New World, the same kind of control was invoked. Small wonder, then, that although the first printing press appeared in America in 1638, 52 years were to pass before the first American newspaper was born. Behind this paper lies a very interesting story.

The publisher, Benjamin Harris, had been editor of a Whig newspaper in London, but because of a severe brush with the law, for which he served a prison term, he emigrated to America where he took up residence in Boston as a bookseller and printer of such safe writings as almanacs and primers. His old desire to print a newspaper, however, reasserted itself, and on September 25, 1690, he came forth with a publication called *Publick Occurrences Both Forreign and Domestick*. He promised to issue his paper "once a moneth (or if any Glut of Occurrences happen, oftener)." In size, the paper was 6 x 9½ inches. It had four pages, but only three were used for printed matter—the fourth was left blank for the reader to use for personal correspondence when he mailed the paper. Little did Harris realize, as his dream of a newspaper became a reality, that his enterprise would be short-lived. Four days later, the Governor and the Council issued a statement in which they not only suppressed the paper, but also condemned it for printing some gossip about the King of France and for criticizing the government for a phase of its conduct of the French and Indian War. Thus, after just one issue, America's first paper came to an end for exercising that which the press now views as its most sacred right—the right of freedom of speech. In suppressing the paper, the Governor and the Council declared that the printing had been done "without the least Privity or Countenance of Authority." This action, of course, served as a warning that the government meant to control printing, and, since it was the first of its kind in America, it established a precedent.

THE BOSTON NEWS-LETTER

Not for almost 14 years did another paper make an appearance in America. Then, on April 24, 1704, John Campbell, Scottish postmaster of Boston, founded the *Boston News-Letter*, the first continually published newspaper in America— a paper that lasted for 72 years under four successive owners. The *News-Letter* was a single sheet, slightly larger than *Publick Occurrences*, with printing on both sides. Two thirds of its news was taken from London papers, while the remainder told of such local occurrences as the arrival of ships, deaths, and storms. In its first six years, the paper suspended publication twice, once for two months and once for eight months. The principal reason was financial, for many colonists considered a newspaper a luxury.

When Campbell lost his position as postmaster of Boston, his successor, William Brooker, claimed that the paper should be the property of whoever held the office. When Campbell refused to relinquish the *News-Letter*, Brooker was indignant, and on December 21, 1719, he started as a rival a news weekly, the *Boston Gazette*. The next year, Brooker was discharged as postmaster, and, strange as it seems, he handed his paper over to his successor. Thus begun, the tradition of having this paper published by the postmaster became fairly well established, for it was duly passed on, being published altogether by five different postmasters, beginning with Brooker. This paper survived until 1741, when it was merged with the *New-England Weekly Journal.*

THE NEW-ENGLAND COURANT

When the *Gazette* was edited by Brooker, it was printed by James Franklin, elder brother of the famous statesman, Benjamin, who at this time was the apprentice boy in the printing shop. Brooker's successor, however, decided to take his paper to another shop, and so Franklin, encouraged by men in opposition to the government of the province, began the *New-England Courant.* With the appearance of the first issue on August 7, 1721, a chapter was written in the history of American journalism, for the *Courant* was a pioneer in two important fields.

First, it was a new departure in American journalism because of its witty, lively, and frequently breezy coverage of items heretofore ignored as newsworthy. "The main Design of this Weekly Paper," it once read editorially, "will be to entertain the Town with the most comical and diverting Incidents of Humane Life, which in so large a Place at Boston, will not fail of a universal Exemplification." In its efforts "to entertain the Town," it became the first paper in America to publish letters, essays, and verse, and thus was a distinct relief from the stodgy quality of its predecessors. But second, and more important, the *Courant* is significant as the first American newspaper to speak out openly and freely without fear of offending the government.

The first important issue on which the *Courant* opposed the government was the question of inoculation against smallpox. (The *Courant* opposed the practice.) But the wrath of the authorities was aroused more by the continual criticism, sometimes subtle, sometimes open, of practically every colonial institution. In all matters, the *Courant* spoke forth frankly and pointedly, though not always wisely.

Historically, the *Courant* is also important because throughout the greater part of the year 1722 it printed Benjamin Franklin's famous "Dogood Papers." The story of their appearance is interesting, indeed. Young Ben, the apprentice boy, feeling the urge to do some of the humorous writing to which the paper was committed, was hampered by the fact that his brother, knowing the source, would be prejudiced. The ingenious Ben therefore assumed the pseudonym "Silence Dogood" and slipped his work under the print-shop door at night. The editors were delighted with the work, and one can imagine the restrained glee of young Ben as he set type for his own writing. The articles, which appeared every two weeks, kept the editors of the *Courant* guessing at the identity of the learned and talented Bostonian who was submitting them surreptitiously. When Ben finally revealed his identity, the elder Franklin was not at all pleased and the series came to an abrupt end.

Eventually, however, the *Courant* did what many a sage citizen had predicted—it ventured too far in criticizing the government. The facts were these: pirates had been engaging in their unlawful activity just off the coast, and finally, when some pirate ships were sighted just off Newport, the *Courant* and the populace became incensed. The governor promised immediate action, but there were citizens who had long suspected a secret agreement between the pirates and the governor. The *Courant*, aware of the situation, duly reported the presence of the pirates and the promise of the governor in a manner that was too thinly veiled. Said they, "We are advised from Boston that the Government of the Massachusetts are fitting out a Ship, to go after the Pirates, to be commanded by Captain Peter Papilon, and 'tis thought he will sail some time this Month, wind and weather permitting." One does not need any great powers of discernment to observe the sarcasm in this passage, nor to realize that its ridicule was not pleasing to the ruling powers. Franklin was brought before the Council the next day, and for this indiscretion, plus an attitude that did not flatter the Council, he found himself in prison.

Franklin was imprisoned for one month, but during his enforced retirement the tone of the *Courant* did not alter. It was just as critical and just as outspoken as ever. After his release, there was considerable discussion of the case, an indication that even at this early period the people were considering the question of freedom of the press. Franklin's freedom from the heavy hand of the government did not last long, however, for the following year, when writing offensive to the government and to the ministers of religion appeared in his paper, he became the object of a ruling by the General Court: "That James Franklin the Printer and Publisher thereof, be strictly forbidden by this Court to Print or Publish the New-England Courant, or any Pamphlet or Paper of the like Nature, except it be first supervised by the Secretary of this Province." Nevertheless, Franklin was not silenced. By virtue of a ruse in which he substituted the name of his brother, Benjamin, in the masthead, the *Courant* carried on for over three years. Its tone became quieter, however, and it faded from existence sometime in 1726.

OTHER COLONIAL PAPERS

During this colonial period, several other historically important papers were established. One of the most significant was the *American Weekly Mercury*, which appeared in

Philadelphia on December 22, 1719. This paper, the first established outside of Boston, was well written and fairly inclusive, especially for the times. Its publisher was Andrew Bradford, who wrote a spirited defense of James Franklin when the latter faced court. This action, prompted in part by Bradford's own difficulty with the authorities, undoubtedly helped in the struggle for a free press.

The first paper published in New York was the work of William Bradford, father of the Philadelphia publisher. His paper, however, which appeared on November 8, 1725, under the title of the *New-York Gazette*, was little more than an official publication. Helped along by the government, it survived for eight years. A far more significant publication was the *New-York Weekly Journal*, founded November 5, 1733. This paper was highly important for three reasons: (1) by virtue of upholding the right of the people for a free government, it set going the discussion that culminated in the Declaration of Independence; (2) in its opposition to the *Boston Gazette*, which supported the government, it occasioned the first battle of newspapers in America; and (3) when its publisher, John Peter Zenger, was charged with printing libelous statements, his lawyer, Andrew Hamilton, established two points having a far-reaching effect on journalism: (a) that the truth or falsity of any libelous statement must be proved (hence, true statements may be printed) and (b) that a newspaper must be allowed to criticize the government.

The first paper in America to attempt publication at intervals shorter than a week was Benjamin Franklin's *Pennsylvania Gazette*. This paper was a continuation of a work entitled *The Universal Instructor in all Arts and Sciences; and Pennsylvania Gazette* which was begun by Samuel Keimer on December 24, 1728. Keimer, facing failure, sold his paper to Franklin after only nine months, and Franklin made the experiment of publishing twice a week. After a short time, however, he reverted to the weekly schedule. A deeper significance of this paper lies in the fact that it contained some of the best prose of its publisher, one of the great literary masters.

SOURCE OF NEWS IN EARLY AMERICAN PAPERS

The early American conception of news was sharply different from that of today. We complain if our modern paper carries a story that has appeared in a previous issue of another paper; but the reader of the colonial paper found himself perusing news that was six months old. In fact, the colonists held two conceptions of the function of the newspaper—that of a publication to dispense news and that of a publication to discuss recent history. Thus, the colonial newspaper was a strange mixture of news, both new and old, and assorted appraisals and narrations of moments in history as well.

News gathering was complicated for the colonial paper by the fact that the greatest source of news was not America but England. The ties with the homeland were still so strong that the colonists were most interested in stories from England. This foreign news was obtained in three ways: by conversations with captains or other reliable persons arriving by boat from Europe; by letters sent from abroad to such persons as merchants and the editors themselves; and by the simple process of appropriating from foreign newspapers whatever the colonial editor chose to use. For local news, the editor and his assistant acted as reporters, and for news from other colonies the paper relied either on correspondents or on the old method of appropriating from other papers.

Local news was influenced by a concept that has since

changed drastically. This was the feeling that, because the towns were small enough to enable everyone to witness the major events, the paper should not write of these events. The colonial editor would be quite surprised to see something we now accept as standard practice—the eight-column streamer across the local paper, "Snow Blankets Entire City." He would argue to no avail that everyone had seen the snow, and he no doubt would be amazed at the emphasis given the story today.

THE STAMP ACT AND THE NEWSPAPER

An important influence on the early history of journalism was the Stamp Act. This act, passed in March 1765, to become effective the following November, required that all legal documents, official papers, books, and newspapers be printed on special stamped paper which provided a tax solely for the British government. To the newspaper, this meant a half penny for each copy of a two-page paper and one penny for four pages. A united cry of protest immediately arose from the papers throughout the colonies.

On the day that the Stamp Act tax was to become effective, no newspaper appeared on the stamped paper. A few, such as the *Maryland Gazette*, suspended briefly, but the others appeared as usual. Some were openly defiant in their manner. Others, feeling a need to be tactful, relied on such excuses as the inability to get stamped paper (which was true, because in many cases the paper had been destroyed) and an unwillingness to subject delivery agents to the wrath of an enraged populace. Some papers resorted to legal trickery by publishing without the usual masthead and serial numbers, thus pretending to be handbills or tracts, neither of which required the stamped paper.

9

Against such opposition, the Stamp Act could not succeed, and so it was duly repealed the following March, although the colonies, because of communication facilities with England, did not learn of the action until May. Historians have pointed out that the newspapers in England had accepted the tax without protest. But they have also pointed out that for the colonies this tax was "taxation without representation."

The Stamp Act protest was a milestone in the history of journalism because it marked for the American newspaper the first unanimous agreement upon a single issue and, more important, the first united front against governmental control. With this experience of successfully criticizing in unison an unpopular act of the government, the newspaper gained a vantage point and an editorial freedom that it has never relinquished.

THE REVOLUTION AND THE NEWSPAPER

As one easily can realize, the American Revolution had a marked effect on the history of journalism. Aside from the physical handicaps of attempting to publish in a nation that had become a battleground, the newspaper was most affected by the influence of the war on editorial policy. Every paper now had to decide on its support of one of the two sides. Although one might assume that all papers backed the cause of independence, such was not the case. Fifteen papers at one time or another supported the Tories.

The most famous example of a Tory paper was James Rivington's publication, established in New York on April 22, 1773. Known as *Rivington's New-York Gazetteer: or Connecticut, Hudson's-River, New-Jersey, and Quebec Weekly Advertiser,* it was so violently pro-Tory that its plant was damaged by mob action twice in 1777. On the second occasion, the damage was so severe that a new press and type had to be brought from England. With the new equipment, Rivington then established The *New-York Loyal Gazette* and continued his pro-Tory writing. A famous example of a paper that was fiercely pro-American throughout the struggle was the *Boston Gazette,* founded April 7, 1755, a publication that was so bold and so forthright that it commanded the greatest respect of the patriots. An example of a vacillating newspaper was the *Pennsylvania Evening Post,* established in Philadelphia on January 24, 1775. This paper at first supported the American cause, then backed the British when they occupied the city, and later rallied to the Americans as they returned. Such vacillation cost the paper its life.

The effect of the war on the ability of papers to publish was genuinely serious. On April 19, 1775, the day of the battles of Lexington and Concord, there were 37 papers in publication throughout the American colonies. Of this number, only 20 lasted for the duration of the war. And of these 20, several were forced to suspend publication for periods varying from a few days to many months. However, some papers were begun during the war, and so, when hostilities ceased, 35 papers were being published regularly in the colonies, plus a few that appeared irregularly.

One of the most trying problems faced by the newspapers during the Revolution was the acute paper shortage. The importation of paper, small before the war, now came to a standstill, thus forcing publishers to depend on the inadequate supply at home. Government subsidies to manufacturers to start paper mills helped the situation somewhat, but the shortage was still felt keenly, chiefly because the mills were unable to get rags from which to make their product. Another serious problem was lack of printing equipment. Because presses and type were imported from England, the hostilities soon occasioned a shortage that handicapped many newspapers.

The coverage of news during this period was poor. There was no organized system so that once again the chief sources for most papers were letters and the old practice of helping one's self freely to news from other papers. A distinct exception, however, was the *Journal of Occurrences*, published by the Boston patriots. This paper collected its news systematically, selling its stories to other newspapers in the form of a daily column. This was the first syndicated column, and as such it is important historically. The column consisted chiefly of a daily account of life in Boston, with all the trials and hardships of the times.

Also appearing during this period of the Revolutionary War was the forerunner of the newspaper editorial. At first, the opinions of the editor were interpolated into the leads of the stories or placed in little paragraphs tacked to the ends. At the close of the period, however, these editorializings were printed in much the position that we find them now.

The way for this editorializing had been prepared by the freedom which the press had gained before the war, notably with its opposition to the Stamp Act. This freedom increased with the struggle between the colonies and the mother country because the editors, knowing that the majority of the populace were behind them, spoke out against the unpopular acts of the mother country. The tendency toward free speech grew even more as the editors saw the colonial governors fail in their attempts to have grand juries indict the editors of such free-speaking papers as the *Boston Gazette* and the *Massachusetts Spy*.

As the Revolutionary period closed, the newspaper was firmly on its way to becoming a permanent and an important institution, primarily because it had asserted its position as the free voice of the colonists. The leaders of the new government now looked upon the newspapers as a power to be recognized; and the people looked to the newspapers to keep them informed and to protect their interests.

THE POST-REVOLUTIONARY PERIOD (1780–1800)

With the Revolution settled and the prestige of the newspaper established, the number of papers began to increase. In the two decades after the war, almost 450 new publications were founded. In number of papers, New York was well ahead of other American cities with eleven. During this post-Revolutionary period, the newspaper also became political in two important ways: (1) it became the medium by which national leaders carried their arguments to the people and (2) in many cases it openly lined up with political groups.

The use of the newspaper by national figures was not a totally new development. Before this time, several newspapers had acted as outlets for the views of prominent leaders, the notable examples being the *Boston Gazette*, which contained the writings of such famous men as Samuel Adams, James Otis, and John Adams, and the several newspapers to which Thomas Paine contributed his famous series, "The Crisis." Now, however, with the problems of the new nation before the people, the important leaders took to the press as never before. Men like Alexander Hamilton, John Dickinson, James Madison, and John Jay wrote little essays for the newspapers which supported them, and their adversaries quickly sought space in other papers. Thus, the newspaper was bound to become political as it opened its columns to political figures.

The association of newspapers with political groups rose principally with the clashes over the framing and the ratification of the Constitution, the controversy that gave rise to the Federalist and the anti-Federalist parties. To support their cause, the Federalists helped John Fenno to establish and maintain the *Gazette of the United States,* an open organ of the new government, which first appeared in New York on April 15, 1789. To combat this paper, Thomas Jefferson and his adherents encouraged the establishment of the *National Gazette,* which was first printed in Philadelphia on October 31, 1791. Each paper, of course, took up the battles of its supporters. With this controversy, the practice of journalistic support of political factions was begun.

As the newspapers began to support political factions, they naturally attacked the leaders of the opposition. These attacks sometimes became downright scurrilous. Benjamin Franklin Bache, grandson of the famous American, was both caustic and untrue in his attacks on Washington in the *Aurora;* and such other journalists as William Duane, successor to Bache as director of the *Aurora,* and William Cobbett, who established the *Porcupine's Gazette,* sank so low that an enraged Congress passed the Alien and Sedition Acts in 1798. These acts, which existed for three years and were almost re-enacted, were aimed squarely at the scurrilous press. The Alien Act provided for deportation of any editor of foreign birth who offended the government and the Sedition Act provided for suppression of any native American editor guilty of the same offense. Under the Alien Act there were no actual persecutions, but under the Sedition Act about 25 persons were arrested and 10 were found guilty. As the proponents of freedom of speech condemn this governmental attempt to bridle the press, they must also remember the low tone of the newspapers of the time.

Despite the blots of this post-Revolutionary period, the newspaper was making significant gains in prestige and in freedom, and editors were determined to hold fast. When the Commonwealth of Massachusetts, with no malice intended, announced in 1785 a tax on newspapers, almanacs, and similar publications, a loud cry arose from both within and without the state. The bill called for a tax of two thirds of a penny for each paper, a stamp to be placed on the paper to indicate that the tax had been paid. Since this, to the newspapers, was simply the hated British Stamp Tax in new garb, they objected vigorously. So loud was their protest that this tax was repealed before it was to become effective. However, in its place a tax was levied on advertisements—sixpence for 12 lines and one shilling per 20 lines for the longer advertisements. Once again a strong protest was made, and the tax finally was repealed in 1788.

In this post-Revolutionary period, another significant gain was scored in freedom of the press. Newspapers now became bluntly outspoken in their demands to view all that occurred within the government. They felt a right and a duty to report all that happened. An indication of their new position is to be seen in their discussion of the Jay Treaty before it was to be ratified (1794), an act that formerly would have been unthinkable. They also clamored loudly for admittance to the sessions of the Senate, and in 1794 a resolution was passed by that body admitting the press to its galleries. Newspapers already enjoyed this privilege in the House of Representatives, or they would have demanded it there also.

However, the press at this time wanted its rights stated more definitely, and many influential citizens agreed. Of the 13 colonies, 9 had constitutional provisions for freedom of the press. And when the Federal constitution was considered for ratification by the states, no less a person than Thomas Jefferson wanted his native Virginia to withhold approval until a definite provision for freedom of the press had been inserted. Opposed to such an amendment to the Federal constitution was Alexander Hamilton, who felt that it would "leave the utmost latitude for evasion." Instead, he would have freedom of the press guided by public opinion. However, the proponents of the amendment were victorious, and the first amendment now reads in part: "Congress shall make no law respecting an establishment of religion, or prohibiting the free exercise thereof; of abridging the freedom of speech, or of the press."

During this post-Revolutionary period, the first daily newspaper made its appearance. It was not a new paper, but rather an already established triweekly publication known as the *Pennsylvania Packet and General Advertiser.* On September 21, 1784, this paper appeared as a daily, changing its name to the *Pennsylvania Packet and Daily Advertiser.*

As this post-Revolutionary period closed, the newspaper was firmly established on the road to progress. Advertising was increasing; circulation was growing, though the greatest circulation of the period was only slightly over 4,000; and by Federal ruling the newspapers could be sent through the mails (Postoffice Act of 1792) for one cent each. But most important, the public had come to view the uncensored newspaper as a part of its life. Freedom of the press was now guaranteed constitutionally, and the public was getting an unfettered newspaper to keep it informed.

FIRST HALF OF THE NINETEENTH CENTURY

The first half of the nineteenth century was characterized by: (1) a substantial increase in the number of newspapers; (2) a heavy political influence on editorial policy; (3) another series of events affecting freedom of the press; and (4) the appearance of the cheap newspaper.

Number of Newspapers

As the century opened, there were about 200 papers in the United States. These papers, however, must not be thought of in the light of present-day standards, for they were smaller, their coverage was much more limited, and their editorial approach was distinctly different from that of today. Also, many of these 200 papers did not publish daily; some published triweekly, semiweekly, semimonthly, monthly, or quarterly. Hence, some of these papers more nearly resembled periodicals.

As the century moved on, the number of newspapers began to increase rather sharply. According to figures computed in 1856 by W. T. Coggeshall, State Librarian of Ohio, the number of newspapers in the United States in 1810 was 359; in 1828, 861; and in 1840, 1,403. This increase is also substantiated by statistics released by the Postal Department in July 1839. On that date, according to the Department, there was a total of 1,555 newspapers and periodicals throughout the nation. Further evidence of the increase is to be seen in the national census figures of 1850, which listed the number of newspapers and periodicals at 2,800.

Political Influence

The political influence on editorial policy that began with the Federalist–anti-Federalist controversy was heightened in the new century. With the defeat of the Federalist Party and the ascendancy of Thomas Jefferson and the Democrats, the split of the newspapers into political camps was sharper than ever. Such subsequent controversies as the Embargo Act of 1807 and the War of 1812 merely served to draw the lines of cleavage more severely. The division was further intensified by the reliance of the political parties on the newspapers to spearhead their attack. By the time of the War of 1812, the press was so divided by the political parties, and so devoted to them, that the years 1812–32 have been labeled the "party press" period.

The close alliance of politics and press during this post-war period caused the newspapers to sink to a new low in name calling and muck raking. The editors, in their fierce desire to support or to blackguard a political party, released their innermost thoughts, and nothing was too abusive to say of one's enemy. The practice became so bad that the term "black journalism" has been attached to the period. The tide of black journalism did not turn until the middle of the decade 1820–30, when some of the more enlightened editors began to free their papers of subservience to party politics.

The influence of politics during this period changed the entire identity of the newspaper. Not only did the paper support its party editorially, but also it frequently used its columns almost entirely for political news. In many cases, the newspaper was nothing more than a straight party organ, devoting its efforts almost exclusively to its party. In thus allowing itself to be influenced so heavily by politics, the newspaper became a political rather than a social institution.

Freedom of the Press

In this period there were some interesting incidents and decisions touching on the all-important question of freedom of the press. An especially notable instance occurred in 1826, when the *St. Louis Enquirer* published a criticism written by a lawyer of a decision made by Federal District Judge James H. Peck. Editor and lawyer were brought before the judge.

The editor received only a reprimand, but the lawyer was fined, sentenced to prison, and barred from practice. Fortunately, this high-handed action did not pass unnoticed. Judge Peck was tried in the Senate of the United States, where he barely escaped the necessary votes for impeachment. The actual count was 21 to 22.

Another significant entanglement with the law occurred when the *Detroit Gazette*, in 1828, criticized the court for waste of time. For his indiscretion, the editor, John P. Sheldon, found himself in jail for contempt of court. This action was another boon to journalism. A group of sympathizers took donations to pay the fine (no one was allowed to contribute more than 12½ cents), and upon his release Sheldon was feted in grand style by the townspeople.

Even P. T. Barnum, the famous showman, had a session with the law. His hometown newspaper in Danbury, Connecticut, having refused to print his contributions, with characteristic Barnum flair the young man bought a press and turned out a paper of his own. Discretion was not a part of Barnum's personality and a libel suit was soon instituted. The townspeople smiled until Barnum was jailed for 60 days for what the court adjudged an indiscretion. Then they became indignant. Barnum wrote his paper from jail and upon his release was given a hero's welcome.

These three instances are important historically because they were further steps in the progress toward freedom of the press. The outcome of these and similar incidents of the period continued to strengthen the newspaper as an independent institution.

The newspaper of this period, however, was not entirely free of public censure. In the early part of the century, the incensed citizen frequently challenged the editor to a duel because of remarks made in print. In fact, the most famous duel in American history—that in which Aaron Burr killed Alexander Hamilton, on July 11, 1804—resulted from statements published in the *Albany Register*. As the political influence upon editorial policy grew, public censure grew, and newspaper plants sometimes stood in grave danger. This public censure of newspapers naturally flared with every significant controversy of the period.

Obviously, the greatest controversy of this period was that of slavery, which was felt as early as the tenure of Andrew Jackson (1829–37). In 1835, a mob beset William Lloyd Garrison for utterances of the famous *Liberator*, but the paper continued to publish as before. In Philadelphia, Cincinnati, and other large cities, the abolition-favoring papers were stormed and in some cases the buildings were set afire. The most serious outburst was that in which the Rev. Elijah P. Lovejoy of Alton, Illinois, was killed as a mob burst into his newspaper building on the night of November 7, 1837. Lovejoy, an abolitionist, was setting up a fourth press after his first three had been thrown into a nearby river by similar mobs. Northern publications favoring abolition naturally found difficulty in maintaining circulation in the Southern states, and in some cases committees of Southern citizens rifled the mails, destroying Yankee publications. On the whole, however, the right of the press to speak freely was accepted by the people, despite the opposition of such literary men as James Fenimore Cooper, who, within a few years, brought 14 private libel suits against newspapers and instituted two prosecutions for criminal libel; and Charles Dickens, who, in his "American Notes" and his novel, "Martin Chuzzlewit," attacked the American press as an unbridled monster capable of almost any misdeed.

The Cheap Newspaper

In the early part of the nineteenth century, papers were sold only by the year. The price of the mercantile papers was $8 to $10, which usually entitled the subscriber to a four-page paper six times a week. This kind of paper naturally was composed chiefly of advertising. However, about 1830 a change occurred in the price of the newspaper. The *Daily Courier* originated at this time in Portland, Maine, the first paper to publish north of Boston, and its price was $4 per year. Noting the success of the *Courier*, Lynde M. Walter founded the *Boston Transcript*, which sold at the same price, and the following year Charles G. Greene established the *Boston Morning Post*, also a $4 per year publication. Another $4 paper, the *Mercantile Journal*, was founded in Boston in 1833.

A more important event affecting the price of the newspaper occurred on January 1, 1833, with one of the best-known names in journalism figuring prominently in the venture. On that day no less a person than Horace Greeley took part in a significant, if unsuccessful, attempt to sell a cheap newspaper for cash on the streets of New York. Associated with Greeley were Francis Story and Dr. H. D. Sheppard, the man who suggested the idea to Greeley. Dr. Sheppard is reputed to have got the idea from his observation of street vendors selling candy, peanuts, and trinkets. The idea of a cheap newspaper had already been tried by a little-known Philadelphia paper, *The Cent*, which had appeared at the penny price for a short time in 1830. The paper published by Greeley, Story, and Sheppard was the *Morning Post*, and its price at first was to be two cents. After two unsuccessful weeks, due in part to very bad weather, the price was lowered to one cent, but sales were still scarce. Consequently, this first project of selling a cheap paper on the streets ended in failure.

Later this same year, however, another paper succeeded where Greeley's had failed. The paper, which appeared on the morning of September 3, 1833, was the New York *Sun*. Its publisher was Benjamin Henry Day, a printer, and its name was reputed to be the suggestion of David Ramsey, a compositor. In its four pages of three columns each were a heavy emphasis on human interest stories and a humorous treatment of police court scenes. Imitating the methods used successfully by the London *Morning Herald*, it jumped to the forefront with a circulation of 2,000 in two months. In four months the circulation was 5,000 and the *Sun* was leading the New York field. Naturally, other papers began to follow a new course.

The influence of the penny paper upon the history of journalism was threefold: (1) the competition for street sales occasioned a stirring competition for news (the newspapers now put added emphasis on the scoop and on the beat, thus stepping up the coverage of news); (2) the newsboy, later to become a familiar sight on the street corner, made his appearance with the advent of the penny paper; and (3) the lowered price made the newspaper available to all classes, rather than only to those able to pay the relatively high subscription price. As the paper became available to the lower income group, it became in a real sense an institution of the people, for it enlarged its field of news coverage to satisfy readers of all economic levels.

IMPORTANT NEW PAPERS

During this period, some of the most successful newspapers of all time were founded. On May 6, 1835, James Gordon Bennett launched the New York *Herald*, the first paper to have a financial page. Bennett had to work against great odds, including a fire in the building where the paper was printed, before bringing his publication to the forefront. On March 25, 1836, the first issue of the Philadelphia *Public Ledger* appeared. This paper continued in operation until it merged with the *Philadelphia Inquirer*, almost a hundred years later. On April 10, 1841, the first issue of the *New-York Tribune* was published under the guidance of Horace Greeley, who had the satisfaction of seeing its circulation rise to 11,000 after only seven weeks of publication. After holding this figure for several years, it began a steady rise, so that by the time of the War Between the States it claimed 45,000 subscribers.

Yet one must not measure the influence of the *Tribune* in terms of circulation figures. Rightly or wrongly, this paper took a firm stand on the important questions of the day and bluntly expressed its views. The power of its voice is evidenced by the fact that the editorials written by Greeley had a heavy influence on the issues which plunged the country into the War Between the States. Also important is the fact that Greeley was a reformer who crusaded relentlessly for his causes. His influence, historians agree, is not to be taken lightly.

Another great paper, the *New-York Times*, appeared on September 18, 1851. Its tone from the outset was much the same as it is today—calm, rational, and forceful, a model of the higher type of journalism. It was launched on a large scale and it was successful from its first issue, even though it soon had to raise its price from one cent to two as the *Herald* and the *Tribune* had done before it. The *Times* struck a new note in journalism by emphasizing foreign news as well as domestic and by adhering to a course of calm, deliberate thought, divorced from fiery passion.

MECHANICAL ADVANCES

The mechanical advances of this period greatly influenced the course of journalism. As the century opened, all newspapers were using the old-fashioned hand press. By 1812, however, Frederick Koenig and an assistant, Thomas Bensley, had invented a press with a revolving cylinder, the press operating by having the cylinder roll over the type bed. Further progress was made in 1822 when Daniel Treadwell, a native of Boston, invented a steam-driven press. His invention, however, had two big disadvantages—its operation was cumbersome and its structure was rather clumsy. These disadvantages were lessened in 1830 when Isaac Adams improved upon the Treadwell press in structure, operation, and effectiveness. But more important, the Adams press also made several of the operations more nearly automatic.

Adding to the improvements on the Adams press, Robert Hoe (who eventually owned the Adams patents in 1858) continued to improve the whole process of printing. His most important contribution was the Hoe Lightning Press, which appeared in 1847. This press held its type on a revolving surface, thus greatly increasing the speed of printing. In fact, with later improvements by its inventor, the press had a capacity of 20,000 sheets per hour. The significance of the Hoe press was threefold: (1) it shortened the time required to print a paper; (2) it affected individual enterprise in that its cost, which ranged from $20,000 to $25,000, ended the opportunity to establish a metropolitan daily with the small capital formerly required; and (3) it changed the make-up of advertisements because the cost of placing a cut on a revolving surface greatly increased the expense of the cut.

LATTER HALF OF THE NINETEENTH CENTURY

By the middle of the nineteenth century, newspaper circulations were reaching a new high. In 1860, the *New York Herald* was the world's largest daily, with a figure of 77,000, and many less significant daily papers throughout the nation had circulations of over 50,000. The largest circulations of the time, however, were enjoyed by the two New York weeklies, the *Tribune* and the *Ledger*. Their totals were 200,000 and 400,000, respectively. The student of circulation statistics should not be too hasty in scoffing at these figures as compared with those of today. He should instead compare them with the circulations of 1833, when all papers were below 5,000.

The growth in circulation during this period was due to several conditions. First, there was an increase in population, which occasioned a corresponding demand for newspapers. Second, because of the growth in public education, illiteracy was decreasing, thus increasing the number of potential readers. Third, oil lamps and later gas lamps were replacing candlelight, so that reading was much easier. Fourth was the all-important consideration of cost. With the lowered price of the newspaper, the demand grew accordingly. But fifth, and perhaps the greatest reason, was the desire of the people to know of the affairs of their country. Democracy dictated a continued interest in the affairs of the government, and the press was the best means of keeping abreast of the times.

THE NEWSPAPER DURING THE WAR BETWEEN THE STATES

With the outbreak of the War Between the States, the newspaper was seriously affected. Not only was the circula-

25

tion of papers in combat and enemy areas cut off, but also frequently the physical plant of the publication was damaged. In addition, there were the usual problems of wartime—rising costs of production, heavier taxes, and restrictions rightfully and wrongly ordered in the name of national security.

News coverage during this period presents an interesting picture, for reporters roamed with the armies, giving eyewitness accounts of the actual battles. For the most part, news was completely uncensored and it was exceptionally prompt and accurate. Because the newspaper of this time was almost the only source of news, the people read its accounts avidly. Consequently, the large New York papers often devoted as much as one third of their columns to the coverage of the war. The newspaper as early as this day was also publishing war maps and casualty lists in small type at the bottom of the story.

Correspondents following the armies were not treated as noncombatants, as they are today. Instead, they traveled as an integral part of the army and were considered as such, taking their chances on being captured, wounded, or killed in the field. (The correspondents, known as "specials," were frequently the editors of the papers who were compelled to take a turn in the field.) In getting their news through, the correspondents had an especially difficult time. Although the telegraph system now made wiring stories possible, correspondents often were forced to take their accounts personally to their offices. Sometimes their work necessitated riding through enemy lines or living in hostile territory, but the correspondents carried on nonetheless.

In some respects, the newspaper now enjoyed the widest freedom of expression ever known—a freedom that actually retarded the Union war effort. Evidence is to be seen in the fact that President Jefferson Davis and his generals were eager to obtain Northern papers to read of troop movements and military preparations. The Union, realizing the danger, in August 1861 cited for the press the 57th Article of War, which provides for court martial with possible death sentence for giving information to the enemy. Even then, however, little change was effected. The view of the military leaders regarding the latitude taken by the press was exemplified in a post-war incident when General Sherman refused to shake hands with Horace Greeley because he felt that the *Tribune* had hampered the war effort by printing information helpful to the enemy.

Before and during the war, editorials—especially in New York—were free, to say the least. So outspoken, for example, was Greeley in the *Tribune* that many persons attributed the militaristic attitude of the North squarely to him, a fact that caused an angry mob to sack the *Tribune* building. Even President Lincoln, who always retained considerable respect for the rights of the press, felt that some papers were exceeding the bounds of propriety.

During the war, the "Copperhead press" was making its power felt. This press was a section of the Northern newspaper field opposed to the war and its purpose. Some Copperhead papers used an open approach. They spoke glowingly of Southern victories, they belittled the national administration, and they criticized adversely the conduct of the war by the Union leaders. Others used softer language and a more crafty method, but they were effective nonetheless. The very fact that these papers could exist indicates the strength of the conception of freedom of the press.

THE POST-WAR PERIOD

The period between the close of the War Between the States and the end of the century was characterized by (1) the emergence of three men who had a strong influence on the history of journalism—Charles A. Dana, Joseph Pulitzer, and William Randolph Hearst; (2) the launching of the most famous of all newspaper crusades, that against New York's Boss Tweed; (3) the lessening of political domination of the newspaper; (4) the staging of the famous Stanley-Livingstone stunt; and (5) the appearance of the linotype machine.

Charles A. Dana

One of the most important figures in nineteenth-century journalism was Charles A. Dana, who bought the New York *Sun* in 1868 for $175,000. Formerly Assistant Secretary of War during the war years and managing editor of Horace Greeley's *Tribune*, Dana was extremely capable both as editor and as publisher. At the time of purchase, the *Sun* had a circulation of 43,000. In two and a half years, Dana raised this circulation to 102,870, and by 1875 he had the paper in the front ranks with a circulation figure of 120,000.

Aside from his role in building this significant paper, Dana is important for his stylistic contributions. More so than anyone else, he broke the American newspaper away from British tradition. He insisted upon a lively, competent news coverage not known theretofore; he demanded that his reporters write in a highly finished style; he innovated the idea of presenting news stories in a condensed manner; he demanded, and received, the most original heads on the American newspaper scene; and he developed the feature story into its present form. These contributions alone insure his importance in any history of journalism.

JOSEPH PULITZER

Another important figure, Joseph Pulitzer, whose name we associate today with annual prizes, made history in 1883 with his purchase of the *New York World*. He stated his editorial policy frankly in the first issue: the emphasis was to be placed on human interest stories and sensationalism, plus a little gossip and scandal. Pulitzer wanted his paper to be democratic but he also wanted it to be different. At the time of purchase, the circulation was 20,000. This figure he doubled in four months; raised to 100,000 by 1884; and to 250,000 by 1886. In 1887, Pulitzer began the *Evening World*, and although the circulation of his morning paper was somewhat affected, the two papers had a combined figure of 374,000 in 1892 and a circulation of 1,000,000 in 1897. Meanwhile, the Sunday *World* had risen to 250,000. The advertising in all the editions continued to grow, despite an increase in rates. Stepping out in front of all competitors, Pulitzer and his *World* achieved the happy distinction of being the most profitable paper ever published.

WILLIAM RANDOLPH HEARST

Just as the entrance of Pulitzer into the field of New York journalism was the most significant event of the eighties, the arrival of William Randolph Hearst with the purchase of the *Morning Journal* was the most significant event of the nineties. Like Pulitzer, Hearst was already a newspaper owner, for he had been publishing the *San Francisco Examiner*, bought by his late father. Having been highly successful in that city by

29

imitating the methods of Pulitzer, he wanted to move to New York, which he viewed as the most challenging city in which to operate a paper. He bought the tottering *Morning Journal* for $180,000, and, by spending lavishly in promotion and hiring, soon effectively challenged the field now dominated by Pulitzer's *World*.

The Pulitzer-Hearst competition gave journalism one of its liveliest episodes. They clashed during the free silver campaign of 1896, and they competed savagely against each other in news beats and stunts. Their treatment of news, which often sank below the line of decency, was ultrasensational, to say the least. Consequently, they drew opposition from churches and civic groups that envisioned a detrimental effect on newspaper readers. As one of their many competitive enterprises, the *World* and the *Journal* each had a single comic drawing of a character known as "The Yellow Kid." From this incident, the adjective was taken to describe the kind of journalism employed by these papers, so that to this day the term "yellow journalism" is a synonym for sensationalism and all that usually accompanies it.

All this was only a starter for the famous Hearst, who was now launched on a tempestuous though successful course. He tried all sorts of stunts, successful and unsuccessful; he played a dominant part in encouraging and criticizing wars; and he continually flaunted his use of the sensational. Despite numerous unfavorable criticisms and concerted opposition to his policies, he remained to his death in 1951 a strong influence on the business that he chose for his own as a young man who withdrew by faculty request from Harvard College.

Boss Tweed

Probably the most famous of all newspaper crusades, that against Boss Tweed, undisputed leader of the infamous Tammany Ring, falls within this period. During the years 1870–71, the *New York Times* and *Harper's Weekly* conducted the campaign that eventually brought this notorious group to its end, but not before the gang had swindled the city of an estimated $200,000,000. A blot on the history of journalism lies in the proof that almost a hundred newspapers were discovered to be on the payroll of the ring in one form or another.

ABSENCE OF POLITICAL DOMINATION

During this period, there was a substantial increase in the number of newspapers that were freeing themselves of commitments to political parties. By 1880, one fourth of the papers in the country were politically independent, and by 1890 the number had increased to one third. This trend was occasioned by the increased desire to criticize the government freely and by the changing conception of the newspaper. The new conception dictated an expansion of the fields of news coverage and the inclusion of more human interest stories. As the fact became apparent that the consistently successful papers were independent, the trend gained momentum.

STANLEY AND LIVINGSTONE

In this period there occurred one of the greatest stunts in the field of making news—one that is famous to this day and one that has led dozens of other papers to imitation. Dr. Liv-

ingstone, a missionary and explorer of international reputation, had been lost in an expedition to find the sources of
Africa's Nile and Congo Rivers. Believing him to be alive and
having some evidence to bolster his belief, Henry E. Stanley,
reporter on the *New York Herald*, financed by his employer,
James Gordon Bennett, Jr., conducted an expedition to find
the lost missionary. The expedition, consisting of 3 white men,
30 armed natives, and 150 pack animals, set out in December
1871 on its quest. After long, weary months of fighting disease, unfriendly natives, and countless other obstacles, Stanley
and his party found Livingstone, thus giving to history one
of the most famous searches for a lost man. Journalistically, it
set a precedent, and today hundreds of papers would pay a
high price for such a scoop.

THE LINOTYPE MACHINE

As the century neared its last decade, a mechanical advance
appeared that was to revolutionize the printing of the newspaper. This was the linotype machine, the invention of Ottmar
Mergenthaler, a German-American resident of Baltimore,
Maryland. Mergenthaler was aided by a company of newspapers organized in 1885 to help financially in perfecting the
machine. The name of the machine explains its work; it casts
its type in lines, thus making obsolete the older and slower
process of arranging type by hand. The machine was first
used extensively in the composing room of the *New York
Tribune* in 1886, and shortly thereafter by the *Chicago Daily
News*. Additional improvements on the machine so increased
its use that, by 1890, it was established firmly in the major
newspaper plants of the country and its acceptance was a solid
fact. With the linotype machine, the whole process of printing the newspaper was changed. Because the type was set so

much faster, the newspaper was able to add more pages and the time between writing and printing was shortened.

TURN OF THE CENTURY TO THE PRESENT

The period from the turn of the century to the present is so complex that it can be appreciated best by studying separately its many aspects. Broadly speaking, the course of the newspaper has been influenced most by the peculiar character of twentieth-century life. But it has been influenced also by journalism's continued efforts to safeguard its freedom of speech; by a gain in prestige; by two major wars; and by the growth of the newspaper chains. Also of significance in this period are the rise of the tabloid, the question of libel, and the use of the cartoon.

TWENTIETH-CENTURY LIFE

The peculiar character of the twentieth century has had a strong influence on the newspaper. This age has been one of technological advances, of big business, and of industry. It has also been an age when cities have grown tremendously, when improved transportation has made vast distances shrink unbelievably, when every phase of life has moved at high speed.

The many technological advances of the age have had their influence on every major department of the newspaper. In the editorial offices the improved typewriters, the advent of the teletype machine and the wire photo, and the heavier use of the telephone and the telegram have changed the whole process of gathering news. Stories are now gathered faster; material comes from more distant points; methods of seeking and editing news have changed. Heretofore, one reporter

33

usually gathered the facts and wrote the story. Now two or three may work on the same story, procuring facts for one or more rewrite men who write the story in the office. The emphasis is on speed, and any device that gains speed must be adopted.

In the mechanical departments of the newspaper, the technological improvements have been even more revolutionary. Not only has the linotype machine been improved, but also a totally new invention, the teletypesetter, has come into being. The teletypesetter, a combination of the linotype and the teletype devices, is now used for one of two operations. Under the first operation, one person operates a master machine which automatically sets type on machines in distant newspaper offices; under the second operation, one person operates a machine which makes a punched tape that is used to activate a device for setting type automatically on a linotype machine equipped for that purpose. Also, the autoplate has been invented to speed the process of printing and the appearance of the high-speed press has enabled the newspaper to print thousands more copies than possible heretofore. The unbelievably high circulations of today are possible only because of the speed with which the paper can be set in type and printed.

The growth of big business and industry has affected the newspaper in two important ways: (1) the large establishments advertise heavily, thus helping substantially to provide revenue for the newspapers and (2) the newspaper itself has become a big business venture. Without the revenue from the increased advertising, the newspaper could never hope to meet the heavy expenses which it now incurs. Thus, it owes its ability to grow financially largely to big business. The newspaper itself has become a big business venture by virtue of the heavy investment necessary to operate. No longer can a paper compete successfully unless it can afford the expensive modern equipment and the staff necessary for such an operation.

The tremendous growth of the cities has affected the newspaper primarily by creating news sources. The hustle and bustle of the city, its many activities, and its variegated population have provided a totally new brand of news. Accidents, suicides, murders, and riots are to be found daily, and drama and pathos for the feature story are omnipresent.

The improvement in transportation has generated a deeper interest in distant places, and thus a deeper interest in news from other places. It has also made possible a direct contact with distant points not possible heretofore. Now a newspaper can send its reporters hundreds of miles for first-hand news, whereas formerly it had to rely on other sources. Thus, improved transportation has helped to change the whole character of news.

FREEDOM OF THE PRESS

The newspaper's freedom of speech has been challenged several times in the twentieth century, but in each instance the newspaper has held fast, so that today it can speak without fear of censure when it states the truth.

Freedom of the press has been challenged in this century largely because of the power of the press itself. Although journalism has long been an important institution, its influence has increased markedly in this century. The newspaper now reaches more people than ever; it contains more varied material than ever; and its editorial voice, despite the competition of radio and television, is a powerful one indeed. Consequently, it stands today as a major force in forming public opinions.

As might readily be assumed, freedom of the press in this period has been challenged by the most important figures in our government. A notable instance occurred in 1908, when the Federal government, at the insistence of President Theodore Roosevelt, had Joseph Pulitzer and his top editors of the *New York World* indicted in a District of Columbia court for criminal libel. The action resulted from the *World's* disclosure of the means by which this government had secured the right to build the Panama Canal. The case eventually was carried to the Supreme Court, where the judges agreed unanimously that, since only documentary evidence had been printed, the *World* was in no sense guilty. This decision, as others before it, re-established the right of the press to print the truth.

Another important clash between President and press occurred with the passage of the National Industrial Recovery Act during the first term of Franklin D. Roosevelt. Under the terms of this act, the President was to have power to license the press, to revoke the license for failure to comply with the law, and to exert a general control by making the press observe the conditions of the license. Those associated with the President insisted that he would never use these powers. The press, however, refused to accept such oral assurances in the face of the written law, and so the law was brought to a test. Actually, there was no real test, because the newspapers had never made any attempt to comply with the law. They simply continued to print as before, regardless of governmental likes or dislikes, and the government, seeing the inadvisability of challenging so strong an institution as the American newspaper, let the matter pass. Thus, the newspapers won this very important round by default.

The press was most uneasy in the twentieth century during the tenure of this same President, Franklin D. Roosevelt. To this day, no one has shown conclusively how long Roosevelt wanted to remain President or how much power he really desired. But the fact does stand that he disliked intensely to be crossed; he was a man who resented opposition in practically any form. At first his relations with the press were extremely cordial, but, as time passed, his temper rose. He was especially caustic at election time, referring to the fact that most newspapers in the nation were opposed to his winning. He also resented the power of the press in helping to defeat some of his major domestic plans, such as the enlarging of the Supreme Court. Consequently, the press was wary of his opposition because his power was so all-encompassing. One major newspaper chain even went so far as to run nation-wide full-page advertisements on the subject of freedom of the press. However, the newspaper successfully rode out this contest, as it did so many others, by holding steadfastly to its right to print the truth.

A later condition in this period that concerned newspapermen slowly gained momentum throughout 1954, 1955, and 1956, finally coming to a showdown in 1957. This was the situation wherein powerful figures in the Federal government began to close off news sources in the name of "national security." Several high-ranking figures in the Federal departments decided completely on their own that certain news sources were to be checked, and they issued orders accordingly. The most famous of all such instances was the refusal of the State Department to grant newspapermen visas to visit Red China. The newspapermen contended that, since the United States was not at war with China, they had the right to visas, especially since they were going as journalists rather than as tourists. The Secretary of State, John Foster Dulles, contended that his department was acting in the best interests of the nation in refusing the visas. Although the most prominent organizations of editors, publishers, and other newspapermen passed formal resolutions condemning the action of the State Department, President Eisenhower would not reverse the ruling of his Secretary of State.

During this time, there were also other smaller instances of friction between government and newspapermen. Reporters resented the "guided tour" aspect of the government in letting them see tests of new and secret weapons, and they once again scored the formal "handout" of news. There was a distinct feeling that "national security" was once again simply an excuse for checking the source of news.

PRESTIGE

During the twentieth century, the field of journalism has come more nearly to represent a profession. Although such an able, though caustic, journalist as H. L. Mencken once said that the newspaperman, for all his dreams, remains "a hired hand," the fact stands that a career in journalism now commands more respect than heretofore. This respect has risen from several conditions.

One of the most important has been the size of the field itself. Although the actual number of newspapers in the United States is decreasing, the field is larger than ever because the remaining newspapers have the largest circulations of all times, they receive more revenue than ever, and they are in every sense a big business. Therefore, the very size of the profession commands respect.

Another important condition in raising the prestige of the newspaper has been the improvement in ethics which has been effected in this century. This improvement has appeared in both the business and the editorial departments. Business ethics began to improve sharply with the adoption, in June

1914, of a code governing advertising by the Newspaper Division of the Associated Advertising Clubs of the World. This code was designed to eliminate all fraudulent advertising. Adoption of the code by such prominent newspapers as the *New York Tribune*, the *New York Times*, and the *Chicago Tribune* led to its acceptance by every other leading paper in the nation. The improvement in editorial department ethics has risen from the several codes adopted by publishers' and writers' organizations and from the self-imposed codes of the best newspapers. Although such prominent papers as those of the Hearst chain sometimes rouse the ire of loftier-minded newspapermen, the profession generally has a higher code of ethics than heretofore. This general rise in ethical standards naturally has occasioned a corresponding rise in general prestige.

Also of significance in raising the prestige of the newspaper has been the genuinely important position which the newspaper has attained. By virtue of its vast circulation, its ability to present up-to-the-minute news, and its strong influence on many readers, the newspaper now stands as one of the most important of American institutions. The daily newspaper is read, respected, and quoted in many quarters. Consequently, those associated with the newspaper are respected accordingly.

Still another influence in raising prestige has been the creation of schools of journalism in our large universities and courses in journalism in practically every college throughout the nation. Now a student can specialize in journalism as his fellow students specialize in medicine, law, teaching, or any other profession. Thus, the university's recognition of journalism as a profession has encouraged a similar acceptance by the general populace.

A final influence in raising the prestige of the newspaper has been the high caliber of many of the persons associated with the profession. In this twentieth century, some of our ablest writers have been professional newspapermen. William Allen White, H. L. Mencken, Heywood Broun, Franklin P. Adams, Walter Lippmann—these and many others have been proud to be known as newspapermen. As a result, the whole profession has commanded additional respect. Today, top-notch newspapermen fill the roles of advisers to the President, college commencement speakers, civic leaders, and many other callings respected by the general populace.

THE TWO WORLD WARS AND THE NEWSPAPER

During wartime, there is always a distinctly noticeable change in the tone of the nation's newspapers. Generally speaking, they become more loyal to the government in power and they slant their news toward creating a note of patriotism. There is considerably less unfavorable criticism, there seems to be a concerted drive to unify the nation, and in many newspapers there is a flag waving that is almost offensive to some readers. All this is due to a desire to help in the war effort, plus some prodding by the government.

However, the government has not always been content to influence the wartime press by prodding. In World War I, more drastic actions were taken. The Espionage Act of June 15, 1917, set up a system of fines and imprisonments for anyone who "shall wilfully cause or attempt to cause . . . disloyalty . . . or shall wilfully obstruct recruiting" into the armed forces of the nation. Publications guilty of breaking this law also were to be denied the use of the mails. The Trading with the Enemy Act of October 6, 1917, required that all messages sent abroad be censored and that any publication printing material in a foreign language file a sworn translation with the local postmaster. The Sedition Act of May 16, 1918, provided heavy fines and imprisonment for writing or publishing "any disloyal, profane, scurrilous, or abusive language about the form of government of the United States, or the Constitution, military or naval forces, flag, or the uniform of the army or navy of the United States." It also forbade the use of language that would tend to bring upon the things mentioned "contempt, scorn, contumely, or disrepute."

The language of these laws was so broad and sweeping that trouble between government and the newspapers was inevitable. Yet, the trouble came not, as one would expect, with the Department of Justice, which is the law-enforcing agency of the nation; the trouble came, rather, with the Post Office Department, which set itself up as censor of all publications using the mails. During the first year of the Espionage Act, 75 papers ran afoul of the Post Office Department, the more fortunate of which were allowed further use of the mails only after promising to print no more discussion of war questions. Since appeals to the courts made no headway, the Post Office became a powerful control on the press.

During World War I, the government established an official agency, the Committee on Public Information, to distribute news and propaganda. The C.P.I., directed by George Creel, had vast powers and was resented in many quarters. Yet there was in the 6,000 releases which it provided during the war a supply of information that was valuable as news.

During World War II, the name of the agency was the Office of War Information, and its director was Elmer Davis, Rhodes Scholar, newspaperman, and radio commentator. This agency carried on primarily in the foreign field, where it attempted to circulate propaganda. It never had the power on the home front that had been enjoyed by its counterpart in World War I, a fact that probably accounts for the higher respect accorded it by newspapermen.

Field correspondents were numerous and effective during World War I, and, unlike the writers with other armies, they were allowed to move freely. In World War I, however, they were merely accepted, as compared with World War II, where they were actually encouraged. In fact, during this latter war, well-known journalists were sought after by generals and admirals who recognized the value of their writings. Correspondents were in constant attendance with all the front-line troops except the Russians, who insisted on restricting their activities to their own newspapermen. Some famous writers lost their lives during these two wars, including Ernie Pyle, who was struck by a bullet from a Japanese sniper on a Pacific island.

Newspaper Chains

The first newspaper chain in the United States resulted from the activity of the Scripps family, an activity which began in 1873 when James E. Scripps launched the *Detroit News*. Noting this success, two brothers, Edward and George H., and a cousin, John Scripps Sweeny, decided to found another paper, the *Penny Press*, which was launched in Cleveland, Ohio, on November 3, 1878. Two years later, Edward W. Scripps launched the St. Louis *Chronicle*, and, in 1881, the Scripps interests gained control of the newspaper that eventually became the Cincinnati *Post*. In 1889, Edward W. Scripps entered into a partnership with Milton A. McRae, who had been advertising manager of the Cincinnati *Post*. This partnership became known in 1895 as the Scripps-McRae League of Newspapers. At that time, the league had control of four newspapers—the St. Louis *Chronicle*, the Cincinnati *Post*, the *Kentucky Post*, and the Cleveland *Press* (formerly the *Penny Press*).

The other important figure in the establishment of a newspaper chain was a man already discussed, William Randolph Hearst. By 1940, Hearst had bought or established 42 newspapers. All these papers, however, he did not retain in the original form. Some he merged; some he sold; and some he suspended because of financial failure.

Scripps and Hearst were not the only figures in the newspaper chains. At the turn of the century there were eight chains of significance. They were Scripps-McRae, Hearst, Ochs, Booth, Kellow, Perkins, Pulitzer, and Belo. At this time, the chains controlled about 10 per cent of the daily circulation. The chains increased in number throughout the next three decades, reaching a total of 60 in the mid-twenties. At that time, they were especially strong in the Sunday field, where they controlled over half the total circulation. There has been little change in the situation since, other than an increase in the number of papers merged.

THE TABLOID NEWSPAPER

The term "tabloid" originally meant simply a small-sized paper, and as such the earliest of American newspapers were tabloids. Today, however, the term has another meaning, one that arose with the appearance of the *Illustrated Daily News* in New York on June 26, 1919. This paper, in size approximately half as large as the ordinary newspaper, has always relied heavily on sensationalism, pictures, and bold headlines. In its first few months it wobbled badly, but then began to pick up sharply. The subway crowd seemed to favor its size and they seemed to like the emphasis on pictorial treatment, crime, and sex. They also liked its breezy style. By 1924, its circulation was up to 750,000, a figure above that of any other daily in New York, and in 1940, as it neared the two million mark, "Editor and Publisher" rated it a tie for second place in circulation for all the papers of the world.

Such success naturally drew others into the tabloid field. Especially significant was the New York *Daily Mirror*, founded in June 1924 by William Randolph Hearst, and the New York *Daily Graphic*, founded a few months later by Bernarr Macfadden. The hot competition of these papers engendered all sorts of devices to gain an edge. Obscene stories and pictures were run; reporters were engaged to dig up facts concerning unsolved murder cases; rewards were offered to readers who could supply evidence concerning baffling crimes; and on one occasion a news photographer strapped a camera to his ankle to obtain surreptitiously a picture of an electrocution in the death house at Sing Sing prison.

In 1930, there were 12 tabloids, in the modern sense of the word, and this number increased to almost 50 in the next decade. The tabloid of the moment is not so daring nor so obscene as the New York triumvirate of the twenties. Today it still puts the emphasis on the sensational, it still employs the breezy style, and it still makes a heavy use of pictures, many of which would never appear in the conservative papers. But the tone of "gutter journalism" has been modified considerably.

LIBEL

In this twentieth century, libel is still a far from settled question. Although libel suits have been staged ever since the first famous one, that in which John Peter Zenger was tried in 1735 for unfavorable criticism of a governor of New York, there is still a pronounced lack of agreement throughout the nation. In this century, however, the United States Supreme Court has made some progress in unifying libel laws. Proceeding on the established "clear and present danger" and the "bad tendency" tests, it frequently has found state laws on libel to be unconstitutional. These decisions, however, have been the only unifying force; otherwise, the entire subject has been handled by law-making, law-interpreting, and law-enforcing agencies in a variety of ways.

To understand completely the present situation in the field of libel, a definition is necessary. Broadly speaking, libel is a published attempt to defame by writing, printing, pictures, images, or any other means that appeals to the sense of vision; that is to say, if one attempts to bring another into disrepute by means of published material, he is guilty of libel.

The first difficulty in adjudging libel arises in deciding when one man has defamed another. Frequently a hair's breadth separates the libelous material from the nonlibelous. The newspaper, for instance, may say that a carpenter who is unable to pay his bills is "bankrupt," but it may not use this term in speaking of a merchant in the same condition if he has not filed a formal statement of bankruptcy. The theory behind the law is that the carpenter will not be defamed but the merchant will.

Libel is also difficult to adjudge because words, especially slang and idioms, have such a variety of meanings. A Pennsylvania woman, for example, sued a newspaper because it had referred to a social occasion in her home as a "hot party." She contended the adjective "hot" possessed an immoral implication; the newspaper contended that the word connotes "loud, hilarious, boisterous," as used, for instance, in the old song, "There'll be a hot time in the old town tonight." The court eventually agreed with the newspaper.

45

Difficulty also arises because of the sharp variance of libel laws from state to state. To see the variety in these laws, one need only make a cursory examination of them throughout the United States. In two Southern states, a newspaper is guilty of libel when it says that a white man is a Negro. In some other states, a libelous action has been committed when the newspaper prints an obituary of a living man; makes light of an individual's deformities; or calls someone a "liar," a "gambler," a "dead beat," or any other name of a disparaging nature.

Also important in any discussion of libel is the fact that most present-day newspapers knowingly print potentially libelous statements.[1] They do so because, otherwise, they would have a very dull paper. Consequently, some of the best stories in the paper would run a chance of being adjudged libelous if examined in court. But the newspaper, in its attempt to present interesting material, is willing to take the risk. It also prints potentially libelous material because many of the people libeled are not in a position to sue the paper, or because the paper can often make a small out-of-court settlement if the outcome appears dark. The wisdom of the newspaper's course is evidenced by the small number of cases won by the plaintiffs as compared with the abundance of material which is potentially libelous.

CARTOONS

The political cartoon as we understand it at present made its appearance in American newspapers before the middle of the nineteenth century. Its use, however, was not habitual; editors simply used cartoons as they felt the need. However,

[1] For an interesting discussion of this subject, see Stanley Walker's "City Editor," pp. 186–206, Stokes, New York, 1934.

as the century drew to a close, cartoons suddenly came into their own. Between 1892 and 1895, there was a decided increase, followed by a genuinely widespread use in 1896, when Bryan and McKinley were staging their famous battle. The precedent thus established, newspapers had another ground for rivalry, and publishers scrambled madly to obtain and retain good cartoonists. Today it is difficult to find a newspaper without a cartoon.

At the height of a political campaign or a crusade, the cartoon may appear on page 1, but, generally speaking, it occupies a regular position on the editorial page. Frequently its tone harmonizes with the leading editorial of the day, and in many newspaper offices the cartoonist attends the meeting of the editorial committee in order to know the attitude of the paper on the questions of the moment.

Although the most famous use of the cartoon in American journalism is undoubtedly the work of Thomas Nast, whose drawings played such an effective part in ending the corrupt rule of Tammany Hall and Boss Tweed, one should not underestimate the influence of the cartoon today. At present, every large newspaper employs a top-notch cartoonist in its efforts to entertain or to influence opinion. Smaller newspapers unable to afford a cartoonist rely on the syndicates for the same service.

MID-CENTURY STATISTICS

To repeat the words of the "Editor and Publisher 1950 International Year Book," "Daily newspapers came through 1949 and entered 1950 in the strongest position in their history." Statistics from this same source present very interesting findings. The total morning and evening circulation, as of October 1, 1949, reached an all-time high of 52,845,551.

47

This figure represents an increase of 1.07 per cent over the comparative 1948 figure of 52,285,297.

Evening newspapers registered a gain of 2.04 per cent. The total evening circulation was 31,840,901, a gain of 637,509 over the 1948 high of 31,203,392. Morning newspapers experienced a slight decline of 0.36 per cent or 77,255 from the 1948 high of 21,081,905. The 1949 morning total circulation was 21,004,650. Sunday newspapers experienced a slight increase of 0.19 per cent as they established another record circulation of 46,398,968. These figures represent a gain of 90,887 over the 1948 figure of 46,308,081.

The total number of daily newspapers in the United States as of January 1, 1950, was 1,780. This figure represents a decrease of 1 from the 1,781 of January 1, 1949. The breakdown on this figure shows that morning newspapers increased by 1, the figure going from 328 to 329. Evening newspapers, however, decreased by 2, the figure dropping from 1,453 to 1,451. Sunday newspapers increased from 530 to 546. The year 1949 was the first since 1944 that showed no increase in the number of dailies.

Advertising figures also represent an interesting picture. In 1949, the total advertising as revealed in the records of 52 representative cities showed a 1.7 per cent gain over the 1948 figure of 28,522,205 lines. This figure represents a 21.3 per cent increase over 1929 and a 116 per cent increase over 1933, which had the lowest figure for the preceding 18 years.

CURRENT STATISTICAL PICTURE

An interesting insight into the current statistical picture of the American newspaper is to be seen in the August 1957 publication of the "Standard Rate and Data Service, Inc.," of Evanston, Illinois. This publication reveals that there are presently 1,588 newspapers in the United States with a net paid circulation of 56,641,575. Of the total newspapers, just four have circulations of less than 1,000, while 13 have circulations of 500,000 or over. A further examination reveals that the 1,588 newspapers are located in 1,453 communities. The breakdown on circulation is as follows:

CIRCULATION GROUPS	NO. OF PAPERS
500,000 — over	13
400,000 — 499,999	8
300,000 — 399,999	14
250,000 — 299,999	13
200,000 — 249,999	18
150,000 — 199,999	22
100,000 — 149,999	28
87,500 — 99,999	25
75,000 — 87,499	23
62,500 — 74,999	18
50,000 — 62,499	48
45,000 — 49,999	16
40,000 — 44,999	20
35,000 — 39,999	32
30,000 — 34,999	33
25,000 — 29,999	50
20,000 — 24,999	77
17,500 — 19,999	39
15,000 — 17,499	57
12,500 — 14,999	74
10,000 — 12,499	126
7,500 — 9,999	143
5,000 — 7,499	260
4,000 — 4,999	145
3,000 — 3,999	175
2,000 — 2,999	76
1,000 — 1,999	31
Under 1,000	4

The News Story

Chapter
2

WHAT IS NEWS?

In any discussion of the news story, the first step should
be to define "news." This, however, is a baffling task, for,
although many definitions have been advanced, few have
gained even limited acceptance. Consequently, most newspapermen make no attempt to define; they simply come to
recognize news by association—by learning the situations that
provide news.

An all-inclusive definition is impossible because news is a relative matter, varying sharply (1) from one paper to another, (2) from one time to another, and (3) from one locality to another.

The variation in news from one paper to another can be seen by comparing the tabloid and the conservative daily of any large city. Many of the stories displayed prominently in the tabloid receive no mention in the conservative daily; conversely, many of the stories in the conservative daily are not used by the tabloid. In each instance, news exists for one paper but not for the other.

The variation from one time to another can be seen by checking the stories in a given newspaper for an extended period. On days when newsworthy items are scarce, a local banquet is news. On days when newsworthy items are more numerous, a similar banquet receives no space whatever. Time thus makes the difference between news and no news.

The variation from one locality to another can be seen by checking the stories in the rural paper against those in the metropolitan daily. In the rural area, a small local fire is news. In the metropolitan area, a dozen similar fires are ignored. Locality makes the difference in the existence of news.

Further evidence of the varying nature of news is to be seen in the manner in which several papers may handle the same story. While they agree that a given set of facts provides news, they may disagree on kind of news, facts to be omitted, and angles to be stressed. For example, the tabloid, the conservative daily, and the neighborhood weekly generally differ widely in their treatment of automobile accidents in which children are killed. The tabloid usually plays up the sentimental side, using one or more gory pictures. The conservative daily most often confines itself briefly to the main

facts, using pictures of the traditional pattern. The neighborhood weekly generally handles the story from a strictly local
angle, interpolating the maximum in local interest (names of
residents involved even slightly, playmates' reactions, schools
attended, etc.). Thus, the story provides a different brand
of news for each paper.

Despite these insurmountable obstacles to establishing an
all-inclusive definition, journalists are in fairly common agreement that the following five qualities characterize news stories.

First, *news is any printable story which, in the opinion of
the editor, will interest the readers of his paper.* A story is
"printable"[1] if it meets the editorial policy standards of the
particular paper; a story will interest readers if (1) it concerns them directly or (2) it makes interesting reading. The
most common stories that concern readers directly are accounts of governmental actions (e.g., tax increases, new laws,
appointments); advances in science (e.g., cures for disease,
new inventions, experiments); and economic analyses (e.g.,
employment studies, price-level explanations, stock-market
predictions). The stories that are news because they make interesting reading run a wide gamut. They tell of executions,
country fairs, neighborhood rows, or anything else the editor
believes newsworthy. How deeply the editor thinks the
reader will be interested largely determines the "play" that the
story receives.

Second, *news is always completely true.* It is the story of
something that has actually happened or a statement that has
been made. In relating news, therefore, the writer may not
resort to conjecture or supposition. He is limited to the cold
facts of the story, told without emotion, prejudice, or personal opinion. Any deviation from these restrictions is termed

[1] See Chapter 7 for a discussion of editorial policy.

"editorializing," a fault that is viewed as a serious error by most newspapermen.

Third, *news has a quality of recency about it.* It is the story of something that has just happened or something being told for the first time. In short, it is a story that possesses the appeal of freshly discovered material. The successful newspaper, therefore, must relate for its readers the latest newsworthy items in places ranging from the police court to the conference rooms of the United Nations. And it must print its accounts as soon after the actual occurrences as possible. The old statement, "as out of date as yesterday's newspaper," is an excellent illustration of the emphasis placed on recency.

Fourth, *news has an element of proximity about it.* People, generally speaking, are most interested in events that are near them in space, time, and general background. This statement means that people are usually most interested in stories from their own city, state, and nation; in stories of or close to the present time; and in stories related to their racial, social, cultural, or national background. The element of proximity thus places a heavy emphasis on stories of local interest, current events, and celebrations by racial, religious, and national groups.

Fifth, *news must have some element of the unusual about it.* Although some few stories, such as routine announcements from public officials, can have little of the unusual, the editor invariably demands stories outside the commonplace. He makes this demand because a newspaper must rely on the unusual to brighten its pages. The importance of the unusual is to be seen in the old saw, "If a dog bites a man, it's not news; but if a man bites a dog, it is news."

The caution to be noted in any discussion of these five qualities is that there can be no "chemistry" of the news story because newspapers do not emphasize the qualities uniformly. The *Christian Science Monitor*, for instance, concerns itself almost exclusively with national and international news; the New York *Daily News*, a tabloid, leans most heavily on sensational stories of New Yorkers; the Philadelphia *Evening Bulletin* strives to cover a wide field of interests. In each case, therefore, is a different emphasis on the qualities that characterize news.

FINDING THE NEWS

THE REPORTER

The greatest element in the gathering of news is undoubtedly the ability of the reporter seeking it. One reporter may cover a district without finding a single story; a second may glean a dozen from the same area. In another instance, one reporter may find barely enough information for a short; a second may get a full column. In each case, the ability of the individual reporter determines the quality and the quantity of news obtained. Many an old newspaperman would summarize by saying that a reporter must have a "nose for news." He would cite case after case where successful journalists obtained stories when others had failed, attributing it all to a congenital news-finding ability. Yet, there is ample refutation for this old argument that reporters are born, not made. Many reporters have been highly successful by learning their job as one would a trade or a profession; that is, by working hard, being alert, and studying the methods of the most successful men in the field.

Undoubtedly those best qualified to pass judgment on the requirements of the good reporter are the newspapermen themselves. The student of journalism, therefore, should know the qualities which the seasoned newspaperman looks for in the reporter. The following points represent the attributes of the successful reporter, as given by 45 newspapermen who have had successful careers on large papers for periods ranging from 11 to 51 years.

1. **Accuracy**—Above all else, the reporters must be accurate, for editors and publishers have little use for a reporter given to inaccuracies. The importance of accuracy stands unquestioned because (1) the only consistently successful defense against libel up to the present has been to prove the statement true and (2) a paper printing inaccuracies loses prestige with its readers.

2. **Recognition of a Story**—The reporter must be certain that he can recognize news as defined by his paper. He must also remember that occasionally the real story may lie deep beneath the superficial facts. He, as a reporter, should be able to sense such a story in the manner that a good hunter senses the presence of game.

3. **Handling a Story**—When "working" a story, the reporter must know the facts to seek, their order of importance, and where to find them. He must get all important names, with correct spelling, plus the addresses and the occupations of the persons involved. In unsolved crime stories, he must know the officials with whom to maintain contact and he must be able to anticipate the movements of the police assigned to the case. In all stories, he must know the procedure best designed to get the facts quickly and accurately.

4. **Clarity of Expression**—The reporter must have the ability to express himself well in both written and oral speech. The need for effective written expression is obvious. The need for effective oral expression exists because the reporter does so much interviewing and because he often gathers news for a rewrite man to whom he must make clear and vivid, usually by means of the telephone, every point in the story. Also,

55

frequently the reporter must give the editor a quick, incisive picture of a situation or happening that he believes to be newsworthy.

5. **Pleasing Personality**—Because so much newsgathering involves personal contact, the reporter must have a pleasing personality. The importance of personality, however, is not limited to gathering news; it is also highly important in one's relations with his fellow newspapermen. Frequently reporters must work together under intense pressure to get a story, and in such instances a pleasing personality obviously helps to make the team work more smoothly. The reporter, in short, must be one who can "get along" with other persons—one whose personality "wears well."

6. **Adjusting Approach**—The reporter must develop versatility in handling people. He must be able to handle with equal facility the residents of the so-called "tough" neighborhoods as well as those from the better sections. He must speak the language of the person he is interviewing, if he can do so without affectation. And he must be especially careful not to imitate the Hollywood versions of the reporter in action. The ability to adjust approach must be developed at the outset, for strange though it may seem, the lowliest reporting assignments (cub reporter, district man, etc.) often cover the widest range of personalities.

7. **Speed**—The reporter must be one who can work efficiently at top speed, one who does not break under the pressure of time. This ability to work rapidly is indispensable because much news breaks fast and must be handled fast. The reporter, therefore, must be able to handle accidents, disasters, and other spot news in the minimum time, or the newspaper is likely to be scooped.

[2] See Chapter 3, p. 97, for a discussion of the attributes of the successful reporter related to interviewing.

Gaining the ability to work quickly is largely a matter of knowing what to do. Many reporters become rattled and lose their efficiency simply because they have never learned to plan a course of action for all types of stories before the actual news breaks.

8. Ingenuity—The successful reporter must be well blessed with ingenuity. He must be able to find the way to obtain the news, if such be at all possible, and he must always be alert in procuring photographs and other material helpful to his newspaper. He must never forget that the newspaper world, like other highly competitive fields, is one wherein intelligence is an essential. The reporter who is constantly outwitted by a rival or outmaneuvered by someone involved in the news source stands little chance to succeed. Ingenuity is also vastly important in finding new and different angles to handle otherwise dull and routine material.

9. Knowing News Sources—The reporter must remember that persons in a position to give news frequently want to withhold stories, either temporarily or permanently. This is especially true of the central figures in scandals, thefts, and other stories likely to provoke unfavorable publicity. Thus, the reporter must know where stories are likely to break and how to get them at the earliest moment. The hospitals, the morgue, the police stations, and similar places must be checked thoroughly and constantly by a reporter who knows how to unearth news.

10. Checking Names—Since persons not wanting their names in newspapers sometimes give false information to the reporter, he must know how to check names and addresses against a source likely to be correct. Among the best on-the-scene sources are drivers' licenses, social security cards, and draft classification cards. Among the secondary sources are police blotters, telephone and city directories, and private

listings (club membership lists, institution catalogs, private directories, etc.).

11. **Building Contacts**—The reporter should maintain a long list of friends and acquaintances who may be of help when stories break, and he should know intimately persons who can give authoritative information on every kind of story. Among the most desirable persons to have on a contact list are police officers, labor leaders, attorneys, governmental employees, and persons associated with hospitals and other places where stories are likely to be found.

12. **Retaining the Favor of the Police**—Because the police are involved in so many situations that become news, the reporter must know how to obtain and retain their favor. This end is accomplished primarily by giving the police favorable publicity, or, in the words of the veteran district man, "taking care of the cops." This statement means that, whenever there is an arrest or other creditable work by the police, the reporter should get the name of the individual officer into the paper—the officer thus gains the notice of his superior at City Hall, a notice that may lead to a promotion. Many a reporter has received a scoop by virtue of help from a policeman grateful for a past favor. And many a reporter has failed to obtain a story because he did not have the necessary help from the police.

13. **Respecting Promises**—The reporter must be one who respects promises, especially promises made to persons who are news sources. If the reporter knows, for example, that he cannot withhold a name from publication, he should not promise to do so. And if someone gives him a story with the understanding that certain facts are to be printed, he must make certain that the stipulated information gets into print. Broken promises invariably threaten the continuance of many news sources.

14. Knowing the City—The reporter must know his city in order not to lose valuable time in handling stories. He must know the streets, the important buildings, and the fastest routes to all places at all hours. He must familiarize himself especially with the locations of hospitals, police stations, morgues, firehouses, public auditoriums, and similar news sources.

15. Working Agreement with Rivals—Whenever a reporter agrees to exchange information or co-operate with a reporter from a rival paper, he should make certain that the agreement is beneficial to him and that it is clearly understood by the rival reporter. If an agreement is not beneficial to a reporter, he is actually helping the rival paper. If a working agreement is not clearly understood by both reporters, unpleasant relations are certain to follow and the co-operation necessary on big stories that break fast will be threatened.

16. Getting Names in the Paper—The reporter must get as many names as possible in the story without obviously overloading it. Names are important because they generate reader interest and because they give stories a note of authenticity.

17. Direct Quotations—Whenever a direct quotation is authorized, the reporter should read the statement back to the speaker in order to avoid misunderstanding and future difficulty. This is standard procedure in interviewing high public officials. When a mimeographed statement is distributed, this move, of course, is not necessary.

18. Editing the News—The reporter must not trespass on the domain of his editor by acting as a field editor, or one who assumes the task of editing the news at its source. The reporter's job is to find news; the editor's job is to pass upon it. When the reporter draws the fire of his editor by assuming the latter's prerogative, strained relations generally arise.

19. Professional Respect—If the newspaper reporter is to be successful, he must have genuine respect for the whole field of journalism. He must realize the significant role that the newspaper fills in society and the importance of his work as a reporter. All too often, a reporter feels that he is doing routine work for an unappreciative public. When this attitude is adopted, the reporter's work is certain to reflect a tone of mediocrity.

20. Improvement—The reporter must always strive to improve, even after long years of varied experience. As in other professions, the reporter will slip backward when he ceases his efforts to improve. A constant effort to be a better reporter is, therefore, imperative.

SOURCES OF NEWS

Newspapers in large cities usually obtain their news from the sources listed below. These sources are also used in varying degree by small dailies, trade publications, and weeklies.

1. District Men—As the term implies, district men (or legmen) are reporters assigned to patrol a given beat. They are responsible for any news that may originate in their assigned firehouses, hospitals, morgues, and other places likely to have first knowledge of events that make news. When the district man has a story, he calls his editor who decides whether the story is to be used, and, if so, the "play" that it is to receive. The editor then assigns a rewrite man to take the story over the telephone and write it up. The district man may also be called upon to check tips on stories given him by his desk or to gather information on a story emanating from another source.

2. Special Assignment—Because of the importance of the news and the complexity of the task, reporters frequently are given the "special" assignment of watching over one spot, such as a city hall, a courthouse, or a state capitol, where news may be found at any moment. Although much of this news may seem routine in nature, the demand for capable reporting is great. Hence, only the best reporters are used in this role.

Another phase of special assignment work is that of having reporters concentrate on definite kinds of stories or "specialties." Sometimes the field is so large that a reporter handles no other type of work; other times it requires only part of his working day. Among the specialties are politics, society, business, religion, drama, labor, education, radio, and stamps. On very large newspapers, these specialties frequently are enlarged into departments, each of which is headed by an editor.

The term "special assignment" is not to be confused with the term "general assignment." The latter term applies to the reporter who is on call to handle any story to which he may be assigned.

3. **Roving Reporters**—The roving reporter is a seasoned newspaperman assigned by his editor to roam the city for news—especially for material for human interest and other feature stories. He usually seeks stories at building constructions, waterfronts, and other places where news is likely to exist, and he also relies on friends in varied walks of life to give him tips. The success of the roving reporter obviously determines his right to hold this attractive assignment, an assignment that is eagerly sought after because of the pleasant nature of the work and the inevitable by-line.

4. **Futures File**—The futures file, as the name indicates, is the repository for notices, letters, programs, and notations of events to come. This file is especially helpful in making assignments, planning the news schedule for the week, and maintaining coverage of local events. The file, usually at the

city editor's desk, generally covers the coming three months.

5. Tipsters—Newspapers frequently maintain a staff of "tipsters," or persons paid for informing the editor of anything that may be newsworthy. The tipster, who is usually paid in proportion to the space given the story in print or to the importance of the tip, must demonstrate both integrity and the ability to furnish valuable information. Tipsters are most often persons whose industrial or governmental positions enable them to have the first inkling of newsworthy events.

6. Press Releases—Any institution, organization, or group wishing publicity distributes press releases.[3] These releases, prepared by a publicity man or a professional agency, are sent to the newspaper offices. Although many are of little value as news, one occasionally can be used. These releases are of most value when they come from such nonprofit organizations as museums, scientific groups, and charitable agencies.

7. Space Writers—Because of the economy effected, newspapers frequently employ writers to contribute stories on a space basis. The space writer is paid by the column inch for material accepted for publication, regardless of amount of material submitted. Space writers are usually aspirants to the newspaper business, students who write of events in their schools, and persons who act as correspondents from their home towns for newspapers located elsewhere.

8. Unsolicited Calls—All newspapers receive unsolicited telephone calls and letters telling them of potential stories. These calls most often tell of accidents, deplorable neighborhood conditions, or illicit activity. Some of the best stories may result from checking these unsolicited tips.

[3] For an exhaustive discussion of this subject, refer to "How to Get Industrial and Business Publicity," by C. E. St. Thomas, Philadelphia, Chilton, 1956.

9. **Death Notices**—By checking the death notices in the paper, the editor sometimes finds one that should be enlarged into an obituary, or he learns of the death of someone who figured in an earlier story. The death notices are also checked against "Who's Who," the social register, and the clippings in the newspaper morgue.

10. **Stories in Other Newspapers**—The top editors of a newspaper invariably study every edition of rival papers as soon as they can be procured. If they find in another paper a good story not in their own, they immediately assign a reporter to work on the story, if such be possible. Or, in some cases, they simply have a rewrite man recast it for their own paper. Consequently, local stories can be exclusive for only one edition unless a newspaper can cut off its rivals from the source of the news. A story in a given newspaper that has a "follow" (i.e., that will create more news in the near future) invariably is worked over by the other newspapers.

In addition to these 10 sources, newspapers rely on the wire services to supply news from other parts of the state, the nation, and the world. The two prominent wire services in the United States presently are the Associated Press and the United Press International News Service. In addition to the wire services, newspapers use the news bureaus of such large papers as the *New York Times,* the *New York Herald Tribune,* the *Chicago Tribune,* and the *Chicago Daily News.* These bureaus sell the news in their publications to papers in other cities. Thus, readers in Cleveland, San Francisco, and other American cities get local news from other parts of the nation.

Campus newspapers, church magazines, trade journals, and similar publications usually know well in advance what they are going to use, and assign reporters to cover the events. In fact, frequently a large part of the copy is written a day or two before their presses start.

WRITING THE NEWS STORY

STRUCTURE OF THE NEWS STORY

In writing the news story, the journalist often employs a structure unique to journalism. Unlike the usual short story, where the events build consistently to a climax, the news story generally states the climax at the outset and then proceeds to enlarge upon it. The news story is divided into two parts, the lead and the body.

The **lead** of the news story is exactly what the term implies. It is the part that comes first, and it tells the whole story in a sentence or two.[4] The story itself may be several columns in length, but the lead must still summarize everything. The lead tells the *where, when, what, how, why,* and *who* of the story. All six qualities are not essential to every lead, but no lead should be without all the necessary ones. Here are four typical leads:

**Teamster Unit
To Give Car To
Palsy Victims**

The 23 children suffering from cerebral palsy who attend South Side Training Center school in the Tuley Park fieldhouse, 90th st. and St. Lawrence av., will be presented with a specially equipped station wagon today by Teamsters Joint Council No. 25, Ray Schoessling, president of the council, announced today.

—Chicago Tribune

**Housing Group
Unveils Home
Despite Rebuff**

Although denied a new loan by the Reconstruction Finance Corporation, the Lustron Housing Corporation today unveiled six new home models, including a five-room house to sell for approximately $2,000 less than the first Lustron house introduced two years ago.

—Christian Science Monitor

[4] This statement refers to the conventional lead.

OFFICIAL CERTIFIES LAUNDRY BALLOTING

A National Labor Relations Board official said here today he is certifying to Washington the results of last week's laundry and dry cleaning election in which the AFL won a 2-to-1 decision over the CIO.

—Indianapolis News

Continued Hot Weather on Tap

The Fourth of July weather Nashville has enjoyed for its long weekend will continue today when everyone goes back to work, Weatherman Jack Merryman said last night.

—Nashville Tennessean

The lead is highly important primarily because it can either lure the reader on or send him off to another story. Therefore, it must be attractive as well as inclusive, and sometimes even an experienced writer may try three or four leads before he is satisfied.[5]

The **body** of the story, which is the part that follows the lead, serves to explain and enlarge upon the facts of the lead and to supply the less important information. The most common methods used in writing the body are the highlight, the chronological, and the pyramid.

When the writer employs the **highlight** method, he dwells on the most important parts of the event, thus "highlighting" the event. The highlight structure is especially suitable for stories of speeches, sports events, and pageants (parades, celebrations, etc.). The following is an example of the highlight method:

[5] For further variety in leads, see Chapter 4, p. 123.

200 Get Overstreets' 'Self' Psychology Prescriptions

More than 200 Baltimoreans were given a hatful of do-it-yourself prescriptions for practical psychology last night by Harry Allen Overstreet and his wife, Bonaro Wilkinson Overstreet, at the First Unitarian Church.

Mr. Overstreet, author of the best-selling "The Mature Mind," and Mrs. Overstreet, a poetess and specialist in parent education and adolescents' problems, spoke on "Learning To Live With Ourselves" in a lecture sponsored by the church's Women's Club.

Speak As One

The Overstreets began their dual discourse by asking their audiences to assume some homework—the listing of all dictionary words beginning with "self." On this peg, they hung their talk.

They chose three word combinations as key phrases for their subject: Self-awareness, self-dedication and self-acceptance.

Mrs. Overstreet wore a two-piece brown-and-white flowered outfit and a shiny jeweled brooch; her husband, whose gray-edged hair recedes halfway back on the left, wore spectacles and a conservative bow tie, slightly aslant. Together, they leaned intimately over the pulpit once manned by Ellery Channing, father of the Unitarian Church in this country, to deliver their carefully rehearsed message.

In effect, they spoke as one.

They described the immature human mental survival pattern of "fight and flight"—a system of meeting problems headon or of avoiding them altogether. They said this pattern is common in the growing person.

The opposite, and better, pattern is one of "loving and learning," they said. Those who have come to utilize this system can take the persons with whom they deal into the fold of their appreciation and understanding, they said—adding that "loving and learning" is simply a matter of projection.

In dealing with the three key phases necessary for successfully living with oneself, they defined self-awareness as the condition of not being deceived by oneself. This is the quality of being conscious of how funny (or worthwhile) one is, how one can be, and especially how one looks to others, they pointed out.

Final Requisite

Self-dedication, they said, is possessed by the person who relates himself to his world with the sense that there are great things to be done in that world. This dedication need not be directed toward oneself, but should be focused on some person or cause outside the individual.

And the final requisite for living with oneself — self-acceptance — was said by the Overstreets to be "a quiet, working belief that one has within himself what it takes to make a good life."

On this inspirational note, the man-wife team closed its presentation on how to appease one's ego.

—*Sun*, Baltimore, Md.

The term "**chronological** method" is self-explanatory; it is the method by which the events in a story are presented in chronological order. This method employs the structure of the conventional short story, building directly up to a high point or climax. The following story is an example:

When Boat Fans Meet, They Sail Into Battle

Special to the Minneapolis Tribune

LONDON—In Britain, for centuries ruler of the waves, ships are taken seriously—even model ships.

So there was, as usual, a big crowd around Long pond on Clapham Common when Bob Cordiner launched his model steamboat, Robbie's Pride, and Ken Piper put into the water, from the opposite side, his model yacht, the Tempest.

The two elaborately contrived craft approached each other. Suddenly the Tempest swung in front of the steamship. Robbie's Pride, ignoring the rule of the sea that steam must give way to sail, plowed into the yacht, rending its sail.

The yacht owner ran over to the steamboat owner, grabbed him, and threw him into the pond. The steamboater, fishing out the yacht, carried it ashore and broke the mast over his knee. The two owners closed and came to blows.

It was a fine fight, until spectators and police broke it up. Then the two model builders were hauled off to court, where the judge imposed fines totaling $22.40 on the pair, both grown men, and gave them a lecture.

—*Minneapolis Tribune*

The **pyramid** method derives its name from the fact that the arrangement of details resembles a series of inverted pyramids; that is, the facts of the story are arranged in a descending order, the most important coming first. Study the following example on p. 68.

Andrew Talandis, the Oakland pest extermi-
nator who escaped from a Florida chain gang 16
years ago, must be returned to the Southern prison,
Superior Judge Donald K. Quayle ruled yesterday.

Talandis, whose real name is James C. Malden,
failed to win a writ of habeas corpus sought by
Assistant Public Defender Enid Weseman in an effort to block his extradition.

The judge ruled the extradition papers from
Florida prison authorities were valid and that
Governor Goodwin J. Knight's order for his re-
turn must be obeyed.

Only one formality remains before Talandis
leaves Oakland's city jail for Florida. That is a
routine hearing on the fugitive warrant, scheduled
in the Oakland Municipal Court this morning.

Talandis came to Oakland after his escape in
1938 and settled down. He is married and has one
child and five step-children. A 1951 attempt to
extradite him failed when Governor Warren refused
to approve the papers.

Knight, however, said he ordered the extradition after an investigation disclosed Talandis
failed to keep pledges about his personal conduct.
Knight said Talandis drank heavily and failed to
support his family.

—*San Francisco Chronicle*

STYLE OF THE NEWS STORY

Conciseness

Generally speaking, the prime consideration in writing the news story is to say everything in the fewest words possible. Stories must be written concisely because most newspapers invariably have more material than they can use, and they want to print the maximum. The reporter, therefore, must learn to phrase his thoughts succinctly, without loss of details or accuracy. Note the following examples:

Long: The man decided after a great deal of consideration that it was best to act then and there.
Better: The man finally decided to act immediately.

Long: The rays of the light extended for a distance of more than 50 feet.
Better: The light shone more than 50 feet.

Long: They do not have any opening at the present time for a man with the qualifications of a stonemason.
Better: They have no openings at present for stonemasons.

Long: This problem is a very difficult one and is baffling to the best mathematicians.
Better: This very difficult problem baffles the best mathematicians.

Clarity

The second consideration in writing the news story is clarity. Although the story may be of a complex nature, it still must be readable to the normal junior high school student.

This clarity of presentation is obtained by sentence structure and by a relatively simple word choice. Note the following examples:

Poor: That Judge Sloan's judicial pronouncements on the somewhat complex and frequently enigmatic subject of professional mendicants vacillates is not readily demonstrable, even by lawyers.

Better: Even lawyers would have trouble proving that Judge Sloan is not consistent in his rulings on the difficult question of professional beggars.

Poor: The chemist immersed an ecru redingote in a saline solution.

Better: The chemist dipped the tan coat in a salt solution.

Poor: A cardiologist extemporized upon the systolic and diastolic activity of the patient's heart.

Better: A heart specialist spoke about the beating of the patient's heart.

If the writer is forced to use a term that may baffle his reader (as, for instance, a legal term), the expression can be explained in parentheses, an "editor's note," or in the context of the story, according to the nature of the explanation. Notice how the writer of the following story has explained a term in the context:

A supply of gamma globulin, the fluid used to combat paralysis caused by polio, will be turned over to the Office of Defense Mobilization today by the American Red Cross.

—*Courier-Journal*, Louisville, Ky.

Forceful Expression

The third consideration in writing the news story is the need for forceful expression. Although the demands for conciseness and clarity often result in simplicity of expression, news writing still must be forceful. The writer, therefore, must constantly seek for the most effective way, within the limits set by journalistic writing, of expressing a particular thought. It may lie in words used, or it may lie in nice turn of phrase. It may lie in an unusual figure of speech, or it may lie in some other rhetorical device. Wherever it is, the reporter must find it. Note the following examples:

Fair: Goering was very proud of the German armed forces.

Better: Goering had a fierce pride in German armed might.

Fair: The captain, a large, heavy, tough-looking man, shouted his orders from the bridge.

Better: The captain, a burly, swaggering, belligerent Irishman, bellowed his orders from the bridge.

Fair: The small, conceited lawyer moved up and down before the unimpressed jurors.

Better: The pompous little lawyer strutted like a ham actor before the unimpressed jurors.

Fair: Samuel Insull, who was now a man without a country, spent his time in a completely new setting of customs, places, and atmospheres.

Better: A man without a country, Samuel Insull whiled away his time in a maze of strange customs, unfamiliar places, and new atmospheres.

71

Cautions

However, there are two cautions to be noted in stating that the journalist must write forcefully; the first concerns *choice of words*, and the second concerns *coherence*. In choice of words, the journalist, already limited to a relatively simple word choice, is restricted further by the need to recognize localisms and the rules of his newspaper concerning doubtful words. He may, for instance, speak of "redding up" (straightening the furniture, cleaning, etc.) a room in a region where that localism is used, but in other localities he must avoid it. As for doubtful words, the writer must check his paper's stylebook to know whether he is permitted to use such terms, for example, as *thug, cop, bum, flophouse, street walker, gun moll, racket, love nest.*

The caution concerning coherence is simply this: the writer of the news story must not strive for the coherence of fiction and other nonjournalistic writing. Coherence in the news story is sacrificed to conciseness and clarity of detail. The following story, taken from one of America's large newspapers, is a typical example of journalistic writing. Despite its lack of conventional coherence, it is, journalistically speaking, quite acceptable.

Grand jurors Tuesday learned first hand how Alcatraz-hardened Floyd Hill and nine other prisoners broke out of county jail after slugging three guards Wednesday night.

The jurors took time out from their duties to investigate county jail and circumstances leading up to the escape.

District Attorney Fender previously announced that the grand jury would be asked to check into the jail break. He has said that as far as he's concerned, there was no criminal negligence involved.

The investigation came on the heels of the grand jury's indictment of the 10 men on charges of escape from jail.

If found guilty the men face a prison sentence of from two to five years. The offense becomes a felony when someone other than the escaping prisoners is hurt in the jail break.

Star-Telegram,
Fort Worth, Tex.

Accuracy and Truth

The fourth consideration in writing the news story is respect for accuracy and truth. The writer must be careful of distortions and inaccuracies, for most newspapers make a heavy point of accuracy and truth.[6] They do so because these qualities are the bedrock of prestige.

Also to be noted in speaking of accuracy and truth is the fact that small errors make an appearance when copy is not edited carefully. These errors, although obviously not so serious as gross misstatements of fact, nonetheless are to be deplored in good journalistic writing. Note the following examples of faulty writing:

Faulty: Physicians say that the new drug is a sure-fire cure for polio. (This sentence implies that medical authorities are in complete agreement that the new drug is 100 per cent effective. Such is probably not the case. Also, this type of flat statement is too often used as a means of giving the writer's or a limited group's opinion.)

Faulty: The farmer lost a thousand chickens in the fire. (Either the exact number should be given, or such an expression as "about" or "an estimated" should be used.)

Faulty: The car careened around the corner at a 45-degree angle. (The expression "45-degree angle" is both trite and inexact. Only a most unusually constructed car could lean at this angle without overturning.)

[6] See p. 78 for a discussion of "slanting" and "coloring."

73

Faulty: The new member of the golf club was a young college professor. (The term "professor" is too often used loosely as a synonym for "college teacher." Strictly speaking, only one who holds professorial rank should be referred to as a "professor.")

Dictional Don'ts

The final consideration in news writing is to recognize the standard dictional "don'ts."

1. **Don't use bromides.** Such expressions as the following have been overworked and therefore are considered trite or hackneyed:

too good to be true	lightning fast
fleecy clouds	pearls of wisdom
raving maniac	host of friends
hall of fame	render a solo
stellar performance	heartbreaking finish
as luck would have it	last but not least
method in his madness	hanging in the balance
few and far between	brown as a berry
a dime a dozen	burning the midnight oil
pleasingly plump	dancing divinely
the flowering of genius	true blue
thick and fast	booming voice
straw that broke the camel's back	waxing poetic
slow as a tortoise	generous to a fault
sly as a fox	never-say-die
quick as a deer	sickening thud
	needle in a haystack

2. **Avoid expressions that are not literally true, or that are obviously overstatements.** Some examples:

Everybody knows this is true. (There is nothing that everybody knows.)

The entire audience was pleased. (Who can be certain of the word "entire"?)

It is the world's most appreciative group. (How can one be certain?)

He is the brightest boy in the school. (Judging by what infallible test?)

There can be no doubt whatever that he is the final authority on the subject. (Too sweeping to be entirely true.)

Like all Irishmen, he has a knack for politics. ("All" should be changed to "many.")

3. Avoid overworked personifications. Some examples:

Mr. Man-in-the-Street	Jack Frost
Mr. Average Citizen	Old Man Winter
Dan Cupid	Mother Earth
Lady Luck	Mr. Would-be
Dame Fortune	Johnny Doughboy
Joe College	G. I. Joe

4. Avoid euphemisms. Some examples:

He passed away July 1, 1936.
   Say simply: He died July 1, 1936.
An odor of perspiration was perceptible about the race horses.
   Say simply: The racehorses sweated (or perspired) freely.
He was so ill that he lost his dinner.
   Say simply: He regurgitated (or vomited).
His mortal remains were interred in the earth.
   Say simply: He was buried.
An aged gentleman entered.
   Say simply: An old man entered.

5. Avoid expressions that editorialize (i.e., give the writer's opinion either directly or by implication). Some examples:

75

She has the most pleasing voice in this community.
It is going to be a most interesting affair.
Fall is undoubtedly the best time of the year to get work done.
The defendant should certainly be acquitted.

REWRITING

An important phase of the news writer's work is that of rewriting. The term "rewriting" includes (1) rewriting or revising one's own copy; (2) taking news over the telephone and writing it according to instructions from the "desk"; (3) rewriting press releases and other material sent to the newspaper; (4) rewriting or revising with a view to trimming or improving the copy of other writers within the office; and (5) checking the writing of others for grammar, libel, style, and general accuracy.

The conditions which most often cause a newspaperman to rewrite his own work are: (1) his superior is of the opinion that the story is not well written; (2) the story must be trimmed because the paper is too tight; and (3) new facts must be added. If the writer is rewriting because of his superior's objections, he recasts, changes, and deletes according to instructions. If he is rewriting because his story must be trimmed, he may gain his end by eliminating the least important facts or by recasting the entire story. If he is rewriting because of new facts, usually he can accomplish his purpose by writing another lead and inserting the new facts in the appropriate places. In rewriting, the journalist simply observes the qualities of good journalistic writing as set forth in this chapter.

When the rewrite man handles a story telephoned to him by

a district man or reporter, he is not "rewriting" in a literal sense. He is, rather, the writing half of a team of two. The first man gets the facts; the second writes the story. This teamwork is employed in order to speed the story into print. Under this system, an editor first listens to the facts as the reporter calls in. Then he assigns a rewrite man to handle the story, telling him how long to make the story, the approach to follow, and the facts to play up. The rewrite man then proceeds accordingly.

In rewriting press releases and other material sent to the paper, the rewrite man is literally re-writing. Although these releases frequently are written by former newspapermen, they must be recast because they may not suit the style of the given paper, they are too long, or they are too obviously publicity releases. When the rewrite man handles such material, he may achieve his purpose by trimming and changing, or he may have to write the story anew, selecting the facts he wants to use. In such instances, he handles the story just as he would one that was telephoned in.

A rewrite man is called upon to revise the copy of others when the editor wants a second writer to work on a completed story. Perhaps he wants a humorous touch that the original writer is not able to give. Perhaps he thinks that the first writer is not capable of rewriting his own story or that the second writer can do the revision better. In such instances, he asks the second writer to trim, point up, or make any other changes which he, the editor, wants. The second writer then revises the work as though it were his own. He cannot, of course, spare the feelings of the first writer; he must hack and change as he sees fit.

When a rewrite man checks the writing of another for grammar, style, libel, and accuracy in general, he proceeds

77

as if he were a copyreader. In the small newspaper office, he is, in fact, a copyreader. The student of journalism, therefore, can understand this phase of rewriting by reading the duties of the copyreader in Chapter 5.

The amount of rewriting done in a newspaper office varies with the size of the particular paper. Thus, rewriting may be one of several tasks assigned to one man, or it may be the single task of many men. On the very small paper, one man may act as copyreader, rewriteman, and general editor, whereas the large newspaper may have several men who do nothing but rewrite.

TREATMENT OF NEWS

Slanting and Coloring

Although the manner in which the news story is written should be straightforward, factual, and impersonal, there are two qualities which the writer of the news story should know —"slanting" and "coloring." He should know these qualities in order to avoid them, or, strange though it may seem, because his paper employs them.

News is said to be **slanted** when the facts of a story are so arranged as to lead the reader to a desired conclusion. In slanting a story, therefore, the writer concerns himself solely with arrangement of facts. The newspaper that cites the progress of the national debt, showing statistically that we are moving toward a danger point, is slanting the news. The newspaper that compares the progress of one city with that of another, even though its manner may be impersonal, is slanting the news. The newspaper that gives a front-page spot to an official communique is, by virtue of the placing of the communique, slanting the news. In each case, the newspaper wants its readers to draw certain inferences and it slants the news accordingly.

News is said to be **colored** when some facts are stressed and others are made inconspicuous or omitted. The newspaperman speaks of stressing facts as "playing up" a given angle of a story. In speaking of making facts inconspicuous, he uses the terms "playing down" or "toning down." To see a good example of coloring, one has only to compare newspapers that support opposing parties at election time. Their reporters may have covered the same event—perhaps the speech of a candidate—but their versions are miles apart. The paper supporting the candidate emphasizes the ovation as he entered the hall. It refers to the applause as "thunderous," "deafening," or "tremendous." The other paper merely states that, "after customary applause, the candidate began his speech." The first paper dwells on the strong points of the speech, those parts likely to win votes for the speaker. The second paper stresses the parts likely to lose votes. In each paper, therefore, is a colored version of the story. This interesting comparison can be carried further by reading the story in a conservative or impartial paper.

In order to understand clearly the difference between slanting and coloring, the student of journalism should remember this distinction: news is slanted when the writer has attempted to influence the reader by arrangement of facts alone; news is colored when the writer attempts to influence the reader by arrangement of facts and by choice of words. The student should also remember, however, that many newspapermen consider these terms as synonymous and that many newspapermen believe that practically all news is slanted or colored to some degree.

Examine the following examples of slanting and coloring.

Slanting the News

City Deficit Being Reduced

Albert K. Leeds, City Treasurer, announced today that municipal revenue for the past year was $524,-829.19, an increase of 12% over that of last year. He also pointed out that for the three years in which the present administration has been in power, the deficit inherited from the former administration has been reduced each fiscal period. At the present rate of reduction, the entire deficit will be removed within ten years.

The above news article is slanted because it leads the reader to believe that the present municipal revenue, which is the result of an unusually good year in the city's industries, is due to good management and that this revenue will continue. The article also ignores the fact that the deficit was caused by the erection of some badly needed municipal buildings. In short, it leads the reader to believe that the present administration is very economical, while the last was not. Actually, the reverse is true.

INJURED ATHLETES TO BE COMPENSATED

The Inter-scholastic Athletic Association announced yesterday its new schedule of payments for injuries received by members of football teams of the association.

Boys receiving fractures or broken bones will have medical expenses paid, plus $5. per week for the period of incapacity. Boys becoming permanently disabled (spinal injuries, loss of arm or leg, etc.) will receive a flat sum of $1000. For loss of life the beneficiary will be paid $2000.

This news article is slanted because it leaves the reader with the unfortunate opinion that serious injury and loss of life are commonplace in football. Thus, it does a serious wrong to the sport. Actually, serious injury is not common when a team has been properly trained and coached. Death, of course, in such instances is extremely rare.

Coloring the News

Study the highly colored news story below, noting especially the words that contribute to the coloring.

Judge Stephens Addresses Group

Speaking in his unusually resonant voice and evidencing his customary charm, Judge Harold L. Stephens, noted authority on the problem of first offenders, addressed the members of the Hillside Community Center last night. Judge Stephens, as always, delivered a very fine address. He drew upon his wide experience and his deep understanding of criminally inclined people to give a sympathetic, scholarly picture of the condition as he sees it.

The benign jurist opened his address by modestly declaring that he would do his best to interpret the problem of first offenders which has become so very serious within the last few years. He then proceeded to phrase succinctly and clearly the various phases of the problem. "The root of the problem," he declared forcefully, "lies in the home. We must have a good start there. If father and mother don't assume their responsibilities, then the child will naturally fall into bad ways." He then proceeded in a rare manner of calm rationalization to outline the work that must be done by the school and the church as well. "And where these agencies fail," he concluded in ringing tones, "society must assume the burden."

Judge Stephens then proceeded to answer questions from the floor with his characteristic ease, never once faltering or groping for words in his answers. The sincerely appreciative response of the audience throughout attested to the real quality of the speech.

CUT LINES

A picture to be used in the paper is referred to as "art" or as a "cut." Thus, the newspaperman speaks of a one-column cut, a two-column cut, and so forth. The line that appears over the picture is called the "caption," and the lines under the picture are called "cut lines."

If the picture accompanies a story, the reporter involved usually is called upon to write the caption and the cut lines. Once the reporter has learned to write a news story, the writing of these lines is rarely difficult.

81

Cut lines, like headlines, vary according to the effect desired. Sometimes the effect is to be humorous, sometimes satirical, sometimes straightforward and impersonal. Thus the writer must strive for the words and the style that best suit the occasion.

EXAMPLES FOR DISCUSSION

On the following pages are news stories taken from some of the leading newspapers in the United States. Make a study of these stories, noting especially the lead and the manner of relating the facts. Also make note of anything that especially impresses you, either favorably or unfavorably.

TWIN SISTERS, 80, MURDERED IN HOME

Virtual Recluses Are Beaten to Death in Their Ancient Staten Island Dwelling

The bodies of elderly twin sisters, members of one of Staten Island's oldest Huguenot families, were found with skulls crushed lying on the kitchen floor of their home at 3344 Richmond Terrace, Mariners Harbor, yesterday afternoon.

They were Misses May and Viola De Hart, believed by the police to be nearly 80 years old. Although their family was well known, they themselves were seen little by their neighbors, living almost as recluses. No visitors ever were permitted in their shuttered, two-and-a-half-story frame house, and even the postman was required to shove their mail under a door.

Determination of the exact cause and time of their death awaited autopsy last night by Dr. Mendel Jacobi, assistant medical examiner of Staten Island.

The bodies, one lying partly on top of the other, were found at 4 o'clock yesterday afternoon by Dolores Schoppman, 11, who lives a short distance away at 3326½ Richmond Terrace. Her attention was attracted early in the afternoon by a brush fire in a field back of the old De Hart house.

On her way home from watching the fire, the child noticed that the lower panel of the kitchen door of the dwelling had been knocked out. Her curiosity aroused, she peered through the kitchen window and saw the bodies on the floor. A few minutes later she confided her discovery to a clerk in a near-by drugstore, who notified Staten Island Police Headquarters in St. George.

Early last night the police were unable to find any clue or disclose a motive for murder.

According to neighbors, the two women rarely left their house. Occasionally Miss Viola, who appeared the more active of the sisters, went out to shop but kept to herself.

Richmond Terrace is the main thoroughfare on the north shore of Staten Island, running from the municipal ferry house in St. George a distance of more than ten miles to Mariners Harbor. The women lived near the end of the thoroughfare where dwellings thin out. Although their house is not isolated, it is somewhat removed from the street. It is an old structure, believed to have been standing a century. Ancestors of the women were among the early settlers on Staten Island. De Hart Avenue in Mariners Harbor is named for them.

—New York Times

Landing of B-36 Thrills Denver

An air force B-36 superbomber made aviation history in Denver at 11:35 a. m. Saturday by landing on the new 8,500-foot runway at Stapleton airfield. It was the largest plane ever to land at the municipal field.

Thousands of people watched from their homes as the giant six-engine bomber circled the city, and several thousand were on hand at the airport when wheels of the big bomber touched the new east-west runway. The visit of the plane highlighted ceremonies dedicating the runway.

The plane arrived in the Denver area about 9 a. m. and circled the region for two and one-half hours.

The plane was brought to Denver through arrangements made by The Denver Post with W. Stuart Symington, air secretary, and other air force officials.

An open house celebration to dedicate the new runway began at 2 p. m. The giant B-36 was to be on display Saturday afternoon and Sunday morning on the concrete apron at East Thirty-second avenue and Syracuse street.

The plane took off from its Fort Worth, Tex., base Saturday morning, and flew over Stapleton airfield shortly after 9 a. m. It was seen by thousands of Denverites who heard it roaring over the eastern portion of the city.

The exhibition flight was turned into a training mission as well, and the plane kept in touch with the Denver airfield control tower.

—Denver Post

SLEET STORM BREAKS STATE POWER LINES

Service to 43 Towns Cut Off; Floods Rage in Dixie

Snow and sleet covered northwestern Oklahoma Sunday, cutting off electric and telephone service and disrupting transportation in some areas.

Oklahoma Gas and Electric Co. officials described the storm as "one of the worst for the company in that section of the state."

Ice formed on power lines and cut off electric service to 43 Oklahoma communities. Southwestern Bell Telephone Co. officials said many of its long-distance circuits were out of order because of broken lines.

TOWNS WITHOUT SERVICE

The power company listed the following communities temporarily without service:

Alva, Woodward, Geary, Greenfield, Loyal, Hitchcock, Eagle City, Oakwood, Canton, Watonga, Ames, Ringwood, Meno, Lahoma, Goltry, Helena, Jet, Nash, Garber, Covington, Lucien, Three Sands, Medford, Douglas, Lovell, Marshall, Billings, Hunter, Lamont, Salt Fork, Deer Creek, Narden, Renfro, Clyde, Gibbon, Wakita, Manchester, Carrier, Hillsdale, Kremlin, Pond Creek, Jefferson and the Medford waterworks.

Residents of Woodward were not inconvenienced by the storm damage to power lines. The city has its own plant sufficient to meet local needs.

Alva has only a small standby plant which officials said was capable of supplying essential service. Alva's service was curtailed because a feeder line tower was blown down by wind.

Power company officials said 125 workmen and engineers had been dispatched to the trouble area and hoped to restore service within 24 hours.

200 PHONE LINES OUT

The telephone company said at one time as many as 200 long distance circuits were down in the northwestern part of the state including sections between Moreland and Woodward, Woodward and Forgan, Woodward and Seiling, El Reno and Clinton, Medford and Blackwell.

All main highways were open but U. S. 66 in the Texas Panhandle was closed because of storms in the Amarillo area, the State Highway patrol reported. Snowplows cleared some drifts in the Woodward area but county roads were all blocked because of snow.

Southwestern Bell said repairs would take two or three days. Forgan, Cherokee, Alva, Fairview and Carmen were without telephone service late Sunday. Also, service was out at about 40 other communities operated by private concerns.

Over 200 extra repairmen rushed to the area to fix an estimated 300 broken poles, 500 broken cross arms and 5,000 wire breaks.

The official forecast for Monday called for fair and warmer with highs from 45 to 50.

—Tulsa Daily World

VOTE HEARING ON TV NETWORK

The Iowa house appropriations committee Tuesday voted to hold a public hearing on whether a 12-station educational television network should be launched at state expense.

Representative G. T. Kuester (Rep., Griswold), committee chairman, said he "presumed" the senate appropriations committee would agree to a joint hearing, but added that he had not yet discussed the matter with Senator J. K. Lynes (Rep., Plainfield), senate committee chairman.

After Recess.

Kuester said any public hearing would be held after the legislature's recess, which starts after the Friday session and will end Mar. 9.

Representative G. M. Ludwig (Rep., Tiffin) said he presented the idea of a public hearing to the house appropriations committee.

He speculated that Harry Boyd, editor of the Cedar Rapids Gazette and chairman of a citizens committee favoring the educational television plan, might organize pro-television forces for a public hearing.

Ludwig said he did not know what persons or groups might represent opposing forces.

The Iowa Broadcasters association is one group which has indicated opposition toward the plan as proposed. Edward Breen of Fort Dodge, association president, and Boyd are scheduled to discuss the plan at a Chamber of Commerce luncheon here Friday.

Bill Is Filed.

Ludwig said he personally favors the plan "with certain reservations." He added that he had "no trouble" in obtaining 12 other representatives to co-sign a bill calling for establishment of the network.

The bill, filed Tuesday for introduction today, does not mention cost, but it has been estimated that about one million dollars would be needed for first stages of the plan.

—Des Moines Register

Divided House Blocks Road, but Mover Stays in Jail

By TODD SIMON

With its dining room hanging out, a four-room section of house was blocking W. 130th Street, the dividing highway between Parma and Brook Park Village, last night.

And the house mover, Frank Mural, of 2317 Denison Avenue S. W., was in a jail cell in Berea. All attempts to bail Mural out had failed because Brook Park's mayor, Louis J. Mares, would not fix bail.

Mayor Mares was at his home, where he and his wife were entertaining friends in honor of Mrs. Mares' and George Washington's birthday.

And two-thirds of the transient house was waiting 700 feet south of Snow Road, in Parma, to be joined by the last third.

Mural was charged with failing to obtain a license and permit to move a structure on Brook Park property, according to the mayor.

According to Mural, Brook Park police came without warning and, saying they were going to help him get his permit, took him in a police car to the Berea jail and locked him up.

Mural said the house did project over the center line of W. 130th, but that the dolly on which the house rides is entirely on the Parma side of the highway, Route 612.

Mayor Mares said the trucks would straddle the center line.

Marked by two flares and a lantern, the itinerant hunk of housing was making automobiles drive onto the Brook Park shoulder of the road, churning it into mucky ruts.

The house was bought from the New York Central Railroad by Allen Thomas, 14045 Lorain Avenue. Thomas was having it moved to his land south of Snow Road, where he was going to rent it out. Eight rooms have been trucked down to that plot and now stand on cribbing there.

But, complete with L-shaped porch and with wallpaper of a delicate pink floral design, the third part to be moved was stalled just as it was turning out of its driveway into the road.

Mayor Mares told it this way:

"No, I haven't set bond. Mural has not been arraigned yet. Today was a holiday, and it would be difficult to dig up the city solicitor to make out a formal charge.

"Besides, it is my wife's birthday and I have friends here at the house for dinner.

"Mural was warned some time ago when he moved the other two sections. He was supposed to get a license and permit and to post a bond in case of damage. He should have applied to the building commissioner of the village for his permit."

Mural's Story

In his Berea cell, Mural said:

"There was a telephone man waiting down there to raise up a lighting pole and wires to let this part of the house in on Mr. Thomas' lot. I sent Mr. Thomas to get the permit so I could stay on the job.

"Then the police came and told me they'd help me get my permit, but they drove right here and put me in jail.

"My bond with the Traveler's Insurance Co. is still good for six months. And we aren't even touching Brook Park territory. Just a little of the house hangs over, about three feet."

Mike Mural, brother-in-law of the prisoner, and Thomas complained that they had tried repeatedly to find out what was the charge and what money or security bond was required to get Frank Mural free, but that both Mayor Mares and Police Chief Glenn Worsley had refused to tell them.

At dark, nobody had moved into the roadbound vacancy, which has two downstairs and two upstairs rooms and a stairway, but no kitchen or bath and no place to rest.

—*Plain Dealer*, Cleveland, Ohio

Extra Cops Meet Mrs. Kirkwood

Extra police were stationed at Pier 90 today when Mrs. Philomene Kirkwood, charged with kidnaping her son, Tommy, 8, by a previous marriage, returned from France aboard the Queen Mary.

The special detail of five patrolmen and a sergeant had been requested by Queens District Attorney Sullivan to prevent any possible Communist demonstration such as occurred in Cherbourg when the Queens woman was placed aboard the Cunard liner.

Sullivan, who obtained Mrs. Kirkwood's extradition through the State Department, went down the bay to meet the ship and questioned the woman before the vessel docked at W. 50th st. and the North River.

Sullivan was to decide whether Mrs. Kirkwood, 27, was to be taken directly to Queens Felony Court for arraignment.

Her former husband, George Kreisler, 29, of 349 W. 87th st., was armed with a court order for Mrs. Kirkwood to show cause why she should not be held in contempt of court for violating a custody ruling last July 30, when she took the youngster out of the country.

—*New York Journal-American*

The News Story

Bakery Drivers
Off Wednesdays

San Diego A.F.L. bakery drivers beginning tomorrow will take Wednesdays off to give them a five-day week. This agreement was nego-

tiated by the sales-drivers division of the Teamsters Union and coast employers. Members of the union negotiating committee are Larry Smith, secretary of Local 683, and Gordon Bourne.

The new agreement also provides for health and welfare coverage, Smith said.

—San Diego Union

EXERCISES

Practice A:

Make the following sentences shorter without sacrificing detail:

1. The color of the house was brown.
2. He then called on a man by the name of Peters.
3. He ran for a long way before he stopped.
4. The course will cover a period that will probably extend over three weeks.
5. All people who are interested should plan to attend.
6. It requires a long time to find out who is the next in line of succession.
7. The opinion of each and every student in the entire school should be considered.
8. We are planning to use the book which we want.
9. He asked his mother, he asked his father, and he asked his brother.
10. He asked us to tell him if we are thinking about or considering the action at the present time.
11. It was decided by the committee to act.
12. The flag was flapping and flapping in the strongly blowing wind.
13. We got our message through to him by the use of the telegraph.

88

14. He will speak at the convention which takes place on Monday.
15. Mr. Smith, who is the man who lives next to me, gets up early every morning in the week.
16. The man with the red hair was shouting and hollering in John's ear.
17. Mr. Howard, who is president of the club, spoke to the club at the meeting held on Tuesday of last week.
18. He put his glasses on in order to read the paper.
19. He was making an attempt to obtain a coat of tan.
20. He was wearing his hat on his head in a manner that was very strange.

Practice B:
From the following notes write news stories:

1. Man arrested this afternoon by Branchtown Police: name, John Henderson; address, 117 Linden St., Heather, Pennsylvania; age, 35; charge, attempted larceny of automobile; anonymous telephone call traced to public telephone in drugstore at 16th and Washington Sts. told police that strange man apparently was trying to force open door of parked car; surprised in act by police, Henderson said he thought car was his; car actually owned by Howard Hester, 2120 N. 8th St., City; check on records shows Henderson doesn't own a car; held by police magistrate at afternoon session in default of bail of $1,000.; to face Grand Jury Monday morning.
2. Woman found wandering in downtown New York this morning (December 17th) without coat or hat; unable to give name or any other pertinent fact; believed to be victim of amnesia; age, about 45; height, 5.5; weight, 145; hair, gray; complexion, sallow; wearing navy blue, frock type dress; muttered irrelevantly to all questions by police; placed in Harper Memorial Hospital for observation pending identification by relatives; photographer has taken picture to be run with story.

The News Story

3. Fire broke out at 1:00 A.M. this morning in Heller Department Store, 15th & Harold Sts., Philadelphia; cause, watchman threw cigarette butt in pile of refuse on first floor as he was making rounds; did not discover fire until next visit at 1:45; coming down stairs he saw a bright flame and discovered that entire first floor was blazing; unable to get past stairs; ran back to second floor; telephone miraculously not dead; called operator who called firemen; watchman jumped from second-story window into net; building now a flaming mass because faulty automatic sprayers did not work; fire finally extinguished at 6:00 A.M.; damage over $500,000.; owners considering prosecuting watchman for criminal negligence, although no one injured.

4. At commencement exercises this morning at Louden University, Louden, Ohio, speaker was Dr. Harvey H. Beister, President, Harrow College, Harrow, Indiana; addressed class of 721; advised them to seek positions with future, shun positions without future even though salary be very high; look for security job; work hard; marry intellectual equal, otherwise be unhappy; above all, go to church; church-going people always happiest; honorary degree of L.H.D. given Beister for work as educator and author; only 10 honor students— Harold J. Palmer, Phila., Pa., John I. Jones, Buffalo, N. Y., Peter H. Boone, Cleveland Ohio, Robert G. Deitrich, Erie, Pa., Morris P. Lester, Indianapolis, Ind., and Harry U. Powers, Robert Williams, Craig Flint, James Thompson, William MacIntyre, all of Louden; salutatory given by Palmer; valedictory by Boone.

5. Automobile accident at 21st & Race Sts., Kane, Texas, this morning; car driven by John K. Roberts, Dallas, sideswiped car of Paul Kyle, 181 Main St., Kane; Roberts attempting to pass Kyle who was going "Too darn slow, you'd think he was in a funeral"; damage, one fender badly bent; no injuries except upset dispositions; Roberts promises to pay damages; released by police on promise to settle privately.

6. Dr. George H. Lyon, Dean, Hillcrest College, Hillcrest, Conn., forbids girls to wear slacks to class beginning next Monday; declares them "unladylike"; threatens suspension for offenders; girls furious; have asked boys to help them by wearing skirts to class next Monday; think this will make issue ridiculous; boys "making no promises"; dean adamant; girls determined; interesting time ahead.

7. Walter O. Ritter, President, Ritter Tea Company, died at home in Laurel, Md., this afternoon of heart attack; age, 72; death unexpected; found lying on bedroom floor by maid; widower with one son, Walter Jr., secretary of father's business; Walter Sr. was active in affairs of Trinity Episcopal Church, Old Peoples Home; familiar figure at local opera and other musical events; lifelong member of the Republican party; rose from newsboy to importer; philanthropist and financial "angel" for local boys with musical talent; funeral to be announced.

8. Eleven monkeys escaped from the Phila. Zoo this afternoon; keeper forgot to lock door after feeding; monkeys made way out of grounds slowly; did not seem afraid of traffic outside zoo; too agile for keepers to catch; bounded across tops of cars on parking lot; climbed trees; scaled porch railings of houses; called by neighbors, police unable to cope with situation; neighbors keeping windows closed so monkeys can't get in; keepers finally coaxed five monkeys into net with bananas; "monkeyshines" predicted until remaining six are caught.

9. Entire city block, Chestnut to Locust, 13th to 14th, Devon, Mass., to be razed to make room for new vocational school; building to cost $3,800,000.; to have all latest equipment for every major type of shop work; emphasis to be on practical experience; enrollment will be 2,000; four-year course; some academic work of practical nature; building to start by June of next year.

10. Thomas J. Kearns, Manager of Hotel La Vue, held up and

robbed of $100. and watch as he left hotel at 1:00 A.M. this morning; robber was tall and heavy; about 40; spoke in heavy tone; face masked; was standing in doorway four doors away from hotel, apparently waiting; jabbed gun in ribs, took money, and jumped in car that evidently by pre-arrangement drove down street; Kearns placed with hands in air facing doorway; told if he turned to look he would be shot; no clues; police baffled.

11. Governor Louis K. Lowe, Nebraska, coming to Boston, Mass., to address Republican organization leaders at annual banquet; will arrive at North Station at 2:13 P.M.; will drive to home of Mayor Jenkins in latter's car; will spend afternoon in conference with party leaders; after banquet will have private party in mayor's home; leaves tomorrow morning on 11:20 A.M. train for Nebraska.

12. Ralph M. Pelot, 38, escaped convict, caught today by Lansing, Mich., police; was trying to board freight train at west-end yard; escaped from Lowton State Prison, Lowton, Ohio, last Monday by concealing himself in garbage truck; was a trusty working in prison kitchen; apprehended today on tip of railroad police who called local police when they heard that "suspicious-looking character" was hanging around yard; railroad police and city police set out for yard at same time but city police arrived first and had Pelot when others arrived; no shots fired; man surprised from behind; was unarmed; gave up without a struggle; said he was "glad it's all over"; hiding from police was "hell."

13. Thermometer today (August 12) reached 97; 14th straight day over 90; no relief in sight; weatherman says this is greatest heat wave since 1910 when 19 days were over 90; 14 people fainted in downtown section; people taking to parks and swimming pools; death of Joseph Combe, 71, 38 N. Titan St., of heart attack induced by great heat; week-end rush for seashore predicted; hotel reservations at Seaside Hotel, Ocean City, already sold out; ice cream dealers unable to keep up

with demand; Dr. Carl O. Hart, Director of Public Health,. warns people to watch diet, avoid undue exertion, don't "gulp ice water."

14. Eugene L. Cort, Republican, elected mayor over John E. Roberts, Democrat, in yesterday's election; great surprise; odds had been 2-1 on Roberts; final count, Cort 543,829— Roberts 499,134; Chestnut Hill section voted 4-1 for Cort; East Side voted 2-1 for Cort; vote about even all other sections; Cort declares results "a victory for reform in municipal expenditures"; Roberts says, "People have spoken. I accept their will"; election occasions great excitement at Republican headquarters; Democrats quiet; say they are waiting for "next time."

15. Explosion of gas tank on farm of Hiram L. Weaver, Teper, five miles from city, at 3:00 A.M. awakens hundreds; no one hurt; cause of explosion unknown; shed near tank demolished; 200 calls to City Hall and newspapers to inquire if earthquake had occurred, city arsenal had exploded, etc. Weaver says he was "blown clear out of bed"; doesn't have any idea of cause of explosion.

16. Two boys caught at 11:30 last night in act of stealing from Herten Bakery, 821 Powelton St., this city; boys are Peter Lawson, 14, 482 Lutlow St., and Thos. J. Ryan, 15, 499 Lutlow St.; Policeman Robert Kope patrolling beat heard noise in building as he passed; investigated and found door had been forced; boys gave up in tears; no police record on boys; placed in House of Detention for magistrate's hearing today; parents are surprised and shocked; believe boys listen to "too many bad T.V. programs, see too many bad movies."

17. Wheels stolen from police car at 2:00 A.M. this morning while officers having a snack in restaurant at 15th & Race Sts.; car jacked up and placed on milk boxes; wheels retrieved at corner of 20th & Arch Sts. by fellow police cruising in locality at 5:30 A.M.; all concerned "red-faced"; police in restaurant were Jacob Stone and Charles L. Ulton, patrolmen

attached to 1st District; police have no clue concerning
pranksters; suspect local college boys; Supt. of Police Herbert
Walton plans to "look into" custom of early morning snack
while on duty.

18. Dr. Lyle W. Turner, chief surgeon at Chester Hospital, ampu-
tated arm of injured worker in accident today at construction job on apartment at 4th and Locust Sts.; workman heard
warning cries too late to avoid having arm caught beneath
steel girder that accidentally fell; workmen unable to move
girder; no machinery available; police summoned surgeon to
unconscious man; arm badly mangled; only hope to free man
lay in immediate operation to remove arm; operation performed on spot; man removed to Chester Hospital, is resting
comfortably; excellent chance for recovery; man is Howard
Potter, 976 Karter St., this city; father of 4 children; age 48;
laborer for past 30 years.

19. Woman committed suicide by leaping from 4th story of
Biddle Bldg., 4th and Callow Sts., this morning at 10:00; no
marks of identification; had ripped all labels from clothing;
about 39 or 40 years of age; 5.5 in height; about 145 lbs;
dark hair; swarthy complexion; appears to be of Mexican or
Italian extraction; elevator operator, Norgert J. Smith, 45,
398 Haverford Ave., this city, remembers taking woman up,
but says he never saw her before; landed in street between
two parked cars; no one saw her leap except traffic policeman
Elmer O. Hayne, 41, 322 S. 11th St.; says he happened to be
looking that way just as she stood in window of lavatory
and jumped; battered body taken to morgue to await identification.

20. Kidnaped child of wealthy oil man George K. Johnson found
in lonely shack one mile from railroad station at Moylan,
Indiana; child is George Jr.; age, 6; taken from Moylan
schoolyard last Tuesday morning; no one saw him go; ran-
som note received Wednesday; father told to drop money
from airplane flying at distance of 1,000 ft. over certain
section of forest adjacent to Hubert, Indiana; terms carried

out, but police found money untouched next day; child remembers only "big dark man" who told him that father
wanted him to come home from school; had got in car and
was driven "long way" into country; man was "kind sometimes, nasty sometimes"; forced to sleep in little room in attic
of shack; cried sometimes; told by man he would be put out
in underground cave if he didn't "shut up"; child unhurt,
although suffering from shock; police refuse to divulge source
of information leading to raid on shack; man not found as
yet; police are "hot" on trail; parents overjoyed, but feel
man must be apprehended "in order to protect other people."

21. Circus coming to town; parade starting from West St. freight
yard at 1:30 tomorrow afternoon; proceeding to Broad St.;
turning left down Broad to Poplar; there turning east to
circus grounds at 4th St.; elephants, horses, and wagons containing wild animals will be in parade; also clowns, and a few
freaks such as fat man; circus to feature usual acrobatics, etc.,
plus captive gorilla that killed three men when being captured; gorilla named Pete, very ferocious; will be shown in
specially constructed cage; circus to stay in town for one
week.

Practice C:

Select 12 pictures from various newspapers and evaluate the
cut lines for general effectiveness.

Interviewing

Chapter
3

Introduction
Attributes of the Successful Interview
Other Important Points

INTRODUCTION

If the reporter is to be successful in his daily work, he must know how to interview. The ability to interview is necessary for the simple reason that most news comes directly from personal contact. From the formal press conference in the White House to the district man's conversation with the bootblack who witnessed the automobile accident, gathering news is largely a matter of interviewing people of all sorts and conditions. Because interviewing is so important in gathering news, the capable reporter constantly strives to develop his ability in this field.

Developing the ability to interview is complicated by the fact that interviewees are so vastly different from each other, thus requiring the reporter to develop a series of techniques rather than a single skill. There are the persons who welcome the chance to be interviewed—the movie actor seeking publicity, the political candidate fighting for votes, the publicity-hungry individual wanting to see his name in print—as opposed to those who want least of all to be interviewed—the swindler detected in his crime, the central figures in illicit love, the arrested patrons of a local gambling joint. There are the well-known personalities—the high governmental figure, the celebrity, the foreign statesman—as opposed to the obscure individuals—the man who witnessed the stabbing, the clerk in the store that has been looted, the boy who telephoned the police to tell of a suspicious character. There are the persons who themselves are the important news figures—the defendant in the murder trial, the visiting dignitary, the hero in the recent disaster—as opposed to the figures who are simply news sources—the janitor who can tell the reporter when the celebrity usually comes home, the hospital orderly who knows the exact number of victims in the recent accident, the inconspicuous desk sergeant who can give the names of the people arrested.

Interviews usually are classified according to kind of story (news, feature, sports, etc.); type of interview (press conference, extemporaneous, exclusive, etc.); subject (crime, politics, accident, etc.); and persons (well known, obscure, etc.).

The reporter should not think of interviewing as a task peculiar to the newspaper business, for, as can easily be seen, it is an important phase of many fields. The personnel director, the guidance counselor, the investigator, and many others whose work involves personal contact must be able to interview.

ATTRIBUTES OF THE SUCCESSFUL INTERVIEW

How much the ability to interview is congenital and how much acquired is a question not easily answered, for newspapermen and others can debate the subject almost endlessly. However, there are certain attributes of successful interviewing upon which there is common agreement. A discussion of these follows.

1. **Favorable Impression**—Although the reporter in the press conference and the one asking routine questions for small stories (minor accidents, purse snatchings, small fires, etc.) need scarcely have dynamic personality appeal, the more involved interviews demand that the reporter make a pleasing impression upon the person interviewed. The interviewee must respond well to the questions, he must evidence some spirit of co-operation, and he must view the whole interview as a pleasant experience. Naturally, these reactions are always dependent on the reporter's making a favorable impression.

Just how the reporter is to make a favorable impression can hardly be reduced to a formula. He may do so by displaying congeniality, respect, sympathy, fairness, or any other of the many qualities to which the interviewee may react favorably. Generally speaking, however, the reporter succeeds by displaying an attractive personality and by respecting the dignity of the interviewee.

2. **Varied Technique**—As shown in the list of attributes of the successful reporter (p. 54), the interviewer must vary his technique according to the particular situation he faces. Since there are sharp differences among the persons interviewed in the course of a normal day, there must be a corresponding difference in technique. The stevedore approached on the morning of the strike, for example, is a problem all in himself. He is resentful, defiant, and reckless. More important, he is especially difficult because he feels that the paper has not or will not present his case fairly. To handle him effectively is a real feat. The best course in such a situation

is probably a straight-from-the-shoulder, man-to-man approach with no attempt to influence or to chide. The mayor speaking at the midday meeting of the service club requires a sharply different approach. The reporter can scarcely expect to be successful by addressing him as he would the stevedore. He must, instead, take some cognizance of the mayor's important position as he speaks with him. In all instances, the reporter must be able to vary his technique as the situation may demand.

Certainly there can be no formalized procedure to guide the reporter in varying his technique. His only course is to analyze his successes and failures in other interviews with a view to improving. A critical analysis and a sincere attempt to improve, coupled with practice, are the best ways to gain the "know how" of varying one's technique.

3. Asking the Reader's Questions—The reporter who is interviewing should always think of himself as an intermediary. He is the representative of the reader; he interviews in order to ask the questions which his reader will expect to have answered.

The reader naturally wants to know the usual facts of every story—names, addresses, occupation, and similar details—but he also wants the answers to other questions. In reading an account of an unsolved murder, for instance, he wants every detail, large or small, in order to try to find the solution. In accounts of court battles, he wants every aspect of the case in order to establish an opinion. Thus, the reporter must obtain all pertinent data as he interviews.

4. Avoiding Routine—In interviewing, the reporter should make a strong effort to avoid a routine procedure, especially in seeking feature story material. In the small stories involving one or two questions, a routine procedure is inevitable. A routine procedure must also be used frequently in such straight news interviewing as the formal press conference, the questioning of the high governmental official about foreign relations, and the questioning of the lawyer about legal implications. But, in the many stories where variety is possible, the reporter should attempt to gain a new approach and treatment. The stock, dull questions should be avoided; and in their place, novel or striking ones should be asked. Examples of routine interviewing are to be seen in the stories of the movie actresses and the sports figures. The actresses are usually asked the same silly questions about their favorite this and that; the sports figures invariably are asked to explain their success. Although these stories may be interesting to many readers, too often they have the atmosphere of having been written many times before.

5. Pre-interview Contact—Whenever possible, the reporter should attempt to make a contact before the actual interview. Generally speaking, a person is better able to give an interview if he knows what to expect. Therefore, the reporter should communicate with the interviewee beforehand, giving some inkling of the questions to be asked. In the case of important persons, making an appointment beforehand is almost mandatory. In the case of less important persons, last-minute arrangements are acceptable.

Sometimes, of course, there are instances where making arrangements beforehand is impossible. An example is the case of the dignitary or the celebrity arriving by boat or train. In these instances, however, the person to be interviewed frequently expects reporters and is prepared accordingly.

6. Preparation—Whenever a reporter is able to plan an interview in advance, he certainly should do so. He should think of the questions that he wants to ask, he should make plans for "drawing out" the interviewee, and he should anticipate any lull or change in the conversation. While he can scarcely cross-examine the interviewee, he should prepare his questions so as to get the material desired.

Preparation is especially important when the interviewee's time is limited, as is true of the busy official, the dignitary boarding a plane, and the athlete after the contest.

7. **Knowledge of the Subject**—The reporter should always make certain that he will know what the interviewee is speaking of. This statement means that the reporter should brief himself on the interviewee's background and position and on the nomenclature of his field. A reporter, for example, interviewing the conductor of the symphony orchestra should know something of music; the sports reporter should know the ins and outs of the game involved; and the reporter questioning the scientist should know the main ideas of the particular subject. When the person being interviewed must explain needlessly, or when he feels the reporter's incompetence, the whole interview is certain to sag.

OTHER IMPORTANT POINTS ABOUT INTERVIEWING

In addition to the requisites for interviewing already discussed, the student of journalism should know the qualities peculiar to interviewing for the major departments of the newspaper. A discussion follows of interviewing for straight news, feature, sports, theater, and society stories.

1. **Straight News**—The important points to be remembered concerning interviewing for the straight news story are: (1) this is the largest single field of interviewing; (2) generally the reporter is pressed for time most severely in this field; (3) the news reporter usually has least foreknowledge of, and hence least chance to plan, the interview.

Straight news constitutes the largest single field of interviewing because it represents the largest part of printed material. Although much of the interviewing may be done by outside reporters (wire service, syndicates, free-lance writers), news stories still represent more interviewing by the staff than any other kind of material.

The reporter handling the straight news story generally is pressed hardest for time because so much of his material is spot news. The news breaks fast, and he must accomplish the interview quickly. He must also work in competition with the other papers' reporters against an ever-descending deadline. Consequently, frequently he must interview with a close check on the clock in order to get his material into print.

Straight news interviewing gives the reporter least foreknowledge because of the very nature of news. A large portion of news, as already noted, gives no forewarning that it will break; consequently, the reporter may find himself interviewing several persons at a moment's notice. Examples of such instances are the interviews with the victims of a swindler, the municipal office holders who unexpectedly have been discharged, and the witnesses of a tragedy.

2. Feature Story—The important points to be remembered about the interview for the feature story are that (1) there can be great latitude in approach; (2) the reporter is rarely pressed for time; and (3) the interview usually seeks to reveal a personality or an atmosphere rather than to present straight factual material.

There can be great latitude in approach because the feature story frequently can be treated in sharply different ways. Consequently, the reporter varies his approach to suit his proposed treatment. The story of the local traction company's decision to remove an antiquated trolley line, for instance, can be handled in at least three ways—humorous, sarcastic, reminiscent. If the treatment is to be humorous, the reporter interviews passengers with a view to obtaining facetious remarks about the old vehicles; if sarcastic, he phrases his questions so as to draw forth slightly nasty remarks about the tardiness of the action; if reminiscent, he plays up the sentimental angle by interviewing oldsters who "remember when." In short, he forces the interview into a pattern that will suit his intended treatment of the story. This approach is in sharp contrast to that of the news story, where the reporter seeks straight factual material.

The reporter is not pressed for time in the feature story interview, as he so often is in the straight news interview, because usually the feature is planned well in advance. The reporter thus can allow himself ample time for interviewing and for writing. In fact, sometimes a feature story is completed and in type a day or more before it is used.

Because the feature story usually seeks to reveal a personality or an atmosphere, the whole course of the interview is affected accordingly. The reporter becomes highly selective. He looks primarily for the material that will contribute to forming a good picture of the personality or creating depth for the atmosphere. Consequently, he will talk at length with a view to selecting the helpful material after the interview. If, for instance, he is interviewing a coal miner with the intention of showing the drudgery of his existence, he may ask many irrelevant questions in order to study the miner's face as he answers. If he is writing of life on a river boat, he may ask many questions of crew members for the sole purpose of gaining atmosphere. Thus, the feature story interview frequently resembles a conversation between friends rather than a formal question-answer process.

3. Sports—There are two conditions characteristic of sports interviewing: (1) interviews are generally very easy to obtain and (2) there is a distinct homogeneity in the people interviewed.

Interviews are easy to obtain in the world of sports because athletic organizations are heavily dependent on public favor. Hence, favorable newspaper publicity is desired—in fact, the newspaper has a distinct advantage over many athletic organizations because, if this favorable publicity is not forthcoming (or, worse still, if unfavorable write-ups appear), the athletic organization may find itself in a very tight position in more ways than one.

There is a distinct homogeneity in the persons interviewed in sports because they have so much in common. The reporter, therefore, can always work from these known facts: sports figures are all striving to reach the top; they are in constant competition with others like themselves; and they are completely devoted to their sport. This homogeneity, however, leads to difficulty, for the big problem of sports interviewing lies in the attempt to gain variety. The entire field is so limited and the facts so often fall into a standard pattern that the reporter finds difficulty in gaining novelty. What, for instance, can a reporter find to ask a baseball player that has not already been asked hundreds of times? What can be said of an up-and-coming athlete that has not been said of many, many others? Many prominent newspapermen have had long and successful careers in the field of sports interviewing, but many have also bogged down in attempting to gain original approaches.

4. **Theater**—Like those engaged in sports, the person connected with the theater leans heavily on publicity in order to prosper. Consequently, interviews are rarely difficult to obtain.

But, once again, the interviewer also has difficulty in gaining originality. A nationally known actress, for instance, being interviewed for the local paper, presents a problem because her interviews have been published so many times before.

Syndicated features, magazines, and other newspapers probably have dealt with her life at length. The reporter for the local paper, therefore, must strive for a new angle.

5. Society—The reporter conducting interviews for material for the society page should have two attributes; he should himself be well established socially and he should enjoy his work.

The reporter himself should be well established socially in order to have an entree into the so-called "best circles." Rarely can he obtain a satisfactory interview with a member of the exclusive social group unless he also is a member. This accounts for the fact that, in the large cities where a social register is printed, the newspaper has as society editor someone listed therein.

The reporter must enjoy society interviewing if he is to be successful because this work quickly tires anyone not rabidly enthusiastic. The idea of keeping tabs on the routine doings of such a relatively dull group holds little appeal for most newspapermen.

However, the importance of the society page is not to be taken lightly. Although the devotee of the sports page may laugh derisively at the two-column cut of the pale-faced, slightly built young man conversing inanely with the somewhat horsy, unattractive young woman, such material represents a strong attraction for many readers, especially among the many "would be's" and the *nouveau riche* of the community. Consequently, the newspaper must include it—which means someone must gather it.

EXERCISE

Examine the following news story with a view to evaluating the interview techniques revealed therein:

Brooklyn Police Seize Fugitive Lugging Battery

8 Witnesses Identify Jail Breaker in $64,000 Queens Bank Robbery

By RAYMOND C. BRECHT

New York, Feb. 19—The law moved swiftly today to put "Slick Willie" Sutton, notorious bank robber and jail breaker, back in prison.

The man who twice broke prison in Philadelphia and was recaptured in Brooklyn yesterday after five years of freedom faced arraignment in Queens County Court, Long Island City.

In a closely-guarded courtroom, the authorities planned to give him a hearing on charges that he led a $63,942 holdup of the Manufacturers Trust Co. in Long Island City on March 9, 1950.

Eight witnesses pointed to him at a police standup last night as the leader of this robbery. And police said that he had made a "statement," supposedly a confession.

Recaptured by Accident

The mild-mannered, 51-year-old robber, one of the FBI's most wanted criminals, was recaptured by accident by two uniformed Brooklyn policemen, after his automobile had been stalled by a dead battery.

He had nearly $8,000, in $100 and $50 bills, and a loaded .38 caliber revolver in his possession.

Ironically, it was Sutton's desire to save a $1.50 service charge for replacing the dead battery that led to his capture.

Sutton, who had been living in a cheap rooming house in Brooklyn for two years, was tinkering with the stalled car—a $1,900 Chevrolet he bought about a month ago—when Patrolmen John J. McClellan and Donald P. Shea saw him.

With no other thought than to help a motorist in trouble, the policemen approached him and offered assistance.

Remember Picture

The policemen didn't recognize him at first. They asked him his name, and he replied, "Charles Gordon." The policemen took a good look at him.

It dawned on them that he resembled the pictures of Sutton that had been plastered in police stations all over the country.

The policemen moved off in their radio car, watched him for a while, then radioed headquarters for help.

Sutton, meanwhile, tinkered with the dead battery. He finally took it out of the car and lugged it to a nearby garage. There he was told that it would cost him $3 to get the car moving again.

This charge included $1.50 for charging his own battery, and $1.50 for installing a rented battery on the street.

Serving Life Here

Sutton decided to take the rented battery back to the car and install it himself and save the extra $1.50 service charge.

He was about to pick up the rented battery when detectives, summoned by the two policemen, grabbed him.

It was the end of five years of freedom that began when Willie went over the wall from Holmesburg County Prison in Philadelphia in 1947. He had been serving a life term imposed by the late Judge McDevitt as a fourth offender.

The sentence was imposed after Sutton pleaded guilty to 13 charges, including a $10,980 holdup on the 60th and Ludlow branch of the Corn Exchange Bank & Trust Co. on January 15, 1934.

Philadelphia Too Hot

Willie said at last night's standup, during which he was stripped down to his shoes, that he had never gone near Philadelphia since his 1947 escape. Philadelphia, he said, was too hot for him.

What did he do in the five years since he jumped out of Philadelphia —five years that made him one of the FBI's first ten most-wanted criminals?

Nothing, said Willie, blandly.

His money "just mildewed," he said, almost without expression. He was working. Just hustling around. But not around Philadelphia.

It was 10.45 last night when Sutton "The Actor," they call him—appeared at New York's Center st. police headquarters.

Arrives at Headquarters

He was driven up in a car, manacled to two young policemen. They were the ones who spotted him.

In that slightly uncomfortable position, Willie walked stolidly up the marble stairs. He was wearing a blue-gray snap-brim hat, a dark blue overcoat, a blue, chalk-striped suit. He had a pencil mustache, a doughy complexion. He was subdued, with eyes downcast.

Surrounded by a half a dozen more detectives, the slipperiest bank thief in the country was walked down the corridor, down a flight of stairs and into the police photographic bureau.

He first went through a room filled with green filing cabinets and a few black, accordion-pleated cameras, and then into a sparse-looking room with banks of glaring lights and a couple of cameras that said they meant business. The lights made Willie and everybody else look purple.

Made to Undress

He didn't say a word. They stood him up beside a vertical measuring stick, for height. A sign in blue and white in front of him said: 51387. It also said February 18, Monday, Police Department, City of New York.

Willie Sutton, who once tunneled his way out of the Eastern Pen and boasted that "no jail can hold me," was poker-faced.

The detectives whispered a little and he began to undress.

He got his suit coat off. Then he squirmed out of a sleeveless maroon sweater. Off came a gray necktie with brightly colored ducks on it. Then off came his white shirt.

The pencil mustache betrayed nothing as he bent over and hauled off the trousers. Then he took off his underwear. The purplish glare was merciless.

An amiable-looking detective the

size of a small truck called to the photographer: "You want him with his shoes off?"

"No," said Lieutenant James O'Brien, of the 108th squadron, Long Island City, "let him keep his shoes on."

'Stand Straight, Willie'

So Slick Willie stood there with his low, polished shoes and dark blue socks on. There were a dozen detectives gathered around, a half a dozen reporters and other officers from the detective bureau. There was an air of undramatic but not unhurried efficiency. Everything was still purple.

Slick Willie crossed his hands in front of him.

"Just stand straight, Willie," said the photographer, tonelessly.

The man with a 20-year record let his hands fall to his sides.

"Turn around," the photographer said. Willie turned sideways, displaying the flat chest and circular stomach of a sedentary man of 51 with things on his mind.

"You want the side?" he inquired almost inaudibly.

"Yeah," said the photographer. "Stand still."

Willie's hair was stringy. It was parted a bit to the left of the middle. Some lifeless strands fell over his left eye. The hair, despite the hideous purple glare, was brownish, not black, but brownish in a sickly way as though it had been dyed but not meticulously tended. It wasn't as trim as the penciled mustache, although there was a little gray in that.

Dresses Again

There were lines in his face, made the sharper by the deadpan

expression. The purple light gave an almost weird cast to the smallish, probably slate-blue eyes. They seemed to look at nothing very much.

They let him get dressed then. He did it swiftly but without visible hurry, while the detectives told about his having been questioned by Police Commissioner George P. Monaghan and later by Assistant District Attorney Thomas McCullen when they got him to Long Island City.

That's the county seat of Queens, where the most immediate charge lay.

Dressed again, the snap-brim hat on, the tie knotted neatly, Willie sat down on a plain bench against the wall between two detectives. He lit a cigarette. He held it without shaking in somewhat stubby fingers with short-cut, squarish nails. They were not manicured.

Never Went Back

"Willie," I said, "did you ever go back to Philadelphia after that break out of Holmesburg in 1947?"

He was leaning over with his elbows on his knees and the cigarette between the first two fingers of his right hand. He looked up from under the gray hat and smiled easily, or maybe it was a half-smile.

"No, I've never been back there," he said. The voice was like dry leaves. It sounded as though it always was that way. The light made his tight smile and the teeth behind it a garish purple.

"It was too hot back there for me," he said. Then, nodding in a knowing fashion: "You know, fellows from the Pen that might know me, and things like that."

"Did you ever live in Philadelphia?"

"Yes," the head came up again. "I lived in Philadelphia about a year—in 1933, out around Chester Av.," he added vaguely.

"What were you doing then?"

"Oh," the trim smile again, ". . . just hustling around, seeing the country . . ."

He lowered his head and flicked an ash from the cigarette.

"Just getting myself 36 years. That's what I was doing."

"I Figure 105 Years"

His head was up and the smile was back, fleeting this time.

"Is that the way it looks now?"

"Things are pretty hopeless . . . I have nothing to look forward to. I'd figure maybe 105 years"—this time it was a wan, violet smile.

Everybody seemed to be in good humor. The detectives were smiling, but edging toward the door.

"Is that your figure?" a reporter asked.

"My figure's about six months," said Slick Willie, the actor.

The detectives were close to a laugh on that one. Lieutenant O'Brien whispered, "Let's go."

They put the manacles on again, one locked to each of the round-faced policemen who had spotted him. The Brooklyn detective who had verified the spotting and helped with the arrest walked grimly behind.

Taken Back to Jail

In the corridor they turned left. A few yards away there was an iron-barred door. Photographers were on the other side. The little group paused while the pictures were made.

Then they walked him out in the same effortless fashion and got in a car again and took him back to the Queens County Jail on Long Island City's Courthouse Square.

The detectives were asked if they thought they would turn him over to Philadelphia authorities.

"Well," they said easily, "if we didn't have anything on him. But he was perfectly identified as the man in that Long Island City hold-up."

One of them added: "About eight people identified him and he's made a statement."

Slick Willie, the actor, pulled up his coat collar and the car pulled away.

—*Evening Bulletin,*
Philadelphia, Pa.

The Feature Story

WHAT IS THE FEATURE STORY?

The typical newspaper reader would be completely lost if he were asked to explain the feature story. In fact, he probably would be hearing the term for the first time. But if his newspaper did not contain several such stories daily he would soon choose another, for good features are essential to maintaining reader interest. Without them, the newspaper simply would not be a newspaper. Just what is the feature story? Journalists invariably define it by comparing it with the news story.

In the news story, the whole atmosphere is impersonal. Straight facts are related in an objective manner. There is no conjecture, no opinion, no delving beneath the surface for a human interest angle. Thus, except for minor stylistic devices, the news story shows no traces of the writer's personality. In the feature story, however, the whole tone becomes personal.

Now there is a distinctly subjective treatment of the aspects that are emotional, dramatic, or personal in character—the aspects that have human interest appeal. The writer, in short, adopts a subjective approach in order to portray the human interest quality. Thus, the difference between the news story and the feature story is one of selection and treatment. The news story writer selects only the straight facts and treats them objectively; the feature story writer concentrates on the human interest angle and treats it subjectively.

Naturally, all stories do not lend themselves to feature story treatment. A writer, for example, would be hard pressed to find a feature story angle in a routine announcement that public buildings will be closed, as usual, on Christmas Day. But, on the other hand, some stories are so obviously features that one would experience the greatest difficulty in treating them as straight news. For example, the story of the old woman defying the authorities by refusing to vacate the condemned house is unquestionably feature story material. So is the story of the man receiving public charity who surreptitiously bought a ticket in the Irish sweepstakes and won $50,000. These stories are clearly feature material because the human interest angle must take precedence over the straight facts. Certainly the reader is more interested in the personal aspects of these incidents than he is in the simple facts of the story.

In the many instances where a story may be used either as straight news or as feature material, a decision naturally must be made. This decision is generally based on the editorial policy of the paper, the number of feature stories already being used, and the value of the story as straight news as compared with its value as a feature. Consequently, one newspaper may use a given set of facts as straight news while another in the same city may use the material for a feature story. An example of this difference can be seen in stories concerning new equipment purchased by the local government. Some papers play up the color of the whole story (employees' reactions, changes necessitated, etc.); other papers merely report the details of the purchase in a perfunctory way.

Still another point to be noted in distinguishing between straight news and the feature is the fact that many stories fall between. An editor, in assigning a story, may tell the writer to give it a "light" touch, a humorous touch, or a satirical touch. The story, in short, is to be neither straight news nor straight feature; instead, it is to have some qualities of each. An example of this kind of story is to be seen in the following account of a steer on rampage. This story is really straight news with a very light touch:

Police Corral Steer Roaming Streets and Help in its Last Roundup

Patrolmen in red cars turned cowboys today long enough to capture a steer which broke away as it was being unloaded at a West Philadelphia abattoir.

Before the animal was finally led into a garage at the home of Bernardo Consorto, 5126 Master st., it had romped up and down Lancaster av., and along the side streets and alleys from 48th to 52d st.

Edward Grace, of Townsend, Del., and his brother, George, brought the steer with a truckload of cattle to the slaughter house of Alec Crisanti, Lancaster av. near 49th st. They had unloaded the cattle without trouble. Then came the steer's turn.

Halfway down the ramp, the steer leaped into the street and hightailed down Lancaster av., with Crisanti and an employe, Charles Sini, chasing after it. George Grace decided it was a case for the police. He telephoned the 49th st. and Lancaster av. station.

Summoned by radio, four red cars arrived within five minutes. The policemen adopted maneuvers to corner the steer.

Even after they got it in Consorto's garage, the steer balked attempts to be put in the truck.

When George Grace borrowed a shotgun from one of the neighbors and was about to shoot, the steer calmly walked out of the garage and up the ramp into the truck.

The steer was taken to the slaughter house, where it will be kept a day or so before being turned into steaks, roasts, etc.

—*Evening Bulletin*,
Philadelphia, Pa.

To make this story a feature, the reporter would concentrate almost entirely on the humorous aspects of the situation. He would poke gentle fun at the police, relate humorous remarks and occurrences of the chase, and stress any other element likely to draw a smile. If the reporter were to handle the story as straight news, he would make no attempt to capitalize on humor. His story would read like the following straight news account of a deer on rampage. This story, of course, could easily be made into straight news or part news–part feature by altering the treatment accordingly.

DEER 'CRASHES' BAR, SCARES RHINELANDER SHOPPERS, DIES

RHINELANDER, WIS. — Deer season drama was brought to the downtown area here Friday when a wounded, frightened 175-pound buck broke a tavern window, scared downtown shoppers and had its throat cut by hunters.

The buck, a nine-pointer, was shot in the back legs and in the mouth in swamp areas just outside the city limits. He made his way into Rhinelander, running down the middle of a street. He turned onto Brown street, this city's main thoroughfare, and went onto a sidewalk. Pausing at a tavern, he saw his image in the window and made a lunge for it, crashing the glass but not entering.

The buck then went half a block farther when three men, two of them red-coated "hunters," converged on him. A barber working at a shop close by took the deer by the horns, another man hung onto the hind feet while the third slit the deer's throat.

—*Minneapolis Sunday Tribune*

A final point to be considered concerning the part news–part feature story is that practically every newspaper uses several very short ones daily to brighten pages or to serve for

113

filler. These shorts, which frequently are akin to the comedian's jokes, are especially valuable for the inside pages containing advertisements. They often make the reader pause as he turns the page, thus increasing the chance that he will read the advertisements. Although the wire services provide an abundant supply of these shorts, editors encourage their reporters to find local ones because of their proximity.

The following shorts are typical of those found daily:

LOW THIEF STEALS A LADDER, MAN IS MAROONED ON ROOF

The meanest thief of the week was walking the streets of Alton today, congratulating himself on his sly humor.

He stole a ladder yesterday, marooning Gene Thiesen on the roof of the Miller Lime & Cement Co. Thiesen, a clerk in the store, had been on the roof putting a light bulb in the electric sign at the front of the building.

Other employes found another ladder and Thiesen got down.

—*St. Louis Post-Dispatch*

Policeman, Hold Back! Final Round Coming Up

SALT LAKE CITY, Nov. 27.—(AP)—The police radio dispatcher's log showed this in the "disposition" column Saturday after a cruiser car was dispatched to quell a family disturbance:

"The lady doesn't want anything done until he hits her again."

—Associated Press story in the *Denver Post*

Assets Unfrozen

QUINCY, Mass. (UP).—A sneak thief dipped into the deep freezer which grocer Samuel Jolas used for a hiding place and stole $90—cold cash.

—United Press story in the *Philadelphia Inquirer*

He's a Heller

CLEVELAND, OHIO—(U.P.)—Mrs. Florence Heller, 33, Friday filed suit for divorce. She charged her husband, Otto, 35, poured water on her while she slept.

—United Press story in the *Minneapolis Sunday Tribune*

114

ABILITIES NEEDED FOR FEATURE WRITING

As one might naturally assume, the first requirement of feature writing is the ability to recognize feature story material. The reporter must have a sense of recognition of the *unusual* and an awareness of the dramatic or human interest quality in the *usual*. In an instance where one reporter would never think of looking for a feature story, another may find an excellent one. To illustrate this, let us take the case of a reporter assigned to cover a routine story of a small warehouse fire. Instead of contenting himself with the usual facts about amount of damage, cause, and similar details, he looks for another angle. In his search, he learns that, for a fireman who has just completed 25 years of service, this is fire number 10,000. Immediately the reporter has not only another angle, but also a really interesting story. He talks with the fireman, learns about his most exciting experiences, gathers some interesting opinions, and obtains some reflections on the progress of fire-fighting methods over the years. Now, instead of having a short of eight or ten lines, he has a story that merits a full column with an appropriate headline and picture. Thus, the ability to recognize feature story material has unearthed a good story and no doubt has helped to strengthen the editor's esteem for the reporter.

The second requirement is the ability to write humorously, for one can safely say that over half of all feature stories appeal to the reader's sense of humor. How, for instance, could a reporter successfully handle the following little feature story without humor?

Mystery of How Four Boys Ate 96 Pies Puzzles Cops

Gastronomical Miracle, Done in Short Time, Bared by Warren Burglary

From the Post-Gazette Correspondent

Warren, Pa., Aug. 9.—Warren police have been busy with pencil and paper endeavoring to figure out the pie capacity of four lads of the Laurel street section.

This was due to a raid on the Warren Baking Company during which 96 pies disappeared. In the days of the school attendance of the police, they learned that "the stomach is an organ holding about one pint" and this just can't be reconciled with the space that would be required to store 96 pies.

The pies were of all flavors, both the fruity and the creamy kind and they were of the accustomed dimensions that allows the pie venders to cut about 10 slices that bring 10 cents each over the counter. The cops figure that the creamy sort would slip down easily and that perhaps the "organ holding about one pint" is rather elastic in small boys. The raid was made about midnight and, as the boys were of the sort that should be in bed at that hour, the coppers figure they must have devoured the pies at a rapid rate. The youngsters and their parents will meet with police and the bakery owner.

—*Pittsburgh Post-Gazette*

The third quality needed is the ability to be **gently satirical**. The writer of the feature story must be able to poke fun without being mean, and he must show clearly his ability to laugh pleasantly at man's foibles. An illustration of this follows on page 117.

43-Year-Old Insult

Called Ugly by Wife in '02, Husband Will Get Divorce

The way Advisory Master William R. J. Burton, of the Camden Chancery Court, figures the situation is this:

Even if it did take 43 years for an insult to sink in Hugh Watson, a 63-year-old steel worker, is still entitled to a divorce if his wife deserted him.

So the Master recommended a divorce yesterday after hearing from Mr. Watson's lips a saga of insult which, he said, began one month after he and his wife, Winnie, were married in 1902.

At that moment (one month later), Mr. Watson, who lives at 1033 Cambridge st., Camden, related in court, the missus looked at him one morning and declaimed: "My gosh, Hughie, you are ugly!"

* * *

But that wasn't the half of it, according to Mr. Watson's testimony. The next thing the little woman said to him, according to his sworn testimony, was, "If I had known how ugly you are, I would never have married you."

And so she went her way, and Mr. Watson went his, he told the judge, and the years dripped by with all the precision of a leaky faucet—43 of them—and Mr. Watson just yawned. He indicated yesterday that he even felt grateful about the situation.

Once, he said, he went to Baltimore a short time after the separation and discovered Winnie living with another man. But that, he averred, didn't bother him at the time.

* * *

Then why in the devil, the advisory master wanted to know, did he wait so long to sue for a divorce? Of course, the Master put it in much more judicial language.

"Well," said Mr. Watson, "I wasn't much interested in other women. I didn't even want to look at another woman. But now I'm getting old and I don't want my wife to inherit my little property."

So Mr. Burton let the situation go with a recommendation for a divorce.

—Philadelphia Inquirer

The fourth and over-all quality which the writer of the feature story must have is a deep sense of the brotherhood of man. He must have that feeling for humanity which enables him to appreciate the hopes, the joys, the sorrows, and

117

the disappointments of others. It is this feeling which helps the feature writer to handle such stories as the interview with the mother whose son has been killed in battle, the visit to the orphanage Christmas party, and the tour of the flooded areas along the Mississippi. However, the writer must be careful of exaggerated sentimentality and emotional overflow. Gushing and sobbing have no place in the mature feature.

Note how the appeal of the following story stems from the writer's ability to feel the experience of his subject. Note, also, the absence of sentimentality.

G. I., a Smile His Weapon, Restores Faith of Korea's Hapless Orphans

By ROBERT ALDEN

Special to THE NEW YORK TIMES.

SEOUL, Korea, Jan. 13—Out of the chaos and confusion of war and the waste and ruin of wrecked lives that result, there is occasionally fashioned a wondrous and ennobling story. One of the modern day true stories is told of Sgt. First Class Werne Krenzer of Rego Park, Queens.

Sergeant Krenzer, like so many called to duty overseas, was unhappy to be going to a far off country called Korea. The 26-year-old sergeant had a sweetheart and their marriage was in the offing. He was stationed at the Brooklyn Army Base, not too far from his home at 82-28 Penelope Avenue. His job as a military escort honor guard for the dead of the Korean war was a choice military assignment.

It was not pleasant for Sergeant

Krenzer to leave all this for an unknown lonely assignment across the sea. On a warm May night before he left he couldn't sleep at all, and drove restlessly about the streets of Queens looking at familiar trees and the rows of private homes that had for long been part of his life.

By the end of June, 1952, the sergeant was in Korea, a country he had heard so much about—a country whose rubble and poverty were constantly being renewed by the fresh wounds of battle. The soldier did not know what type of assignment awaited him, but he did know his enlistment was to expire the following March and in order to get him back in the United States by that time the Army would have to ship him home in January. Seven months did not seem too long to wait, and then there would possibly be marriage and life would be happy and normal once more.

Sergeant Krenzer was assigned to the Seoul city team of the United Nations Civil Assistance Command and given many jobs. One was working with Korean orphans. The sergeant, along with Kim, his 12-year-old interpreter, would go down to the railroad station. There they would find many waifs orphaned and made homeless by war.

The children gathered there because there was some shelter and frequently someone would light a stove so they could get warm. Also, a lot of soldiers passed through and they were always generous with food and candy.

The sergeant and his little friend Kim would pass among the hapless abandoned orphans and try to win their confidence. They would offer candy or a warm smile and sometimes the smile would mean more than gold to the child for whom no one cared and who had no place to go. If one of the children seemed content to share their friendship, Kim and Sergeant Krenzer would ask the youngster to come with them to one of the orphan homes in the city.

The children liked the American sergeant and many went with him. That confidence was in its own way a perfect tribute, for these children —some as young as three years old— had learned to really trust no one.

Waiting For A Miracle

They roamed the country like poor unhappy vagabonds, passing a month or so in Seoul, then perhaps moving to some other town where they hoped things would be better. Always in back of their minds was the thought that by some miracle of chance their parents or someone else they loved would magically appear to save them from all the suffering and hardship they had known. Their freedom and that hope was all in the world they possessed and it was hard for them to give these precious gifts up to live in the confines of any orphanage.

However, Sergeant Krenzer with little Kim enjoyed good success. "For me it was like opening the gates to wonderland," the sergeant said. "I was doing something and then in short time I would come back and see how much good I had accomplished."

The sergeant told of a frozen little 5-year-old girl he picked up at 1:30 on New Year's morning. She was covered only with a bit of burlap and she sat on a stoop shivering with her head pressed on her lap for warmth. "We took her to one of our orphanages and sat her on a bench near the stove. At first she could not stop shivering. But then the warmth took hold and as we watched, she slowly sat up and then stood up. It was just as if we were watching a little plant that had withered slowly come alive and grow again."

A Lifetime of Happiness

Now wherever Sergeant Krenzer goes among the orphanages of Seoul he finds many little friends. "Hello, Sergeant," they say in broken English and Sergeant Krenzer returns the greeting in broken Korean.

Those exchanges of greetings are apparently worth a lifetime of happiness to the sergeant. Although he could now return to the United States, Sergeant Krenzer has agreed to remain over here so he can help the children and other destitute people of Seoul. The sweetheart he left behind in the United States has entered a convent and the sergeant regards all that has happened as God's will. "It is all part of life; it is all part of living," he will tell you in a soft, sincere voice.

—New York Times

SOURCES OF THE FEATURE

For the sake of convenience, the sources of the feature story have been divided into the 10 groupings discussed below. The student of journalism should remember, however, that these groupings are purely arbitrary. They are intended merely as broad classifications.

1. The Usual—As already stated, many of the stories handled by the newspaper can be treated either as straight news or as features, and the writer accordingly relates the facts in the straightforward, impersonal style of the news story or he adopts the subjective approach and treatment that characterize the feature story.

Typical instances of such stories are the demolition of a once-famous building, the death of a well-known blind news dealer, the razing of the last covered bridge in the locality, and the implications of a recent election.

2. The Unusual—In every day's crop of stories come those so predominantly features that they must be treated as such. To treat them otherwise would be almost impossible.

Examples of this type of story are the interview with the new circus freak, the visit to the home of the 400-pound man, the interview with the man who has regained his sight, the antique automobile parade, and the hailstorm in mid-August.

3. The Seasonal Story—A never-failing source of feature stories is the events that come with each change in the calendar, and even though the resemblance of these stories to

those of previous years is frequently strong, this kind of feature is popular nonetheless.

Among the common seasonal feature stories are the account of the first arrival of Christmas trees in the big city, New Year's Day celebrations, ground-hog day, the Easter parade at fashionable places, Memorial Day celebrations, the July 4th parade, the crowds at the beaches during the heat wave, and the opening and closing of the schools.

4. **The Supplementary Story**—Where a story has received a great play, there is invariably another story or series of stories related to this main story. This lesser story, sometimes called a "color" story, is in reality a supplement to the larger one.

Outstanding examples of the supplementary story are the account of the crowd at the Army-Navy game, the biography of a man about to be executed, the story on the members of the President's family at his inauguration, the caterer's story of his work at a famous wedding, and the eyewitnesses' accounts of their reactions to such newsworthy events as serious accidents, disasters, and other uncommon sights.

5. **The Dramatic Situation**—When a story is high in dramatic quality, it is invariably treated as a feature. Scarcely does a day pass without several such stories.

Examples are the accounts of the tiny terrier that awakened the family when their home was afire, the faithful servant who has been left a fortune by his grateful employer, the physician who is called upon to save the life of a member of his family, and the man of low estate who suddenly is introduced to the President of the United States.

6. **The Guidance Story**—Newspapers frequently have one of their staff members or an eminent authority write a story which gives advice or explains an important problem. Such a writing is appropriately termed the "guidance story."

Examples of this type of feature writing are explanations of hidden issues in a forthcoming election, accounts of proposed legislation, and advice on filling out governmental forms (income tax, social security, veteran questionnaires, etc.).

Sometimes feature writing on a given topic appears regularly, and the newspaper may treat it as a column. The most common examples of such writing are the buyer's guidance story, advice to the lovelorn, aids to dieting and better health, advice to aspirants in a particular field, etiquette talks, and writings on psychology.

7. Personal Experience—One of the most popular feature stories is that in which a reporter or someone outside the newspaper field writes from the standpoint of personal experience.

Reporters employ this first-person approach in such stories as those which tell of the meeting with a famous person, the demonstration of a new invention, and the visit to an interesting or unusual place. The stories by outsiders, many of which are frequently ghost-written, include such writings as those of famous baseball players who write of their big games; military men who recount their experience under fire; and plain citizens who have been eyewitnesses to major disasters.

8. Arts and Crafts—On many occasions, one finds in the newspaper a story which explains a fad or trends in a particular art or craft at a given moment. The story is really a little essay to explain.

The music critic, for instance, writes of the record sales for the past month; the radio editor holds forth on the entertainment for the coming season; and the women's page editor tells of the crafts which are currently popular among the children's groups of the city.

9. **Popularizing Facts**—Rarely does one examine a large metropolitan newspaper without coming upon the feature story which explains the below-surface facts of an institution, a craft, or an interesting place. Perhaps the reporter has visited a famous restaurant. He tells of the quantities of food, the unusual details of its preparation, and any interesting statistics on number of diners and eating habits.

This type of feature story is employed to a great degree by those working on the magazine section of the Sunday paper. Here one can find story after story explaining places of historical interest, unusual vegetation, and institutions and places which one passes daily without knowing much about them.

10. **The Utility Article**—When the editor sees the advisability of teaching the readers how to perform in a given field, the utility article is employed.

On the women's page, one comes upon the article concerning new dishes and other phases of improving the home; on the music page, one finds articles teaching the reader how to interpret music or how to play an instrument; on the sports page, one sees the article telling readers how to play golf, how to tie flies for trout fishing, or how to understand the various sports.

THE LEAD IN THE FEATURE STORY

Writing the feature story lead differs from writing the news story lead in that there is much greater latitude. The writer can now use one of several kinds of leads, depending on the material and the style of the story. One lead, he finds, creates suspense. Another creates sympathy. Another gives just the humorous beginning he wants. Consequently, he chooses the one that best suits his needs.

The Feature Story

The most common kinds of leads are listed below. In studying these leads, the student of journalism should note that not all are strictly feature story leads; several can be used in the straight news story or in the part news–part feature story.

1. The Contrast Lead:

A race in alms giving to promote world peace through the influence of spiritual leaders rather than an arms race for war was called for by Rabbi Samuel M. Segal in his sermon yesterday morning at Mount Neboh Temple, 130 West Seventy-ninth Street.

—New York Times

2. The Question Lead:

GAYLORD—Why did three boys take turns shooting at a friendly, 66-year-old woodcutter until a bullet in the back killed him?

A psychiatrist will try to answer that question Wednesday.

Probate Judge Frank Libcke said he would take the trio to the Central Michigan Children's Clinic in Traverse City.

—Detroit Free Press

3. The Astonisher Lead:

Cincinnati, July 8—(UP)—A Cincinnati sociologist today suggested that people stop "falling in love."

Roy E. Dickerson, executive secretary of the Cincinnati Social Hygiene Society, said it just isn't so—we don't "fall in love." Nor do we "love at first sight."

Dickerson told University of Cincinnati students that love is the product of a growth process.

"It isn't an accident or a sudden visitation," he said. "If there actually were such a thing as love literally at first sight, it surely should be carefully tested by the passing of time."

—United Press story in the *Evening Bulletin*, Philadelphia, Pa.

4. The Suspended Interest Lead:

What appeared to a Claypool Hotel room clerk to be a serious housing shortage was quickly solved the other day.

Richard Condon and Mr. and Mrs. E. G. Fitzgibbon, representing Paramount Pictures, arrived in Indianapolis to do some promotion work on the new Cecil B. DeMille production, "Samson and Delilah." They went to the Claypool Hotel, where they had reservations, and presented themselves to the room clerk.

Frowning mightily, the clerk said: "You have reservations for two bedrooms with twin beds and a living room. That isn't enough for all five of you."

Puzzled, Condon took a look at the reservation slips in the clerk's hand.

One said: "Mr. and Mrs. E. G. Fitzgibbons." A second: "Richard Condon." And a third: "Samson and Delilah."

* * *

—Indianapolis News

124

5. The Figurative Lead:

By Frank Lowe

MONTREAL Airport at Dorval is shaking out its fall wardrobe for the greatest day in its history. And the Montreal public is planning on the gayest, biggest reception it has been invited to in 12 years.

—Montreal (Canada) *Star*

6. The Epigram Lead:

NEW YORK—AP—Robbery is a very unsatisfactory occupation for a man. The pay is poor. Retirement is early, invoked either by death or iron bars.

On paper, it looks easy. A carefully selected group of men, usually masked, walk up to a lot of money. They cow guards and bystanders with weapons. They make a clean get-away.

That's what happened in Boston a couple of weeks ago. That's the pattern for big-time robberies since the days of the bow and arrow. Nevertheless, any ambitious literate thief is invited to look at some of the major hauls of the past 30 years. The record is grim enough to make him head abruptly for the straight and narrow.

—Associated Press story in the *Trenton Sunday Times-Advertiser*

7. The Parody Lead:

Clock Has A Face That Stops A Girl

Bedford, Pa. (U.P.)—The clock in the office of Bedford county Prothonotary Howard J. Koontz has a face that stops a girl.

Koontz had to pull the plug on the electric clock because a temporary stenographer is allergic to florescent light from its dial. It made her break out in a rash.

So time will stand still in Koontz' office until his regular stenographer returns.

—United Press story in the *Daily Local News,* West Chester, Pa.

8. The Quotation Lead:

"Don't argue with a young man who has lost God. Take him out to supper."

This was the simple philosophy of Sir George Williams, founder of the Young Men's Christian Association, which today in America alone has 3,500,000 members and an operating budget of more than $100,000,000 a year.

—*The Journal-Every Evening,* Wilmington, Del.

9. The Dialogue Lead:

By RICHARD L. COE

WASHINGTON.

"If I'm gonna be a sittin' duck, I might as well sit for the big guns," said a girl from Independence, Mo., in Washington last week. And her name isn't Margaret Truman.

She's Ginger Rogers, a freckled kid of 40, candidly unconcerned about how the critics will receive her play when it arrives at New York's Plymouth Theatre on Oct. 16, twenty-one years after "Girl Crazy" propelled her to Hollywood.

—*New York Times*

125

10. The Cartridge or Capsule Lead:

American arms now can begin flowing to western Europe.

The last two roadblocks preventing the delivery of $1,000,000,000 in American military to Europe have been removed, with:

—*Christian Science Monitor*

11. The Pun Lead:

Music Lover Locked in Store

DULUTH, Minn., Feb. 3 (UP).— Nancy Wisklund really lost herself in her music.

She stopped after school at a music store yesterday to play the organ and became so engrossed she didn't notice when the clerks locked up and went home.

Police had to call employes from their homes to get her out.

—United Press story in the *Philadelphia Inquirer*

12. The Rhymed Lead:

By DAMON RUNYON Jr.

With one belt the Celt rose from zero to hero. Today Bobby Thomson said it seemed like a dream.

"I still can't believe it happened," reported the Giant whose bat nailed the National League pennant to the Polo Grounds pole in baseball's most sensational finish.

In this dazed state the brawny Scotsman was joined by millions of baseball addicts who thought Brooklyn had won for sure, only to find the Dodgers couldn't weather the Gael.

—*New York Journal-American*

The student of journalism should know that leads are also frequently classified according to their grammatical structure. Hence, one finds such leads as the infinitive lead, the prepositional lead, and the participial lead. The reason for these terms is simply that the lead opens with the grammatical form for which it is named. Examples follow:

1. The Infinitive Lead:

To meet the holiday needs of the traveling public, Quaker City Bus schedules will be increased substantially this week.

—*Evening Bulletin*, Philadelphia, Pa.

2. The Prepositional Lead:

Under the heading, "Menu of 1929," startling low prices Thursday greeted the customer who ate at the Columbine Coffee Shop, 823

15th St. A hot roast beef sandwich was only 15 cents, and the top dinner on the list was 65 cents.

—Denver Post

3. The Participial Lead:

Recognizing the important role played by the thousands of boys and young men who serve and sell newspapers in Maryland, Gov. Theodore R. McKeldin has proclaimed next Saturday as "Newspaperboy Day."

—Baltimore News-Post

4. The Dependent Clause Lead:

Although Calvert County is long on history and tradition, it never has had an official song or seal.

—Evening Star, Washington, D.C.

5. The Compound Sentence Lead:

Memorial Day is only a few weeks away, and with it comes the informal opening of the vacation season in nearby Connecticut.

—New York Herald Tribune

EXAMPLES FOR DISCUSSION

Study the following feature stories. What makes them features rather than simple straight news? What quality necessary to the feature writer is evidenced in each story?

Boys Turn Tables on 'Debs,' Plan Swank 'Dub Cotillion'

BOSTON, Dec. 25 (UP)—Six college boys, who think debutantes have the right idea, make their bow to society this week at a swank "dub cotillion."

They'll "come out" Thursday at a strictly formal gathering of 500 Boston blue bloods in the lavish Louis XIV ballroom of the Hotel Somerset.

Since debutantes are introduced to a public swelling with males, the six students figured a turnabout would give them a fair play, so they abolished the stag line. Instead there will be a "doe line."

"We're all eligible bachelors," said dub Douglas S. Burns of Boston, "and we want as many girls as possible to have a chance to meet us. But they must be nice girls. We're limiting the invitations to those whom our parents approve."

So far the "doe line" and girl ushers include vacationing students from Skidmore, Wellesley, Bradford Junior College, Radcliffe, Smith and Simmons.

127

"It makes a very nice selection, too," said dub Milton E. Stone of Waban. "We couldn't come out in nicer company. But we're shelling out a thousand bucks for this debut, and for that kind of money we ought to get introduced to the best there is."

Burns, a student at Babson Institute, and Stone, a sophomore at Colby, will be joined in the receiving line by Donald P. Butler of Hartford, Conn., another Babson student; Boston University sophomore Charles V. Fitzgerald; John D. Glass of Springfield and Kevin H. White, a Williams sophomore.

They'll greet their guests in evening clothes, their top hats crowned by a corsage. Burns said the only deviation from formal attire will be the ties. They will be polka-dot ties, instead of plain black, but it hasn't been decided whether they'll be the kind that light up.

Being a little more direct than female debutantes, the boys plan to follow the reception with an auction of themselves.

They'll be put on the block by orchestra leader Sammy Eisen, but not for money. The girls may offer a couple of week ends of dates, a prom invitation, or maybe an office boy's job in their father's office. It's up to the girls at that point. The boys will be there, "waiting to be dragged off."

When the girls make their selections and get acquainted with society's latest additions, they'll be asked to select the "dub of the year."

"That," said dub Fitzgerald, "should be a close race."

—United Press story in the *Florida Times Union*

Alexandria's City Hall Losing Capt. Davis by Retirement

By Mary Lou Werner.

When Charles "Buck" Davis went to work for the City of Alexandria in 1904, his first task was pulling grass from between the cobblestones on Washington street.

Now 65, he is retiring, and it is hard even for him to visualize that first job. Washington street has become the city's busiest artery—a link in the heavily traveled Mount Vernon boulevard and a major route for north-south traffic. One blade of grass wouldn't stand a chance, even if it could push through the smooth asphalt that has buried the old cobblestones.

Capt. Davis—he picked up the title when he served as a fire captain and drove an engine for the city—was only 15 when he got that first job during a summer vacation from school. He has had a variety of municipal assignments since then, serving since 1929 until the present as superintendent of City Hall, market master and custodian of the old City Hall clock.

Five Cents an Hour.

"I was paid 5 cents an hour for that grass pulling," recalled the popular little man with the friendly blue eyes, as he pondered events of the past half century. "And it took one hour's pay to buy a straw hat from Howell's Hattery to keep the sun out of my eyes."

Capt. Davis' schoolmates were able to return to classes at the Alexandria Academy after that first summer of grass-pulling. But the aging grandmother who raised Capt. Davis needed financial help. Her only income came from her small lunchroom next to City Hall. He found it necessary to keep on working instead of returning to school.

For the next seven years, Capt. Davis remained with the street department. In 1911 he was transferred to the city gas works. One of his tasks was lighting gas lamps that illuminated city streets. He remembers two occasions when gas street lamps served as yardarms for lynchings. One of the lynching poles was acquired by Capt. Davis when gas lamps were replaced by electric lights. That same pole, only a few years ago, was installed by the city in front of the remodeled Juvenile and Domestic Relations Court as a Colonial decoration.

Became Fireman.

Interest in fire-fighting led Capt. Davis to his next city assignment. He spent every spare moment rushing to fires as a volunteer until 1916 when the city transferred him from the gas works to the fire department

as a captain and driver of No. 5 Engine Co. He drove engines that were pulled over the cobblestone streets by horses.

"We had those horses so well trained they would back right into the rig when the alarm sounded," he reminisced. "We were fast, too. Each company raced to see who could reach a fire first."

When motorized equipment replaced the horses, Capt. Davis drove the city's first gasoline-driven fire engine. He taught the city's present fire chief, Bernard Padgett, how to drive a fire engine. Chief Padgett always hung around the firehouse as a boy until Capt. Davis finally gave him a chance to drive the big red wagon.

Fire-fighting brought Capt. Davis a serious injury that has helped force his retirement. He suffered severe internal injuries when struck by a high-pressure hose at the Southern Railway coal chute fire in the early 1900s.

Acquired Several Jobs.

In 1926 Capt. Davis was transferred back to the gas works. He remained there as a serviceman until the gas company was sold to become a private utility, and in 1929 he fell heir to the combination of jobs around city hall that he has held ever since—superintendent, market master and clock custodian.

The post of market master once was a big position. Farmers' stalls occupied practically the entire first floor of City Hall, plus the market square behind. The coming of supermarkets and the growth of city offices gradually has squeezed the city market into a few remaining in the courtyard. A handful of farmers from nearby Fairfax County drive

The Feature Story

into the market each Saturday for a few hours of business, arranging with Capt. Davis for their stall spaces.

"It wasn't always like that," said Capt. Davis. "They used to come on Friday night by ox cart and mule wagons and stay all week end. Every one shopped at the market. I just wonder how much longer it can last at all."

Care of the old City Hall clock has been increasingly difficult for Capt. Davis in recent years, but he has managed to keep the cranky old timepiece fairly accurate. This sometimes has involved chipping off solid ice from the giant hands during the bitterest weather.

Brings Worry Now.

"That's one thing that worries me," said Capt. Davis. "Who will take care of the clock? Alexandria just wouldn't be the same without it."

The City Council and other city officials who have known and worked with Capt. Davis for years think City Hall won't be quite the same without him, either.

"I guess I'll be around if they need me," he promised. "You'll see me around."

—*Evening Star*, Washington, D.C.

SPCA Moving Very Tactfully To Ease Skunks Out of Town

Great Care Taken to Avoid Hurting Sensitive Feelings Of Occasional Visitors Here Sampling City Life

By JACK D. HUNTER

"Dear Mr. and Mrs. Skunk and all little skunks:

"This is to notify you that serious negotiations are under way to evict you from your premises in various sections of Wilmington and environs.

"Inasmuch as your occupation of dwellings under porches, in hedges, and in back yards constitutes a mental hazard and otherwise threatens the well-being of other residents of the area—human, canine, and feline

—you, as the English say, have had it.

Very Respectfully

"Respectfully—very respectfully— the SPCA."

It's doubtful whether such a communication will actually be sent out by the Wilmington SPCA, and even more doubtful that it would be read and acknowledged by New Castle County's more pungent citizenry.

But the fact remains: Skunks must go!

130

Miss Alice Warner, treasurer of the SPCA here, assures that there has been no sudden influx of the odoriferous animals.

Few Requests Each Year

But the society receives from four to six requests for aid a year from Wilmington householders whose homes have become the temporary addresses of skunks with a liking for urban living.

For this reason, Miss Warner says, she has placed an advertisement seeking the services of skunk trappers, so that when word comes from a citizen in distress, the society can dispatch a man equipped to take the animals with a minimum of perfumed ado.

The reason the SPCA can't handle the complaints itself, Miss Warner asserts, is that the only traps it has suitable for the purpose would, quite obviously, need scrapping after one application.

Need for Professional

Since the SPCA traps are needed for other pursuits than evicting the four-legged chemical warfare units, she is negotiating with professional trappers to use their equipment.

The "negotiations" are necessary, she points out, to make certain the trappers would use only humane instruments, and not devices that would cripple the skunks or endanger children, dogs, cats, or other pets.

In other words, the orders are this:

"Trap 'em and get 'em out, boys—but don't hurt 'em."

Man-Sized Task

This is, of course, a man-sized task, seeing that the animals to be trapped are known to defend themselves first and ask questions later.

But Miss Warner says she has received three or four answers to her ad from men "who are obviously very responsible and who would meet the requirements set down by the SPCA."

The trap authorized by the society, she points out, is a box-like affair with a sliding door at one end. The prowling black-and-white atomizer is caught when he enters the box to investigate bait left at its far end.

Theoretical Procedure

When the bait is touched, the sliding door is released, and Brother Skunk is on his way out of town.

How the trip to less populated areas is contrived without the trappee putting up a—that is, exercising his God-given right—is a technical matter, apparently.

Under the arrangements under study, Miss Warner says, the SPCA will act as a sort of clearing house for skunk-threatened householders and the trappers.

"If a resident finds he has a skunk living around his place," Miss Warner explains, "he can call us and we will refer him to our SPCA-approved trappers. Financial arrangements between the customer and trapper are their own affair."

Do skunks damage property?

"Well," Miss Warner smiles, "not necessarily."

Then their main nuisance value is the nervous strain they engender among non-skunks?

Again Miss Warner smiles.

—*The Journal-Every Evening*, Wilmington, Del.

EXERCISES

Write a feature story for each of the following. Use the given material only as a basis. Supplement the material as you see fit, supplying names and additional facts where you think that they will make a better story.[1]

1. Two nine-year-old boys have been apprehended by the police in the act of taking a dip in the basin of the large fountain outside the public library. The date is August 10th, the temperature is 91, and the city pavements are sizzling.
2. Write the color story for the Harvard-Yale game. The date is November 19th, the weather is clear and cold, the game is being played in the Yale Bowl, and all tickets were sold two weeks ago.
3. The city government in your home town has just installed voting machines. This is election day. Cover the story. Remember to stress the human interest angle.
4. Peg Leg Pete, notorious gate crasher, was baffled last night for the first time in his 22-year history of getting into big events without paying when police caught him on three occasions trying to crash the Barton-Kenyon fight in Madison Square Garden. They took him into custody because they were "tired of watching him." He was released by a police magistrate this morning.
5. A patent has just been issued to a local inventor for an electrically operated apparatus for reading in bed. The apparatus holds the book at any angle and turns the pages. It is controlled by a series of buttons on a small board at the reader's fingertips.
6. Write a feature article containing advice to a future teacher,

[1] You, the student, are permitted to supplement the material in the exercises so that you may develop your ingenuity in handling the feature story. You must not conclude that such a procedure is permissible in actual feature writing.

doctor, lawyer, or other professional person, basing your remarks on your "years of experience."

7. You are present when a man blind from birth has the bandages removed from his eyes after a successful operation to give him sight. Write the story. Remember, not too "gushy."

8. Visit the dog pound and write a story. The dogs have looked at you imploringly, there has been no end of noise there, and you have seen many, many kinds of dogs.

9. It is Easter Sunday morning on New York's Fifth Avenue. The crowds are returning from the churches, and the Easter parade is at its height. The weather is perfect for the occasion.

10. Write a story about a hermit who has lived in an old shack five miles from your home town for the last 48 years. Known as the "Old Man of the Mountain," he used to come to town only once a year to buy provisions. He was found dead this morning, January 10th, by a police officer who broke down the door when a neighbor reported seeing no trace of life about the house for the last two weeks.

11. Write a story about a 14-year-old girl who is about to undergo her twelfth operation to cure a peculiar growth of her left foot. Physicians are baffled in their attempts to keep the foot growing normally. It shows a tendency to twist badly. The little girl is very cheerful about it all.

12. A very poor laborer, father of seven children, living in the slum section of town, decided to patch the wall in the dining room of the home that he has finally managed to buy. In chipping off the cracked plaster, he came upon a strange opening in the wall. Investigating, he found a small metal box containing $22,000. in old bills and coins. The former owner threatens to sue, but the laborer claims all the money.

13. Write a color story for Christmas, which is just five days away. Visit the toy departments, travel down the main streets, get reactions of merchants concerning purchase of gifts, and any other details you think should be in a story of this kind.

14. A local produce merchant who has just been defeated for his party's nomination for mayor for the fifth successive time an-

nounces that he is going to try for the nomination for governor at the next convention. He says that he "might as well lose for big stakes as for little ones." He espouses the payment of pensions for all people over 50 years of age, basing the amount to be received on the amount of "good" the applicant has done. He measures "good" by attendance at church, ability to stay out of prison, and number and quality of character references which an applicant can obtain. Points are to be given for each phase of an applicant's record, and the judging is to be done by an impartial board.

15. Visit the home of a local business man who has 12 children. There is no problem of support because the father has a good income. Write an interesting story on the family at dinner, on the purchase of food, and on all the interesting aspects of their life together.

16. An eccentric spinster, very wealthy, plans to launch a nation-wide campaign to restore the bustle to feminine attire. At present she is having literature printed on the subject, and next she plans an attempt to enlist the aid of movie actresses and other prominent people. She plans a speaking tour for herself.

17. An actress now 65 years old—on the stage since she was 12—gives the feature writer an interview. She advises girls and boys to know what career they want and to strive for that career, come what may. She believes that "there is always room for a good one, no matter how crowded the occupation may be." She believes the home and the church are the foundation of society and advises everyone to develop more respect for each.

18. A local insurance broker has heard that his brother who he believed was killed in action in the last war is a patient in a veterans' hospital on the West Coast. He checks the report and finds it to be true. The brother, who has lost both legs and part of an arm, has chosen to allow the news of his supposed death to stand because he doesn't "want to be a burden to anyone." Write the story as if you were the insurance

broker from the time he comes face to face with his brother.

19. This is September 5th and the first day of school. Try to avoid the stereotyped feature story on this subject.

20. Worshipers at the local Baptist Church are in a constant state of unrest during the services because two small blacksnakes are at large in the church. They escaped from the pocket of a 15-year-old boy six weeks ago during a service, and all attempts to capture them have failed. They were last seen a week ago as they disappeared into two of the numerous holes between the floor and the wall, after scaring the women in the church almost to death. They have at times appeared during services, at strange places and under strange conditions.

Copyreading

Chapter

5

THE COPYREADER

One of the most important positions in the newspaper office is that of the copyreader. This fact is true because the copyreader is actually an editor responsible for the final checking and editing of copy before it is set in type. He must pass judgment on the quality of the writing, the tone of the story, and the accuracy of the facts. When the story leaves him, its fate has been decided.

In the case of the very small newspaper, a few copyreaders may be sufficient to handle all the copy for the entire paper. In the instance of the larger papers, however, the work may be so heavy that every department has its own copy desk. Thus, the size of the particular newspaper determines the number of copyreaders and the assignment of specific copy-reading duties.

The copyreader sits at a large circular table, commonly called the "rim," where he works along with his fellow desk men. The head copyreader is called the "slot man" because his position at the traditional copy desk is a section cut inward to enable him to address, or throw a story to, any copyreader around the rim. The slot man assigns the stories to be read, keeps a record of their status, and acts as general supervisor of the entire desk.

To be a copyreader, one must be quick, intelligent, well informed, resourceful, and confident. But above all, he must be a good newspaperman in every sense of the word. He must know the ins and outs of the world of journalism, and he must be thoroughly familiar with every department of the newspaper. In most cases, therefore, the copyreader is a former reporter advanced to this important position.

Because the copyreader is the link between the editorial department and the composing room, he must be especially aware of the problems of both. To the editorial department, he is responsible for checking and editing the story. To the composing room, he is responsible for making the wishes of the editorial department clearly known. To the slot man, he is responsible for the duties discussed later in this chapter.

Functions of the Copyreader

As the copyreader takes his seat on the rim, he must be prepared to execute his duties with a proficiency that is almost perfection itself. This being the case, one can readily understand the demand for good copyreaders. The duties of the copyreader are:

1. **To Make the Story Readable**—Where the reporter has written a phrase that is involved or ambiguous, the copyreader must recast it, for journalistic writing must be clear and forceful on the first reading. Making the story readable is difficult because, while newspaper readers represent a wide range of intellectual backgrounds, the story must be intelligible to all without offending any. The laborer will cast the paper aside if it baffles him; the college professor will look for a more mature paper if this one insults his intelligence. To the copyreader, therefore, falls the difficult task of attempting to please readers from all intellectual levels.

2. **To Keep the Story Brief**—Since most newspapers rarely have enough space for all the material on hand, the copyreader must make certain that everything is stated as briefly as possible. He may infuriate the reporter, who feels that his art is being weakened, but, nonetheless, he must attain brevity. Frequently there are even occasions when the copyreader must eliminate facts. Here is a typical instance: the paper is "tight"—i.e., it has a great many stories—when an important story not anticipated is phoned in by a reporter covering a district. Immediately the make-up editor and the editor confer. They decide to make the new story a column in length, and they instruct the copy desk to cut certain stories already written. The copyreaders handling these stories are told to "trim" them or "boil them down." This

means just what the term implies—to eliminate facts in order of least importance until the story has been cut to the length desired.

3. To Guard Against Libel—The copyreader must delete or recast any statement that smacks of libel. To define libel is rather difficult because legal interpretations vary from state to state, but the copyreader must have a working knowledge of it nonetheless. Loosely, libel can be understood best by comparing it with slander: if one calls a man a "thief" orally, he has slandered him; if he calls him the same thing in writing, he has libeled him. The only consistently successful defense against libel has been to prove the statement true.

Frequently, the copyreader takes refuge in such statements as "police say," "it is rumored," and "many people believe," but on many occasions such prefatory statements have failed to defend newspapers in libel suits. The copyreader, therefore, must be on guard for statements that may expose his newspaper to libel suits.

4. To Check the Accuracy of Facts—Because the reporter sometimes makes mistakes in facts, the copyreader must be prepared to make corrections. To aid this process, the copyreaders are frequently given specialties, or kinds of stories on which they are well informed. One copyreader, for instance, is the specialist in local politics, and all stories in that field are read by him. He usually knows every major political figure, so that if the reporter states that John J. Kelly is political leader in the 27th precinct, whereas it is really the 37th, the copyreader can make the correction. Another copyreader may be the specialist in local crime, and he is certain to know the correct spellings and middle initials of most of the police officials and the records, the aliases, and many colorful details of major criminal figures. With this knowledge, he acts as a check on the reporter.

If anyone thinks that small mistakes are inconsequential, he should sit at the telephone of the city room after an error has appeared in print. Or he should make a study of reporters who have been discharged because of such mistakes.

5. **To Make Stories Conform to the Style of the Newspaper**—Every newspaper office has definite policies regarding usage of questionable words, punctuation, spelling, and capitalization. These policies are to be found in the stylebook used by the particular paper. The policy covering questionable words governs the use of such terms, for example, as *cop, hoodlum, thug, gigolo, boy friend, racketeer, love nest, gun moll.* The punctuation policies govern the use of the comma, the dash, paragraph indentation, precedes on stories, and any detail having to do with special punctuation marks (stars, asterisks, arrows, etc.). The spelling policy pertains to such words as *thru, nite, boro, catalog,* and *theater,* while the capitalization policy governs all instances where the capitalizing of a word is optional. For further study, see the section in this chapter on the stylebook.

6. **To Keep a High Tone to the Stories**—The copyreader must always be on the alert for facts that either cheapen the paper or do not contribute to an already established policy of dignity and restraint. Where he is in doubt about killing such a fact, he should consult the slot man. Such facts usually make their appearance in stories describing shapely movie actresses; in accounts of defendants in criminal courts; and in stories of divorced persons.

7. **To Write Headlines**—Because of its complexity, this phase of the copyreader's work is discussed separately (see p. 164).

THE COPYREADER HANDLES THE STORY

Once the student of journalism understands the functions of the copyreader, he is prepared to follow the progress of the story as it arrives at the copy desk.

All stories coming to the copy desk are handed first to the slot man, who notes on his schedule the slug, the time of arrival, and the name of the copyreader to whom the story will be assigned. This schedule will also eventually bear the kind of head and the time that the story cleared the desk. After making his initial record, the slot man hands the story to the copyreader to carry out the functions previously described.

To make clear the manner in which the copyreader handles the story, this section tells something of the stylebook and the symbols used by the copyreader, and it presents a story that has "cleared" the desk.

THE STYLEBOOK

A stylebook is a newspaper's set of instructions for writing and editing copy. The reporter must know his paper's stylebook so that he can do his work well; the copyreader must know the stylebook verbatim for he cannot work without it. A typical stylebook that might be adopted by a newspaper follows:

1. General Instructions:

a. PREPARING COPY—All material must be typed; longhand articles are not acceptable. Typing must be done clearly, without strike-overs or blurred erasures. Only regulation copy paper should be used. Typing must be on one side only. Typing must be double spaced in order to leave room for corrections. Ample space should be left at top and bottom and margins should be wide.

b. MAKING CHANGES—All changes should be made clearly and positively. The reporter should not make changes in longhand. The copyreader should use a standard copy pencil and standard symbols in making changes. When corrections have been made in longhand, the letter "n" should be overscored and the letter "u" should be underscored.

c. PAGE MARKINGS—Reporters should put the slug (name of the story) in the upper left-hand corner of the first page and on every succeeding page. The reporter's name should follow the slug. Every page should be numbered when a story has more than one. The slug, usually given by the editor, should be short and expressive.

When there is to be more than one page, the reporter should write and encircle the word "more" at the bottom of all pages except the last. The end of the last page should bear the mark (30) or (#) or (///) .

If the copyreader plans to write the head for the story after finishing the last page, he should mark the first page "hed to cum" so that the composing room will know the situation.

d. STYLE—All writing should be in accepted journalistic style. It should not be bombastic, trivial, overenthusiastic, or gushy.

The reporter should not place important details in the last paragraph because this section is usually the first affected by trimming. Where the reporter has done this, the copyreader must be careful as he trims.

e. ACCURACY—The writer must be accurate at all times. When in doubt, he should check. The standard sources for checking are the dictionary, the "World Almanac," "Who's Who," the telephone directories, and the numerous catalogs and publications of such places as universities and churches. Newspapermen must remember that most persons are extremely sensitive about the spelling of names, correct titles, and many other details that seem trivial to the person not concerned.

f. OFFENSIVE EXPRESSIONS—The reporter should not use and the copyreader should delete expressions and nicknames that are likely to give offense. Some examples are: *dago, Polack, shanty Irish, ward heeler, small fry, schoolmarm, high-pressure salesman, yes man.* The offending expression is most likely to appear in a quotation, but, nonetheless, it is certain to offend some readers. The reporter and the copyreader also must be careful of words or slantings that are indecent, either directly or by implication.

2. Punctuation Marks:

a. THE PERIOD:

The period is used AT THE END OF A SENTENCE as it is in ordinary writing. Where the reporter has struck the typewriter key lightly, the copyreader should make the period heavier. Where the copyreader inserts a period, he should encircle it or use one of the standard devices—either ⊙ or ⊗.

The period should be omitted after headlines, captions, figures, the names of radio stations, and letters standing for well-known agencies.

The period is used WITH ABBREVIATIONS, as, for instance, the following: the *Rev. Dr.* Robert L. Peters, *Capt.* John K. Rossen, *Supt.* Earl P. Thomas, Chrysler Motors *Inc.*, Smith *Mfg. Inc.*

A series of periods is used TO INDICATE OMISSION, as, for instance, "Many a flower is born *to . . . waste* its sweetness on the desert air."

b. THE COMMA:

The comma is used IN A SERIES. *Ex.:* He chose *toys, baskets, ties, and vases.* (The last comma is optional.)

The comma is used TO SEPARATE UNRELATED ADJECTIVES. *Ex.:* It was a *long, difficult* pull.

The comma is used TO SET OFF THE NONRESTRICTIVE CLAUSE. *Ex.:* Senator Davis, *who leaves office next year,* predicts a hard fight.

The comma is used TO SET OFF THE APPOSITIVE. *Ex.:* Representative Connally, *the chairman of the committee,* spoke to his group.

The comma is used TO SET OFF THE DIRECT QUOTATION. *Ex.:* "*The time,*" said he, "*is now at hand.*"

The comma is used TO SET OFF THE INTRODUCTORY ELEMENT. *Ex.: Therefore,* the disaster was forestalled.

The comma is used TO SET OFF THE PARENTHETICAL ELEMENT. *Ex.:* Algebra, *how I hate that subject,* gives me a great deal of trouble.

The comma is used TO SET OFF THE NOUN OR THE PRONOUN USED IN DIRECT ADDRESS. *Ex.:* That course, *John,* is very important.

The comma is used IN THE COMPOUND SENTENCE. *Ex.:* *Jones spoke for a long time, but he did not disclose his final plans.*

The comma is used IN THE COMPLEX SENTENCE if the dependent clause precedes the independent clause. *Ex.:* *If Thompson is to be re-elected,* he must work now.

The comma is used TO SEPARATE THE ELEMENTS IN DATES AND PLACES. *Ex.:* The candidate was born on *August 1, 1901, in Bay View, Potter County, Maine.*

The comma is used TO SET OFF CONTRASTED EXPRESSIONS. *Ex.:* The president, *not the advisory board,* is responsible.

Generally speaking, the comma should be used also IN ANY SITUATION WHERE: (1) the meaning is doubtful without one and (2) the presence of one makes for easier reading.

c. THE COLON:

A colon is used AFTER A STATEMENT INTRODUCING A DIRECT QUOTATION. *Ex.:* *He made his point tersely: I am not going to accede.*

A colon is used TO INTRODUCE A LONG SERIES. *Ex.:* Those present included: *Katherine Thompson, secretary; Mary Williams, treasurer; etc.*

A colon is used TO INTRODUCE A FORMAL RESOLUTION. *Ex.:* *"Resolved: That this assembly . . ."*

A colon is used TO INTRODUCE A SPORTS RESULT. *Ex.:* *Score:* Whitney, 20; Harrow, 12.

A colon is used TO SEPARATE CHAPTER AND VERSE in scriptural references. *Ex.:* I Corinthians *13:1.*

d. THE SEMICOLON:

A semicolon is used TO SEPARATE TWO CLOSELY CONNECTED CO-ORDINATE CLAUSES. *Ex.:* *The Trojans were outclassed; they were beaten from the start.*

A semicolon is used IN A SERIES that would not be clear by the use of commas. *Ex.:* The president spoke to *Johnny*

Kirk, our captain; Pete Smythe, our manager; and Mr. William Meyer, our coach.

The semicolon is used, generally speaking, as THE NEXT PUNCTUATION MARK AFTER THE COLON. *Ex.:* The apparatus is used thus: *to combat, if necessary, any unexpected disaster; to aid in the regular work; and to supplement the equipment already on hand.*

e. THE DASH:

The dash is used TO REPLACE THE PREPOSITION "TO" IN SCORES. *Ex.:* The final score was *2–1.*

The dash is used, without a period, FOR THE UNFINISHED STATEMENT. *Ex.: "Why, if I had known ——"*

The dash is used TO DENOTE THE OMISSION OF OFFENSIVE WORDS. *Ex.:* The senator said, *"You can go to ——."* (Note– Some newspapers either use the offensive word or avoid this construction.)

The dash is used FOR AN EMPHATIC PAUSE. *Ex.: John got his answer–fired.*

The dash is used occasionally FOR THE LONG APPOSITIVE. *Ex.:* Pete Jeffers–*who was a winner, a runner-up, and an also-ran in previous tournaments*–never had a chance this year.

The dash is used FOR THE LONG, INVOLVED, PARENTHETICAL ELEMENT. *Ex.:* The team captain–*and in my calm, considered judgment I say I have never seen a better one, on this field, at least*–fought from start to finish.

The dash is used FOR EMPHASIS IN DIRECT ADDRESS. *Ex.: John*–I think you are right! (Quotation marks are not needed with this form.)

The dash is used AFTER QUESTION AND ANSWER in verbatim testimony. *Ex.: Q.–Where do you live? A.–Chicago.*

The dash is used in such instances as these: *First–, Second–, Table 4–Continued, Note–.*

f. THE HYPHEN:

The hyphen is used TO COMBINE TWO OR MORE WORDS

INTO ONE WORD. *Ex.*: a *Truman-like* gesture, a *through-the-house* chase, a *bent-on-murder* move.

The hyphen is used WITH FIGURES DENOTING MEASUREMENT only if the figure is part of an adjectival expression. *Ex.*: a *5-in.* pipe, a *12-ft.* board a *4-lb.* weight.

Do not use the hyphen in writing figures, as *fortysix, eightyone, thirtyeight*. However, use the hyphen WITH FRACTIONS, as *two-thirds, one-sixth, two-eighths*.

Write as one word: *baseball, football, today, tonight, tomorrow, homecoming, textbook, bookcase, downstate, upstate, snowstorm, lineup, newsstory copypaper, newsman, writeup, makeup*.

Use the hyphen WITH PREFIXES USED WITH PROPER NAMES. *Ex.*: *post-Roosevelt, un-American, anti-Truman*.

Words compounded of the following prefixes and suffixes are not hyphenated: *a, after, ante, auto, bi, demi, ever, grand, holder, in, inter, intra, less, mid, mis, non, off, on, over, post, re, some, sub, super, trans, tri, un, under, up, ward, wise, with*. *Ex.*: *ever present, grand march, mid afternoon*.

Words compounded WITH THE FOLLOWING PREFIXES AND SUFFIXES are hyphenated: *able-, anti-, brother-, by-, cross-, -elect, ex-, father-, great-, half-, -hand, mother-, open-, public-, quarter-, -rate, self-, semi-*. *Ex.*: *semi-monthly, anti-Democrat, president-elect*.

However, if the word is used widely, it may be written as a single word, or without the hyphen, as usage dictates. *Ex.*: *antitoxin, byway, quarter final exam*.

g. THE APOSTROPHE:

The apostrophe is used TO DENOTE THE POSSESSIVE CASE OF NOUNS. *Ex.*: *John's* book; *Mr. Smith's* house; *Mrs. Roberts'* daughter.

The apostrophe is used TO DENOTE A CONTRACTION OR AN OMISSION. Strictly speaking, this mark, although the same as an apostrophe, is an omission mark. *Ex.*: *He'd* put his house in pawn! He aims *t'* please.

The apostrophe is used TO MAKE LETTERS PLURAL. *Ex.:* The student earned two *A's.*

The apostrophe is omitted where general usage has already done so. *Ex.:* State *Teachers* College, the *Engineers* Club, the *Lawyers* Guide.

IN THE CASE OF PARTNERS, the second name is apostrophized. *Ex.:* Dunn and *Bradstreet's* index.

h. FIGURES:

Numbers from one to ten are spelled out; numbers from 11 on may be written in their arabic numeral form.

There are, however, several exceptions. Time should be written as *8:15 a.m.* this morning; *11 p.m.,* Thursday; *1:35 p.m.* next Tuesday afternoon.

Sums of money should be written as $12. (not $12.00); $5,000.; $15.80.

Street numbers are always figures: 2158 N. 14 st.; 821 Roosevelt blvd.; 61 Barton pl. Figures are also used for scores, degrees of temperature, automobile license plate numbers, telephone numbers, distances, numbers in election returns, prices, dimensions, and all similar situations.

A sentence should never begin with arabic numerals if any other course is possible. If the first word in a sentence is a number, it should be spelled out. *Ex.: Twelve* members were present.

If a sentence contains a number below ten and one above ten, use arabic numerals for both. *Ex.:* The ages varied from *6 to 20 years, 2 months.*

Phrases should be spelled out. *Ex.:* One man in a *thousand.*

i. PARENTHESES:

Avoid parentheses as much as possible.

Parentheses may be used sparingly FOR EXPLANATION. *Ex.:* John spoke last (*the first time this year*), but he was effective nonetheless.

Parentheses may be used sparingly FOR THE PAREN-

THETICAL ELEMENT. *Ex.:* Harold said the answer was five (*Boy, was he wrong!*).

A caution to be noted is this: Brackets, not parentheses, must be used for any words interpolated by the editor into a direct quote. *Ex.:* Said the President, "We [*Americans*] . . . must be ready for the battle."

j. THE QUESTION MARK:

The question mark is used, in general, as THE END PUNCTUATION IN A QUESTION. *Ex.:* Is that *all?* Are you *ready?*

The question mark is used TO CREATE DOUBT FOR THE SAKE OF HUMOR. *Ex.:* The actress will be a *raving* (*?*) *success.*

k. QUOTATION MARKS:

Quotation marks are used FOR A DIRECT QUOTATION. *Ex.:* "*Here,*" he said, "*is the table.*"

No quotation marks are necessary for a quotation when it is set in smaller or different type to indicate the fact that it is a quotation.

Single quotation marks are used FOR A QUOTATION WITHIN A QUOTATION.

Place "weak" punctuation marks—periods and commas—inside quotation marks. Place the "strong" marks—question marks, exclamation points, colons, and semicolons—outside.

Use quotation marks FOR TESTIMONY, CONVERSATION, AND STATEMENTS GIVEN IN DIRECT FORM. The one exception is the quotation which employs the dash.

Use quotation marks TO SET OFF A WORD OF UNUSUAL MEANING or an unfamiliar or coined word used for the first time. *Ex.:* The "tagee" then becomes "it."

Use quotation marks FOR THE NAMES OF BOOKS, PLAYS, PAINTINGS, SONGS, MAGAZINE ARTICLES, etc.

Use quotation marks AT THE BEGINNING OF EACH PARAGRAPH OF A QUOTATION extending to two or more paragraphs. Place marks at the end of the last paragraph only.

Use no quotation marks for names of newspapers or periodicals, as *New York Times*, or for common nicknames, as *Sad Sam* (except when they are used with the full name, as *Samuel "Sad Sam" Smith*).

1. ABBREVIATIONS:

Abbreviate the following TITLES WHEN THEY PRECEDE: *Dr., Mr., Messrs., Mrs., Mme., Mlle., Prof., Rev., and all military titles except Chaplain.*

Abbreviate NAMES OF STATES when they are preceded by the names of cities. *Ex.: St. Louis, Mo.* The generally accepted abbreviations are:

Ala.	Fla.	Md.	Nev.	Oreg.	Tex.
Ariz.	Ga.	Me.	N. C.	Pa.	Va.
Ark.	Ill.	Mich.	N. D.	P. I.	Vt.
Calif.	Ind.	Minn.	N. H.	P. R.	Wash.
Colo.	Kans.	Miss.	N. J.	R. I.	W. Va.
Conn.	Ky.	Mo.	N. Mex.	S. C.	Wis.
D.C.	La.	Mont.	N. Y.	S. D.	Wyo.
Del.	Mass.	Nebr.	Okla.	Tenn.	

Abbreviate the NAME OF MONTHS having five or more letters when used in dates and datelines. *Ex.: Dec. 24.*

Abbreviate the word NUMBER before figures. *Ex.: No. 16.*

Abbreviate UNITS OF MEASURE when preceded by numerals. *Ex.: 21 ft. 6 in.*

Abbreviate common designations of WEIGHTS AND MEASURES in the singular only. *Ex.: lb., in.* Exceptions: *Figs. 1 and 2, Vols. 1 and 2, Nos. 1 and 2.*

Abbreviate COLLEGE DEGREES. *Ex.: A.B., S.T.D., V.M.D.*

Abbreviate avenue, street, alley, drive, boulevard, road, and place when used in an ADDRESS. *Ex.: 28 Firth ave., 29 Warden dr.*

Abbreviate MORNING to a.m. and AFTERNOON to p.m.

Abbreviate NAMES OF COMMON ORGANIZATIONS. *Ex.: R.O.T.C., G.A.R., D.A.R., W.C.T.U.* (Note—Omit period in names of radio stations and very common abbreviations. *Ex.: WJZ, PX*)

Do not abbreviate *Christmas* to *Xmas,* christian names, or such titles as senator, congressman, bishop, president, secretary, and chairman when used with a last name.

m. TITLES:

Men's initials or first names should be used when the name appears for the first time. Thereafter, use simply the last name except in the case of high-ranking people. Where only initials appear, the reader assumes that the name is that of a man.

First names of unmarried women should always be given. Thereafter, the title *Miss* and the last name are to be used. If no title is given before the name of a woman, the reader assumes that she is unmarried.

Divorced women and widows are given the title *Mrs.* and their christian names unless they wish otherwise.

Men in religious orders should always be given their proper titles. A clergyman is *the* Rev. Mr. Jones.

Foreign Titles

The following are approved forms for foreign titles:

EAST INDIAN

Maharaja	Maharani (or ee)
Raja	Rani (or ee)

ENGLISH

King	Queen
the Duke of	the Duchess of
the Marquis of	the Marchioness of
Earl (or the Earl of)	Countess
Viscount	Viscountess
Baron	Baroness
(more commonly, Lord)	(more commonly, Lady)
Sir Paul Barry	Lady Barry
(thereafter, Sir Paul)	

Baronet is a hereditary title. Baronets are distinguished from *knights* by the abbreviation *Bart.* or *Bt. Ex.:* Sir John Turner, *Bart.*

Use the *Right Honorable* rarely. Say *Captain Sir Clarence Peters;* thereafter in a story it is *Sir Clarence* or *Captain Peters.* The Lord Mayor's wife may be called the *Lady Mayoress.*

French

Prince	Princesse
Marquis	Marquise
Vicomte	Vicomtesse
Comte	Comtesse
Baron	Baronne
Monsieur (M., plural MM.)	Madam, Mademoiselle (Mme., Mmes.; Mlle., Mlles.)

German

Herr	Frau, Fraülein

Italian

Principe	Principessa
Duca	Duchessa
Marchese	Marchessa
Conte	Contessa (sometimes Contesina)
Barone	Baronessa
Signore	Signora, Signorina (Miss)

Use the last name with these titles (Signore, Signora).

Russian

Grand Duke Boris Vladimir (father's name plus ovich, for son)	Grand Duchess Marie Vladimir (mother's name plus ovna, for daughter)

SPANISH

Principe	Princesa
Duque	Duquesa
Marques	Marquesa
Conde	Condesa
Baron	Baronesa
Señor	Señora, Señorita (Miss)

SWISS

M.	Mme.

The Swiss also use German and Italian forms.

n. CAPITALIZATION

Do not capitalize:

Names of national, state, and city bodies, boards, etc. *Ex.: assembly, council, legislature, house, senate, department of welfare, highway commission, tax office, city hall, capitol.*

The words "street," "avenue," etc. *Ex.:* 10 Downing *st.,* 241 Maple *ave.* However, it should be: 241 *Boulevard of the Allies,* 833 *Avenue of the Pacific.*

Seasons of the year: *spring, summer, autumn, winter.*

Points of the compass: *north, east, south, west, northeast, southwest.*

The subject of debate. The standard style is: *"Resolved: That the minimum age requirement for voting in national elections should be lowered to 18 in all states."*

These prefixes: *von, de, di, la, le,* except where they begin the sentence. *Ex.:* Hermann *von Bulow,* Henri *de la Rouge.*

Time: *a.m.* and *p.m.* Write *12 o'clock noon* or *midnight.*

Names of school departments and all studies except names of languages and subjects containing a proper noun. *Ex.: mathematics department, philosophy, Latin, American history.*

153

Titles when the name precedes. *Ex.: Howard Thomas, professor of chemistry*.

Names of classes: *freshman, sophomore, junior, senior*.

College degrees written out. *Ex.: bachelor of arts, master of arts, doctor of philosophy*. However, it is *A.B., A.M., Ph.D.*

Titles in lists of officers: *Ex.:* The newly elected officers are: Peter Johnson, *commander;* George Harris, *vice-commander*.

Widely used common nouns or adjectives derived from proper nouns. *Ex.: phoenician alphabet, russian dressing, macademize, german measles, swiss cheese*.

o. INDIVIDUAL PUNCTUATION MARKS:

The copyreader should consult the slot man before approving any distinctly individual punctuation marks (stars, asterisks, arrows, etc.).

The Copyreader's Symbols

On pages 156–159 are shown the symbols used by copyreaders throughout the country, followed by a story that has "cleared" the copy desk. The student should study these symbols as they appear in the chart. He should then study the story with the corrections made by the copyreader, shown on pages 160–163.

Before studying the symbols, the student should recognize three important facts. He should note first that these symbols are a specific language—the language employed by the copyreader to give instructions for preparing material for print. Next, to facilitate learning, the student should attempt, wherever possible, to see a reason for the nature of the symbol. The symbol for transposing words, for example, is clearly logical, as are the symbols for moving type. However, when symbols lack a logical basis, as do those denoting the end of the story, the student should strive for some association by which to remember the symbols. Finally, the student must learn all symbols for every situation; he must not content himself with learning only those he plans to use. The three symbols for the end of the story, for instance, must be known because all three are employed widely.

The student should also learn to make symbols with the standard pencil used in copyreading. This pencil, appropriately termed a "copy pencil," has a soft lead in order that it may be used easily on standard copy paper. The harder lead of the commonly used pencil makes too light a mark and often tears the paper used in most newspaper offices. Ink is not used in copyreading because of the difficulty in erasing and because it has a tendency to run on copy paper.

Copyreading

SYMBOL	MEANING	EXAMPLE
⌐ or ⌐ or ℋ	Start new paragraph	⌐It was then that the man
		⌐It was then that the man
		ℋIt was then that the man
≡ or ⫫	Make capital letter	Said mr. Smith in answer
		Said mr. Smith in answer
\ or /	Make lower case	In answer to the Question
		In answer to the Question
⊙ or ⌄	Insert comma	across the dull hot desert
		across the dull hot desert
ᵛ⁾ ⁽ᵛ	Insert quotation marks	"Come," he said loudly.
⊙ or ⌄	Insert apostrophe	Johns book was lying there.
		Johns book was lying there.

156

SYMBOL	MEANING	EXAMPLE
Ⓧ or ⊙	Insert period	That was all he said Ⓧ That was all he said ⊙
/	Separate words	quickly came into the/room
◯	Abbreviate or spell out	Fifth (avenue) the (prof) turned
◯	Write out or use arabic number	the ③ judges leaned forward had (sixty-four) cups there
Ⓧ	Kill but allow for possibility of restoring	The old man then left the judge's chambers amid a silence and an atmosphere of bewilderment.
∿	Bring copy together	The car careened madly
⌐ or ⊐	Delete letter	The pasture was white The pasture was white

Copyreading

SYMBOL	MEANING	EXAMPLE
℈	Delete word	speaking ~~very~~ softly
stet or	Kill correction	speaking ~~very~~ softly *stet*
		speaking ~~very~~ softly ......
⌒	Bring letters together	Rising qui_ckly to her feet
∿	Transpose letters	th~~ier~~ men were now ready
∿	Transpose words	their men were ready now
ʌ	Insert letters	Har*r*y spoke to me
℘	Insert words	Harry *spoke* to me
∿∿∿	Set in boldface	By Norman J. Doe
___	Set in italics	Smith says that he knows.

158

SYMBOL	MEANING	EXAMPLE

[

]

Indent left

Indent right

By a unanimous vote the jury has decided that the defendant must die in the electric chair.

(#)

or

(///)

or

(30)

The end.

down came the curtain. (#)

down came the curtain. (///)

down came the curtain. (30)

Copyreading

STORY THAT HAS CLEARED THE COPY DESK

Singer - Jones #4 | Slug; reporter's name; head.

Facing a battery of news cameras and a mass of | Paragraph; separate words.

Miss

cheering people, Alma T. Johnson, Montville's great | Insert title; insert apostrophe.

lyric soprano, returned home in triumph today. The

attractive 18 year old brunette appeared at Munici-

prize

pal hall to formally receive the $5000. check for | Capital; transpose words; delete and insert.

contest for

winning the recent competition to select the best | Delete; delete and insert.

Nation's

feminine voice in the high schools of the Nation. | Insert; period; delete.

Contest

The money, according to the rules of the contest, | Insert and delete; comma; delete.

is to be used in furthering the winner's musical | Insert apostrophe.

education. Miss Johnson was formally presented | Delete.

to the audience by Mayor Richard L. Tomkins who | Insert comma.

paid glowing tribute to her ability.

Accompanying her were her mother, M rs. Mary | Paragraph; bring letters together.

Johnson, and her sister, Mrs. Ronald H. Campbell,

both of whom were visibly affected by the honnor | Strike out letter and bring letters together.

to

being accorded this famous member of their family. | Delete and insert; transpose letters.

Miss Johnson's father, Richard T, was confined to | Insert period.

more | Encircle word "more."

160

The Copyreader Handles the Story

2 Singer - Jones	Page number; slug; reporter's name.
his home ~~with a severe case of~~ /arthritis. Mrs.	Delete and insert.
Johnson reported that ~~that~~ "he'll certainly be	Line out reporter's deletion.
listening in."	Mark quotation.
Following the ~~introductory~~ speech ~~in which~~	Paragraph; restore deletion; insert and delete.
Mayor Tomkins ~~stated the purpose of the gathering,~~	Insert comma; delete.
Miss Hazel H. Smithers, teacher at the local high	
school ~~here in Montville,~~ told of her happiness	Insert comma; delete.
concerning her former pupil's success. Miss	
Smithers explained ~~to the audience~~ that the un-	Delete.
usual quality of Miss Johnson's v*oi*ce was *always* appa-	Transpose letters; insert word.
rent ~~from her earliest years.~~ Miss Smithers ex-	Insert period and delete.
pressed her ~~firm~~ belief that ~~international suc-~~ *world fame awaits*	Delete; insert and delete.
~~cess is in store for~~ Miss Johnson.	Delete.
After Miss Smithers' speech, May*or* Tomkins	Paragraph; insert apostrophe; transpose letters.
introduced ~~Mr.~~ Howard L. Jenkins, ~~representative~~	Delete; delete.
of the Sherrill Woodwork Company, sponsors of the	
contest, who explained briefly the method by which	
~~the winner of the contest was selected~~	Line out reporter's deletions.
more	Encircle word "more."

Copyreading

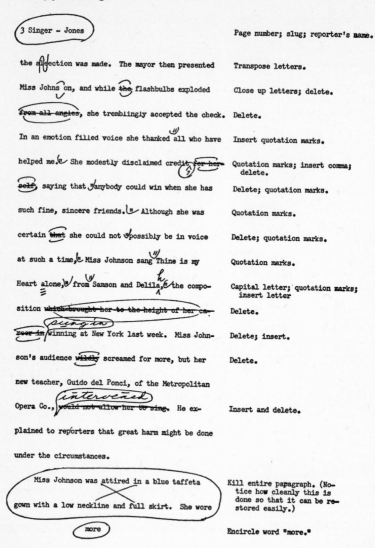

3 Singer - Jones   Page number; slug; reporter's name.

the seclection was made. The mayor then presented   Transpose letters.

Miss Johns on, and while the flashbulbs exploded   Close up letters; delete.

from all angles, she tremblingly accepted the check.   Delete.

In an emotion filled voice she thanked all who have   Insert quotation marks.

helped me. She modestly disclaimed credit for her-   Quotation marks; insert comma; delete.

self, saying that anybody could win when she has   Delete; quotation marks.

such fine, sincere friends. Although she was   Quotation marks.

certain that she could not possibly be in voice   Delete; quotation marks.

at such a time, Miss Johnson sang Thine is my   Quotation marks.

Heart alone, from Samson and Delila, the compo-   Capital letter; quotation marks; insert letter

sition which brought her to the height of her ca-   Delete.

reer in winning at New York last week. Miss John-   Delete; insert.

son's audience wildly screamed for more, but her   Delete.

new teacher, Guido del Ponci, of the Metropolitan

Opera Co., would not allow her to sing. He ex-   Insert and delete.

plained to reporters that great harm might be done

under the circumstances.

Miss Johnson was attired in a blue taffeta   Kill entire papagraph. (Notice how cleanly this is done so that it can be restored easily.)

gown with a low neckline and full skirt. She wore

more   Encircle word "more."

162

The Copyreader Handles the Story

4 Singer - Jones	Page number; slug; reporter's name.
silver slippers, and in her hair she wore a large diamond pin to match her bracelet.	Kill paragraph.
Miss Johnson has told friends that she	Paragraph.
has already declined more than seventy-five	Use arabic numerals.
offers from commercial firms for radio entertainment.	
- 30 -	Encircle "30."

Copyreading

HEADLINES

One of the tasks the copyreader enjoys most is that of writing headlines. He enjoys this work because it gives him a chance to be creative, a chance to express his personality. He may have to revise the headline four or five times before the slot man and the editor are satisfied, but he likes his work nonetheless. Even though the copyreader usually sees his headlines in proof, he eagerly awaits the first papers to see his work in the finished product.

One should remember that, journalistically speaking, the term "headline" (or "head") means the words over the story. The layman, on hearing of headlines, has a tendency to think only of the large lines that cross the entire page. These lines are correctly termed "streamers," "banners," "banner lines."

Most newspapers distinguish their heads by giving them numbers, #1 being the largest, #2 the next size smaller, and so on. As the copyreader sends the head copy to the composing room, therefore, he places in the upper left-hand corner the number of the head and any other pertinent information (family of type, heaviness, caps and lower case letters, etc.). Some newspapers, however, use individual terminology. A paper, for instance, may call a #1 head an "A flare" and a #2 head a "B flare." Whatever the system, the newspaper usually has all its heads pasted together in book form for the new copyreader to study. This form is called a "schedule" or "hed sked," and, where not available, the copyreader should make one for himself.

FUNCTION OF HEADLINES

The function of the headline is fourfold:
1. To Summarize the Story for the Reader—Because most newspaper readers have only a fraction of the time required

to read every item, they want to read the stories that interest them most. Thus, the headline serves the reader by summarizing the story. If the headline holds the reader's attention, he begins to read the story; if not, he usually turns his attention to another headline.

2. To Appraise the Importance of the Story—As the editor decides upon the size of the headline to be given a particular story, he places a relative importance on the story. Thus, many stories with large headlines are read thoroughly, whereas, with smaller heads, they might never be read at all. Generally speaking, the larger the head, the more important the story—or, at least, the more desirous the editor is of having the reader peruse it.

3. To Attract the Reader—The headline serves to attract the reader to the printed page. Many newspapers are sold because a passerby has been attracted by a headline, or because a car rider has seen a headline over a fellow passenger's shoulder. And many stories have been read because of an attractively written headline. This is especially true of the feature story where the head is often humorous, questioning, or astonishing. In the straight news story, of course, the writer of the head tries to generate interest in a more conventional manner.

4. To Give an Attractive Quality to the Newspaper—Attractive headlines, well written, give beauty to the newspaper by presenting a pleasant relief to a field of gray. They serve to break the monotony of looking at column after column of type. In fact, this quality of attractiveness is highly important in causing a newspaper to adopt certain kinds of headlines (see p. 173). It also causes newspapers to use a variety of headlines (full line, stepped line, etc.) on a given page and to employ two or more families of type throughout their pages. Attractiveness, therefore, is an important consideration.

165

Writing the Headline

Aside from mastering the mechanics of writing headlines, the copyreader must develop the *art* of writing headlines. He must acquire those esthetic qualities necessary to recognize and to write a good headline. Like all arts, headline writing cannot be reduced to a formula, but there are some basic abilities upon which any success in this field is built. A discussion of these follows.

1. **Command of Synonyms**—The first requirement for writing headlines is a command of synonyms, especially short ones for long words. Since many newspapers frown on abbreviations in heads, short synonyms are especially important when a headline demands that a long name or term must appear. (For instance; a headline where the name "Richardson" must appear leaves very little room for any other word on the same line.) Some standard synonyms, many of which are overused, follow:

rob for steal; *quiz* for question; *grill* for questioning continually; *hit, rap,* or *flay* for criticizing unfavorably; *ire* for anger; *vie* for compete; *go* for contest; *rip* for denounce; *flee* for abscond; *laud* for praise; *wed* for marry; *raze* for demolish; *scan* for examine closely; *probe* for investigation; *top* for defeat.

Sometimes there are synonyms for names, as, for instance, appellations given the many athletic teams throughout the country: *Quakers* for University of Pennsylvania; *Gophers* for Minnesota; *Rams* for Fordham; *Phillies* for the Philadelphia National League baseball team; *Cubs* for the Chicago team in the same league.

Occasionally, the synonym of a city or a state is invaluable in writing a headline, as, for instance, *Twin Cities* for Minneapolis and St. Paul; *Hub* for Boston; *Bay State* for Massachusetts; *capital* for Washington, D.C.

Although abbreviations frequently are prohibited, those that are immediately clear to the reader are often permitted, especially where they replace a title too long to be practical. Examples: *DAR, WCTU, GOP, YMCA, USSR.*

Then, too, there are many papers which circulate only among readers who know certain abbreviations immediately. In these cases, journalists use these abbreviations. Examples: *PIAA* (Pennsylvania Inter-Scholastic Athletic Association); *AAU* (American Athletic Union); *PSFS* Building (Philadelphia Saving Fund Society); *NYU* (New York University); *UCLA* (University of California, Los Angeles); *NEA* (National Education Association); *AAUP* (American Association of University Professors).

2. Command of Vocabulary—The writer of the headline should have a vocabulary that is extensive and attractive. He must know and be able to use words that create interest, that arouse curiosity, that have a picture-making quality about them, and that can summarize concisely.

Imagery plays a part in this quality, and so we find many of the following personifications in headlines. In fact, that is just the trouble—we find them in too many newspapers, thus wearing them thin from overuse. Examples: *Adonis* for well-built man; *Venus* for beautiful girl; *Man Friday* for faithful servant; *Bluebeard* for wife murderer; *Nero* for one who wastes time in the face of important work; *Alexander* for one who is looking for another field to conquer; *Don Juan* for faithless lover; *Romeo* for ardent lover; *John Q. Public* for every citizen; *Izaak Walton* for ardent fisherman; *John Bull* for England; *GI* for veteran of World War II.

The important fact to remember, however, is that there can be no rule of thumb for gaining the right word. It is a faculty which the copyreader has or hasn't. And, once again, the old-time newspaperman will say that if one isn't born with it, his case is hopeless. And, once again, many a modern teacher will say that, granted native ability, this quality can be developed. Yet, through this controversy emerges the cold fact that the copyreader must know the right word for the particular situation. "Bard" for "poet" may be just right in one instance but may be hopelessly out of place in another. "Snooper" for "detective" would be all right where the effect was meant to be humorous, but it definitely would be out of place in a straight news story. "Yes man" would be permissible in a derisive statement but it could hardly be condoned in any other instance.

3. Ability to Summarize—The copyreader must have, in addition to the qualities mentioned, the ability to write a headline that summarizes the story. In the case of the news story, the headline is essentially the same as the lead. It contains or implies the "w's" and the "h." In the case of the feature story, however, the headline may depart from this pattern in order to arouse curiosity, to be humorous, or to do whatever will lure the reader into the story. Consequently, the feature story head does not always summarize.

Although this ability to summarize may appear easy to acquire, it really comes only with long experience.

4. Ability to Make Headlines Readable—What one of us hasn't at some time or other read a headline two or three times before understanding it? This head was written by a copyreader who either temporarily lost his ability to write a readable line, or, worse still, never had that ability. A headline must always be clear and readily intelligible. Aside from the mechanical aspect (making the headline attractive and uncrowded), two important facts to keep in mind are: (1) try to make every line in the head a logical thought within itself and (2) try never to split a word or a phrase over two lines. Study these examples of good headlines:

German Factory　　**Eased Tax Rate**
Keeps Producing　　**Goes in Effect**
Under Russians　　　**With New Year**

It is not always possible, of course, to make every line a natural break in thought, but this should be kept in mind as an ideal.

The necessity for making the headline readable has greatly increased the use of the verb "to be" in headlines. Heretofore, many newspapermen—especially "old-timers"—have scored this practice bitterly. Now, many large dailies condone the practice as a means of making the head readable. Thus, many heads now resemble declarative sentences. The following are examples:

U. S. Skiers Are Among Favorites For World Jumping Crown Today

---

Coach Hopeful of Placing Three in First Seven at Lake Placid—Swedes, Finns Also Threats to Norse Supremacy

---

—New York Times

St. Luke's Offer of Beds For TB Is Outlined to City

—Philadelphia Inquirer

Copyreading

The Headline Counting Process

Well known to compositor and copyreader is the fact that nothing is so unyielding as type. A headline will either "go"— i.e., fit—or it will not. Consequently, the novice frequently finds his headline returned by the composing room with the explanation that it "won't go" or that it is "too tight." Even headlines already in type are sometimes discarded because the editor thinks that they look too crowded. The simplest way to know whether a headline will fit or not is to "count in" the letters.

Every kind of headline allows a definite number of units per line, depending on family of type, size of type, and particular letters involved. Generally speaking, the following facts may be taken as absolute guides in counting the letters in a head.

1. All capital letters, excepting "M," "W," and "I," count as one unit. "M" and "W" count as 1½ because of their width. "I" counts only as ½ because it is narrow.
2. The space between words counts as a half unit.
3. If the headline is in capitals and lower case letters, every letter counts as a unit with these exceptions: lower case "i," "l," and "f" take only a half unit; lower case "m" and "w" are still 1½ units in width.
4. The full quotation mark (") requires a full unit. Therefore, the copyreader uses the single quotation mark ('), which takes only a half unit.
5. The period and the comma take only a half unit each. Other punctuation marks (dash, brackets, stars, etc.) vary according to the style of the paper.
6. All figures except "1" are 1½ units. The figure "1" is a half unit in some fonts.

170

TYPE

In speaking of type, the newspaperman considers (1) size, (2) family, and (3) heaviness.

Size of type is measured in points, each point being ⅟₇₂ of an inch. Thus, type ¼ inch is 18 points; ½ inch is 36 points; one inch is 72 points. The smallest type used by most American newspapers is 5½ point, or "agate" as it is more frequently termed. Type sizes throughout the newspaper naturally vary with the printed matter. The smallest type is used in the classified advertisements and in the jump lines; the largest is found in the display advertisements and in the banner lines. The type ordinarily used in the body of most stories is 7 or 8 point. The following are examples of type sizes:

This is 4 point, also called Brilliant

This is 5 point, also called Pearl

This is 5½ point, also called Agate

This is 6 point, also called Nonpareil

This is 7 point, also called Minion

This is 8 point, also called Brevier

This is 9 point, also called Bourgeois

This is 10 point, also called Long Primer

This is 12 point, also called Pica

This is 14 point, also called English

This is 16 point, also called Columbian

This is 18 point, also called Great Primer

171

This is 24 point type
This is 30 point type
This is 36 point
This is 42 point

The expression "family of type" refers to style, the word "family" thus covering all the variations within a given style. Most newspapers limit the use of type to two or three families. They base their choices on attractiveness and on families already in use by rival papers. This latter fact is true because the typographical appearance of a given paper is its distinguishing characteristic to the reader. The most common type faces are shown here, set in 12 point:

Bodoni Book	Goudy
Bookman	Karnak Lite
Bruce	Modern
Caslon	Scotch Roman
Century	**Spartan Medium**
Erbar Light	Tempo Medium
Franklin Gothic	Times Roman
Garamond	**Vogue Bold**

The term "heaviness" pertains to the thickness of the linear formation of a letter. Some families of type are obviously heavier than others, but there are also variations within a given family. These variations enable the editor to emphasize by using types of contrasting heaviness. Some newspapers, for instance, always accentuate the name of the paper in the body of a story by setting it in boldface; some emphasize all titles by setting them in boldface or italics; some always set subheads in boldface.

The width of letters may vary within a family. Thus type can be

Regular　　　　**Extra Condensed**

Condensed　　　　**Extended**

The heaviness of type may vary within a family. Thus, for example, type can be

Regular　　　　Lightface

Boldface　　　　**Extra bold**

Type may also be varied by italicizing.

This sentence is italicized.
This sentence is not.

KINDS OF HEADLINES

For purposes of individuality, attractiveness, and necessity, a paper adopts a fixed method of writing and printing headlines. Complete familiarity with the method of the particular newspaper is naturally a "must" for the copyreader. As stated previously, the paper usually has a schedule, but when there is none, the copyreader must make one for himself. The most common headlines are:

1. The Full-Line Head—The basic idea of this head is to make every line full without giving it a crowded appearance.

Plane Crash
Killing Four
Of 23 Aboard
To Be Probed

—*The Journal-Every Evening*, Wilmington, Del.

2. The Stepped or Drop Line—The reason for the name of this line is apparent at first glance. This, incidentally, is one of the most popular of headlines.

RAIL WALKOUT
SPREADING TO
OTHER POINTS

—*News-Times*, Danbury, Conn.

3. The Inverted Pyramid—Once again, the name of the headline is apparent at first glance.

New Housing Loan Bill
Attacked as Unsound

—*Evening Bulletin*, Philadelphia, Pa

4. The Flush Left Head—This headline, which gives considerable freedom to the copyreader, begins every line at the immediate left, leaving the blank spaces to the right.

Grandparents,
Divorced 3 Years,
Remarried

—Seattle Daily Times

5. The Hanging Indent—This head is written with a full first line and shorter lines thereafter. The succeeding lines are indented.

U. S. Planes, RAF Craft Test
Britain's Air Defenses

—Los Angeles Examiner

6. The Jump Head—The part of a story continued on another page is called the "jump" and naturally the head over the continued part is known as the "jump head." Since it is shorter, it strives to take the most important part of the original head. The student should note that some papers use as jump heads a line that more nearly resembles a slug.

SOLONS O.K.
WATER BILL
(Continued from Page 1)

—San Diego Union

Rose Robbery

—Indianapolis News

7. **The Crossline or Keyline**—This is simply a one-line head written straight across the column. It is most popular as a subhead or as a jump head.

Lilliputian Rooms

—Christian Science Monitor

BANKS

When a story is very long or very important, the editor frequently decides to have more than the simple headline. In such cases, banks are written below the main head, enlarging upon the details already given or supplying new ones. These banks are also referred to by newspapermen as "decks." Below is the headline with banks:

SPEEDY REPAIRING OF STREETS URGED

Epstein Tells Borough Heads to Get the Jobs Done as Quickly as Possible

---

WILEY DEMANDS ACTION

Tells City Hall Conference He Is Blamed for Traffic Delays Not of His Doing

—New York Times

SUBHEADS

In long stories, the copyreader frequently is called upon to divide the story into logical units by writing single lines or subheads that are inserted where they divide the story nicely for the reader. The type used in the subhead is slightly larger than that of the story and usually is set in boldface. Here are the subheads for the preceding story.

Borough Heads' Problem — Cavanagh and Gulick Attend

Here is a headline with banks as the copyreader would state it. On p. 178 is the same headline as it appears in type.

West asks Soviet
To Geneva Parley
Of Big 4 On July 18

U. S., Britain, France Send
Notes Proposing Conference
of Heads of Government

Preliminary Talks Set

3 Powers' Foreign Ministers
Meet in New York June 16-17
to Prepare for Session

WEST ASKS SOVIET TO GENEVA PARLEY OF BIG 4 ON JULY 18

U. S., Britain, France Send Notes Proposing Conference of Heads of Government

PRELIMINARY TALKS SET

3 Powers' Foreign Ministers Meet in New York June 16-17 to Prepare for Session

—New York Times

Below is part of the hed sked of the *New York Times*, taken directly from that newspaper's stylebook:

PRESIDENT SEEKS BILLION INCREASE IN DEFENSE FUNDS

Request for $35.5 Billions Is Indicated in Conference With Congress Leaders

AIR FORCE TO GET BULK

Missiles Also to Be Stressed —Democrats to Support Bipartisan Program

STATE WILL CLEAN POLLUTED HUDSON, ENFORCING CURBS

Names Offenders in Specific River Area and Demands Purity Improvements

CATHOLICS EXPAND MODERNIZED BIBLE

Issue Second of 5 Volumes in New Translation Using 'More Reliable Sources'

DROP QUAINT LANGUAGE

Publication Has Seven Books of Old Testament, Changes Title of Ecclesiasticus

ALL R.K.O. MOVIES SOLD FOR TV USE

Entire File of 740 Features and 1,000 Short Subjects Bought for $15,200,000

(Continued on next page)

C HEAD

Top, 24 point Latin Antique Extra Condensed, 14 Units. Banks and Crosslines, 10 point News Gothic.

RETARDED PUPILS
AWAIT STATE AID

**Severely Handicapped Rely
on Private Assistance for
Their Education Here**

½C HEAD

Top, 24 point Latin Antique Extra Condensed, 14 Units. Bank 10 point News Gothic.

POLAND TO WIDEN
PRIVATE BUSINESS

**To Encourage Limited Group
of Service Industries**

TEXT REFERENCE
8 point Italics

*The text of the President's
budget message, Page 17.*

X HEAD (PAGE 1 BOX)

18 point Cheltenham Bold Italic Condensed, 16 Units.

U. S. Rebuffs Soviet
On Prelate's Powers

3X HEAD

18 point Cheltenham Bold Italic Condensed, 16 Units.

Bonn's High Court
Outlaws Red Party
And Front Groups

F HEAD
12 point News Gothic

FINANCIAL NOTES

G HEAD
8 point News Gothic

CORPORATE CHANGES

1 COL. BOX (INSIDE)

14 point Cheltenham Bold Italics Condensed, 20 Units.

New York Poet Wins
Academy Fellowship

[NOTE: A precede box with border takes a one-line 14 point Cheltenham Bold Italics Condensed, 16 Units.

M HEAD

Top, 14 point Cheltenham Bold Italic Condensed, 16½ Units.

ARREST MAY REVEAL
THEFT UP TO MILLION

D HEAD

Top, 12 point News Gothic, 20 Units. Bank, 9 point News Gothic.

CAUSES SON'S ARREST

**Brooklyn Man Charges Boy, 16,
Took $350 and Went on Spree**

L HEAD

8 point De Vinne. Used only as follow head.

TWIN CITY RAPID TRANSIT

**2-for-1 Stock Split Is Proposed
—Regular Dividend Declared**

P-SUBHEAD

12 point Cheltenham Bold Condensed. Used over bylines on 3-em dash matter and to head some texts.

U. S. Officials Leave Today

K HEAD

9 point News Gothic, 24 Units.

Salvation Army Plans Drive

OTHER WORK OF THE COPY DESK

EDITING WIRE COPY

On the copy desk of the large newspaper is a man known as the telegraph or wire editor. If the size of the paper warrants, he may have one or more assistants. The principal duty of the telegraph editor is to copyread the wire stories that arrive via teletype from the news services supplying the particular newspaper. Because wire copy is nearly always in capital letters, this editor must distinguish between capital and lower case letters. By pre-arrangement with the composing room, all letters in wire copy are considered as being small unless marked with one of the standard symbols (≡ or ⩶) for caps.

The telegraph editor, naturally, must be completely familiar with the agreements between his newspaper and the wire services. Some stories may be edited, some may not. Others may be used only under certain conditions—as, for instance, a predated story or one with a "hold for release" order. The telegraph editor must be careful to respect the laws of the wire associations, or the service may be discontinued.

Within the last several years, the wire services have increased the practice of using by-lines on their stories. Consequently, the names of their top-flight writers are now familiar to thousands of readers. The wire services have also sought after famous writers outside the newspaper field to handle assigned stories.

A typical piece of edited wire copy follows:

¶ NEW ORLEANS, DEC. 21...PETER K. ROBERTS, WEALTHY
NEW YORK CITY IMPORTER, REACHED HERE TODAY IN HIS
NATION WIDE TOUR TO FORM A THIRD PARTY, FORM A THIRD
PARTY FOR THE PURPOSE OF WINNING THE NEXT NATIONAL
ELECTION. AS USUAL, HIS FIRST REMARK WAS THAT THE
PRESENT MAJOR PARTIES HAVE BEEN IN THE SADDLE TOO
LONG."

(30)

READING PROOFS

The copyreader should know how to check proof because
he is expected, when time permits, to read the proofs of the
stories which he has handled, even though the composing
room proofreaders check all printed matter routinely. The
copyreader must also know how to check proofs because
there are instances when he must change something already
in type. Obviously, these changes must be noted on the proof.

The following chart constitutes the principal marks used
by the proofreaders throughout the nation. Although these
marks are somewhat similar to those of the copyreader, there
are several sharp differences necessitated by the closeness of
the type.

SYMBOL	MEANING	EXAMPLE
tr	Transpose	He (ready is) for the trip. *tr* /
⸌ ⸍	Quote marks	He said, Come. ⸌/⸍ /
⸌ ⸍	Single quotes	He said; "I am touchy now." ⸌/⸍
⸍	Apostrophe	He had his brothers book. ⸍/
⌄	Comma	He was a short stocky man. ⌄/
?/	Question mark	Is that all ⌄ ?/
⊙	Period	The firm is Smith Bros, Inc. ⊙/
ital	Italics	He never <u>denied</u> his guilt. *ital*
bf	Boldface	<u>Now</u> is the time. *bf*
|²⁄ₘ|	Two-em dash	That was all ⌄ he was finished |²⁄ₘ|
w.f.	Wrong font	BAN<u>k</u>ER INDICTED *w.f.*
ↄ	Turn over letter	The mat⟨ɹ⟩on spoke to the woman ↄ
rom	Use roman type	She spoke in A̲ct 3. *rom*/
!/	Exclamation mark	The day was lost⌄ !/
l.c.	Make lower case	Soper and his /Brother Now HE lives in New York. *l.c.*

Copyreading

SYMBOL	MEANING	EXAMPLE
Delete	Delete	Mr. Joines was president.
		Mr. Joines was president.
stet	Leave as was	He never denied his guilt. *stet*
∧	Insert	He was leader. *the*
¶	Paragraph	That was all he did. ¶Rugby ended the inning as Adler struck out all the heavy hitters.
no ¶	No paragraph	Clark finished the first inning. no ¶ Then he went to the showers.
⊏	Move left	Clark finished the first inning. ⊏ Then he went to the showers.
⊐	Move right	Smith plans to talk with Rickey early.
‿	Less space	Smith plans to talk with Rickey early.
#	More space	Smith plans to talk with Rickey early. So he ∧ #/
⌒	Close up	When h e is ready, he will begin.
≡	Make a capital	Harper and peters stood guard. ≡
═	Make small caps	Chicago, Illinois

Other Work of the Copy Desk

SYMBOL	MEANING	EXAMPLE

See copy

Just then the man entered the room and ∧ to the woman sharply. *see copy*

□ — **Indent one em**

he left the town early.   But □ — for all his care — he made a mistake.

Straighten line

The story was a <u>very exciting</u> one. The main character was a man who never thought of any

⌐ **Move up**

There was never a really dull

moment from the time that he entered the room until the time The storm kept lashing the coast

⌐ **Move down**

from the early hours of the morning. By noon the entire populace

(?) **Is this correct?**

Back and forth. Forth and back. Back and forth. Back and forth.   (?)

X **Bad letter**

The defendant never wavered in his testimony. He averred that   X

/=/ **Hyphen**

In the post ∧ war era the council   /=/

⬭ **Spell out**

The firm is Smith ⬭Bros Inc.

EXERCISES

Practice:

Copy the following articles just as they appear. Use standard copy paper, and double space. Then copyread them.

1. On her third nation wide concert tour miss Anne Brown, soprano will again appear in the college auditorium, November 13, at 8.15 pm. She last presented a recital here on October 14, 1942. Miss Brown is also a talented painter; has studied costume designing in New York city and is currently featured in "Rhapsody in Blue." Critics have called Miss Brown "Queen Ann of Song" and "The Female Chaliapin."

   Miss Brown, who sang before she talked, had ideas of her own about an operatic career before she was ten. She even composed an opera, words and music her own, and acted it out for hourse before a mirror.

   A debut was made at the age of four when, just before demobilization in World War I Anne was brought to Camp Mead, stood on a table and sang for the soldiers. As time went on, she sang the leading roles in her school operettas and was soloist in her church. The only discordant note in this happy household was the obstinate opposition of her father to a stage career.

   When Anne was fifteen, her mother went off with her to New York to apply for admission to the Institut of Musical Art of the Julliard School of Music. Anne was accepted. It marked one of the happiest days in the life of her mother, she relates.

   In the spring of 1934, just as she was about to be graduated from the Julliard School, Anne applied for and got the starring role in Porgy and Bess, George Gershwin's famous work. From that day to the present, she has been a bright light in the world of music.

   "From Bess to Beethoven" was one reviewers comment,

when Anne Brown appeared as soloist with the N.B.C. syjphony orchestra under the direstion of Leopold Stokowski, while she was still starring in "Porgy and Bess." Miss Brown is presented as the second feature in a series of six programs under the direction of the Cultural Life program of the college.

2. The study of American Literature is neglected in colleges and universities throughout the United States and as a result students are unaware of many of the significant fields of their native arts and culture, according to a survey conducted under the auspices of the National Council of Teachers of English. Few of the seven hundred cllleges that responded to the councils questionnaire require courses for B.A. or B.S. degrees.

   However, 30 per cent of the universities and colleges require American literature for majors in English and for those who are perparing to teach English. But the total number of students who fall in those catefories is less than 10 percent. Emerson, Hawthorne and Whitman are teh three most popular American authors judging by the frequency with which they are studied. Others are Peo, Thoreau, Mark Twain, Franklin, and Washington Irving.

   Many of the educators who attended the recent convention of the Council in Minneapolis, Minnesota expressed genuine concern over this situation. They feel that if we are to hold the things for which we have fought, we must increase respect for our nation and its heritage in the arts.

3. Bayonne, New Jersey, police are seeking a dangerous intruded these days. It is a mouse with an unfortunate appetite for the most important papers in the desk drawers at police headquarters in city hall.

   He has caused already no ned of embarrassment to city officials. Last Saturday, for instance, ,Police Captain John O'Donnell had to race allover town to get the signature of District Attorney Lewis J. Kolb on the committment papers for Joseph Torrence, convicted of larceny and sentenced to five years in the State Penitentiary. Imagine the embarrassment of the captain when, as he reached for the paper in his top desk drawer last Monday morning he found that the mouse had eaten a hole right through the signature.

Then there was that sad occasion on Tuesday when Patrolman George Potter stood red faced in the court room of Judge Oliver T. Rosen where Thomas Warren, 312 S. 2nd Street is being tried as an accomplice in the numbers racket. Patrolman Potter declared that when he arrested Warren he found five slips of paper in the latter's possession. On the papers were numbers and names and addresses. Those papers, Potter sadly declares, were taken from my top desk drawer or else that mouse ate them." With this the courtroom burst into laughter and Potter slunk back in abject misery.

Thus far all efforts to capture Mr. Mouse have failed. A trap baited with cheese has been spurned, a little wire house with an inviting piece of bread inside has not been visited, and a big cat imported for the sole purpose of capturing the criminal has reported "no progress."

In the meantime, Captain O'Donnell has ordered that all important papers be kept in the metal filing cabinet.

4. Smarting under a ver poor batting average for the past week, Harold Upton, Weatherman for the town of Harshaw, Pennsylvania refused to predict the weather for more than a day at a time in the future. Upton has been wrong for six of his last seven predictions. For Monday he prophesied snow; it rained. For Tuesday he forecast continued showers; it was clear. For Wednesday he saw countinued fair weather; again it rained. For Thursday he announced continued rain; again it cleared. Friday, said he will be clear and cold; it was cloudy all day. For Saturday, he foresaw contineued cloudiness, but he didn't go far enough for that day saw the heaviest snowfall in years. His prediction for today is bound to be correct; he says the snow is going to remain for a while before it melts.

5. The first Chirdren's Concert presented yesterday morning by Eugene Ormandy and the Philadelphia Orchestra, was as full

of surpreses as a christmas stocking and equally delightful. Even the Academy of Music wore an unespectedly festive air with Christmas trees and a colorful winter scene on stage and many eager youn members of the filled auditorium looking like Christmas cherubs themselves.

A bust of Beethoven directly in front of the podium reminded the audience that the great composer who would have been 175 to-day was sharing honors with the coming holiday event.

The program was composed of "The Nutcracker Suite, Beethoven's first piano Concerto in C major, and the traditional C h ristmas carols.

Make-Up

**Chapter
6**

Introduction
Principles of Make-Up
Other Guiding Points

INTRODUCTION

The most casual of readers is aware of the difference in format of newspapers. He knows that some papers use banners, large heads, and cuts profusely, while others use these devices sparingly. He knows that some papers use a definite family of type and an individual set of punctuation marks, while other papers use sharply different ones. He knows that one paper always boxes or panels late flashes, while other papers place these same flashes in precedes or inserts. He may also be vaguely aware of balance or some other attempt at orderly arrangement of material. To the reader, these practices are all part of appearance; to the newspaperman, they are part of the self-explanatory term "make-up."

Although newspaper make-up has much of the science about it, in the final analysis it is an art. It is an art because it is a distinctively creative work, a work wherein one relies on his innate sense of order and beauty, a work wherein one expresses his artistic personality. As is the case with all other arts, there is an endless amount of disagreement and controversy about make-up. A page considered by one newspaperman to be an example of perfect make-up is viewed disdainfully by another; practices favored by one paper are taboo with a second. Consequently, one finds a wide disagreement over the use of such devices as the eight-column streamer, the bleeding cut, the read-out line, and the shifting of the name plate or the masthead. These arguments are not likely to be settled easily—no more than are the arguments concerning the well-dressed man, the properly furnished living room, the world's most beautiful woman, or the greatest musical composition. As long as newspapermen are human beings, there will be the disagreement about make-up that characterizes creative work.

The procedure for making decisions regarding make-up varies from paper to paper. On the very small newspaper, where there are an editor and two or three assistants, the editor makes the decisions. On larger papers, there is one man, appropriately called the make-up editor, who handles this work. He, however, is not the absolute authority, for he must be guided by the established policies of his paper and his work must be approved by his superiors. Usually, he attends the editorial conference that reviews the day's news so that he can draw up the dummies for the important pages (generally the front, the editorial, and the split pages). He then submits these dummies for the approval of the top editors. The make-up of the other pages containing general news is his decision. The make-up of the specialized pages— sports, society, theater, etc.—is usually done by the top editor in the particular department.

PRINCIPLES OF MAKE-UP

Although there is a sharp divergence of opinion concerning the well-made-up paper, there are some basic principles upon which agreement is fairly common. These principles concern (1) attractiveness, (2) balance, and (3) readability.

ATTRACTIVENESS

Attractiveness is the first consideration of make-up because the reader knowingly or unknowingly looks for a pleasantly arranged page. He is unlikely to favor one as black and unattractive as a page of the telephone directory, or as jumbled and as illogical as an unassembled puzzle. Thus, the material on a given page must present a pleasing appearance. The problem of defining "pleasing appearance" is, of course, obvious. It is, like attractiveness in other fields, something that can never be completely defined; it is simply sensed. It is recognized when met and noted when absent, and the degree to which it is present is always determined on a purely subjective basis.

The opportunity to make a page attractive is naturally affected by editorial policy. A very conservative paper, for example, may not allow streamers, large heads, or more than two small cuts on page 1. Thus, the make-up editor is limited in his attempt to gain variety. The sensational paper, on the other hand, may demand so many cuts and banners that the make-up editor is at a loss to find a really attractive arrangement.

BALANCE

Balance is what the term implies—the attempt to arrange material so as to gain symmetry and hence beauty of the page. Headlines, cuts, boxes, and type are selected and arranged with a view to accentuating each other. As might be assumed, there are several variations within the realm of balance, the most common of which will now be discussed.

Balanced Make-Up

The first of these variations is referred to simply as **balanced make-up**; actually, it should be called **true** or **perfect balance**. Under this pattern, an attempt is made to approximate a perfect pairing of material. Each item is the counterpart of another in head, position, and length, and everything may be ruled over by an 8-column head. The great advantage of balanced make-up is the orderly appearance given by the regularity of the page; the big disadvantage is that other important qualities may be sacrificed to gain this regularity.

Balanced Make-Up

A second variation of balanced make-up is the **inverted pyramid.** Under this pattern, material is so arranged that an inverted triangle can be constructed with its base across the top of the page and its vertex near or at the center of the page.

Inverted Pyramid Make-Up

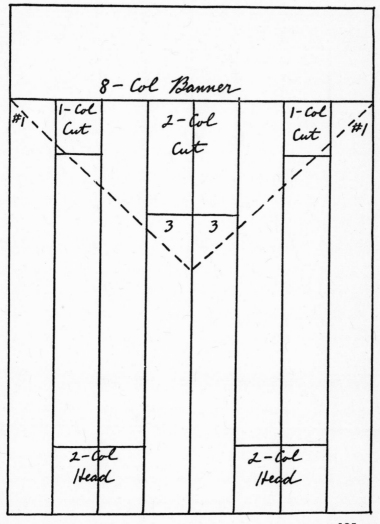

A third variation is **brace make-up.** Under this pattern, one of the upper quarters of the page, usually the right, is given the heaviest concentration of type. This procedure thus creates the impression of a brace or a bracket.

Brace Make-Up

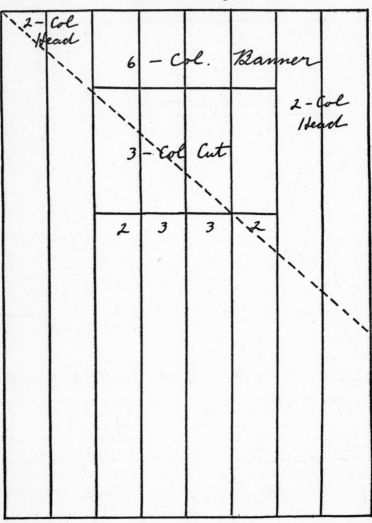

A fourth variation is broken **column make-up**, so called because each column is broken by two or more heads. This make-up is employed in order to have as much material on the page as possible, meanwhile retaining some semblance of order and beauty. Achieving attractive broken-column make-up is difficult, but a capable make-up editor can do it.

Broken Column Make-Up

Unbalanced Make-Up

Although generally balance is viewed as an essential of make-up, there is a fairly large segment of the newspaper world that deliberately avoids it. This group openly revolts against balance in any form. In its stead, they favor the unbalanced page. Under unbalanced make-up, there are two prominent forms. The first is frequently called "circus" make-up, and the second, for an immediately apparent reason, is termed "panel" make-up.

"All the News That's Fit to Print"

The New York Times.

CITY EDITION

VOL. CVII...No. 36,638.

NEW YORK, SATURDAY, OCTOBER 26, 1957.

FIVE CENTS

U. S. AND BRITAIN WEIGH NATO TALK BY TOP LEADERS

SPAAK URGES PLAN

President, Macmillan End Talks on Note of Free World Unity

Text of the communiqué will be found on Page 2.

By DANA ADAMS SCHMIDT
Special to The New York Times

WASHINGTON, Oct. 25—President Eisenhower and Prime Minister Harold Macmillan concluded today pressing forward problems of the free world to have a meeting of the heads of government of the North Atlantic Treaty Organization powers.

GOMULKA ASSAILS PARTY'S SKEPTICS; PURGE IS ORDERED

Polish Leader Says Ousting of Selfish May Halve Red Membership

By SYDNEY GRUSON
Special to The New York Times

WARSAW, Oct. 25—Wladyslaw Gomulka has conceded that an "atmosphere of doubt about the prosperity of Socialism" exists within the Polish United Workers (Communist) party.

Abel Guilty as Soviet Spy; Could Get Death Sentence

Brooklyn Jury Deliberates 3 Hours and 35 Minutes—Judge Praises Verdict and Sets Nov. 15 for Sentencing

By EDITH EVANS ASBURY

Col. Rudolf Ivanovich Abel was watched war front craftily yesterday of the jury being polled until the moment of exit when he was led from United States Brake the Broad Court.

SEARS LABOR ROLE DEPLORED BY AIDE AS 'DISGRACEFUL'

Official Tells Senate Inquiry Concern Won't Tolerate Repetition of Acts

By ANTHONY LEWIS
Special to The New York Times

WASHINGTON, Oct. 25—An official of Sears, Roebuck & Co. told Senate investigators today that his company had engaged in "reprehensible, unnecessary and disgraceful" anti-union activities.

ANASTASIA SLAIN IN A HOTEL HERE; LED MURDER, INC.

TWO FIRE 10 SHOTS

Masked Killers Escape —11 Witness Attack in Barber Shop

By MEYER BERGER

U. S. DEFIES SOVIET ON MIDEAST POLICY

Lodge Tells U. N. Moscow's Threats Won't Alter Aims —Welcomes Inquiry

By LINDESAY PARROTT
Special to The New York Times

UNITED NATIONS, N. Y., Oct. 25—Henry Cabot Lodge said today that threats of the Soviet Union would not sway the United States from carrying out its established policy in the Middle East.

BIG VATICAN RADIO ON AIR TOMORROW

Pope to Inaugurate Station Thought to Be Jam-Proof

By PAUL HOFMANN
Special to The New York Times

SANTA MARIA DI GALERIA, Italy, Oct. 25—The Vatican is about to begin a world-wide radio crusade.

STRIKES DISRUPT FRENCH SERVICES

Wide 24-Hour Walkout Cuts Transport and Mail—New Violence in Brittany

By HENRY GINIGER
Special to The New York Times

PARIS, Oct. 25—France's economic life was disrupted today by the one served time in little more than a week by twenty-four hour strikes in transport and other public services.

DU PONT-G.M. SPLIT IS OUTLINED BY U.S.

Plan Would Give Chemical Concern's Stockholders Right to Auto Shares

Text of Government judgment is printed on Page 16.

By RICHARD J. H. JOHNSTON
Special to The New York Times

CHICAGO, Oct. 25—The Government proposed today that E.I. du Pont de Nemours & Co. and its principals be forced to distribute their 63,000,000 shares of General Motors stock.

GANGSTER MURDERED

Umberto (Albert) Anastasia, who died of wounds.

A.F.L.-C.I.O. WARNS TWO MORE UNIONS

Says Baker and Textile Units Must Clean Up by Nov. 15 or Stand Suspended

By JOSEPH A. LOFTUS
Special to The New York Times

ATLANTIC CITY, Oct. 25—The A.F.L.-C.I.O. executive council today warned two more unions.

PRICE INDEX RISES FOR A 13TH MONTH

Decline in U. S. Food Costs Is Offset in Other Areas

By EDWIN L. DALE Jr.
Special to The New York Times

WASHINGTON, Oct. 25—The United States Consumer Price Index rose in September for the thirteenth month in succession.

Satellite Is Unheard On Short-Wave Sets

Monitors of the Soviet earth satellite reported yesterday that its signals could no longer be detected.

24-Hour Trace Set In Guatemala Crisis

Special to The New York Times

GUATEMALA, Oct. 25—The military junta and Gen. Miguel Ydigoras Fuentes signed an agreement today for a twenty-four-hour political truce.

RUBBISH begins to pile up at the Place Deux Ecus in the market section of Paris as Sanitation workers strike.

BALANCED MAKE-UP

NORFOLK LEDGER-DISPATCH
The Portsmouth Star

LATE
HOME
EDITION

The Weather
Tonight
Clearing; low about 68.
Tomorrow
Mostly fair; high 88.
Full report and index on Page 1
Section 2

VOL. 292, NO. 6   Dial Portsmouth: EX 3-7371   Norfolk-Portsmouth, Va., Tuesday Afternoon, July 9, 1957   Dial Norfolk: MA 5-1431   14 Pages—Price Five Cents

WHERE ARE THE VOTERS? Officials at the 14th Precinct in the 5th block of Olney Rd. today had plenty of time to relax with the polls deserted of voters. At noon only 62 had cast their Democratic Primary ballots there. Left to right are Mrs. Josephine Edwards, judge; Mrs. Della Nabokov, clerk; Mrs. Sadie Johnson, clerk; and Henry C. Odom Jr., senior judge. (Staff Photo.)

Almond Urges Whitehead To Withdraw From Race

Defense Cautious On Jurors
College Teachings Made Point in Clinton Race Trial

Spies' Claim to Asylum Denied by French Official

Don't Break Solid Front, He Pleads

Voting Lines Missing In Lethargic Primary
At Many Precincts Before Noon Officials Outnumber Ballaters

Cooler Tonight But Still Dry

Showers Give Way For All-Star Play
By JOE REICHLER

Ranger Heads for Atlantic For First Time in Trials
By J. GOODENOW TYLER
Ledger-Star Staff Writer

Court Reverses Singer Conviction

$40,000 Mink Herd Stolen From Farm
GREENLAWN, N.Y.

Motion to Quash Subpoena Heard
RICHMOND

Today's Index

RANGER SEA TRIAL—The 1,046-foot Ranger, third of the Navy's Forrestal-class aircraft carriers, passing through Hampton Roads en route for sea trials. Scheduled for delivery to the Navy in August, the Ranger is the 17th aircraft carrier built at Newport News Shipyard. (AP Wirephoto)

Israeli Spray Plane Damaged by Gunfire
JERUSALEM

UNBALANCED MAKE-UP

End War or Die! Einstein's Last Warning to World

LONDON—(INS)—Eight prominent scientists, including the late Albert Einstein and five other Nobel prize winners, warned mankind today to renounce war or face extinction.

The warning was in a statement, prepared by Lord Bertrand Russell and Einstein and signed a week before the latter's death on April 18.

It declared that nuclear weapons threaten the continued existence of mankind, adding:

"Here is the problem we present you: stark, dreadful and inescapable.

"Shall we put an end to the human race or shall mankind renounce war?"

The group called for a world scientific conference to study the dangers facing the world as a result of the development of nuclear weapons.

THE OTHER SIGNERS were Prof. P. W. Bridgman of Harvard University, Prof. L. Infeld of the University of Warsaw, Prof. H. J. Muller of the University of Indiana, Prof. C. F. Powell of Bristol University, England, Prof. J. Rotblat of London University and Prof. Hideki Yukawa of Kyoto University, Japan.

The statement continued:

"The people will not face this alternative (war or extinction) because it is so difficult to abolish war."

The scientists foresaw that continued progress in happiness lay ahead for mankind and added:

"Shall we instead cherish death because we cannot forget our quarrels?"

Russell, British mathematician-philosopher, in making public the statement at a London news conference, also released a letter addressed to the world's "heads of state" urging a public expression of approval on the statement.

IN THE LETTER, Russell said the statement, "signed by some of the most eminent scientific authorities on nuclear warfare," pointed out "the danger of utter and irretrievable disaster which would be involved in a mass war" and the consequent lessening of finding some way by which international disputes can be settled.

The said copies of the letter were mailed today to the governmental chiefs of the U. S, Russia, France, England and Canada.

The declaration said obliteration of cities would be "most of the minor disasters which would have to be faced." It continued:

"If everybody in London, New York, Moscow were exterminated, the world might in the course of a few centuries recover from the blows . . . there is a fear that if many H-bombs are used it would be universal death—sudden only for a minority, but for the majority slow torture, disease and disintegration."

RUSSELL TOLD the news conference that the statement originated with Einstein and Russell. He said that since the latter's death "I have approached all of scientific competents in both the East and West, for political disagreement should not influence a matter of science . . ."

"We found that the men who have most are the most gloomy," he said.

The scientists agreed that hope of banning nuclear weapons is "illusory" since peacetime agreements covering H-bombs "would no longer be considered binding in time of war"

They declared that this leaves the outlawing of war as the only answer.

The Nobel prize winners in the group were Einstein, Bridgman, Powell and Yukawa in physics, Muller in medicine and Karl Bose . . . in literature.

HUMID
Warm, humid Saturday, Sunday with thundershowers likely. High Saturday about 90°. Low during night 70°.

CINCINNATI ✦ TIMES-STAR

STATE EDITION
LATEST SCRATCHES
OHIO VALLEY

Cincinnati's Home-Owned Newspaper—Founded 1840

VOL. 116—No. 161 — Phone CH 1-1700 — SATURDAY, JULY 9, 1955 — 20 Pages — 5¢ 30¢

Walnut Hills Home Intruders Beat Victim

MASKED THUGS ROB WAITER

Boy, 9, Dies In Private Swim Pool

A seven-year-old Burlington, Ky., lad, who told a private pool-owner he could swim, drowned Saturday.

He was James Kain, son of Mr. and Mrs. Walton, Route One, Walton, Ohio, Burlington, Ohio, Airport.

It was the second child her . . .

JAMES KAIN

for drowning for the air that . . . Are Kain Burlington.

HE TOLD authorities he . . . plays drowned in 1951 . . .

The self-declared the first tragedy occurred a few Walton youngsters swam . . .

The youngster reached the end at Ridge Avenue. It held them his own swim, . . .

The boys have said with the boys could swim.

A Burlington attorney in . . . in Dieater Hospital at a result of . . . an accident carried to the surface . . .

He is Joe Congress, 30, who lives at 4811 Montgomery . . . and remove the Colonial Bank . . .

HE WAS STRUCK by a . . . a heavy thunderstorm and . . . Friday and dragged 30 feet backward into unconsciousness.

Kroger Official Mystery Deepens

One mystery replaced another Saturday with discovery that a body found at Edgewater Beach, Cleveland, might be that of Joseph H. Howard, 49, of Joseph H. Howard, 34, Kroger Co. official.

New relatives are convinced he is the Joseph . . . but will be in Cleveland to view the body . . .

Trio Forces Way Into Apartment

A 44-year-old Walnut Hills man was beaten and robbed early Saturday by an armed trio who forced their way into his apartment when he answered a knock at the door . . .

Lloyd Clifton, 1419 Wall Place . . . waiter, told police he answered the door about a.m. when three men, wearing black handkerchiefs over their faces forced their way in . . .

IF IT HAPPENED LIKE THIS. Lloyd Clifton, Walnut Hills, shows how three robbers forced him to lie down while ransacking his apartment. He holds the telephone with line ripped from wall. His trousers are spattered with blood.—TIMES-STAR Photo.

$50,000 Hoax!
Youths Admit Sending Phony SOS
—Set Off 30-Hour Sea Search

WOODMERE, N. Y.—Two youths were held today as police uncovered the mystery of the flashing boat Blue Star.

An SOS signal, purportedly . . . coming from the vessel, went off Sunday and touched off a wide search involving . . . Coast Guard rescue craft, on a . . . 100,000-search of the Atlantic.

2 West End Persons Die In Car Crash

Two West End persons died . . . early Saturday in a car . . .

Porter Scans Stock Market

New York . . .

Today's Games

NATIONAL LEAGUE
Cincinnati at Milwaukee, 2
St. Louis at Chicago
Brooklyn at New York, 1 P.M.
Philadelphia at Pittsburgh, 2

AMERICAN LEAGUE
Cleveland at Chicago, 2
Washington at Detroit
Baltimore at New York, 2
Boston at Philadelphia, 2

Local GI's Bride Escapes Red Captors

BERLIN—(INS)—Pretty German-born Mrs. Zita Adams was engaged to West Berlin said today she was imprisoned for six months by East German Communists because she married an American, Pvt. Earl Adams.

RITA TOLD THIS STORY
Special to Adams Sun

Man Missing In Flash Flood

LANCASTER, Ky.—(INS)—A 40-year-old man was reported missing today in a flash flood which caused an estimated $1,000,000 damage in the vicinity of Lancaster, Ky.

Lancaster, a town of 2,500 population, is the seat of Garrard County in central Kentucky.

MRS. RITA ADAMS

Man Mails Note to T-S; Hangs Self

At Press Time

WHITFIELD WITHDRAWS—WASHINGTON—(INS)—Allen Whitfield today said President Eisenhower to withdraw his nomination to be a member of the Atomic Energy Commission (AEC). The President is expected to withdraw it next week.

SPORTS EDITOR DIES—CHICAGO—(INS)—Arch Ward . . .

TIMES-STAR
"LADY AND THE TRAMP"
DOG SHOW
MONDAY
SEE PAGE 2

Hourly Temperatures

CIRCUS MAKE-UP

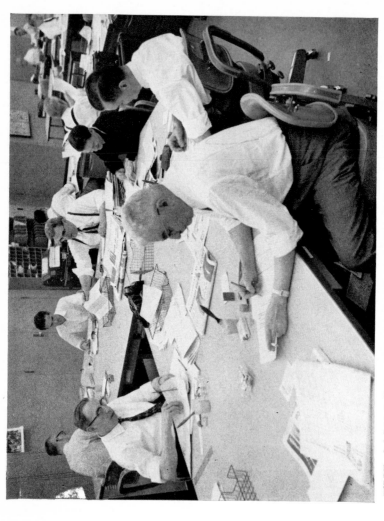

THE COPY DESK OF *THE PLAIN DEALER*, CLEVELAND, OHIO

Under **circus make-up,** stories on the same page are given a variety of heads and type, and cuts and boxes are used liberally. The idea is to make each story different from the other in appearance. In gaining this difference, the stories become like the many barkers at the circus who all scream at once for the patron's attention. When handled skillfully, it can have a pleasantly fresh and appealing appearance.

Circus Make-Up

Panel make-up means using a 2-column panel along one side of the page. Its advantage is that the panel can be used for important material—last-minute dispatches, the big story of the moment, a special feature. Panel make-up also guides one to important news: the reader habitually looks in the panel for late flashes, the most important story, or whatever the editor customarily puts there.

Panel Make-Up

8-Col Banner

1   5   2

3-Col Box   2-Col Panel

3   2-Col Head

2   2

2

3

4   1-Col Box

5

READABILITY

Readability affects make-up because good journalism demands that stories be arranged and headlined logically and clearly. The make-up must enable the reader to "take in" the entire page in one sweep so that he can read stories in order of preference, and his reading must not be impeded by such barriers as closely placed lines of type and illogical placement of heads and jump material.

OTHER GUIDING POINTS

Although there are in vogue many systems of newspaper make-up, there is a general acceptance of certain guiding principles which are applicable to any system. A discussion of these principles follows:

1. **Headlines**—The size of the head should be proportionate to the length and the importance of the story. In making up a page, the editor must be careful that heads do not cancel out each other. If, for instance, there are too many heads at the top of the page, they tend to crowd each other out of the reader's attention. If in three or more successive columns there are similar heads side by side, they tend to obscure or "tombstone" each other.

2. **Position**—The position of stories should be determined by their relative importance and the newspaper department concerned (news, sports, society, etc.). This statement means that, with one exception, the biggest stories get the most prominent positions in their respective departments. The one exception concerns the non-straight news story that is so important that it must be placed on page 1. Examples of such stories are exceptionally exciting sports accounts (World

201

Series, Army-Navy game, etc.), unexpected transfers of well-known clergymen, and "best of the year" awards in movies, literature, and music.

3. Accentuation—The ideal situation is to place all material so as to accentuate all else. On every page there must be an abundance of white to offset the black, and heads must be so written and placed as to set off each other and other heads as well. Cuts and boxes should be used to brighten the page, especially the dull ones. Line after line of close type should be relieved by the generous use of slugs and subheads. Attractiveness, that elusive quality, should be present to the maximum degree under the particular circumstances.

4. News Values—The make-up of the newspaper, especially of the front page, should be adapted to the importance of the news; the news should not be adapted to the make-up. The editor, for example, should not decide to have an 8-column banner, several large heads, and a generally sensational make-up until he is certain that the news justifies these devices. The newspaper that uses banners and large heads every day is hard pressed to label really big news properly when it occurs. The make-up editor must always remember that make-up evaluates news.

5. Inside Pages—Inside pages must not be neglected. All too often, the emphasis on make-up is confined to the front page, while the inside pages are composed with little thought. This is especially true of the pages which contain advertisements. The most important points to remember about inside page make-up are: (1) cuts should be used to brighten the pages; (2) as many pages as possible should have some genuinely lively news stories; (3) if filler is to be used, it should be interesting; and (4) dead ends of type (type without heads) should be kept at a minimum. (However, dead ends

of type are practically impossible to avoid when ads cover almost the entire page.)

6. **Clarity**—Make-up must be clear and logical. The reader does not like to go treasure hunting for the story that goes with a head or for a story continued in the next column or on another page. Therefore, make-up must always serve to guide the reader unerringly to the material sought.

7. **Section Make-Up**—Make-up must vary according to section, for there can be no absolute similarity in all sections of the newspaper. The sports section, for example, is generally the most sensational. It uses more and larger cuts, and it uses the large heads more profusely. The society page, on the other hand, generally has the most conservative make-up in the paper. Its news is of such a staid, routine nature that sensational make-up would be distinctly out of order. Consequently, the make-up of a particular section should vary according to the kind of news therein.

8. **Individuality**—The make-up of a given newspaper should reflect a note of individuality. It should not be so like the make-up of another paper, especially that of a competitor, that the reader can note no difference. How this individuality is to be obtained may present a challenging problem, but it should be found.

Editorial Policy

<table>
<tr><td>Chapter

7</td><td>What Is Editorial Policy?
Conditions Affecting Editorial Policy
Effect of Editorial Policy on the Editorial
and the Column</td></tr>
</table>

WHAT IS EDITORIAL POLICY?

The habitual reader soon comes to know his newspaper as thoroughly as he knows another person. He recognizes the kind of stories used, the stylistic practices employed, and the attitude of the paper on all leading questions. He is also aware of make-up policies for the use of headlines, banner lines, punctuation, and typography; and he is cognizant of a story-to-story and a day-to-day similarity in the portrayal of news. Eventually, he comes to think of the newspaper as a personality, as a collection of writings emanating from a single mind, rather than as the writings of many people; and he quotes his newspaper as if it were a person, approving or reproving the paper as he would a friend.

The consistency in outlook and in publishing practices which this reader recognizes results from what is termed "editorial policy." Stated in its simplest form, editorial policy is the

204

course a newspaper elects to follow as it answers the two all-important questions: What shall we print? and How shall we print? It is composed of the practices, rules, and principles which the newspaper sets as a guide for itself in doing its work. Editorial policy, therefore, governs every phase of the newspaper from the kind of news sought after to the size of type used in printing. The editorial policy of the conservative daily makes it reject the story of a gangster's love affair; the editorial policy of the tabloid causes it to give the story a big play. The editorial policy of the Southern daily rejects the Associated Press round-up of opinions about a recent lynching in the deep South; the editorial policy of the New England daily puts the story on page 1. The editorial policy of one metropolitan daily permits all-inclusive information about horse racing; the editorial policy of another allows only a story containing the results.

Rarely are the most important phases of editorial policy expressed in writing; they are simply understood. Consequently, the newspaperman comes to know by experience, rather than by directive, the editorial policy of his paper. Thus, after working for a relatively short time on a given paper, the reporter can determine almost immediately the importance of a story; the feature editor can evaluate a proposed comic strip at a glance; and the copyreader can write a head consistent with the others in his paper. Each has learned to sense the pattern of editorial policy. The smaller details of editorial policy, however, are recorded in the stylebook. There the newcomer may learn the paper's policy regarding writing stories and preparing them for print.[1]

The editorial policy of a particular paper is established when the paper is founded, and it is maintained or changed, over the years, as a result of editorial conferences. These con-

[1] See the sample stylebook on p. 142.

ferences, as one might assume, are gatherings of publisher and top editors to discuss the day's news, the successes and the failures of recent editions, the editorial view to be taken on leading questions, and means of increasing circulation. Usually the conference is held just before the beginning of the working day so that the various editors may instruct their subordinates accordingly.

The conferees discuss the day's news to determine the coverage to be given the various stories and the slant to be taken. (Even the so-called "impartial" papers discuss slant because there can be no pure impartiality in handling most stories.) The successes and the failures of the recent editions are discussed with a view to improving the paper. (One phase of this discussion is the invariable comparison with rival papers.) The editorial view must be discussed so that the portrayal of news may be consistent with the editorials; and means of increasing circulation are discussed for the simple reason that financial condition is the all-important consideration of the newspaper.

CONDITIONS AFFECTING EDITORIAL POLICY

The editorial policy of most newspapers is affected by the 15 conditions now to be discussed. Although some of these conditions are far more significant than others, all usually have some bearing on the choice of material for the paper and on the manner in which it is presented.

In reviewing these conditions, the student of journalism must beware of oversimplification. He must realize that there is no single formula for editorial policy everywhere because the exact strength of the conditions varies from paper to paper and from day to day. In fact, one can safely say that no two papers have completely similar editorial policies because no two papers are affected in the same manner by these 15 conditions.

1. **Finances**—The condition which above all others influences editorial policy is finances. The newspaper is ever the business proposition; it must make money or retire. Such papers as New York's *P M* and the Chicago *Sun* were operated over long periods of financial loss, but they were carried in the vain hope that eventually they would become solvent.

Because the newspaper must be financially profitable, the publisher usually demands that editorial policy be directed primarily toward increasing circulation. The coverage of news must be all-inclusive, a constant attempt to satisfy readers of all levels must be made, and new elements of appeal must always be sought. The publisher may make further demands upon his editors. He may call upon them to justify an established editorial practice, or he may insist that they adopt new features which he thinks will increase circulation. The financial consideration is especially important in the choice of syndicated features (columns, puzzles, comics, etc.) because they are chosen primarily for their ability to increase circulation.

So serious is the financial question that many papers hold regularly scheduled three-way conferences of publisher, business manager, and top editor to discuss the general condition of the paper. Each hears the reports and the opinions of the others in an attempt to increase revenue and reduce expenses through co-operative efforts.

The importance of the financial consideration may be summarized by saying that, generally speaking, every line of type and every feature must be pointed toward increasing the appeal of the paper. Old readers must be held and new readers must be gained, for circulation is the lifeblood of the newspaper.

Editorial Policy

2. Responsibilities of the Press—Editorial policy is deeply influenced by the newspaper's conception of its responsibilities to (*a*) society, (*b*) individuals, and (*c*) government. According to its conception of these responsibilities, the newspaper varies in its conception of what is to be printed and how it is to be printed. In fact, the view taken of these responsibilities gives rise to one of the most striking differences between newspapers. Thus, as a given newspaper formulates its attitude toward these three responsibilities, a major influence on editorial policy is determined.

RESPONSIBILITY TO SOCIETY

The responsibility of the press to society is tremendous, for the newspaper can be an infinitely good or a horribly bad influence on the reading public. The newspaper that runs an exposé of a political swindle, that constantly sets a tone of calm rationalization on important issues, that treats unsavory scandal merely as a news item is working a good influence on society. The newspaper that constantly plays up stories of crime, divorce, and scandal, that puts a romantic note on the activities of gunmen and robbers, that encourages gambling by running race results and Treasury Department figures (the basis for the numbers racket) is working a bad influence on society. These, naturally, are the extremes, and, in between, one finds the various gradations of good and bad.

The responsibility of the press to society frequently tears the newspaper between using and withholding a story. What, for instance, should be the position regarding rumor? Should the newspaper take cognizance of a false story by printing it, even though printed as rumor? Several years ago, for example, a story was whispered about the country that a large cigarette company had discovered among its employees several victims of a dreaded disease. The newspapers had to decide whether they could be of more service by attempting to discredit the rumor or by ignoring it. Since any attempt to discredit might well aid in spreading, no definite answer could be given. Newspapers are also baffled about printing pessimistic stories of diseases. Should the public be given the discouraging facts about research in incurable illnesses, or is society best served by printing only the good news? Over the editor's answer to these questions always hangs another question. What is the rival paper going to do? If one paper prints a story, the second paper frequently has no alternative but to handle the story also.

Another aspect of the responsibility of the press to society is the manner in which the paper imparts information likely to constitute negative lessons. Among such facts are the names of poisons used in suicides, procedures in abortions, techniques of burglars, and methods of evading the law. Journalists can often agree that some facts should clearly be omitted, that others may be mentioned without elaboration, and that others can be treated fully without serious damage. But since there is no standard guide for every situation, this phase of the responsibility to society is certain to vary.

RESPONSIBILITY TO INDIVIDUALS

The responsibility of the press to individuals should be divided into (1) the responsibility to public figures and (2) the responsibility to the obscure man.

The responsibility to public figures is a far more troublesome question than a first glance indicates. Editors disagree sharply on such questions as: Is the public figure entitled to any privacy? When should his wishes be respected concerning withholding stories? Should he be given special treatment in print, as, for example, always referring to him by official title? Some public figures, such as the high governmental figure, can pressure the newspapers occasionally, but generally the editor decides on the treatment to be given. Consequently, as news stories of public figures arise, a decision is made regarding the use of the story and the slant to be taken. Naturally, this decision varies from paper to paper. Among the stories on which newspapers differ are those which tell of questionable activities of the public figure's relatives, unfavorable opinions of the public figure as voiced by trades people, and off-guard moments of the individual himself.

The responsibility to the obscure man, or the figure who is newsworthy for the first (and probably the last) time in his life, rests on the use of any and all data in such stories as cases of criminal attack, juvenile delinquencies, and serious embarrassments. Here are the facts of three stories, followed by questions which the editor must answer.

a. A 16-year-old girl acting as baby sitter has been criminally assaulted by an intruder. The intruder has stolen nothing, and there is relatively little chance that the police will ever detect him. Should the story be used? If used, what details should be included? What names should be printed?

b. A first-offender in juvenile court is the 13-year-old son of a small business man. The boy has fallen into bad company and has been arrested for shop-lifting in a department store. All concerned are agreed that the boy is not likely to stray again. Should the boy be stigmatized by running the story in the local paper? Why?

c. A local clergyman has been forced by an armed depraved intruder to remove his clothing and dance about the living room of his home. What parts, if any, of this story should be used?

The editor's answers to these questions will show his conception of his responsibilities to the obscure man, and thus they will show also a field in which newspapers may differ sharply.

RESPONSIBILITY TO GOVERNMENT

The responsibility of the press to government is difficult to analyze because of the vagueness of the entire question. To draw the line between allegiance to one's nation and freedom of speech is a very difficult task. Where one paper feels justified in criticizing the government, another may withhold a story because, in the opinion of its editor, the prestige of the nation is involved. Just before World War II, for example, a syndicated writer held forth on the caliber of the U.S. Senate. He presented a documented article to prove the mediocrity of many senators and their general lack of fitness for their high office. Although his arguments were somewhat specious, the article was convincing and highly readable. Several papers, however, killed the story because they felt duty-bound to propagandize our democratic form of government, especially at such an uncertain time.

Also to be noted is the fact that some papers use any story which enhances the glory of the nation, whereas other papers judge the story strictly on its value as news. As a result, one newspaper will run a long account of a run-of-the-mill speech by a local college professor on great Americans; other papers, finding nothing new or striking in the speech, will use it as a short or ignore it.

211

SUMMARY OF RESPONSIBILITIES

In viewing these three responsibilities—to society, to individuals, and to the government—one sees that variations are certain to exist. Stories will be used or rejected and facts will be suppressed or emphasized according to the judgments of the men guiding a given newspaper. Therefore, a newspaper's conception of its responsibilities constitutes a major influence on editorial policy.

3. **Desired Tone of the Paper**—When a newspaper is established, its founders attempt to define the predominant atmosphere or tone of the paper; that is, they decide on the adjective which they want the public to associate with their paper. Thus, the paper becomes radical, belligerent, brash, conservative, scholarly, crusading, hairshirt, or whatever else the founders may desire; and it assumes a position in the gamut that runs all the way from ultraconservatism to extreme sensationalism, or yellow journalism, as it frequently is called. Once this tone has been decided, editorial policy must be so constructed as to obtain and retain it.

As can readily be seen, the desired tone of the paper is related to several of the other conditions affecting editorial policy, but one should note especially the close relationship of tone to the newspaper's view of its responsibilities. These two conditions are so akin as to be really inseparable, for tone results largely from the paper's view of its responsibilities and its role in the world.

The tone of the paper is affected by (1) the kind of stories used, (2) the manner in which the stories are written, (3) the approach or treatment of the subject, and (4) the make-up of the paper. To see how kind of story used affects tone, one need only examine the effect created in the tabloid by the use of sensational and risqué stories as compared with the tone of the conservative paper where such stories are conspicuously absent. The tabloid thus often acquires the air of a cheap gossip, whereas the conservative paper reflects good taste and restraint. To see how difference in manner of writing affects tone, one should make a collection of the same story as recounted by the several newspapers in the large city. One may be related in a manner that is cavalier or superficial—a story written for a light reader. Another may have writing that is solid and thorough—in fact, almost scholarly in tone. And between these extremes may be all the gradations. Naturally, each manner of writing gives a different tone to the newspaper. To see how difference in treatment of subject affects tone, one need only read the same story as handled by several newspapers. He will probably find that each has chosen to play up a different angle, and consequently each gets a different tone. To see how make-up affects tone, one should compare such conservative publications as the *New York Herald Tribune*, the *New York Times*, and the Philadelphia *Evening Bulletin* with a typical Hearst paper. The Hearst paper makes great use of the streamer or banner, frequently making one of the lines red, whereas a front-page streamer on any of the three papers mentioned is a rarity. The result is that tone is profoundly affected.

Another important phase of tone is the art (pictures) that the paper uses. Readers soon notice that newspapers vary sharply in amount of pictures used. The tabloid usually makes a heavy use of pictures, covering the two outside and the two center pages completely and placing cuts generously elsewhere. The conservative paper habitually uses much less art per line of print. But in kind of pictures used, the difference between papers is more apparent. The ultraconservative paper, on the one hand, uses only the most conventional of art.

There are the usual photographers' portraits of people in the news, the customary pictures of dignitaries, and the conventional shots of important events. At the opposite extreme is the tabloid with its pictures of the slain gangster lying in his coffin, the pretty showgirl displaying her well-curved legs, and the truck driver's wife exhibiting her blackened eye in the police court. These obviously are the extremes. The position between these extremes elected by the newspaper shows something of the tone it desires.

4. **Demands of the Readers**—Since any successful business handles the merchandise its customers want, editorial policy is influenced by the readers' demands.

Newspapers try to learn what readers want by many methods. One is to study the contents and the practices of the most successful newspapers with a view to establishing a correlation with circulation. (A rather interesting result of such a study is the disheartening but true fact that many people buy a newspaper primarily for the comics.)

Another method is to send investigators from door to door asking subscribers to name the features they like best and the ones they read regularly. The great disadvantage of this procedure is that readers give false answers. The man of the house, attempting to appear intellectual, will declare that he always reads every editorial—actually, he may rarely read one. The lady of the house, now in her mid-forties, will deny reading the movie gossip column—in reality, she devours it.

A third method is the "pull out." This is simply the procedure of removing a feature without notice, and then keeping an account of telephone calls and letters protesting or inquiring. (This method should be used cautiously with the comics. When "Little Orphan Annie" failed to appear in a Chicago newspaper one Sunday, the switchboard was jammed all day.)

A method that has gained in popularity during the past decade is that of having professional organizations analyze reader interest. Such organizations have evolved scientific approaches for evaluating the phases of the newspaper which have most appeal in given localities. Editors and publishers also attempt to analyze reader demands by checking the letters to the editor and by having staff members conduct casual interviews with fellow passengers on street cars, patrons in restaurants, and others from whom one can get an opinion readily.

Despite the newspaper's unceasing attempt to determine reader demands, the subject remains fairly enigmatic. There always seem to be present certain shifting conditions that make a final analysis impossible. A feature, for instance, such as a column, that is highly popular for a prolonged period may suddenly sag, and an approach, such as a sentimental treatment of a story, that pleases readers in one instance may fail in the next. Consequently, many newspapermen, especially the "old-timers," rely on a use of material that has been appealing over the years and on their own innate judgment.

5. Political Outlook—The influence of political outlook on editorial policy is significant because many of the major questions in the news are affected by political action, and consequently the newspaper finds itself supporting or opposing a political group as it takes a stand on these questions.

The influence of political outlook, as might readily be assumed, is of many varieties. On the one hand is the independent paper which usually weighs every election and every issue very carefully before giving its restrained, qualified support. On the other hand is the newspaper that is violently in favor of one political party. Its editorials screech like an eagle on high, and its headlines and stories ring loudly for its candidate. For the opponent, however good he may be, there is only the screaming, denunciatory banner and the acid comment concerning his shortcomings. Between these extremes are all shades of support and opposition.

Also to be noted is the fact that many newspapers line up with political parties in order to survive. A paper supporting a Republican in many Southern states would find hard going, just as a pro-Democratic paper would have difficulty in many a New England town.

Editorial policy is influenced most directly by political outlook when a newspaper openly admits its affiliation with a political group. It is influenced least when a paper seriously attempts to be impartial in all political questions. Yet, however great or small the influence may be, it is always present. Consequently, editorial policy is always affected by political outlook.

6. **Business Reasons**—Although not always to be condoned, the fact remains that editorial policy is often affected by the firms or the individuals to whom the paper sells space. One of the cardinal rules of some newspapers is that the good customers must never be hurt. To comprehend this fact, one should look for any unfavorable comment in the metropolitan daily concerning a large department store or other big advertiser. The fact is that where department stores are responsible for accidents, the store rarely is mentioned by name, if the story "makes" the paper at all. A few years ago, for example, a woman was about to enter an antiquated elevator in a large metropolitan department store. As she did, a faulty piece of equipment failed, the car dropped, and the woman was decapitated. The newspapers had to run the story because of its seriousness. But when they did, they simply said "a mid-city department store," never once giving any inkling of the name or the location of the store. Since at least 20 stores could

be so described, the reader was left, as the papers wanted him to be, in the dark.

Then, too, a story is often run because the big advertiser asks for it. In this category are such stories as those telling of new products or buildings to be erected.

7. **Religious Reasons**—Whenever any unfavorable comment is to be made concerning a religious organization or a clergyman, the reporter sees a red light. Where he misses it, the copyreader sees it. Members of religious organizations, newspapers have found to their sorrow, will not tolerate unfavorable criticism of their church, regardless of how sound the criticism may be. People who, on other occasions, are fair and objective close their minds to unfavorable comment about their religion. As a result, a strong influence is felt on the source of news. This influence varies according to the size of the particular organization involved. The large organizations, the newspaper soon learns, are beyond criticism. Recently, for example, a San Francisco clergyman of a large organization was arrested for speeding, driving while intoxicated, and reckless driving. Only one paper in the city decided to use the story. As it called to check facts, it was told to "beware the well-known weight of the church." The paper persisted, however, and when the story appeared in print, the members of the organization were told by their clergymen to refrain from buying the paper because of its "anti" sentiments. Thus, a newspaper was brought to the realization that a reporter is not free to "call a spade a spade" where religion is concerned.

The influence of religion also works in another direction; it causes many stories to be printed that are not especially newsworthy. The small-town daily, for example, reserves space for religious news in order to retain the favor of the

217

various denominations. The churches are given space to fill as they please, regardless of how valuable as news their material may be. This principle also functions in the large city, where the newspaper, to prove its impartiality, includes stories of all the major denominations.

Still another influence of this condition upon editorial policy lies in the pressure brought to bear by organizations. The various citizens' committees for the observance of Good Friday, the several organizations for the promotion of better inter-faith relations, and the many other religious groups are constantly making their strength felt on editorial policy. They may want publicity for their particular work, they may have an objection to a story printed, or they may want the paper to take a particular editorial stand. Sometimes these organizations have an uphill battle, but usually they are relentless in their struggle.

8. **Racial and Social Reasons**—When a paper runs a story that is distasteful to a large racial or social group, it faces trouble. The protest may come from an organized group or from scattered citizens, and it may be concerted or sporadic. But it is usually a strong protest, and it invariably makes itself felt to some degree. When the representatives of the offended group are not satisfied with the newspaper's explanation or apology, a boycott of the paper is often begun.

This boycott will vary according to the seriousness of the offense, the number of people offended, and the effectiveness of the organization behind the boycott. Naturally, the most feared boycott is the highly organized one, for without organization it is often relatively ineffective. A good illustration of the importance of organization can be seen in a complaint of the colored people of the United States. For many years they seethed with resentment as the newspapers placed the word "Negro" after the name of any colored person. This practice continued until the National Association for the Advancement of Colored People began to make demands upon the newspapers. Since that time, most papers have discontinued the practice.

Because a boycott can be a serious deterrent to circulation, the editorial policy of most newspapers calls for an elimination of any statement likely to offend a large group or at least a policy of extreme caution.

Cognizance of the influence upon editorial policy of racial and social conditions always appears in stories of race riots, persecution of minorities, and class *vs.* class struggles. In such instances, the newspaper must be especially careful of its presentation because some members of the two groups are certain to be offended. The ideal solution, of course, is to offend the minimum.

Also to be noted is the fact that many newspapers include features and stories designed to increase circulation among racial and social groups in their areas, and many papers strive to convince their readers that they are tolerant of all races, nationalities, and groups.

9. **Patriotic Reasons**—Throughout the United States, the many patriotic organizations have appointed themselves watchdogs over the newspapers of the nation. They scrutinize the papers, as they do the theaters and the motion pictures, for anything that resembles a lack of loyalty to the country. Once they detect such a lack, their ire rises.

As a result of this condition, all newspapers must be especially careful not to be deemed unpatriotic. Parades, celebrations, and all other events commemorating great moments in history must be given a prominent play, and no fact or innuendo must appear that can be challenged effectively as disloyal.

One must not conclude, however, that organizations alone

219

are responsible for the influence of patriotism upon editorial policy. Actually, many newspapers display loyalty because the editors feel so minded or because it is always good business.

The degree to which the newspaper shows its loyalty varies from mild to rabid. While some papers are restrained and dignified, others flaunt their patriotism on every page. In place of ears, one may find American flags, and in the masthead one may find a patriotic quotation. Also to be noted is the questionable insistence of some newspapers on beating the drum of patriotism. They call constantly for purges of the schools, the government offices, and similar agencies.

There is also a sharp difference between the loyalty of a given newspaper during peacetime and wartime. During the latter period, almost every newspaper becomes more vociferous in its patriotism. In this they are usually prodded by the government, even though they may need no help.

10. Personal and Group Reasons— Very often, a story or a picture must appear in the paper simply because an interested individual or group wants it there.

Someone known and respected by the newspaper calls and begins with the customary "I want you to do me a favor." The result is a story or a picture, or both, of a wedding, a prize won at a distant college, or an anniversary. Although most stories in this category are of little value as news, one occasionally appears that deserves space. Examples are stories about the local charity drive, an event to raise funds for a worth-while cause, or the activity of a public-spirited group.

Also appearing in the paper as the result of this kind of pressure are many of the press releases of such large organizations as labor unions, fraternal societies, and lodges.

Stories appearing in the newspaper because of personal or group reasons appear, generally speaking, in proportion to the prestige or the friendship of the person or group seeking the publicity.

11. **Whims of the Editor**—No small matter in the determination of editorial policy are the whims of the editor. By virtue of giving commands to a large force and heading a successful paper, the editor rarely lacks confidence in his own judgment. In fact, he frequently overrides the judgment of his subordinates. Consequently, the paper is bound to reflect in some way his little whims and peculiarities. One editor may like stories of the seamy side of life, another may like subtly humorous stories, another may like tales of horror. The reporters, striving to please the editor, look for his favorite stories. Thus, the paper is affected accordingly.

The top editor also plays the dominant role in make-up, choice of features, pictures, and cartoons. Consequently, his personal likes and dislikes have strong bearing on every phase of the newspaper.

12. **Sectionalism**—The editorial policy of a given newspaper is always affected by the part of the nation in which the paper circulates. The newspaper must show some pride in its section; it must evidence concern for the welfare of its section; and it must handle news in keeping with the over-all atmosphere of its section. A paper in a heavily industrial area, for example, must emphasize news of its industry. It is also expected to support editorially any attempt to improve the position of that industry. Helpful tariffs, regulation of imports, and government aid to the industry must be approved. Conversely, any attempt to weaken the position of the section's industry must be fought. Consider the case of the miner, for instance, in Pennsylvania's soft coal belt who was fined by his union for having an oil burner installed in his home. A local newspaper wanted to support the miner, but

the editor, fearing repercussions, by implication sustained the union. This, of course, is an isolated illustration of a significant condition that affects the inclusion and treatment of news. Broader illustrations can be seen in the agricultural districts where the newspapers not only support everything designed to help agriculture but also include features designed to attract the farmers.

Sectionalism is also defined very clearly in political matters wherein one section of the country differs with another. The question of racial equality, for example, has a heavy influence on editorial policy. Although many Southern editors dislike segregation, they feel that an open avowal of their belief would ring the knell of their papers. Consequently, they confine themselves to weak support of equal rights, they ignore the issue, or they oppose their own consciences by supporting the status quo.

Then, too, there is no doubt that a man's thinking is influenced by the section of the nation in which he lives. As a result, sectionalism affects editorial policy by influencing the thinking of the men who direct the policy of the paper.

13. **Taboo Subjects**—Some newspapers, probably motivated by extreme sensitivity, prudishness, or false modesty, have drawn up a list of subjects which their writers are not permitted to mention. An example of such a subject is venereal disease, which, until fairly recently, could only be hinted at in many papers. Some other taboos are: a prostitute is never to be mentioned as such; crime stories may not be on page 1 unless they are of national significance; swear words must never be used—not even by the old process of using the first letter and a dash; reputable persons may not be referred to by last names only; the names of gambling games (pinochle, euchre, craps, etc.) must not be given; an infant is not to be

spoken of as "it"; "cheesecake" (pictures of shapely women displaying themselves) is always to be omitted.

Some taboos are foolish, as one can readily see, but some are instituted with definitely altruistic intent. Such a taboo was that of the late William Allen White, who forbade the naming of a juvenile delinquent on the first offense.

14. Publisher's Associations—Because the publisher is an important man in his community, usually he is invited to join many prominent organizations. At the meetings and in the other activities of these organizations, he meets people who have axes to grind or are desirous of publicity. These people, and in many cases the organization itself, strive to influence editorial policy by having the paper support or oppose some plan before the public. Perhaps the exclusive golf club has been told that the right of eminent domain is to be exercised, and a highway is to bisect the course; the publisher is asked to spearhead a protest. Perhaps an organization is staging a membership drive; the newspaper is asked for space. Perhaps the local businessmen are fighting against the installation of parking meters; the newspaper is asked to aid in the battle.

The publisher consequently may find himself influencing editorial policy by dictating a stand for his paper.

15. Crusades—When a newspaper is conducting a crusade, frequently its whole editorial policy is affected seriously. The best spots in the paper are reserved for stories relative to the issue; stories helpful to the cause are used while otherwise good ones are discarded; art and cartoons lean toward the particular question; and editorial after editorial beats the drum for the cause.

Some famous crusades launched in the United States have been: the *New York Times* and the *Harpers Weekly* crusade against Boss Tweed and Tammany; the *New York World's* campaign throughout the eighties and the nineties for free ice and medical care; the *Kansas City Star's* campaigns for community improvement programs; the many current crusades throughout the nation for better housing; and the innumerable campaigns for combating juvenile delinquency.

EFFECT OF EDITORIAL POLICY ON THE EDITORIAL AND THE COLUMN

The Editorial

The most obvious reflection of editorial policy is naturally seen in the editorials of a particular paper. Here, as the paper openly states its opinions, one sees how it stands on a given issue. Most editorials, therefore, are really statements of phases of editorial policy.

Because every issue that arises cannot be measured readily against the established policy of the paper, a daily conference of editorial writers is often held to discuss the slant to be taken on leading issues. This conference, usually attended by the editor, his immediate assistants, and the writers themselves, generally decides by a vote upon the view to be adopted. When an editorial writer does not agree with the slant decided upon, he naturally is not asked to write the editorial pertaining to that question.

The Column

Very interesting to note is the effect of the columnist upon the editorial policy of a particular newspaper. Usually, the philosophy and the political leanings of the columnist are well known before his first writing appears in the paper. This is especially true of the syndicated columnist whose material is studied carefully before the publisher decides to buy his column. But often a paper finds itself with a hot potato on its hands. The editorial policy of the paper takes one stand; the columnist takes another. If the situation grows too bad, the newspaper either withholds certain columns or cancels the contract. This has happened in many instances in the recent past.

Also to be noted in this question of the columnist versus editorial policy is the fact that the newspaper often reserves the right to edit the column. An example of such editing occurred when a nationally known columnist continually referred to the widow of a President of the United States in derogatory terms. Many editors simply substituted the woman's proper name for the derisive epithet.

Of further interest is the fact that some papers run a little box on the editorial page explaining that "the opinions of the columnists are their own and do not necessarily reflect the opinion of this newspaper." Sometimes this explanation serves to give a note of fairness or lack of prejudice to a newspaper.

Nevertheless, one should also note that this freedom given to a columnist can be used as a method of printing material that common politeness might otherwise withhold. Once, for instance, a woman columnist of a large New York paper told its 2,000,000 readers that when Mrs. Truman, wife of the President of the United States, was supposedly in Missouri, she was actually in the White House. She simply was not at home to Madame Chiang Kai-shek, wife of the Chinese leader, who was visiting at the time. Usually such a story would be withheld by a paper out of deference to the President. But the columnist's breaking of this story gave the newspaper a clean bill. Yet who can dispute that for many papers this was a tidbit that they were delighted to print?

225

EXERCISES

Directions—As a result of your study of editorial policy, write your answer to each of the following problems. Explain your stand fully.

1. A man comes into the city room of a New York daily to protest a deception by a large department store. There is unmistakable evidence that the store is not selling several of its products as advertised, and hundreds of people are being cheated. The store, of course, is a heavy advertiser.

   What do you, as a member of the editorial policy committee, suggest that the paper do?

2. The rector of a fashionable church in your city is a godly but hot-tempered man. Last night he became angry with a parishioner who was visiting him in the rectory and struck the parishioner over the eye. Six stitches were required to close the wound. The parishioner prefers "to let the matter drop." Your district man got the story at the local hospital to which the parishioner was taken.

   What do you, as editor of your local paper, plan to do with the story?

3. A new conservative daily is about to be launched in Detroit, Michigan, a typical large American city.

   What do you as publisher say about including information concerning (1) horse racing, (2) dog racing, (3) major league baseball "runs for the week," and (4) daily Treasury Department figures?

4. Imagine yourself as editor of a large metropolitan newspaper during World War II. One of your reporters has gathered conclusive proof that a high-ranking admiral is awarding himself seagoing pay on the basis of his use of a Navy yacht

anchored in the Potomac as his sleeping quarters. Actually, he could use land quarters already provided. He probably prefers the yacht because it is more comfortable, especially during the summer months.

What should you do?

5. The most important charitable organization in the United States has a rather lax director of your local unit. You, as editor of a large daily, have been given an exclusive story showing that this director has spent an exorbitant amount in furnishing his private office.

What are you going to do with this story?

6. As editor of a Democratic paper, you have just been told via the telephone that the wife of the Republican governor, a staunch teetotaler, is "rolling drunk" at a local night club. You have a good reporter and the paper's best photographer on hand.

What are you going to do?

7. The 18- and 20-year-old sons of a local college professor have been arrested and fined at a distant seashore resort for changing into bathing suits in their car. The professor is admired and respected in the community and at the college. His wife, however, is a badly class-conscious social climber whose come-uppance is long overdue. You are the editor of the only newspaper in this community of 10,000. If you do not use the story, it will not appear in print, and consequently it will go unnoticed.

What are your plans?

8. A local college president addressing a small group of close friends last evening made some startling pro-totalitarian government remarks. There is strong reason to believe that he had participated freely in an early evening cocktail party,

and there is no other evidence to indicate that he subscribes to totalitarianism.

As editor of the one local newspaper, what action do you plan to take?

9. You are the editor of a Republican paper during a very heated political struggle for the mayoralty of a New England town. A reporter has just learned that a distant cousin of the Democratic candidate, a resident of Utah, has been jailed for drunken driving in his home state. Except for his connection with the Democratic candidate, the cousin would not rate a second thought.

What should your paper do with this story?

10. A local quack doctor has just been arrested. His particular specialty has been "beating" the insurance companies. He has a list of simple yet effective methods of concealing cases of high blood pressure, diabetes, and liver ailments. Over a two-year period he has obtained medical approval for almost 500 people who should have been rejected. The complete story would make highly interesting reading as a feature article.

How should a self-respecting paper handle this story?

11. The picture editor of a large metropolitan daily must pass judgment on the one available shot of a young mother who has just been told that her only child has been killed by a truck. Upon being told, the woman became hysterical. She fell to the ground and began to scream and kick wildly. The picture shows her arms and legs flailing the air, her clothing disarranged, and her face contorted into a maniacal expression.

Thinking of yourself as picture editor of a newspaper of your choice, make and defend a decision.

12. A local dentist has been unfortunate enough to have three patients die in his chair within a month. Since all three were chronic heart cases, the dentist obviously was not at fault.

    How would you, as editor, have your reporter write the news of the third death?

13. The discharged housekeeper of the very able governor of your state has a wealth of embarrassing but highly readable stories about the private lives of her former employer and his family. You are editor of a paper that respects, but does not support, the governor.

    What should your paper do with the story?

14. The Governor of Michigan has just refused to sign extradition papers for a man wanted by a Southern state. The man, a Negro, was convicted on a questionable charge of rape. He broke out of the jail where he was to have served a 20- to 30-year sentence.

    What slant should a New York daily take on this action?

15. The research director of America's largest medical clinic has just given a press conference to speak about the progress in combating the leading incurable diseases. His picture is a very dark one, indeed. He sees only the slightest hope of checking the most dangerous incurable diseases within the next decade.

    How much of the story should be printed?

16. A once-brilliant scientist of national renown, a man who has contributed greatly to the welfare of society, is now completely senile. When a reporter was visiting a nearby home yesterday, the scientist accosted him and engaged in all sorts of childish behavior before being taken into custody by a nurse. The public has already been told that the scientist has

failed mentally. The reporter, however, wants to write a long account of the experience as a feature story.

Which parts of this story, if any, should be used by a self-respecting newspaper?

17. The paper has just stumbled across absolute proof that a local garage owner, known and respected in this community of 15,000 for over 25 years, is a fugitive from justice. Immediately before coming here, he had been sentenced to a 10- to 20-year term for his part in a drunken brawl in which a neighbor accidentally had been killed. No local resident has ever known him to drink; he is strong in his support of the town's churches and civic affairs; he has shown genuine altruism in helping less fortunate citizens.

    What should the paper do?

18. A committee representing nearly every parent-teachers group in this city of 500,000 has just visited the publisher of the paper to demand the discontinuance of a daily comic strip. They insist that this feature is seriously demoralizing to their children because it portrays a majority of disreputable people. They are backed in their judgment by many prominent psychiatrists, psychologists, educators, and children's leaders. The comic strip, however, is distinctly popular with children and adults alike, and its presence is a decided help to circulation. Requests to the cartoonist to change his material have always elicited the unofficial answer that he "would be crazy to cripple a going proposition." Officially, he says, "There's nothing wrong with this comic—it's what people read into it. I can't be responsible for people's thoughts."

    What would you, as publisher, do in this instance?

19. A notorious gangster, high on the "public enemy" list for many years, is soon to be executed. A wire service which sells its material locally to your paper has bought his auto-

biography, a serial of 12 episodes. Although the gangster hits hard in the last chapter the idea that crime does not pay, the earlier chapters are filled with braggadocio, explanations of how to evade the law, and various methods of safecracking. The autobiography makes fascinating reading, especially in the light of the gangster's recent news value.

What would you have the paper do about using this material?

20. The state police have just staged a surprise raid on a suburban barn where a cockfight was in progress. Because cockfights are illegal, the 54 patrons arrested were fined $15 each and given a stern lecture by the local magistrate. Among those arrested were the Boy Scout leader for the entire city, a member of the local charity board, several executives of large firms advertising in the paper, a high school principal, and a layman prominent in his church's affairs. Naturally, there were also the usual gamblers.

As editor, what names would you print?

The Editorial

WHAT IS THE EDITORIAL?

When most newspaper readers hear the term "editorial," they usually think of a strongly worded opinion by the editor upon some important question. Actually, this is merely one of several kinds of editorials, for the term covers a field that varies widely in purpose, structure, and treatment. And it is the breadth of the whole field that prevents hammering the term into a concise, pointed definition.

To see how editorials vary in purpose, one need only read the editorial column of a metropolitan daily on a typical day. There he will probably find at least three of the six types of editorials discussed in this chapter. Perhaps the lead editorial is a militant call to support a particular candidate for office. This may be followed by one that congratulates a prominent citizen on a recent success. And the column may close with a little humorous essay on how to kill mosquitoes or how to beat the heat. In a single column, therefore, are three editorials with three distinctly different purposes.

To see how editorials differ in structure, one should examine a representative sampling. One may be cast in the conventional structure discussed below. Another may employ the suspended interest approach, and a third may be written in the chronological (short story) style. In short, the writer of the editorial, like the writers of the news and the feature story, adopts the structural approach that best suits his purpose.

To see how editorials differ in treatment, one has only to realize that the writer of the editorial, like the effective writer in other fields, must vary his treatment according to his subject and his purpose. Hence, one may find an earnest, passionate treatment in the editorial that is attempting to influence, a sarcastic treatment in the editorial that is attempting to deride, and a whimsical, cavalier treatment in the editorial that is attempting to amuse. Thus, one easily can see that treatment of subject is as varied in the editorial as in other prominent types of writing.

The only all-inclusive statement to be made of the editorial, therefore, is that it is an expression of the editor's opinion or observation, so written and placed in the newspaper as to be recognized for what it is.

WRITING THE EDITORIAL

The conventional editorial generally is composed of three parts. The first part, which resembles the lead of the news story, makes a statement of a situation or of an argument to be defended. The second part, appropriately termed the "body," then proceeds to develop the statement. The third

The Editorial

part, or the "conclusion," suggests a remedy, makes a plea for action, or attempts to summarize the writer's main purpose in a short, forceful paragraph. Although some writers prefer to incorporate the conclusion with the body, this three-part arrangement is the general pattern of the conventional editorial.

The following is an example of the conventional editorial:

ELECTORAL RITE

Now that Congress has again gone through the quadrennial travesty of counting the votes of the Electoral College, it is time to renew serious efforts to reform this archaic system. The Electoral College as it now functions is not simply a quaint but harmless institution; it is a potential danger to democratic selection of the nation's Chief Executive.

Since the entire electoral vote of each state goes to the candidate who wins a majority of the popular vote of that state, it has always been true that a President could be elected who had actually received fewer popular votes than his rival. Such an event has occurred only twice in our history; but a system that makes it possible is out of line with our ideas of democratic government today.

Furthermore, even when such a drastic inversion of the popular will does not take place, the electoral results frequently give a grossly distorted picture of the actual Presidential contest. In one-party states the Presidential election is an empty gesture and their relatively small popular vote reflects it. The present system enhances the evil potential of a determined local machine, and increases the dangers of corruption. There simply is no sense in retaining the system as it is.

Various reforms have been proposed. One of them, known as the Lodge-Gossett amendment, was actually passed by the Senate in 1950, only to be defeated in the House. It would have apportioned the electoral votes of each state in accordance with the popular vote. Under another proposal, put forward by Representative Coudert, each state would have two electors at large, who would vote in accordance with the majority in the state, while the remaining electors would be chosen by popular vote in each Congressional district.

This is the ideal time for Congress to get seriously to work on this question. In the nearly four years before another Presidential election Congress ought to be able to devise a satisfactory solution for what is now a most unsatisfactory state of affairs.

—*New York Times*

If the editorial is not of the conventional type—that is to say, if it is written in the suspended interest or another ap-

proach wherein the writer does not state his main facts or
stand at the outset—then obviously the lead and the body vary
accordingly. Note how the following editorial does not employ the conventional structure:

The Project For Restoring The Flag House

The Flag House on East Pratt
street is probably better known in
other parts of the country than it is
to Baltimoreans. We natives are so
taken up with routine duties that
we seldom think of our local places
of interest until we have out-of-
town guests.

Certainly no spot has a better
right than the Flag House to call
itself a national shrine. For, as everybody knows—or should know—
Mary Pickersgill and her daughter
made the flag which flew over Fort
McHenry during the bombardment
in 1814 and inspired Key's poem
which since has become our National Anthem.

The Flag House receives some
8,000 visitors a year. They come
from all the states of the Union and
from many foreign countries. Since
the place enjoys this popular appeal

it is gratifying to learn that Mayor
D'Alesandro, in cooperation with
the Star-Spangled Banner Flag
House Association, is going to see
that the building is restored to what
it was when Mary Pickersgill lived
there in 1814. The museum and
office space which now mar its original aspect are to be transferred to
a "dependency" adjoining the present one.

Only a few years ago the site of
the Flag House was improved when
the grounds around it were cleared
and converted into a park. It is
hardly necessary to remark that the
success of a restoration depends
upon its fidelity to the original, a
house which was in every way
typical of the Baltimore of its day.
The designation of a competent
firm of architects is an assurance
that the work will be done with care.

—*Sun*, Baltimore, Md.

As is the case with the news story, the lead of the editorial
is highly important because with it the reader is often either
held or lost. The writer of the editorial, therefore, seeks for
the lead that will best suit his purpose. Thus the editorial may
open with a short, crisp sentence, with a single long sentence,
or with whatever other device the writer feels is most effective. Here are the leads from four conventional editorials, all
of which take the same stand on the same question:

The Editorial

Four years ago this week the big news out of Minnesota was that more than 100,000 voters had written in the name of Dwight D. Eisenhower on the ballots of the Republican party primary. The big news out of Minnesota this week comes from the Democratic side. It is that Estes Kefauver, the lone wolf among Democratic Presidential aspirants, has won an amazing victory over Adlai Stevenson and the Democratic state organization.

—*New York Times*

The results of the Minnesota primary fall heavily and directly on Adlai Stevenson, indirectly on the harmony hopes of the Democratic Party. Mr. Stevenson says the very sharp setback in Minnesota will not halt his bid for the nomination. But the upset there is enough to force both him and the national Democratic leadership to carefully reassess their positions.

—*Christian Science Monitor*

Adlai E. Stevenson has been given a staggering setback in his campaign for the Democratic Presidential nomination by Senator Estes Kefauver's impressive victory in the Minnesota primary election. Not even the most ardent Stevenson supporter can find any comfort in the results of this first head-on contest between the former Governor of Illinois and the Senator from Tennessee.

—*Philadelphia Inquirer*

Principal results of the primary election in Minnesota has been to throw new complications into the contest for the Democratic presidential nomination.

Adlai Stevenson entered the primary fully aware of the dangers which always face a front-runner. The fact that he lost has by no means taken him out of the race, though it may cause many lukewarm supporters elsewhere to begin turning their eyes in other directions.

—*Evening Bulletin*, Philadelphia, Pa.

Although the lead of the editorial is highly important, the development and the summation of the main purpose are even more so because therein the writer succeeds or fails in his main purpose. If the writer is attempting to influence, these parts carry the weight of his argument. If he is attempting to inform, they convey the main facts. If he is attempting to amuse, they sustain or weaken his humor. Thus, the writer must be especially careful with these parts of the editorial.

To see the function of every part of the editorial, the student of journalism should study the complete examples given in this chapter. He should then evaluate the writer's ability to correlate the parts effectively.

LANGUAGE

As one studies the actual composition of editorials, he must remember two important facts about language: (1) many words are relative in meaning and (2) choice of words largely determines the tone of the editorial.

The fact that many words are relative in meaning is immediately obvious in any study of language. Words, for example, like "big," "rich," "building," "difficult," and "heavy" have such broad meanings that, unless helped by other words, they can never convey precise meaning. The editorial writer, therefore, often faces a real problem as he attempts to express to all readers the exact idea he has in mind.

The fact that choice of words largely determines the tone of the editorial must be recognized because the writer naturally wants to create a specific tone. If, for example, an editorial is to be written to condemn a tax collector found guilty of graft, one of several tones may be desired, and that tone will result largely from the language used. If the tone is to be dignified, the editorial might call the convicted man "an office holder who has betrayed the confidence of the electorate." If the tone is to be caustic, he might be referred to as a "common ward heeler," "a henchman of an arch political boss," or even worse, "a swine feeding at the public trough." If satire is in order, he might be referred to as a "public servant who has gathered in a few dollars on the side by assisting a taxpayer."

A good example of varying language to suit the desired tone is to be seen in the two following editorials, taken from the same issue of the same newspaper. The first is a passage

237

The Editorial

from a highly serious editorial on the subject of dominion status in the British Empire; the second is a complete editorial on the subject of the annual beauty contest held in Atlantic City, New Jersey. Notice how the language is in sharp variation because of the difference in tone desired.

The geographical position of Ireland and Great Britain has led through the centuries to economic integration. The Irish Government was neutral in the recent war but the Irish people weren't. They volunteered in the British armed forces in greater numbers in proportion to population than any other unit of the Empire. At least 2,000,000 Irish men and women crossed over and helped the British keep their home fires burning.

The recent dropping of "British" from the Commonwealth's title was, admittedly, an accommodation to Ireland, India, Pakistan and Ceylon. Concessions have to be made to historical evolution. The "melancholy path" which Mr. Churchill sees the Empire treading may still have a happy ending. There are stronger ties than Crowns.

—Detroit Free Press

The characters who run the Atlantic City beauty contest have dealt Detroit the insult deadly, and we aren't going to take it.

They have ruled that in the future, we can't enter a Miss Detroit in their old beauty show as a contestant for the title of Miss America. In the past, we could send a Miss Detroit and a Miss Michigan to compete for the crown. But no more. From now on, we have only one entry—a Miss Michigan.

Only New York, Philadelphia and Chicago can have city beauties. All else is on a state basis.

We don't know whether this is intended as a slur at our fair City because we aren't big enough or metropolitan enough. Or whether it's a slap at the pulchritude of our local gals.

After having looked over some of the stuff that passes for beauty in other cities, we're almost positive it isn't the latter. Our gals are much more shapely, much better looking than the drab hags of New York, Chicago and Philadelphia—especially Philadelphia.

So we can only conclude that we're insulted as a city, not worthy to be classed in the big time.

If Mayor Van Antwerp ever stays home long enough, or if we can catch him between dances, we're going to propose that he issue an official boycott against Atlantic City salt water taffy.

—Detroit Free Press

CONSISTENCY IN THE EDITORIAL

The kind of editorial, the style of writing, and the attitude taken are determined for a newspaper by its editorial policy committee. Consequently, one finds a definite consistency in the editorials of a given newspaper. Those of such conservative publications as the *New York Times*, the Philadelphia *Evening Bulletin*, and the *Christian Science Monitor* are generally quiet and thoughtful in tone. The editorials of the sensational papers, the papers consistently supporting a political party, and the tabloids are likely to be vigorous and loud in tone.

The devices of the editorials are also determined by the editorial policy committee. Hence, some newspapers use heavy sarcasm; others avoid it. Some newspapers give nicknames to such high figures as the President of the United States; others use only accepted titles. Some newspapers present heavy, scholarly editorials; others use short, sprightly ones. These devices, naturally, are consistent with those used in the other sections of the paper.

CLASSIFICATION OF EDITORIALS

The only satisfactory way to classify editorials is on the basis of function. Even this approach, however, presents difficulty because function is not always immediately clear. An editorial, for example, which appears to be a light, humorous treatment of a serious subject, written for the sole purpose of entertaining, may in reality be a vicious attack; and an editorial written for the announced purpose of clarifying a difficult question may actually be a veiled attempt to influence opinion.

However, when purpose is fully clear, one can conveniently

239

classify editorials under one of six headings. A discussion of such a classification follows:

1. To Influence Opinion—When a newspaper wants to influence the opinion of its readers, it generally runs an editorial for that purpose. This, the most common type of editorial, outlines the paper's position and the supporting evidence. The editorial usually closes with a plea for action.

The editorial to influence is used to support political candidates, to arouse backing for or against proposed legislation, or to sway the reader's opinion on any other controversial issue.

The writing of this editorial demands primarily the ability to analyze and present arguments forcefully. Because it is the most important kind of editorial, it usually leads the editorial column.

An example follows:

The Dixon-Yates Review

The Senate-House Atomic Energy Committee has begun the long awaited review of the Dixon-Yates power contract and we respectfully urge it to proceed with the utmost care.

From the moment of its broaching, this transaction has been subject to violent controversy, breeding insinuations that have not stopped short of the White House. It was utilized as an issue in the recent political campaign, and unless treated with due respect at this juncture might exert irresistible influence upon future campaigns.

Under the circumstances, the present inquiry requires absolute thoroughness. Hasty or perfunc-

tory or partisan procedure will not suffice. Questions that have arisen need answering in minute detail—questions concerning the unpublicized negotiations, the lack of competitive bidding, the factors that persuaded the administration to put costs in a secondary position in awarding this $107,000,000 power contract to the Dixon-Yates syndicate.

Thus far, the answers to such questions have been put forth piecemeal or vaguely or in terms meaningless to the layman. The public is patently entitled to a clear and authoritative and detailed explanation to the Dixon-Yates contract and the facts behind it.

—*San Francisco Chronicle*

2. To Call Attention to a Wrong—Frequently, a newspaper sees something that it believes to be a serious wrong, and it calls attention to this wrong editorially. It may be a dangerous aspect of a new law, a threatening condition in sanitation, or an error committed by a person in high place. When possible, the editorial is expected to suggest some constructive way to eliminate the wrong.

This kind of editorial differs from the editorial to influence opinion in that it concentrates on factual material rather than on a viewpoint; that is, it is really a straight presentation of facts rather than an argument.

An example follows:

Make Air Raid Signals Clear

The complaint voiced at a meeting of State directors of civilian defense in Washington about a sudden, unheralded change in the Air Force signals for warning against air raids points to a lack of cooperation which cannot be permitted to continue.

Whether the elimination of the "blue" or intermediate warning signal is a good or bad thing is not the main issue. It may be that the Air Force is acting wisely in cutting out this early indication to the public that hostile planes are approaching, but may or may not attack.

The important point is that there should never be any misunderstandings between the Air Force and the various State and local defense directors on a warning system. It could be disastrous if those charged with responsibility for defense of localities waited for a signal which had been discontinued by the Air Force.

—Philadelphia Inquirer

3. To Enlighten Readers—When a newspaper feels a need to explain to the reader some pertinent question or event, it often runs the editorial to enlighten. The subject may be a proposed constitutional amendment, a distant war, or any other issue which the newspaper wants to make clear to the man in the street. Thus, in its true form, this editorial is an unbiased explanation. The reader, however, must often beware the identity of the paper running the editorial, for sometimes the writer may color or slant the material. Politically affiliated newspapers, for example, are rarely impartial in political matters, and regional papers seldom present an unbiased picture of Federal legislation concerning their areas.

An example of the editorial to enlighten follows:

World-Wide Communion

Members of Christian churches all over the world join tomorrow in the observance of the sacrament of Holy Communion, thus signifying the bond of Christian fellowship that unites hearts and hands in the work of Christ's church in every part of the world.

World-wide Communion is just what its name implies, the distribution of the sacred elements to all believing Christians and in accord with the plan instituted by Christ Himself when He met with His disciples in the Upper Room centuries ago. As the disciples looked to Him for comfort and guidance in a time when men plotted against His life, so do Christians today look to the same Christ for inspiration and leadership in a time when the forces of evil in the world seem bent on destroying the very foundations upon which our Christian faith rests.

And so throughout the world wherever the name of Christ is honored men and women will gather at the Lord's table tomorrow and again dedicate their lives to the furtherance of His kingdom here on earth.

—*Daily Local News,*
West Chester, Pa.

4. To Help a Cause—Whenever a newspaper desires to aid in some worth-while cause such as a charity drive, a safety campaign, or a memorial program, it frequently uses its editorial voice. The editorial informs or reminds the public of the importance of the cause and makes a plea for help. Thus, this kind of editorial is actually an advertisement or "plug" for the cause involved.

An example follows:

Freedom's Spire

THE WEATHERVANE of the steeple of Boston's historic Old North Church is on display in the North Gallery of New York's Grand Central Terminal. It will remain there through January and then continue across the country for exhibition in several other cities.

The exhibit is tied in with a national drive for funds to restore the steeple, destroyed by Hurricane Carol. We live by symbols, and the Old North Church steeple is a symbol of American liberty. It was from there that Paul Revere hung his lamps in the birth night of the revolution.

If you care to contribute, the address is Old North Church, Box 1776, Boston, Mass.

—Milwaukee Sentinel

5. **To Praise or to Congratulate**—When a citizen or a group has performed an outstanding deed or received an honor, the newspaper may run an editorial to praise or to congratulate.

An example follows:

The U. of Virginia's Vast Collections

The priceless collection of WALT WHITMAN manuscripts recently given to the University of Virginia's Alderman Library by CLIFTON WALLER BARRETT, of New York, puts that repository near the top among American libraries in the value of its literary holdings. The Alderman Library's great historical collections take comparably high rank.

The amazing WHITMAN collection, with the manuscript of the 1860 edition of "Leaves of Grass" has been placed beside the comprehensive ELLEN GLASGOW collection, which recently was deposited at the Charlottesville institution. The other major literary treasure there is the invaluable assemblage of POE materials, much of which also was given by MR. BARRETT, and has been described as "America's richest collection of the writings of EDGAR ALLEN POE and of materials about him."

Many Virginians are doubtless unaware of the remarkable variety in the Alderman Library's holdings in both literary and historical fields. Not only does it have by far the largest manuscript collections in the South, comprising literally millions of items, and a collection of Jeffersoniana which is indispensable to any student of that great Virginian, but it contains other extremely diverse materials which, like those

243

concerning WHITMAN, seem to have no direct relationship to the University of Virginia, or even to the United States.

These last include the huge CHARLES DARWIN collection, said to be the greatest in the world, and the one having to do with COTTON MATHER, the New England divine, which some consider the best in this country. These and other similar acquisitions from the collection of the late TRACY MCGREGOR, from CLIFTON WALLER BARRETT, and others, have given the University of Virginia library one of the truly impressive treasure troves on this continent.

MR. BARRETT, whose benefactions to that institution have been so conspicuous, is a native of Alexandria, and alumnus of the University who became a successful businessman in New York, and retired not long ago. Virginia stands greatly in his debt.

—Richmond Times-Dispatch

6. **To Comment Lightly on the News**—This kind of editorial is used when the editor sees a need to lighten the column. It is valuable, purely and simply, in proportion to its ability to entertain.

An example follows:

For Adults Only

We note that the correct moves in that complicated game of skill (not chance) called getting junior to bed without fuss have been placed on motion picture film by a New York concern. The intended audience: Baby sitters.

We're willing to risk a reasonable sum that more parents than baby sitters will demand a viewing on the grounds that the saturation point of good ideas for outguessing the bed wary offspring has yet to be reached—if it ever is.

—The Journal-Every Evening,
Wilmington, Del.

GUIDING POINTS FOR EDITORIAL WRITING

Although writing editorials is largely a matter of individual ability, there are five significant points which even the best of writers must respect. A discussion of these points follows:

1. **Thinking the Issue Through**—If the issue be at all controversial, the writer must think the question through before

so much as making an outline. He must make certain that he has *all* the facts, and that he has these facts in a clear, undistorted form. He must also make certain that he has applied the science of logic in examining the whole issue from every possible angle. The writer who is given to hasty or rash judgments should not write editorials on controversial subjects. But if he feels that he must, he should allow himself at least a day to think the issue through.

The great obstacle to thinking an issue through is lack of time, for editorials must frequently be written quickly. An unexpected governmental action, for example, demands an editorial immediately because the reader looks for it. The best course in such instances is to write an editorial on the picture of the moment, guarding one's self against reaching conclusions that future evidence may reverse.

2. Consistency of Viewpoint—The editorial pronouncements of a given paper must evidence a note of consistency. If the editorial of today is inconsistent with that of yesterday; if the editorials on the same day are inconsistent with each other; or, worse still, if the editorial itself is inconsistent, the newspaper faces trouble. The reader does not merely look for consistency; he demands it. When inconsistency exists, he immediately suspects a poor mind or a base motive.

The word "consistency" naturally admits of several definitions. One view of the word may mean a blind support of a political party. Hence, a newspaper may be consistent in its political outlook but inconsistent in an announced intention to expose corruption. Another definition may mean opposing every act of a particular public official. Hence, the newspaper may be consistent in its opposition but inconsistent in its announced intention to be fair. To most readers, however, the term means an honest attempt to be consistently impartial, sincere, and straightforward.

3. Aggressiveness—If the editorial is a serious writing about an important subject, it should have a note of aggressiveness without belligerency. The editorial should reflect the attitude of fighting for what is right in a fearless, unhampered manner, rather than simply fighting for the sake of being in the midst of a combat. Although the editorial should imply that the writer has examined all aspects of a given question, it should take a firm stand one way or the other. Very few readers, newspapers have learned, are interested in innocuous editorial writing.

4. Dignity—For the self-respecting paper, dignity is indispensable. Although tabloids and other papers leaning toward the sensational frequently transgress the limits of good taste in language and approach, a good editorial demands a note of dignity. The dignified editorial, like the dignified man, creates a note of calm, authoritative judgment; the undignified editorial, like the undignified man, too often creates a note of belligerent, reckless thinking. Even in the lighter editorials wherein the writer unbends, a certain note of dignity is essential.

5. Note of Authority—As the reader follows the editorial, he must have the feeling that the writer knows his subject. Very few persons will read an editorial if they get the impression that the writer is not well informed and intelligent. Without a note of authority, an editorial cannot be stimulating. Consequently, it stands little chance of being read.

EXERCISES

Write editorials on the following subjects:

1. Condemn a resolution just passed by City Council to levy a sales tax on all purchases made in the city.

2. Uphold or refute the statement of a leading educator that parents are largely to blame for juvenile delinquency.
3. Enlighten your reader on a dangerous amendment to a recent tax bill in your municipality. The amendment provides an additional tax on property if present revenue is not enough to meet all budgetary items. There is to be no public hearing before the tax is levied.
4. A society of educators is making a drive to put all public schools completely under Federal control. Express your view editorially.
5. The fact is established that radio does not enjoy the same freedom of speech enjoyed by the newspaper because the Federal government controls the airways. Write an editorial on this subject.
6. Condemn or uphold the Governor in his granting of a parole to a man who has served only two years of a 50-year sentence for murder. The prisoner had a long record of petty thievery and unlawful entry before being convicted of shooting an accomplice in a dispute over spoils received in a hold-up. The Governor acted against the advice of the Board of Pardons, contending that the evidence in the trial showed that the man had shot in self-defense.
7. A university in your city wants to take over a large public park for a new building. There are no other parks in the immediate neighborhood. Comment as you see fit.
8. Write an editorial on the subject of compulsory military training.
9. Write an editorial in which you advance a plan for slum clearance in a large city.
10. Write an editorial on the need of a vocational school in a community where there is none.
11. Defend or attack the mayor of a large city for his oft-repeated belief that the city is as nearly perfect as it is possible for it to be.
12. Condemn a city for its failure to support an orchestra or some other cultural institution.

The Editorial

13. A small child has been electrocuted by a wire blown down during a storm. The equipment of the electric company is old, the city is not forcing the company to replace it, and this kind of accident easily can happen again. Write an editorial.

14. Write an editorial supporting a particular candidate for the office of Mayor, Governor, or Senator, or President of the United States.

15. Condemn the present laxity of the police in enforcing the laws against double parking, overtime parking, and illegal parking in downtown streets.

16. Write a light editorial on the recent announcement by the Chairman of the Park Commission that the city parks need at least 200 more benches.

17. Over 500 of the city's 725 high school seniors have received shockingly low grades in a simple American history examination given by a national magazine. This is the month of May, so that in three weeks these people will be high school graduates. Write an editorial on this subject.

18. There has been some agitation to reduce the size of the Art Museum on the grounds that few people visit it. The space saved is to be used for storage purposes by the highway department. Write an editorial as you see fit.

19. Write an editorial in which you explain to the readers how much additional tax each person is going to have to pay under the recently approved tax bill.

20. Write an editorial congratulating a distinguished citizen for an outstanding contribution to the community, the state, or the nation.

The Column

| Chapter 9 | Introduction
Sources of Material for the Column
Attracting Readers to the Column
Style of the Column
Qualities of a Good Column |
|---|---|

INTRODUCTION

One of the most pleasant, satisfying, and rewarding assignments in journalism is the writing of the column. The task is pleasant because the columnist generally has a free hand to compose as he pleases; it is satisfying because he is doing highly creative work; and it is rewarding because some of the highest salaries in the newspaper world are paid to columnists. This being true, the position of columnist is eagerly sought after by many, many newspapermen. The path to success, however, is a hard one, and columnists, like other writers catering to a fickle public, often rise quickly and fade quickly.

Columns are written on a multitude of subjects. There are syndicated and nonsyndicated columns on politics, sports, news, gossip, religion, radio, movies, television, music, stamps, words, general information, legal advice, and a host of other

249

subjects. In fact, the newspaperman is seldom surprised to hear of a column on a new subject, for just about any field is fair game for the columnist.

The great criterion for passing judgment upon the success of the columnist is his ability to attract and hold readers. To be successful, therefore, he must possess a strong appeal to the reading public. Just how a columnist appeals to his readers is frequently difficult to determine, although sometimes the reason is fairly clear. The late Ernie Pyle, for instance, was outstandingly successful as a war correspondent because in his column was the ring of a likeable man. His readers responded to his genuine humility and deep sincerity. Some leading political columnists of the moment attract readers by their tone of scholarly rationalization. Others draw readers by their aggressiveness, by their penetrating analyses, by their ability to reveal behind-the-scenes facts, or by some little pleasing quirk in their style. Generally speaking, a columnist holds readers as an orator does listeners—by saying in a forceful or a unique way something that others want to hear.

Very interesting to note is the fact that signed columns have become increasingly important in the past two decades. Some newspapers now place them on page 1, and many papers have a full page or more in every issue. Columnists are quoted on every hand, and many have become so important that their opinions are sought after by national figures. Then, too, some columns have replaced the news story as the place to look for the scoop.

SOURCES OF MATERIAL FOR THE COLUMN

The source of material varies with the nature of the column for which it is being sought. Consequently, gathering material may be a very simple or a highly complex task.

The least difficult material to gather is that used in the reflective column. This is the column wherein the writer reflects, lightly or seriously, on an event, a change, or some other part of the vast canvas of life. The material is easy to gather because the columnist merely passes along his thoughts on the subject. Perhaps an old theater building is being razed; the columnist reminisces. He writes of famous performances he saw there, of little anecdotes in its history, or of the great actors who trod its boards. He, of course, is successful in proportion to his ability to make his reflections appealing. When well done, this type of column is always highly popular. It is employed by the sports columnist to rehash past baseball seasons, by the political columnist to evaluate the great figures of past or present times, and by all other columnists who write appraisals.

Also fairly easy to obtain is the material for the specialized column (health, stamps, books, etc.). The material for this column is easily gathered because it is always readily available. The physician writing the health column simply gives information on current illnesses; the philatelist writes of the recent issues of stamps; and the book columnist tells something of the new books.

The material for the column of anecdotes, tidbits of news, gossip, and patter is much more difficult to gather. The columnist, like the reporter, must dig hard for material, for the competition in this field is keen. The syndicated columnists who use this kind of material have staffs of reporters to do their leg work; the lesser lights must do their own. The columnist in this field, however, is usually helped by friends who supply tips, by publicity agents of those persons (actors, entertainers, etc.) who must stay in the limelight to prosper, and by tipsters who are paid in proportion to the material used.

Still more difficult to gather is the material for the philosophic column, the column wherein the author probes into the complexities of life. To be successful, the philosopher-columnist must have an air of originality about his work; that is to say, the reader must not be able to trace the writer's ideas directly to other sources. Because presenting philosophy in an original way is a most difficult feat, especially when the writer must turn out six columns a week, very few columnists have been highly successful in this field.

Another column for which material is extremely difficult to gather is the humorous one. The difficulty exists because genuinely humorous material is hard to find or invent. Few persons can do it consistently. Like the comedians of stage, screen, and radio, the columnist who relies chiefly on humor is usually short lived. There have been, however, columnists who successfully wrote humorous columns for many years. Two good examples were Will Rogers and Irvin S. Cobb.

The material for the column which answers readers' queries is, contrary to popular belief, frequently difficult to locate. This condition is true because writing this column is not always a simple matter of extracting questions from the mail and answering them. Too frequently, the questions mailed in cannot be used by the columnist because (1) they have been asked and answered very recently, (2) they are too stupid to be given a reply, (3) the phraseology is so badly muddled as to be unintelligible, (4) important data are missing in the question, or (5) there is no answer available. Where the columnist cannot get his questions from readers, he must invent them. Although this may seem a simple process, it entails a constant effort to unearth interesting material and is, therefore, a real challenge to the columnist.

ATTRACTING READERS TO THE COLUMN

Since the primary aim of the columnist is to have the greatest number of readers, the student of journalism should know the five common ways in which a columnist can attract readers.

First, he can accomplish this end by *originality*. If, in his column, he constantly strikes a new note, he is certain to draw readers. He may have new material, a unique use of language, the ability to coin new words, or an unusual twist of thought. If this quality is attractive and he can maintain it consistently, he will hold his regular readers and draw new ones.

Second, a columnist can attract readers by coming through with an *occasional scoop*. In the past several years, some columnists have divulged stories that have precipitated national scandals and congressional investigations. One syndicated columnist has been instrumental in arresting top-flight criminals; another has sent a congressman to prison; another has blocked presidential appointments. A columnist cannot hope, certainly, to have a scoop every day, but, when he does, he will have many readers. Between scoops, he must rely on his other abilities to hold these readers.

Third, a columnist may build up a large following by exhibiting an *attractive personality*. Such a columnist was the late Will Rogers, who was read and quoted by thousands. Another was a columnist already referred to, Ernie Pyle, who was the most widely read war correspondent of World War II. An attractive personality is important in proportion to the subjectivity of the column. When the column is highly personalized, as is the column of humorous observations, an attractive personality is absolutely necessary. When the column

253

is strictly factual, as is the general information column, the demand on personality is at its lowest.

Fourth, a columnist can gain readers by exhibiting a note of *authority*, by consistently showing that he knows whereof he speaks. What he tells his readers they accept without reservation because he has said it. The columnist, therefore, must beware of rash judgments, immature thoughts, half-truths, and obvious propaganda. Being absolutely accurate is an indispensable quality of any column which has as its first purpose the imparting of facts. Examples of such columns are those on general information, answers to queries, and legal advice.

Fifth, a columnist can win readers by attaining a position of *eminence* before turning to the writing of a column. Syndicated columns have been written by a widow of a former President of the United States, a former presidential cabinet member, and a high-ranking churchman. Then, too, one finds columns by great figures in the military field, the sports world, and similar places familiar to a large portion of the population.

STYLE OF THE COLUMN

In writing the column, there are five general styles which can be employed. In each case, of course, the columnist chooses the one which best suits his material and his personality.

1. **The Unified Style**—When the columnist wants to speak on a single subject throughout, pointing everything toward convincing the reader of his central idea or thesis, he employs the unified style. This column is really an essay, formal or informal, according to the topic and the approach. The unified style is employed by the political columnist, the sports columnist who discusses a single subject each day, and others

who feel a need for a column to dwell upon one main idea. The following two columns are examples of the unified style. The first illustrates *reflective writing;* the second illustrates *serious discussion.*

Strictly Personal

One Needs to Know Why to Be an Expert

By Sydney J. Harris

CHICAGO, ILL.—A friend of mine who happens to be a trustee of his college invited me to attend the "homecoming" football game with him this season. I replied that I don't understand football and that a high school game looks as good (or bad) to me as a Rose Bowl championship.

He snorted derisively. "That's a silly statement," he said. "A little experience and close observation would give you the fine points of the game. Let me tell you, football is quite an art—and nobody who really knows the game could mistake a great team for a poor one."

He is right, of course. But what surprises me about men like him is their unwillingness to apply the same objective standards to other fields, in which they have little or no knowledge.

One Man's Opinion

He would defend his liking bad music instead of good as merely a matter of taste. He would defend his attendance at ill-made plays as "one man's opinion," and call me a cultural dictator for insisting that

only knowledge gives us a right to hold an opinion.

* * *

When the situation is reversed, however, he has no doubt that his evaluation of football teams is better than mine—as, indeed, it is. He has studied the game, knows its fine points, and appreciates things I do not even see on the field.

Then why do so many people have a terrible defensiveness about the arts? Painting, music, drama, literature—these are all crafts, like football and baseball and sailing. They have their rules, their standards, their form.

A Need to Know Why

If it is a matter of *fact* that Notre Dame's football team is better than that of Siwash Gulch High School; it is equally a fact that Beethoven's music is better than Grieg's, and Picasso's paintings better than Grandma Moses'. To become an expert in music or painting is merely to learn the reasons *why.*

* * *

In some things, of course, there is no disputing taste. If I like chocolate ice-cream and red-headed women, and you like vanilla ice-cream and dark-haired women, there is no "better" or "worse."

Levels of Value

But all the arts and crafts, from football to music, have their own

255

levels of value. We can make objective judgments, in a broad sense. We cannot say Beethoven is "better" than Mozart, but we can say that either of them is better than Humperdinck—just as Notre Dame and Northwestern may be roughly equal, but either is better than Siwash.

Most people, of course, defend "personal taste" in the arts because it permits them to be lazy and ignorant without losing face. But they are the same people who look upon me with a great contempt because I can't see the plain fact that one team is infinitely superior to another.

(Copyright, 1954.)

—General Features Corporation

Don't Take My Word For It

By FRANK COLBY

Let's Learn A New Word

In the December, 1949, issue of "Word Study," a publication of G. and C. Merriam Company (Webster's dictionaries), Dr. Thomas Elliott Berry, a college professor, coins a most interesting and useful word to designate the literary device of naming fictional characters after their occupations, appearances, or personal traits, such as Mrs. Malaprop, a character in Sheridan's "Rivals." She is noted for her blunders in the use of words. The word Malaprop was coined from the French phrase mal a propos, "inappropriate."

Dr. Berry's new word is charactonym, formed from the Greek charakter, "impression, mark, characteristic," plus onyma, "name." Charactonym is pronounced: KAR'ik-tuh-NIM, the first syllable as in carrot, carry.

Dr. Berry observes that charactonyms are as old as literature itself. He cites many such interesting examples as Aaron Thousandacres, Admiral Bluewater, and the seaman Harry Ark, from the works of James Fenimore Cooper, Ben Jonson's Cutbeard, a barber, Lady Haughty, and her servant, Mistress Trusty.

Greek fables are rich in charactonyms, and they are to be found in the folklore and legends of almost every race. Indeed, untold millions of persons today bear surnames that began as charactonyms: Little, Strong, Bernard ("bold as a bear"), Leonard ("strong or brave as a lion"), Philip ("lover of horses"), Wise, Goodman, Handy, Long, Short, Longfellow.

In a manner of speaking, then, charactonyms are nicknames.

Teachers of literature will, I feel sure, be very happy to discover Dr. Berry's new word charactonym. And I am more than glad to pass the good word on to the readers of my column. Here's a paste-in item for your dictionaries:

Charactonym: KAR'ik-tuh-NYM. A name given a person or fictional character in keeping with his occupation or most pronounced characteristics. Charactonym, from the Greek charakter, "impression; characteristic," plus onyma, "name," was coined by Dr. Thomas Elliott Berry, State Teachers College, West Chester, Pa.

—*Bell Syndicate, Inc.*

2. The Anecdotal Style—The term "anecdotal style" explains itself. It is used by the columnist who wants to tell a series of little unrelated stories or make several observations which have no bearing on each other. The writer usually has between six and ten of such anecdotes or observations in a column, and he generally separates them from each other by asterisks.

An example follows:

Songs of a City

By EDWIN MARTIN

TIP OF THE HAT TO: George Duros, genial tavern owner of Carlsbad, who gives a big free picnic each year for kids between 5 and 13, at the Buddy Todd Memorial Park in Oceanside. He raises the money for the annual event through the use of a large Mexican pottery bull placed conveniently on the counter of his bar, to which he and his thoughtful customers contribute regularly throughout the year.

* * *

COUNTY PAPERS: We enjoy reading the many fine newspapers that are being published throughout San Diego County—They're very warm and very American. For instance, in a recent copy of the Coronado Journal-Compass was this thoughtful little item headed, "Still in the Running: 'I am twenty-five cents . . . I am not on speaking terms with the butcher . . . I am too small to buy a quart of ice cream . . . I am not large enough to purchase a box of candy . . . I am too small to buy a ticket to the movies . . . I am hardly fit for a tip, but—believe me, when I go to church on Sunday, I am considered SOME MONEY!' "

* * *

Street Scenes

A rather pompous lady gets the salesman of a big Broadway store to take the diamond she is buying out in the sun so she can get a better look at it . . . And your reporter, and three interested lads in the uniform of a Mexican military school, also get a flash of the big stone as the sun's rays are reflected on it in a myriad of colors . . .

Also waiting outside this same store for his wife is a dignified-looking army colonel, rather embarrassed by the lusty cries of his baby, whom he is holding while the

257

good wife does her shopping. In true fatherly manner, he tries to whisper sweet words to the unimpressed infant, changes to sterner tones when he sees passersby watching him, but the lad still cries on with the tones of a little marine sergeant . . . And we grin to ourself, thinking that "every officer-father finds out sooner or later that you can't pull your rank on a crying baby!"

* * *

DO YOU REMEMBER: When Peter B. Kyne, the noted novelist, used to sit in Horton Plaza, and jot down some notes for future stories, while stationed at Camp Kearny, and before going overseas as a captain of artillery in World War I? He grew to love this section so much that he settled down at Del Mar, after he came back from the wars.

* * *

VISITORS IN TOWN: Wilbur Clark, president of the Desert Inn in Las Vegas, and his lovely wife, Toni, who still call San Diego their home, stopped over between planes last night, long enough to pick up Wilbur's brother, Harold, and his mother, and take them with them to Toronto, Canada, where they'll attend the big Variety Club meeting. Later they'll visit their old home town in McKeesport, Ill., after which Wilbur goes to New York and Chicago for some television appearances, then returns to Las Vegas to prepare for the national convention of the Variety Clubs, which will be held there next year.

* * *

SHORT INTERVIEW: Ruth Hussey, that excellent actress, gave a cute one in La Jolla, when a reporter asked her if her son, Ralph, would be an actor when he grew up. "Of course," Miss Hussey replied. "He was on the stage with me in New York in "The State of the Union." That's why I had to leave the show!". . . . Adios!

—San Diego Union

3. **The Departmental Style**—When the columnist has material that is easily separable into "departments," he often employs the departmental style. The departments may be given such names as "In the Mailbag," "Lest We Forget," "Things to Remember," and "Passing Parade"; or they may simply be separated by asterisks or some other typographical device. The departmental style is especially effective for random observations, little-known information, and provocative bits of news of general interest.

Departmental style columns are highly popular with readers because of the ease with which they can be read and the interest they often hold. Consequently, most newspapers have at least one such column. An example follows:

Life With Salt On The Side:

How Long Is A Kiss?

By E. V. DURLING

In this country a film kiss is limited to 16 seconds.

The average screen kiss lasts five seconds. How long does the "good-bye" kiss you give your wife in the morning last? What is the length of the kiss she gives you when you arrive home?

If you don't know, you better clock this osculation. According to our Horses & Women experts, the morning kiss should last 10 seconds. The evening kiss, 15 seconds. Both to be accompanied by a vigorous hug.

* * *

It is usually spelled "porterhouse steak." Should be Porter House steak. Was named after the Porter House, a hotel in Sandusky, Ohio . . . Am strongly in favor of compulsory automobile insurance. Have yet to read or hear a convincing argument against it. However, I am not stubborn. If you are against it, tell me why.

So They Say

Men born under the sign of Leo have unusual executive ability. So say the stargazers. That the astrologers may have something there is indicated by the fact that both Leo Durocher, manager of the New York Giants, and Al Lopez, manager of the Cleveland Indians, were born under Leo. So was "Casey" Stengel, brilliant skipper of the New York Yankees.

Passing By: Richard Maney. Colorful theatrical personality. Celebrating his thirtieth year as a Broadway press agent, during which he has publicized such personalities as Billy Rose, Tallulah Bankhead and Jed Harris. Maney must be added to the list of small-town boys who have made good in the big city. Is originally from Chinook, Mont., a town of about 2,000 population and some 50 miles from Shelby, where Jack Dempsey fought Tommy Gibbons.

Standing Room

To purchase standing room for the opening night of the old Vic production of "A Midsummer Night's Dream" at the Metropolitan, many people waited in line for five or more hours.

No sense in that. Standing room could be reserved. Just draw circles in the standing room section and number them. These circles to cover an area sufficient for standing room for one person. Then the space could be reserved and sold in advance.

* * *

259

There are over 1,600 music publishers in New York city. Yet only about 50 money-making song hits are published each year.

Queries From Clients

Q. One, who was the model used by Bartholdi for the Statue of Liberty? I claim is was Ada Rehan, the actress. Two, is there a statue in Paris of St. Catherine, the patron saint of spinsters? A. Model for the Statue of Liberty was a French girl named Jeanne Bayeux, who later become the wife of the sculptor. There is a statue of St. Catherine in Paris. It is visited annually on St. Catherine's Day by a parade of Paris midinettes who are twenty-five or older and still single.

—Baltimore News-Post

4. The Unrelated Facts Style—When the object of the column is to present a mass of facts which have little or no bearing on each other, the unrelated facts style is generally the best approach. This style enables the columnist to present his facts without any apparent order. He simply separates the facts with one or more periods, depending on the length of pause desired. To relieve the monotony of the reading, the writer or the copyreader may use an occasional subhead.

The success of the unrelated facts style column springs from its author's ability to sustain interest by variety, surprise, or whatever other device may be suitable.

An example follows:

New York Cavalcade:

Manhattan Round-Up

By LOUIS SOBOL

GRADUALLY, West 52nd street between Sixth and Fifth avenues is beginning to look like jaws from which most of the teeth have been extracted. Big gaps where new business buildings are to rise or where smaller structures have been torn down to give way to parking lots. It's the end of what was once a lane devoted solidly to amusement traps. Currently, there still remain a few die-hards featuring strippers but these are doomed too. What was a gay, if tawdry, diversion center will be just another street dedicated to Big Business. It's the death of another colorful era. . .

* * *

Grace Kelly, whose likeness adorns one of the current movie mag covers, now holds the cover record —having passed Greta Garbo and in more recent years, Marilyn Monroe...It happened on Fifth avenue. Jean Wallace and her husband, Cornel Wilde, ran practically smack into Franchot Tone who was Jean's ex. But if they saw each other, there was no indication of recognition. ...A flock of showfolks are among the "angels" for Shepard Traube's forthcoming "Goodbye Again" (opens at the Helen Hayes Theatre April 24th)—included are Peggy Woods, Myron McCormick, Helen Menken, Dorothy Patten, Max Liebman, Norman Lear and Ed Simmons. Not a role in the play for any of them...I don't think I have ever read finer writing than that which decorates Jim Bishop's pieces, so dramatically illustrated by Burris Jenkins, Jr., in the current series on the Negro in the South now running in this newspaper. An expert reportorial and analytical job, too...

* * *

Comedian Herkie Styles recovering after surgery...Well, lookie, lookie: Bridie Murphy, in the flesh, is a hat-chick at the Aztec Room in Jackson Heights, Queens...A picture magazine is notorious for taking hundreds of pictures for a contemplated series—and never using them. Comedian Peter Donald ("Masquerade Party") has posed for many of these and waited vainly thru the years to see any of them printed. Last week, the publication called again and arranged for a photographer to invade his home. But Peter's picture will still be among the missing. It was his dog, Cookie, that the lens were trained on—for a layout on mongrel pups ...Ted Husing coming along excellently after his surgery in the New York Hospital, Thursday... At Eddie Condon's, Jack E. Leonard, who melted off some 80 pounds, referred to himself as "A Fugitive from a Chin Gang"...

* * *

There's a bit of a rustle in Democratic circles to push General Matt Ridgway as a compromise candidate. Local politicians see Harriman coming out on top when the convention smoke is cleared but the Midwest odds are beginning to climb on Kefauver...Oddity in recent Academy Awards is that this was only the second time in 28 years that a song bearing "love" in the title had won the Oscar. The further oddity is that the only other time (1953) it was won by the same two who turned out the current winner, "Love Is A Many Splendored Thing." The other was "Secret Love." The winning pair of writers on both occasions were Sammy Fain and Paul Francis Webster...

* * *

Ran into Singing Gal Elise Rhodes Wednesday nite at 21. "We really have a great thing in common," she said. "It isn't that we both come from New Haven—but years ago my grandmother used to play checkers and poker with your mother."...Rainier has organized his own film company to shoot the wedding in color. Will sell it to a distributing company...

—*New York Journal-American*

261

5. The Question and Answer Style—The reason for the term "question and answer" is immediately apparent—the columnist gives a question and then answers it. This style is employed in all columns answering questions for readers and in columns where the author poses questions. An example of the author-posed question is to be seen in the bridge column, where the writer answers the questions which he believes are most often asked.

An example follows:

The Kibitzer — — Canasta
By SAM GORDON

No. 417—Black Threes

Q. Ever since we have played canasta we have been melding two black threes with a wild card at the time we meld out. Now we are told that black threes are never melded with wild cards. How come?

A. Before the 1951 laws, at the turn in which you meld out, you were permitted to meld four black threes, or three black threes, or two black threes with a wild card. It was then permissible.

This was changed in the 1951 laws, which read: A player may meld three black threes or four black threes (but no wild card may be melded with black threes) when going out at that turn, but at no other time.

Thus, the new laws prohibit any kind of a meld of black threes with a wild card. And, since black threes may be melded only at the time a player melds out, never is there a chance to add a wild card.

Laws in Conflict

Q. Last year we were told we could meld a canasta of black threes when we meld out. We are told this is not permitted in the 1951 laws. What can you tell us about this?

A. The laws before 1951 were not clear on this subject. So, there were different interpretations by experts (alleged and actual). Much confusion existed because of conflicting opinions.

My own contention with members of the committee at that time was never refuted by anything the laws said. But this point was clarified in the 1951 laws to block all future disputes.

The new laws say that no wild card may be melded with black threes. Since this is so, it would be impossible to make a canasta of black threes, because only four black threes are in a pack.

—*Oregonian*, Portland, Ore.

QUALITIES OF A GOOD COLUMN

There can be no set of rules which, if followed diligently, will guarantee a successful column. But as a result of interviewing several outstanding columnists and many general readers who follow columns intelligently, the author has compiled a list of 10 qualities which these persons believe to be essential to the good column.

1. A column should be interesting. The writer should always make certain that his material is going to be interesting to many readers. Thus, he must guard against judging subjects as interesting simply because they appeal to him. A nationally syndicated columnist, for instance, may be very much interested in a minor political dispute in his little home town in Massachusetts, but, before writing of the incident in his column, he had better know that most of his readers are interested also.

2. A column should reflect a note of authority. The reader should have the feeling that the writer knows his topic thoroughly. Consequently, the columnist should avoid launching on subjects in which he is not well informed, and he should never set down conjecture or guesswork as fact. In displaying a note of authority, however, the columnist must be careful not to pontificate or become overbearing, for readers react unfavorably to such attitudes.

3. A column should be newsworthy. Even though some columnists have become very successful by dealing with subjects outside the circle of decency, a columnist should always make certain that his material is in accordance with the standards of good taste. Readers of even the lowest intellectual level eventually weary of the risqué or the crude element.

4. A column should be personable. A column should always reflect a pleasant personality. Pettiness, jealousy, and similar human failings should never characterize a column. The reader must always have the feeling that the columnist is above the failings of the man in the street.

5. **A column should have a tone of newness about it.** The reader must never have the feeling that he has read a particular column before. Consequently, whatever his material may be, the columnist must have some note of newness about his work. The busy reader of the newspaper simply will not read anything that has a second-hand atmosphere.

6. **A column should be consistent.** If a columnist reverses his position on an important question, he had better have a sound reason to offer his readers, for one of the prime requisites of the good column is consistency. The Republican turned Democrat, for instance, may well lose many of his Republican readers because they feel that he has deserted their camp, and he may fail to attract new Democratic readers because of his lateness in seeing their view. If, however, this columnist can make his readers see his viewpoint, a minimum of damage will be done.

7. **A column should reflect intelligence.** The reader must always feel that there is a good mind behind the column. The columnist, therefore, must show breadth of vision, grasp of subject, and keen thinking. Once his readers feel superior to him, the columnist is on the decline.

8. **A column should be thought-provoking or entertaining.** The serious column must always provoke for the reader some question or thought, and the light or humorous column must always be satisfyingly entertaining. The reader should feel, on completing the column, that he has read something stimulating.

9. **A column should have a note of aggressiveness about it.** The column should be characterized by a pleasing degree of aggressiveness. The writer should be bold without being rash

and aggressive without being belligerent. A Uriah Heep has never been a successful columnist.

10. A column should have some note of individuality. A column should never be a stereotyped copy of another. It should reflect, somewhere, however slight it may be, some quality that gives it individuality. This individuality may be in style, approach, treatment, or content, but it must be there. Also, the writer must strive constantly to retain it.

EXERCISES

Write a column for each of the following:

1. Discuss the last major election in the nation, the state, or your city, with a view to its implications.
2. Think of yourself as an ardent devotee of the theater (legitimate stage) and write of the offerings of the current season.
3. Compare the leaders of the United States Senate of the moment with those of 10 or more years ago. Are they of as fine quality? Are they as shrewd? Do they have as much vision and grasp of current problems?
4. Write a column for a school paper in which you discuss the controversial question of compulsory attendance at chapel or assemblies.
5. As a columnist for a metropolitan daily, discuss the strength or the weakness of the modern high school or college education. Remember that you are writing for laymen.
6. As a columnist for a large college publication, write a column composed of observations made about the campus on a particular day.
7. As religious editor for a metropolitan daily, compose your regular Saturday column on the news in your field. Tell of guest speakers in various churches tomorrow, new churches to be dedicated, changes in pastorates, and any other interesting fact having to do with the religious life in your city.

8. Visit the opening of the opera season and write a column on what you see.
9. Write a humorous column on your inability to make your morning train, the baffling questions that your four-year-old son asks, or how to avoid helping your wife with the spring housecleaning.
10. It is January 20th and there is little doing in the world of sport. Rehash last year's World Series.
11. Give a round-up of the nonmalicious gossip of your school, your neighborhood, or your town.
12. As a columnist of national reputation, write a column on some important current question.
13. Picture yourself as a columnist who has lived in your town or city for the last 25 years or more. Write a column of reminiscences concerning changes of all sorts.
14. Gather six or seven interesting anecdotes and put them in a column.
15. Write a humorous column on some trivial subject such as how to get rid of door-to-door salesmen, how to retain the status quo of your waistline, or how not to slip on icy pavements.
16. As a roving reporter, write a column on the very interesting places in your city of which many residents are not aware.
17. Write a sports column in which you discuss the problem of subsidizing college athletes.
18. Write a column in the departmental style composed of material concerning your school or your community.
19. Write a column on the subject of the changing position of women in the scheme of things.
20. Write a column in which you discuss some major speech that has been given recently.

The School Paper

INTRODUCTION

Educators have long since come to recognize the school paper as an indispensable part of a well-developed school life. An effective paper helps to build the pride that is the basis of school spirit; it properly interprets the newsworthy events in the life of the institution it serves; and it provides a medium of expression for students interested in writing for publication. As such, the newspaper is one of the most important phases of the school's activity. But if the school paper is to fill its important role, all concerned must recognize three basic facts.

First, everyone from the adviser to the lowest reporter must realize that the paper, however small it may be, *must be a*

267

real work of journalism, not merely a toy for the amusement of a privileged group. The paper must always aim for the highest standards of the good publication, toward being approved completely by those competent to judge. Every phase of the work—coverage, writing, content, make-up—must be executed carefully, and the staff must think of the paper as highly as if it were a professional undertaking. All too often, a little clique gains control of a paper and uses it in an immature or selfish way. The group prints the small talk they consider sophisticated, they take malicious digs at other students and faculty, and all in all they defeat the purpose for which a paper should exist. Certainly, in such cases, the true function of the school paper is overlooked.

Second, the good school paper *must fill a need.* It must be so important to the institution it serves that, if a single issue were to be omitted, its absence would be sorely felt. The school paper must be anticipated, enjoyed, and discussed if it is to be successful. The school paper that fills a need informs, entertains, and explains in a readable, thought-provoking manner.

Third, the school paper *must have competent faculty direction,* for, without careful guidance and instruction, it seldom points toward high ideals. Rarely does one find a student staff with the maturity and the judgment necessary to conduct the affairs of the paper, for the obvious reason that few students have had sufficient journalistic experience. Such being the case, sympathetic direction is necessary. This direction, as the faculty adviser soon learns, may entail all sorts of difficulties because many students believe that a school paper should be completely unbridled. Athletic teams have coaches whose words are law; musical organizations have conductors who rule with absolute authority; and dramatic productions have directors whose orders are unquestioned. Yet, many students believe that the school paper should be placed unqualifiedly in their hands. Because of this, the faculty adviser may face difficulty as he attempts to guide his paper. If, however, he strives to make his students "see the light" of good journalism, his task will be easier than if he censors the paper ruthlessly. Many good papers, one eventually learns, are turned out with little or no faculty censorship because the adviser has worked hard in properly training his staff. A good point for the adviser to remember is that a minimum of control with a maximum of quality in the finished product is the ideal situation.

Another important point to be noted concerning faculty direction is that the adviser's role varies according to the particular situation. In the case of the secondary school paper, the adviser usually has complete jurisdiction. He is the final authority on every question, and he is expected to be, in the exact sense of the term, a censor.

In the instance of the college paper, however, the adviser's role may vary from that of absolute censor to that of pure adviser—that is to say, the student staff may be required to subject themselves completely to his judgment or they may be expected to turn to him only when they want his advice. Between these extremes, various gradations of control are decreed by college administrations.

Generally speaking, private universities and colleges are most likely to have uncensored papers. Consequently, one may find in many of their papers a complete freedom of speech. When the administration feels that the newspaper has "gone too far," the editor may be called to task, but these occasions are generally rare. In state-controlled institutions, however, the newspaper must often be wary of offending the taxpayer. The paper, for instance, must be careful of aiding one political party at the expense of another, offending a religious group, or straying outside the bounds of good taste. Taxpayers, it seems, believe they have the right to pass judgment on any agency supported by their money, and college administrators, in their desire to keep the public satisfied, censor such newspapers.

The philosophical bases for the various degrees of censorship would necessitate a long and perhaps fruitless discussion. The discussion would be long because of the complexity of the arguments for the various stands; the discussion would be fruitless because opinions are generally pre-established on the entire question. Therefore, the student of journalism should think of the role of the faculty adviser in terms of individual situations.

QUALITIES PECULIAR TO THE SCHOOL PAPER

To understand the school paper, one should know the three important ways in which it differs from the ordinary newspaper.

First, like other house organs, the school paper *relates news of a single institution.* Practically every item tells of some activity in which the school has a direct or an indirect interest. Consequently, nearly all news comes from the school and its related activities, and it is valuable in proportion to student interest in the event described. The fact that the school paper relates news of a single institution makes the entire procedure of gathering and handling stories different from that of the ordinary newspaper.

Second, the school newspaper *serves a distinctly homogeneous group.* Unlike the regular newspaper, its principal readers are generally from the same age bracket, are on approximately the same intellectual level, and have relatively similar interests. Thus, the problem of reader interest is not nearly so puzzling as in the ordinary paper.

Third, the school newspaper *operates in a manner sharply different from that of the ordinary newspaper.* Most noticeable is the longer time lapse between writing and printing. The school paper, except in the large colleges where a daily is maintained, generally has a 24-hour period between writing the last news and seeing the paper in print. Other items may be in type three or four days earlier. This situation poses the problem of giving a "hot-off-the-griddle" aspect to news that may be a week old. Another noticeable difference in operation is the ever-changing personnel of the school paper; positions are usually held for only one year or one term. No sooner does one staff become competent than its term ends and another takes over. A final difference in operation concerns repercussions. Whereas the regular newspaper operates with a view to avoiding censure from many quarters, the school publication is responsible almost solely to the school authorities. Hence, the problem of avoiding censure is much easier to analyze.

PROBLEMS OF THE SCHOOL PAPER

The problems of the school paper, for the most part, can be overcome by experience, the greatest of teachers. Yet, if added to this experience one tries to learn from the experience of others, handling the school paper becomes much easier. A discussion of the major problems follows.

1. Personnel—In staffing the school paper, the success or the failure of the publication is often determined. A competent, eager staff can raise the paper to new heights, while an incompetent, diffident staff can relegate the paper to a surpris-

271

ing depth. The greatest care naturally should be given the choices of editor and business manager. The former is important because on his shoulders rest the responsibilities of publishing a good paper; the latter is important because on him falls the task of providing the finances for printing the paper.

THE EDITOR

The editor should be a person who has risen from the ranks, a person who has *earned* this important position. In addition, he should know thoroughly the business of turning out this particular paper; he should be capable of handling other students so that any friction may be kept at a minimum; he should be well acquainted with every phase of life on his campus so that he can catch immediately any error in fact or procedure made by his reporters; he should be able to write well so that he can help others and correct bad copy; he should be a person of vision and good judgment so that the editorial policy of the paper will reflect a lofty tone; and he should be absolutely reliable in order that schedules may be respected, deadlines may be met, and accuracy may be maintained. But, above all, he should be a person who is doing the work of editor because he is deriving great satisfaction from his labors. Without enthusiasm, he can rarely do acceptable work.

THE BUSINESS MANAGER

The business manager must be a person with a sound business sense, one who can handle the problems entailed in keeping a school paper solvent. He must have an understanding of the intricacies entailed in budgeting expenses and balancing receipts and expenditures, and he must be able to keep accurate records, to operate his department smoothly, and to maintain a close check on an endless amount of small details. He must be able to appraise changing business conditions, and he must be able to handle his staff efficiently. Above all, however, like the editor, he must be a person who is doing work that appeals to him.

OTHER STAFF POSITIONS

The positions immediately below the two top offices of editor and business manager should be given to those students who were runners-up to the successful candidates. They, like those who hold the top positions, should possess in great degree the qualities already discussed, and they, too, should have earned their positions. Also of importance is the fact that these first assistants should be given significant responsibilities to discharge. Too often an unsuccessful candidate for the highest position feels that he has been defeated completely, that he must take orders unquestioningly from his successful rival. This situation can be overcome by so delegating responsibilities and authority that the first assistants have important offices.

In filling the lower positions, the most important consideration should be that of the student's potential value to the staff. A serious attempt should be made to evaluate the student's interest, ability, and reliability. Interest and ability can be appraised by the use of the tryout method; reliability can be determined by appraising the student's work after he has been given some responsibilities. Because the tryout is an important phase of staffing the paper, some discussion of it is in order.

When the would-be staffers report for tryouts, the entire process of selection should be explained. This should be done to convince any doubting candidates that the selection will be fair and open. The actual tryout can evaluate the student's interest by asking him leading questions about his reasons for wanting to join the staff, his extracurricular activities, and his background for the position sought. His ability can be appraised by asking him to write two or three shorts, the facts for which are given him, and by giving him a standard test in usage and mechanics. His work can then be evaluated for style, clarity, mechanics, and the other important phases of journalistic writing.

Once the student has been admitted to the staff, he should retain his position or be promoted according to a clearly explained merit system. This system should be so constructed as to reward the student according to his merit and to aid the paper by placing the best students in the various positions. A merit system should also be constructed with a view to keeping any chances of favoritism at a minimum. Further, merit systems should take cognizance of such important qualities as punctuality in handling assignments, thoroughness in work, and reliability in executing major and minor details.

Personnel Problems

In dealing with the student staff, the adviser must be aware of the immaturity that naturally accompanies youth. He must be on guard for the indiscretions, the rash judgments, and the radical ideas that longer life soften. There will be the student who wants to blast editorially the entire administration of the school or college; the student who wants to discuss some taboo or delicate subject in an open or brazen manner; the student who wants to use the paper as a sounding board for his pet ideas; and the student who wants to print the hopelessly dull material which he thinks is screamingly funny. These students must be suppressed painlessly, if possible, and any talent of theirs diverted into the proper channel. The adviser must also be careful to impress upon his students the responsibility of their work. All too many students display an irresponsible attitude. Deadlines, they seem to think, are elastic things to be stretched at will, and all errors in facts or procedure are to be considered small mistakes.

2. Finances—Before attempting to publish a school paper, the adviser and his staff should establish the financial pattern for the entire school year. Contracts should be signed with printer and advertisers, subscriptions should be solicited vigorously, and all expenses to be incurred should be understood and anticipated. The financial adviser should make certain that there will be enough money, with some to spare, to pay all bills. Where a paper fails financially, advertisers are reluctant to buy space when the publication is ready to resume, and embarrassing situations are always certain to arise.

In considering the financial situation of the school paper, one should know the most basic facts. First is the self-evident truth that, the larger the school, the less financial strain there should be. This is true because, the larger the enrollment, the larger the potential circulation and the higher the advertising rates. Hence, potential revenue varies in proportion to enrollment. Second, on sales days the paper should appear simultaneously throughout the school or campus, preferably under conditions where students cannot share a copy. Once a student has given a newspaper even a cursory examination, he will rarely buy it. Third, every effort should be made to sell the paper by subscription. This guarantees revenue for the entire year, especially through periods where sales might ordinarily be low. Fourth, the opportunity to advertise in a given paper should be made as attractive as possible. This is done by attractive placing of ads and by presenting a good sales talk to the potential buyer. A situation to be avoided is that of accepting complimentary ads. This type of ad should be omitted because it has the effect of weakening the sales talk to a potential advertiser, and it reduces the paper to the patronage level. Fifth, and most important, is the fact that, the stronger the paper journalistically, the greater the chances for wide circulation. In other words, the best way to increase revenue is to turn out a good paper.

One should also know that many schools do not depend solely on revenue from sales and advertising to balance their budgets. In fact, in many small schools, this would be impossible. Instead, the paper is given definite assurance of income from another source. Sometimes the revenue from a play is given to the paper; sometimes it is the profit from a sale; sometimes it is the income from a special athletic event. Then, too, in some schools the students pay a flat sum known as the "activity fee" at the beginning of the year. This payment entitles the student to admission to athletic events and social affairs and to copies of the various publications. In this way, definite revenue is guaranteed to the paper.

3. **What to Print**—When the staff and the adviser face the question of what is to be printed, they are handling a difficult problem. On the one hand, they have the students with all their likes and dislikes; they want the paper to be everything from a joke book to a literary magazine. On the other hand, the paper has its responsibilities to the school and to good journalism in general. Accompanying these situations are the all-too-frequent forces that have axes to grind. A faculty adviser wants a big play for a story that concerns his sphere of activity, even though the story may be dull; the school administration wants the paper to preach long sermons and administer sound warnings; a small segment of the student body would like to see more chatter and much more scandal—provided,

of course, that they are not the object of ridicule. In short, everyone's idea is sharply different.

Amid such conditions, the paper should set up a policy based on good journalism and service. This statement means that every newsworthy item should be given space in proportion to its value as news; after this, the policy may be tempered by such important factors as financial expediency and reader interest.

4. **What Not to Print**—As editors ponder the question of material to be omitted, they should remember primarily that no fact should be used that takes unfair advantage or willfully sets out to injure. This caution is especially important because the student writer, realizing his power over other students who cannot strike back in print, is often tempted to use this advantage. Another important caution concerns gossip. If the editor feels that gossip is in order, he should confine it to one clearly labeled column; it should never be spread throughout the paper, and a definite attempt should be made to keep it nonmalicious. In the hands of a clever writer, gossip can be entertaining and amusing, but too often it becomes dull and inane.

Another type of writing to be avoided is that wherein the student expounds on subjects treated by the daily papers. An example of such writing is the political column. Too often the student-columnist attempts to theorize about the international situation, recent legislation on monetary problems, or presidential appointments. Although the student himself may profit by writing such a column, the subject has probably been covered more authoritatively by a journalist of national stature. In fact, herein lies a grave danger, for all too often the student merely rehashes, knowingly or otherwise, the opinions of these well-known writers. Then, too, the opinions of student writers on such subjects are generally taken lightly by other students. Consequently, such writings are of little value to the school paper.

Also of questionable value for the school newspaper are book reviews, criticisms of motion pictures and plays, and editorials on subjects completely unrelated to the school. The reviews and the criticisms are of little value because they have probably been done better by the metropolitan papers or the leading magazines; the editorials fail because there is a question of the editor's grasp of the subject and of the appropriateness of the editorial in a school paper.

Considering further the subject of material to be questioned, one comes upon humorous writing. This material must be examined closely because more persons have failed in this field than in any other. Few students, the adviser soon learns, can write humorously, despite the fact that many think they are so gifted. The fact that few students can write humorously is not surprising, for genuine humor is extremely rare, even in the best of the large newspapers. Actually, American newspapers are always ready to employ a writer with an appealing sense of humor. If there is a scarcity in the professional field, there is little likelihood that many humorous writers are to be found for the school paper.

A final aspect of what not to print is to beware of the student looking for a quarrel. All too numerous are the individual with a grudge against someone, the radical who wants to make drastic changes, and the person who enjoys disagreeing for the joy of a heated argument. The writings of such students should be throttled vigorously.

5. Instruction—One of the most time-consuming tasks of the adviser is that of teaching the newer members of the staff. They must be taught to write in the journalistic style, to

follow the established practices of the paper, and to hunt for and recognize news.

The ideal way to instruct is to have a class in journalism. In this way, students can be prepared for their work on the paper and given valuable academic material. Failing such a class, the adviser should have a period of formal instruction for newcomers and a procedure for improving the work of the older members of the staff.

At all events, the adviser should never blandly assume that the students eventually will learn to write well. Nor should he refer his students to the files of the old issues for instruction, for, when he does, every issue soon comes to look like a former one.

6. **Schedules**—A real problem in handling the school paper is that of making students respect the various schedules and deadlines. Many staff members, unaware of the importance of adhering strictly to a schedule, will hand in copy late, miss stories, or in some similar manner upset the routine of the paper. This condition is especially prevalent at examination time, immediately before and after vacations, and at the end of the school year. Other than maintaining a staff of reliable students, there is no set pattern for making students respect the calendar and the clock. The adviser, however, must make certain that every key man understands his responsibilities. These key men, in turn, must make certain that their subordinates act accordingly.

Of vast importance in this regard is a smoothly run editorial office. Schedules must be posted and checked regularly; files must be kept absolutely up-to-date; and every tool and device used by the staff must be operated efficiently.

ADVICE TO ADVISERS

As a result of interviewing over 50 advisers, all of whom have been actively engaged in handling secondary school and college papers for 10 years or more, the author lists herewith the points most often given as "advice to advisers."

1. **Financial Situation**—Make certain that there will be no financial worries in publishing the paper. Have a definite, contractual relationship with all concerning financial matters. This includes the printer, the advertisers, all who supply the newspaper with equipment, and the subscribers. When possible, have written agreements.

Because schools and colleges are part of the public domain, be especially careful of the manner in which the paper spends its money. All contracts should be let as a result of open bids, and all expenditures should be listed carefully in accounts open for public examination. The expenditure of funds by the paper of the tax-supported school is an especially important matter because the public frequently watches very closely. Also important is the approval of the budget by the principal, the headmaster, or the president. This protects you from any repercussion.

A final point to remember is that you must budget the expenditures that vary. Among such items are cost of cuts, travel and other expenses of staff members, and photography costs. You must be careful to apportion your allotment, or you may find that you have overdrawn your account early in the year.

2. **Merit System**—Devise a merit system satisfactory to students and faculty alike for selections to staff positions. The usual procedure is to give points on the basis of ability, length of service, and background for the position sought. This tends

to put the best persons in the jobs and to remove the protests of favoritism that frequently accompany direct appointments.

In the absence of a merit system, direct appointment by the adviser is the next best course. The least desirable system is that of allowing students to elect the top officers of the publication. Such a course is unwise because personal popularity, rather than ability, becomes the chief criterion.

3. **Prestige**—Establish a policy designed to enhance the reputation of the paper so that many people want to serve on its staff. Staff membership must be vigorously sought after. In this way, there will be more candidates for the positions and consequently a wider choice in filling them.

The best way to gain prestige is obviously to publish a good paper, for students always like to be a part of a thriving activity. Another way is to award some sort of insigne, such as a pin, for service on the staff. The caution to be exerted in this regard is that the insigne must not be earned too easily. A third way is to award points toward membership in the senior honor society, the number of points being awarded in proportion to length and value of service to the newspaper.

4. **Staff Meetings**—Have regularly scheduled staff meetings presided over by the editor. Try to make every member of the staff feel that he is a part of the policy making of the paper. Try to have the staff think of itself as a unit with a major responsibility to discharge.

Attendance at staff meetings should be compulsory, with only the best of excuses accepted for absence. By making attendance compulsory, the adviser frequently will eliminate the students whose lack of interest does not warrant their being on the staff. This practice will also eliminate the overloaded student, the student who wants to spread his energies thinly over every activity in the school.

281

5. Instruction—Because students must be taught in order to serve the paper well, you should strive to have a journalism class in your school. Failing such a class, try to teach journalism in the curricula of the better English classes. The time spent in instructing students properly will save much time and effort later, and it will result in a better paper.

6. **Faculty Responsibility**—Divide the faculty responsibility for the paper into at least two departments, editorial and business. Do not attempt to assume responsibility for both phases. In large schools, try for a further division so that no one adviser has too much work.

Have a clear-cut agreement with other faculty advisers and students about responsibilities and authority. Such an understanding is absolutely necessary for harmony and efficiency.

7. **Variety**—Try to get into each issue some feature that does not appear regularly. It may be a poll of student opinion, it may be an unusual picture, or it may be an exclusive interview. Whatever else you do, avoid making your paper routine.

An effective device in avoiding routine is that of gaining control of the source of important announcements. When a paper can make exclusive announcements in every issue, it is certain to have variety. A pleasing variety can be gained also by the use of features (cartoons, puzzles, etc.), interesting feature stories, and timely letters to the editor. A final way to gain variety, one that must be used cautiously, is that of varying make-up. This end can be achieved by using catchy ears, changing the position of the masthead, and varying the over-all mechanical composition.

8. **Co-operation**—You must have the co-operation of your students, your colleagues, and your superiors. Aside from being co-operative yourself, you gain co-operation best by establishing the prestige of the paper. If the school paper is

well written, inclusive, and readable, others are bound to respect it, and, as a result, will be glad to co-operate with the staff when the need arises.

9. **Time**—Make certain that you have enough time to do your work. Without adequate time for guidance, editing, and proofreading, there can be little chance of a finished publication. You must be prepared to convince your superiors of this necessity, for few persons outside the field realize the time involved in handling a paper.

10. **Scrapbook**—Keep a scrapbook of stories that are models of good journalism. Although the stories should be chiefly from your own paper, others should not be excluded. Such a book is valuable to the learner.

The caution to be sounded in maintaining a scrapbook, however, is that it is to be used as a guide—not as a collection of models to be imitated.

11. **Exchanges**—Maintain a good supply of exchange publications, especially of outstanding ones, to see what other papers are doing. There is always an excellent chance that you can learn something valuable. Also, an exchange column, if well planned, constitutes an interesting item for your paper.

12. **Press Association Conferences**—Join a press association with a view to attending conferences. Thus, you and your staff can gain the benefit of others' experiences and keep abreast of the developments in your field. You also have the opportunity to present your questions to persons who should know the answers.

13. **Pictures**—Too many school papers are weak in their art (pictures). Don't make the mistake of using pictures taken by unskilled photographers. Avoid the use of pictures that are either too light or too dark, and never use a blurred picture simply because you think that a photograph of some sort is necessary.

Be especially careful of would-be photographers, for there are many students who are extremely eager to learn photography at the expense of the school newspaper. They can spend the paper's money faster and more uselessly than any other staff member.

14. Literary Efforts—Encourage students to attempt the usual literary forms—short stories, poems, and essays—and when they are good, use them. This should be done especially in schools where there are no literary magazines.

15. Commendation—Don't expect to have everyone appreciate the fact that you are turning out a good school paper. Remember that the number of persons who recognize good journalism is surprisingly small. Consequently, you are working for a paper that meets the requirements of good journalism, rather than for one that attempts the impossible feat of pleasing everybody.

SOURCES OF NEWS

As with the professional newspaper, the amount and the quality of news available for the school paper vary with the seeker. The good student reporter, like the good professional reporter, is able to find excellent stories where a less able person finds none. In fact, the good student reporter often finds a story where even the faculty adviser never thought of looking. Consequently, the most important statement to be made of source of news is that made earlier: the amount and the quality of news depend most heavily on the ability of the reporter seeking it.

Proceeding further, one finds more difficulty in saying what is *not* news than what *is* news because the source of news for the school publication is almost limitless. Just as the outside world always has a good story hidden somewhere for the able reporter, so does the world of the school. Highly interesting stories have been written about such apparently routine doings as the window cleaner at work, the janitor emptying the waste baskets, and the pigeons nesting under the eaves. Because so much about the school interests so many in the school, the searching reporter can find news everywhere.

The big difference between the source of news for the regular newspaper and that for the school publication is that the school furnishes very little spot news. The regular newspaper has reporters visiting police stations, hospitals, and other such places where spot news is likely to break at any moment, but the school paper has almost no opportunity for such news. Instead, it must rely for its stories on events that occur with regularity and foreknowledge. To offset the deficiency in spot news stories, the school paper uses many feature and part news–part feature stories. Consequently, no detailed attempt will be made to treat separately the source of news for the feature story and the news story.

There are several broad classifications of sources of news, a discussion of which follows. The reader should remember, however, that many of these stories can be used as straight news or feature material, depending on the effect desired.

1. **Events to Come**—The greatest source of news for the school paper is to be found in writing of events to come. Usually, the most prominent spot in the paper is given to the big event of the forthcoming week. Whether it be the senior play, the spring dance, or the award assembly, the event is generally the most newsworthy item of the moment. The student likes to read of the event in advance so as to learn all details, and the wise paper plays upon this interest to the maximum.

There are several significant points to be noted concerning the writing of events to come. First, the story should be written as interestingly and as attractively as possible because it is an important news item and because the event may need the publicity. A dance, for instance, relies heavily on a favorable preview, as do all other events that depend on student revenue or attendance. Second, the story should not be overplayed; that is, the story should not be padded out to fill several columns, thus squeezing out smaller items. Also, it should not deal in superlatives. The paper that overpraises every event soon loses prestige with its readers. Third, the newspaper should contain as many advance notices of newsworthy events as possible. This serves to keep the reader informed, to cater to a wider group of readers, and to make the paper an important source of information. Fourth, small routine events do not merit a story in every issue. They should be confined to the calendar box. Fifth, the writer must work hard to avoid dullness in the less significant stories of events to come. Never should the story of events to come read like filler.

The following list of stories covers the events to come common to most schools. Therefore, it can serve as a broad guide to show possible sources of news.

a. *Sports:*
 1. Announcement to candidates to report for tryouts.
 2. Announcements of scheduled games and meets, varsity and intramural
 3. Announcements of individual tournaments and contests (tennis, golf, fencing, foul shooting, etc.).
 4. Announcements of exhibitions and sports carnivals.
b. *Dramatics:*
 1. Class plays—stories announcing tryouts, rehearsals, and ticket sales, and a build-up story for the actual performance.

2. Assembly plays—any of the above stories that may pertain.
3. Dramatic Club productions—any of the above stories that may pertain.

c. *Assembly:*
   1. Outside speakers, entertainers, performers, etc.
   2. Award and other special assemblies, pep rallies, school group performances, etc.

d. *Clubs:*
   1. Announcement of formation—purpose, requirements for eligibility, general plans, etc.
   2. Announcement of candidates for offices.
   3. Announcement of meetings.
   4. Announcement of any special event or program.

e. *Class News:*
   1. Announcement of meetings.
   2. Announcement of any regular or special event to come (election of officers, trips, programs, etc.).
   3. Build-up story for any activity.

f. *Unusual Activity of Any Group:*
   1. Field trips.
   2. Class trips.
   3. Interclass contests.

g. *Grounds and Buildings:*
   1. Changes to be made—new construction, repairs, painting, etc.

h. *Social News:*
   1. Announcement of parties, dances, fetes, bazaars, etc.

i. *Exchanges:*
   1. Any especially interesting event to come in another school.

j. *Musical Organizations:*
   1. Announcement of tryouts.
   2. Announcement of calendar for each group.
   3. Build-up story for each event.
   4. Any previously unscheduled event—interschool contests, trips to other schools, etc.

k. *Debating and Other Nonathletic Teams:*
  1. Announcement of tryouts.
  2. Announcement of contests.
  3. Any previously unscheduled event (special programs, visitations, etc.).

l. *Contests:*
  1. Announcement of all contests open to students (essay, poetry, short story, etc.), whether sponsored by school or by outside group.

m. *Yearbook and Other Publications:*
  1. Announcement of tryouts.
  2. Any announcements pertaining to publication itself—date on which pictures are to be taken, dates of issues, contracts to be let, subscriptions to be solicited, etc.
  3. Build-up story for appearance.

n. *Faculty:*
  1. Any group activity—play, picnic, outing, etc.
  2. Any newsworthy story—teacher to address group, to take interesting trip, to engage in unusual project, etc.

o. *Administration:*
  1. Standard announcements—important dates, curriculum changes, new regulations, etc.
  2. Open letter to student body—greetings at opening of year, Christmas, Easter, etc.
  3. Scholastic record summaries.
  4. Board of trustees' proposals and plans.

p. *Miscellaneous:*
  1. Announcements of charity drives, donations for worthy causes, outside organization events given on campus, parent-teacher events, alumni events, etc.

2. **Past Events**—Another large source of news lies in describing past events. In this category are the stories of dances, parties, celebrations, and other extracurricular activities. The most important pitfall to avoid in writing of the past event

is the tendency to overplay. The spring dance, for instance, attended by three fourths of the school and now almost a week old, certainly does not merit a page-1 spread. Yet the student reporter who had a highly pleasant time at the dance is ready to write several columns. A further caution concerning news of past events is to use cautiously the device of writing of an event before it takes place. When the paper appears, only the most naive of students is deceived, and the publication frequently loses face. Then, too, a long history of embarrassments could be written about papers that have used this device to their sorrow. One such paper belonged to a mid-West high school where a glowing account of a play was written for an issue to appear the day after the performance. The article was to be displayed prominently on page 1, and, as the editor looked at the final proof six hours before the curtain was to rise, he congratulated himself on his cleverness. However, an hour before curtain time, the heating system in the building failed and the play had to be postponed. The paper was now in print, so the staff was faced with the unpleasant situation of retiring a whole issue (in which case they would have to make refunds to advertisers and lose revenue from sales); postponing the issue until the printer could make the correction, thus necessitating many other changes and great expense; or distributing the paper as it was. Since they were limited financially, they could only distribute the paper. There is no need to detail their embarrassment and loss of prestige.

By examining the list of events to come, the staff of the school paper can select those stories which will have a follow—that is to say, the events which will merit another story when they have occurred. Frequently, however, there are other newsworthy events which have not been preannounced. Some examples are the unannounced visit of a dignitary, the winning of a contest where entry was not announced, accidents, and other spot news.

3. The Classroom—A third source of news for the school paper is the classroom. Under this heading we find interesting discussions or observations, classroom blunders, and little items of general interest such as reactions of individual students to lessons. This type of news is the most difficult to make new and interesting, and only the most capable of reporters can usually handle it. In lesser hands, it frequently becomes dry, meaningless, or trite. Yet a good reporter can give it individual treatment that is both new and interesting. Therefore, this source of news must not be overlooked.

The most interesting classroom news usually comes from the science laboratory or the shop. The reason is that these stories tell of tangible objects. The student can visualize the apparatus for the interesting experiment or the construction of an unusual piece of furniture easier than he can follow an account of a discussion. Then, too, news from the laboratory and the shop are interesting because they are more likely to have an element of the unusual.

4. Sports—A source of news that should be given great attention is sports. Since sports is invariably the overwhelming choice as the most interesting extracurricular activity, a large section of the paper should be reserved for sport stories. Intramural as well as varsity sports are also valuable in providing material for many columns and features. Another interesting phase of sports material is the interest aroused by running little boxes of statistics—wins and losses, total points to date compared with opponents' points to date, and individual scorings, for example.

5. Feature Stories—The source of news which demands the most ingenuity in handling is that of the feature story, for, in unearthing and writing feature stories, individual enterprise and ability are indispensable. Like the professional, the student reporter must be alert to the possibility of the story and capable in his handling of it. The feature story, if well handled, represents for most house organs the most interesting kind of material. Consequently, the school paper should rely heavily on its use.

Because of the nature of the feature story, there can be no stock list of sources. In fact, the minute a story becomes stock it loses much of its appeal. However, there are some broad fields to be mentioned as rich sources of feature story material. The best of such fields is that of the unusual student activity. One student may have a singular hobby, such as collecting automobile license plates from every country in the world; another may have a highly interesting collection of autographs; another may be a special student of some sort (greatly overage, extremely handicapped physically, from some distant country, etc.). Such students represent feature material ready-made.

Another abundant source of feature material is the faculty. Contrary to popular belief, many faculty members do live interesting lives. They may have fascinating hobbies, they may have extraordinary accomplishments, they may have interesting observations to pass along. Where these stories exist, they should be unearthed and used.

Interesting feature stories can also be written about colorful employees (janitors, cafeteria employees, groundkeepers, etc.), renovations in the school buildings or on the campus, history of buildings and departments, and changes over the years as shown in old publications and records.

The important fact to be remembered concerning the feature is the one already cited—the feature story, like all creative work, depends most heavily on individual ability and enterprise.

The School Paper

The following is a partial list of the feature stories found in 10 representative school papers for a one-year period. It should serve merely as a guide to show the kind of story used by most school papers.

a. *Unusual Student Activities:*
1. Student is professional radio announcer.
2. Student meets President of the United States.
3. Student wins $1400 on radio quiz program.
4. Student tells of being lost in severe snowstorm.
5. Forty-one-year-old man becomes college freshman.
6. Triplets (all boys) enter college.
7. Father and son graduate from college together.
8. Ten of school's 12 faculty children take courses under fathers.
9. Student commutes to college by helicopter.
10. Youngest of eight brothers enters school from which other brothers have been graduated.
11. Students challenge faculty to barbershop quartet contest.
12. Student acquires suit of medieval armor.
13. High school senior wins amateur boxing championship of entire state.
14. Student has returned from round-the-world trip.
15. Student exhibits amazing collection of autographs.

b. *Scheduled Activities:*
1. Students receive photographer's proofs for yearbook.
2. Ridiculous answers to examination questions.
3. Seniors visit Washington, D.C.
4. Lecturer on snakes loses blacksnake backstage—snake still at large.
5. Reactions to forthcoming graduation.
6. Color story on visiting football team.
7. Student confusion regarding new regulations covering dining room, library, and student social room. (Humorous treatment)

8. Dramatic Club tries center-stage performance of famous play in gymnasium.
9. Blind gymnasts to perform in assembly.
10. Student club corresponding with students in foreign land.

c. *Faculty:*
1. Professor makes unusual mountain-climbing trip.
2. Shop teacher and wife build eight-room house for themselves.
3. Latin professor retires after 50 years of teaching.
4. Teacher buys 1914 Ford to drive in antique automobile parade.
5. Story on unusual faculty hobbies.
6. Story on faculty men who were former athletes.
7. Physics professor invents device for automatic home laundry.
8. English teacher publishes volume of poetry.
9. Color story on new headmaster.
10. Exchange teacher returns from abroad.

d. *Miscellaneous:*
1. Squirrels found nesting in old attic storeroom.
2. Forty-five-year-old newspaper found under floor of headmaster's office.
3. Popular janitor celebrates twenty-fifth anniversary in service of school.
4. School bus driver (man) defeats all other contestants (women) in cake-baking contest.
5. College librarian tells of many love notes, etc., left in books returned by students.
6. Faculty member explains architecture on campus.
7. Little-known facts of feeding students in college dining room explained.
8. New equipment in science laboratory explained.
9. Professor of ornithology explains mysterious appearance of snowy owl in eastern Pennsylvania town.
10. Stories in 50-year-old issue of college paper printed with comments.

293

6. **Polls**—A never-failing source of news to the school newspaper is the poll of student opinion. If conducted properly, this type of news is always interesting, because students like to know how others feel about leading questions. Straw votes on presidential and other important elections, surveys of opinion concerning a recent or proposed change, and even tabulation of answers to such trifling questions as "The Movie Actress or Actor I Should Most Like to Date" provide a highly interesting source of news.

There are five cautions to be exerted concerning polls. First, the poll should be as exhaustive as possible. As many students as possible should be consulted if the poll is a sampling, and all students should be approached if the poll is an election. Second, the issue should be stated clearly and simply. There should be no ambiguity or evasiveness in the manner of asking the question. Unless the question is stated clearly, the answers are likely to be of little value. Third, the poll should be taken on an interesting subject. "The Classics I Most Admire" is a fine subject for the bookish student, but, for the great mass, it may be less than a fascinating topic. Fourth, if the poll is of the interview type, the paper should generally concentrate on newsworthy students. Fifth, in the poll of opinions, the dull answers should not be printed or the interest of the reader will be lessened.

7. **Interviews**—A source of news which is very interesting, if used properly, is the interview with students, faculty, or others of interest to readers of the school paper.

Students are interviewed because they are newsworthy (they are top figures in some school activity or they have interesting material to give), or they are interviewed at random to express their views on some pertinent topic of the moment. Faculty are interviewed because they are instrumental in guiding some school activity or because of some outside activity that merits space in the paper. Other news-worthy individuals may be speakers in assembly, interesting or outstanding figures in the outside world, or anyone who has a good story to tell.

The one caution concerning the interview is that it must be done effectively. The interviewer must try hard to avoid routine approach and treatment. Questions must be so phrased as to draw forth interesting answers, and all newsworthy elements must be gathered.[1]

THE COLUMN AND THE EDITORIAL

The procedure for writing the school column can be much the same as that for the regular newspaper. The same methods of gathering information, the same styles, and the same sources of appeal can be observed. Generally speaking, the most successful school columns are written on sports, observations on school life, and patter.

There are, however, several other kinds of columns which can be quite interesting. Capable writers turn out good columns on stamps, hobbies, exchange material, and little-known information about the school. The column in the school paper, like so many other features, varies in proportion to the ability of the person writing it.

Like the column, the editorial for the school paper is handled in much the same manner as that of the professional newspaper world. However, in addition to the material covered in the chapter on the editorial, the student should note some other important facts. Above all else, the tone of the school paper editorial should always be high, and the message should always have a definitely constructive note about it. The editorial should not sound as though it has been

[1] See Chapter 3 for a discussion of this point.

released through the president's or the headmaster's office, but neither should it sound as though it is a recording from a local gathering place for students. The writing of the editorial should be entrusted to a student of fairly mature judgment and broad vision, the ideal situation being one wherein the faculty adviser or the administration never has to censure the writer for exceeding his right to express himself.

Usually, the person best qualified to write editorials is the editor himself, but the task should not be thrust upon him entirely. Assistant editors and even good reporters can be drafted into this work.

Writing for Radio
and Television

Chapter
11

INTRODUCTION

With the emergence of radio in the twenties as a medium
of mass communication, the need for another type of journalistic writing arose. This new type of writing was to be
leveled at an audience listening in their homes to an unseen
speaker. Hence, it was to be writing prepared for one per-

son to read to thousands of others. Because there could be no printed page or other visual aid for the listener, the importance of clarity, interest, and general effectiveness of presentation became apparent at the outset. With the emergence of television in the forties, the writer gained the assistance of visual aids (maps, blackboards, drawings, etc.), but essentially he still produced writing to be read to an audience.

Like all institutions, radio and television have undergone a period of extended development. The programs and the techniques of the earliest days have long since changed or disappeared, and mechanical advances have been truly amazing. Also, because of the constant need for novelty, many innovations have arisen. For example, the dialogue commercial, the testimonial commercial, and the singing commercial—many of which border on the nauseating—have come into being. Then, too, as a result of scientific studies of listeners' interests and reactions, program offerings are now altered more quickly and more sharply than ever. With every new development, a need to modify writing arose. Thus, many new styles and types of writing have developed in the relatively short life of radio and television.

BASIC PRINCIPLES

Certainly the initial step in learning to write for radio and television is to examine the basic principles applicable to all writing for these media. This chapter, therefore, will treat first the broad general principles; then it will consider specifically the writing of news, commercials, program continuities, commentaries, sustaining announcements, and miscellaneous types. Only the "workday" types of writing—the kinds done by regularly employed station writers—will be discussed. The full-length play, the short story, and other highly creative types of writing cannot be discussed because they are, in themselves, extensive subjects.

The first basic principle to be noted is that *the radio and television writer prepares material for listeners rather than for readers.* Consequently, his whole approach is affected accordingly. Whereas the newspaper reader, for example, has banner lines, banks, and above all the printed word to rely on, the radio audience is limited to the spoken word alone and the television audience is limited to the spoken word and any visual aids (signs, drawings, etc.) employed by the speaker. The newspaper reader may peruse stories as he wishes, reading and rereading according to his desires and his abilities, but the listener must follow a pattern prepared for him. Therefore, the first principle of writing for radio and television is that the material must make "good listening"—that is to say, it must be material that listeners of varied backgrounds can follow easily, enjoyably, and intelligently.

The second principle, closely related to the first, is that *the writing must make "good speaking."* Hence, the material should be cast in the style of the speaker rather than in the style of the writer. In fact, the test of the effective broadcast is that it never sounds like writing or reading; it sounds, rather, like a fluent conversationalist addressing a small group in a clear, interesting manner. To see clearly the nature of writing prepared for a speaker as opposed to that prepared for a reader, a simple test is helpful. One need only take a well-written radio script and read it aloud, followed by a similar reading of a page of a science textbook. This exercise will demonstrate immediately the difficulty encountered in attempting to make clear to listeners material not designed for oral delivery.

Third, because material is to be prepared for listeners and speakers, *certain considerations of vocabularly must be observed*, the most important of which are listed:

1. Short, crisp words are preferable to longer, "difficult to pronounce" ones. Compare "The players stood around the injured halfback" with "The competitors circumscribed the fallen gladiator." Note the difference in both clarity and ease of delivery.

2. Simple, immediately meaningful words are preferable to less used, less well-known words—even though the latter words may be more precise. "The rushing waters flooded the field" is preferable to "The turbid tributary inundated the pasture." The first sentence is preferable because of the clarity and ease of delivery gained.

3. Highly technical terms, if they must be used, should be explained as tactfully as possible. Such terms as "minister without portfolio," "multiple sclerosis," and "escrow," which often must be used in newscasts and similar writing, need definition for many persons. In such instances, definitions should be given unobtrusively by such constructions as: "The will held in escrow—that is, the will to be held by the lawyers until the stated time—was delivered as directed." . . . "The judge objected to the word 'anent,' which, as crossword-puzzle fans will tell you, means 'about'." . . . "The separator, a tank 15 feet wide and 10 feet deep, was examined for blood stains."

4. Euphony must take precedence over cacophony wherever possible. The "s" sound, for example, should be avoided, as also should any combination of words that makes a harsh or unpleasant sound. Note the undesirable quality of the following: "The soldiers slipped surreptitiously past the shops." . . . "The gelatinous globules made a

glub-glub sound in the gluey mixture." . . . "To two twosomes, at least, the music was too tiresome."

5. Doubtful words must be examined carefully. Doubtful words include the usual ones found in common use ("dope," "craps," "bum," etc.); slang, especially that which is known to have a vulgar or obscene meaning; and localisms and other words likely to present difficulty or ambiguity in meaning.

The fourth consideration in writing for radio and television is that *certain stylistic practices must be observed*. The purpose of these stylistic devices is to gain a maximum of intelligibility, interest, and pleasure for the listener. The most important stylistic considerations follow:

1. Strive for short, immediately meaningful sentences because long involved ones are difficult to follow. Be especially wary of lengthy dependent clauses, involved structure, and parenthetical elements. Note the differences between the following two versions of the same incident: "The arrested man was angry. He protested; he stormed; and he berated the officer. But he was still helped into the police van and delivered to the city jail." . . . "The arrested man was, to say the least, angry. Although he was eventually helped into the police van, this action did not become a reality until after he had protested and stormed, followed by a berating of the arresting officer."

2. Use the active, rather than the passive voice. The active voice is usually more direct, while the passive voice frequently creates delayed reference. Compare the following: "The shortstop misjudged the ball." . . . "The ball was misjudged by the shortstop."

3. Use the most effective device obtainable for impressing essential data. If, for example, a name is to appear in a

commercial, it must be repeated or spelled out as effectively as possible. If an unusual term must be used, it can be spelled, syllabized, or spoken slowly in order to be made impressive.

4. The positive approach is generally stronger than the negative. Unless negatives are emphasized strongly, they are often lost. Compare the following versions: "The driver was proceeding at a lawful speed."—"The driver was not exceeding the speed limit." . . . "Now is the time to act." —"This is not the time to delay action." . . . "Rely on a tested remedy."—"Do not rely on an untested remedy."

5. Strive for originality whenever possible. Although certainly no formula can be given, the good writer can recognize originality at sight. An unusual phrase, a catchy rhetorical device, or a pleasantly humorous line can be very effective. The following instances of originality were once striking. Now, of course, many have been used to the point of triteness. "The right time is 6 o'clock. The right time to have your car checked is now. The right place to take it is Smythe's Garage, Main Street and Sixth Avenue, Worcester." . . . "Look at your shoes. Everybody else does. Do they need Griffith's Polish! Just 15 cents in the handy tin at your neighborhood store." . . . "Safety is no accident. Be safe—not sorry."

NEWS

The clearest evidence of the importance of news to radio and television stations is seen in the distinct emphasis accorded it. Station directors have long known the newscast to be a strong source of attraction to many listeners, and they have planned their broadcast day accordingly. Seldom does a broadcast hour pass without a newscast of some kind, and many stations attempt to hold listeners with the reminder that a newscast will follow the program being aired. The appeal of news is further established by scientific investigation which reveals that 10 to 25 per cent of adult listening time is devoted to newscasts.

How stations gather, edit, and prepare news naturally varies with the size of the station. In the small station, a staff announcer may have as one of his duties the entire handling of news. He gathers, prepares, and delivers all news. In the larger station, however, there is usually a full-time news director with staff assistants. When one announcer handles all the details, he generally works in a small room with a wire service teletype. State, national, and world news he obtains from the wire service; local news he gets by telephone (from police stations, hospitals, etc.), as tips from friends, as publicity releases, and as letters requesting announcements (banquets, plays, dances, etc.). Also, he seldom feels any compunction in appropriating from local newspapers any item he desires. When a station has a news director with a staff, the process more nearly resembles the procedure of the newspaper. The news gatherer functions as a district man or reporter; writers and editors in the office prepare both local and wire news for broadcast; and the news director supervises the entire staff.

Whether the handling of news is to be the function of one person or of a staff, certain competencies must be present. They are, in order of importance, (1) the ability to recognize news, (2) the ability to prepare news, and (3) the ability to determine audience demands at every hour of the broadcast day.

Recognizing News

The need to be able to recognize news is fundamental, for the newscast must reflect soundness of news values. The general qualities of interest and appeal necessary to the newspaper also hold for radio and television. Consequently, the person selecting news for broadcast must have the journalist's soundness in appraising stories.

To develop the ability to recognize news for radio and television, the writer should first re-examine the qualities that constitute "news" for the paper; then he should examine the newscasts of representative stations for a given day. This latter step will give him an insight into general trends. For purposes of examination, stations can be classified as (1) large metropolitan, (2) smaller metropolitan, and (3) small town.

The newscasts of the large metropolitan station usually emphasize foreign and national news. Although local news is used, it is only the most significant brand (major changes in municipal policy, serious accidents, new laws, etc.). Sometimes a large metropolitan station may have a program devoted entirely to local news, but such is the exception. The reason for this condition is that the large metropolitan station serves an area extending well beyond its immediate city. Hence, local news broadcasts interest only a portion of its listeners. The large metropolitan station generally has at least one newscast each hour, aimed at the most likely audience of the moment.

The smaller metropolitan station, because of competition, often aims to capture a specific audience. It may seek, for instance, to attract the high school population in the late afternoon and the young adults in the evening by a heavy emphasis on popular music. The smaller metropolitan station may even seek to capture national groups by using music from specific foreign lands in full-length programs ("The Italian Hour," "The Irish Program," etc.). In such instances, the newscasts are written with the particular audience in mind. The newscast of the smaller metropolitan station naturally includes world and national news, but generally it places a heavier emphasis on local news than does the large station.

The small-town station has a newscast entirely different from that of the larger stations because it caters to a distinctly local audience. Because its power is limited, the small-town station is restricted to its own area, and consequently it must make its appeal to that area. Thus, it often has an overbalance of local news. In fact, the small-town station frequently has local news broadcasts three or more times daily—even though it may have nothing more significant to report than minor automobile accidents, births at the local hospital, and grass fires.

In developing the ability to recognize news, the writer for radio and television should note two peculiarities of his field. First, he is not free to divide stories over the several newscasts of the day. Most stories must be used almost immediately, and many stories, by virtue of their importance, must be used several times. An example of such a story is the announcement of an appointment to the United States Supreme Court. Although the station may get the flash in time for the 10 A.M. news, the story must be used again at least twice. Usually some new facts can be added, but, in any case, the story must be used several times. If no new facts are available, the story should be re-cast in order to avoid the monotony experienced by the many listeners who hear the material more than once. The second peculiarity of the field of radio and television newscasting is that the newscaster generally has an abundance of material from which to choose. This statement is true because the wire services always provide much more news than can be used. The newscaster's primary problem, therefore, is one of selection.

PREPARING THE NEWS

In preparing news, the writer should remember the basic principles of writing for radio and television already discussed. The need for clarity, interest, and general effectiveness treated at the outset of this chapter assume special importance for the newscast, as do the advice and the cautions cited. Then he should turn to the principles peculiar to the writing of news.

First, he should note that, although his work differs from that of ordinary journalistic writing, the appeal is essentially the same. The listener looks for the qualities in the newscast that the reader seeks in the newspaper. He wants to be interested, informed, and entertained. Therefore, the newscast *must have the basic appeal of the newspaper.*

Second, the writer of the newscast should note that the listener has no power to select. Whereas the newspaper reader may scan and choose, the newscast listener must accept everything in the manner presented. He may change stations, of course, but he is still restricted to a pre-established pattern. The writer of the newscast, therefore, *must select material that will interest and thus hold the listener.*

Third, the writer of the newscast must realize that he is restricted in length. Whereas the newspaper may vary length according to play, the writer of the newscast *must keep every story brief.* True, the more important stories run longer than the less important ones, but still every story must be told briefly. Thus, every story, however important, is really a capsule of the most important data. In fact, the typical newscast is a series of capsules, with no noticeable difference in comparative length.

Finally, the writer of the newscast must observe certain qualities of (1) structure, (2) style, (3) vocabulary, and (4) objectivity.

Structure—The most important fact concerning structure is that the story prepared for a newscast follows a narrative, rather than an inverted pyramid, structure. Because the story must make good listening, it cannot have the tightly packed quality of the newspaper lead, nor can it employ any structural device that prevents the easy flow of the narrative. To see this quality, compare the following story as it was used in the newspaper and as it was broadcast:

Family Doctor Says Roberts Child Healthy

A statement by James T. Roberts, charged with the murder of his daughter, Judith Ann, that she was "a healthy, normal, intelligent child" was confirmed today by the Roberts' family physician, Dr. B. W. Sollod, of 2900 Dunran road.

Dr. Sollod said:
"That is correct."

In Florida Roberts, striking at rumors that Judith Ann's death was "a mercy killing," said she had been pronounced in good health by Dr. Sollod before the Roberts family made the trip to Miami on which she was kidnaped and slain July 7.

* * *

SAID DR. SOLLOD today:

"The child was in good health. She was awaiting a little tonsillar surgery but only for a little residual tonsillar tissue."

Dr. Sollod declined to discuss the matter any further.

In declaring in Florida that Judith Ann, six, was healthy and normal, Roberts said the fact would be verified by Dr. Sollod, the Roberts family's physician for years.

—Baltimore News-Post

A Baltimore physician today agreed with the statement of James T. Roberts, who is charged with the murder of his six-year-old daughter, Judith Ann, that the little girl was a "healthy, normal, intelligent child." Dr. B. W. Sollod, of 2900 Dunran

Road, said that Judith Ann "was in good health. She was awaiting a little tonsillar surgery, but only for a little residual tissue."

Roberts, a resident of this city, is now awaiting trial in Florida on a charge of kidnaping and slaying his daughter on a family trip to Miami last July. He made the statement to answer rumors that his act was a "mercy killing."

Dr. Sollod made his statement to reporters when told that Roberts had said that he, Dr. Sollod, would verify the fact that Judith Ann was normal and healthy. Dr. Sollod has been the Roberts family physician for many years.

—Station WTLU

Style—The considerations to be noted concerning style are all part of a major point already stressed—the newscast is for listeners, not readers. Consequently, the newscast must depend on short, clear sentences; it must have an easy flowing style; and everything must blend smoothly into a whole that is often termed "the news picture of the moment." Because of these considerations, the writer of the newscast often uses standard transitional phrases such as "From the Nation's capital comes . . .", "In the world of show business today . . .", "On the labor front . . ." These transitional phrases serve the double purpose of blending one item into the next and creating a pattern for the listener. This pattern, incidentally, has been found to be exceedingly important. The listener, it seems, is pleased by the grouping effected; he prefers it to the jumbled arrangement of the unorganized newscast.

Also to be recognized is the frequency of expressions found in spoken rather than in written language. The device of asking a question in a conversational tone, for example, is often quite effective. ("What is the feeling of the plain people, you and me, about this question? Here's the answer.") Other oral language expressions, such as the colloquialism, may also

308

be used within limits. Thus, such expressions as "put up with," "gag (practical joke)," and "odds-on favorite" can be used when certainty of comprehension is present.

Examine the following newscast, noting especially the stylistic devices employed:

BRUNHILDA---THE HEROINE OF WAGNER'S FAMED OPERA "SIEG-FRIED"---PROBABLY NEVER THOUGHT SHE'D END UP IN WASHINGTON'S SMITHSONIAN INSTITUTION.   BUT THERE SHE IS---THE STAR OF THE SMITHSONIAN'S NEW HALL OF HEALTH SCHEDULED TO OPEN NEXT SUN-DAY.

BRUNHILDA---A LIFE-SIZE "PLEXIGLAS" MODEL GIVEN HER NAME UNOFFICIALLY BY MUSEUM WORKERS---IS TRANSPARENT. SHE IS A ONE-GIRL LESSON IN ANATOMY---WITH ORGANS THAT LIGHT UP AND VEINS THAT GLOW IN THE DARK.   THE MODEL IS ONE OF THE MOST COMPLICATED OF ITS KIND IN THE WORLD.   ONE BY ONE ... 25 OF HER ORGANS LIGHT UP ... AND A VOICE DESCRIBES THEM TO MUSIC.

—United Press Newscast

Vocabulary—As the writer of the straight newscast prepares his material, he finds that a knowledge of the qualities of vocabulary already discussed is sufficient for his purpose. However, as he turns to the specialized newscast (sports, theater, etc.), he must also possess the ability to use the appropriate terminology precisely and authoritatively. This ability is necessary in order to gain the all-important attribute—note of authority.

To understand this point, one need only consider any of

309

the specialized newscasts. Suppose, for example, that the writer of the sportscast were to make errors in the nomenclature of baseball, or that the writer of the women's program were to confuse the terminology of cooking, sewing, or any other such activity. There is no need to detail the fate of any such program!

Objectivity—Throughout all newscast writing, the keynote must be objectivity. Stories must be written with a detachment that clearly demonstrates impartiality, thus making the newscast usable without hesitation by any major station in the land. For this reason, coloring, slanting, or any other device that leans toward the biased or the partial must be removed. Radio and television stations, unlike the newspaper, rarely take a stand on political questions or controversial issues. True, the local station is likely to favor the activities of its area (e.g., playing up farm quotations in a rural area), but essentially the station is calm and impartial.

To see the basic impartiality of most newscasting, one need only examine the news given by an impartial newscaster, followed by that of one sponsored by a special agency or group (e.g., a labor union, a political party). The differences in arrangement of fact, vocabulary, and inclusion of detail often make the story barely recognizable.

The two types of stories demanding the most care in insuring objectivity are crime and politics. Crime stories present difficulty because of the writer's natural tendency to score wrongdoing and to dramatize. A kidnaping story, for example, occasions a strong tendency to express resentment and to overpaint the picture. Politics presents a problem because the news writer, like most others, often has a settled opinion that approaches the passion of the crusader. Therefore, he is certain to reflect his bias unless he is exceptionally careful.

Determining Audience Demands

A knowledge of radio and television audience demands is necessary for the simple reason that stations, like other businesses, must recognize the likes and the dislikes of their customers. Therefore, the stations must know the programs that attract and the programs that lose listeners.

Although analyzing listener demands is an enigmatic problem, some strong influences are discernible. They are (1) sex of probable audience, (2) age of probable audience, and (3) background of probable audience.

Sex of probable audience is important because men and women often display sharply different interests. Consequently, program offerings must be arranged accordingly. Newscasts, for example, are more likely to be composed of straight news and sports in the early morning and evening because of the probability of many men listeners. Women's news (fashions, shopping tips, etc.) are best suited to mid-morning and afternoon because of the probability of many women listeners. Thus, sex is a distinct influence.

Age of probable audience is important because many programs are pointed toward children, teen-agers, young adults, or other such groups. The child's program, for example, is broadcast in the late afternoon, early evening, or on Saturday morning because those are the times children are most likely to be listening. Age of probable audience usually can be determined easily by the process of elimination; e.g., children cannot be reached in the morning because they are in school, elderly persons seldom listen after 10 o'clock in the evening.

Background of probable audience is the most difficult of the influences to evaluate. It is difficult because it involves an attempt to "weigh and consider" such baffling conditions as educational background, religious affiliation, national origin, and common interests. Naturally, such facts as these are not easily appraised, and consequently most stations are forced to rely on conjecture.

A further difficulty encountered in learning listener demands arises with the off-day and the off-hour cross-section. What, for example, is the nature of the Saturday and the holiday audience? What is the nature and the extent of the audience that listens in cars, restaurants, and waiting rooms? Does this audience remain numerically consistent from day to day, or does it fluctuate sharply? If the answers to these questions were available, they would be helpful indeed.

The program director should always check two sources in ascertaining listener demands. First, he should check the programs of competing stations, because they reflect the opinions of someone faced with the same problem. If the competing station has been at all successful, he can be certain of sound judgment in choosing programs. Second, he should check the scientific studies made by professional organizations which usually are discussed in the trade magazines. Most stations, however, prefer a third procedure. They prefer to make their own analyses of listener interest in their area, followed by a trial-and-error process. Programs which they find successful they retain. Those which do not draw are dropped. The success of a station over the years, they believe, is possible only if the station develops a thorough knowledge of its area and its listeners.

SPECIALIZED NEWSCASTS

In addition to the facts concerning the general newscast, there are specific points pertaining to the special types of newscasts. Besides the general newscasts, most stations usually have programs concerning women's news, sports, and special activities.

Women's news programs most often concern home activities, shopping tips, fashions, and stories of well-known women. Although the wire services provide some women's newscasts, stations sometimes have to gather additional material to fit the local situation. When such is true, the most important caution is to recognize the woman's viewpoint. Consequently, stations often employ a woman to gather, prepare, and deliver the material. A second important consideration is that of novelty. Like devotees of most fields, the woman is a specialist in fashions, foods, and other items concerning the home and her sex in general, and so she does not want to hear facts she already knows—she wants something new and interesting. Hence, the writer must strive to meet her demands.

The newscast of sports, more often termed a "sportscast," must be as specialized for the men as the women's newscast is for its audience. The sports devotee is a species unto himself. He demands accuracy, an enthusiastic but impartial treatment, and an extensive knowledge of all kinds of background information. Throughout all, he demands news that is recent, pertinent, and factual—the kind of news that will give him background material for discussion and argument with other sports enthusiasts.

DIFFERENCES BETWEEN RADIO AND TELEVISION NEWSCASTS

Except for two basic differences, writing for the radio and the television newscast are essentially the same. The first difference is the obvious fact that the radio newscaster is unseen while the television newscaster is on view. The second difference is that the radio newscaster is held to the spoken word while the television newscaster often uses films and other devices.

The fact that the television newscaster is on view makes some changes in his written material. Unlike the radio newscaster, he cannot simply sit back and read. Instead, he must bring something of the lecturer and something of the actor to his performance. He must point, gesture, smile, and be generally appealing to his public. The script, therefore, must contain appropriate instructions for physical action. The fact that the television newscaster uses films and other aids divides his script into two kinds of writing—"on-camera" and "off-camera" writing. On-camera writing is that which is read while the speaker is on view; off-camera writing is that which serves as a running commentary for the material (films, objects, etc.) on view.

Because the television newscaster has a more involved performance, he must plan his program as an actor rehearses. The radio newscaster, of course, need only be certain that he is going to read correctly and appealingly.

THE COMMERCIAL

The inevitable supplement of the radio and the television program is the commercial. Although most Americans now accept the commercial as inevitable, the most casual of listeners recognizes differences in commercials and may even attempt to classify them. Some he considers completely offensive; some he views as tolerable; and some he seems to like. Obviously, the writer of the commercial should strive to create the last type. Because the commercial enjoys the all-powerful position of being both the most common and the most necessary type of writing for radio and television, special consideration should be given it. Let us, therefore, first consider the ways in which commercials offend. Then let us consider the writing of the effective commercial.

The first way in which commercials may offend is through *poor choice of language*. Many words, as can easily be seen, are in themselves offensive. Notice the repugnant quality of the following excerpts from the broadcasts of a representative day: "This cream is good for pimples and blackheads." . . . "Does your stomach feel queasy and uncertain?" . . . "Guard against bad breath!" . . . "Be careful of those ugly layers of fat." Whatever the reason for using such expressions may be, the fact stands that they are clearly unpleasant.

The second way in which commercials offend is by *insulting the intelligence of the listener*. The emotion-charged commercial telling the listener that he "owes it to his theater-going soul to see the most stupendous, the most colossal, the greatest motion picture of all time" impresses only the most naive. The commercial informing the listener that a furniture store is selling its entire stock at "a fraction of its wholesale cost to make room for new merchandise" does not deceive many persons. The commercial that contends that such-and-such a car is "the greatest value, dollar for dollar, the industry has ever known" falls, for the most part, on deaf ears. These and similar commercials lose their effectiveness for many listeners before the announcer has read half the message.

The third way in which commercials offend is by an *excessively intimate delivery*. The announcer coos personal questions at his listeners in a disgustingly oily voice. He asks them, for example, "How long has it been since you felt *truly* glamorous?" . . . "Do you really want to impress your guests, or are you fooling yourself?" . . . "Are you satisfied when you take a good look in the mirror?" He then proceeds to explain the remedy for the horrible condition described. Although one's first thought is to condemn the announcer for this type of commercial, one should score the writer instead. He, actually, is the one guilty of the offense.

As one thinks of these reasons for the offensive commercial, an interesting truism is worth noting: the more widely accepted the product, the less likely is the commercial to be offensive! The best known brands of merchandise—the products that sell well year in and year out—usually have dignified commercials. Conversely, the less well known and frequently inferior brands—the products that have limited sales—often rely on a sensational, emotional commercial. This truism also holds for the advertising of department stores, markets, and other commercial establishments.

THE EFFECTIVE COMMERCIAL

Certainly the first step in writing the effective commercial is to learn to avoid the offensive qualities already treated. The next step is then to recognize the attributes of the good commercial. A discussion of these attributes follows.

First, the effective commercial must be *characterized by brevity*. Because of the detail necessary, commercials generally average 60 seconds. However, the listener cannot be held this long unless the commercial is written and presented attractively. The push-button dial—especially on car radios, for example—is used extensively to avoid commercials. To create an atmosphere of brevity, the writer should observe two guiding principles: (1) He should not let the commercial give a pre-indication of great length. Such sentences as the following should never be used: "I want to speak to you for a few minutes about a brand-new product." . . . "Let me give you five good reasons why you will want to try this wonderfully revolutionary drug." . . . "I should like to trace out for you the steps our bakery follows from the time it receives the flour used in our fine bread until the bread is ready for delivery to your favorite store." (2) The commercial should not have the structure of the short story, nor should it possess any other device that reveals structure. The reason is that the listener, detecting a structural pattern, tires before the commercial is finished, and thus he is lost, even though he may not turn the dial. He simply ignores the rest of the message or he braces himself for the ordeal. An important guide is to make every sentence sound like the last one. Note for instance, how the following commercials present and emphasize all detail, meanwhile making every sentence sound like the last.

What does a bride need for her wedding day? Aside from the groom, of course. Something old . . . something new . . . something borrowed . . . and something blue. Yes, and something a little more practical—in the way of money saved up in the bank for all the extras that help make it a day to remember. A *P-S-F-S Bride's Account*—a saving account specially designed for June Brides, December Brides, next year's brides, and enterprising ladies-in-waiting. This special P-S-F-S Bride's Account helps you keep *one* goal in sight . . . and that makes it easier to save regularly. You're likely to put money in, and less likely to take it out for trifles. Yet you have regular deposit and withdrawal privileges, and your interest rate is three percent. The Bride's Account is one of ten P-S-F-S Convenience Accounts designed to make your saving easier. Stop in at P-S-F-S, the Bank of Convenience, and open your account . . . or accounts. Or just call Miss Henry at P-S-F-S . . . Walnut 5-5800.

—by *Gray & Rogers* for WCAU

Beautiful flowers are our faithful friends. When you're in doubt about a gift, you can be sure that flowers from Joy's are appropriate . . . and when you can't find the right words to express

317

yourself, flowers from Joy's say them for you. In fact, flowers express your love, sympathy, appreciation, and all sentiments. One of the most appropriate ways to say it with flowers is the saddest of all times . . . when death takes one of your friends or relatives. So, too, flowers are sent to greet newborn babies and congratulate their mothers. They share in our happiness through the years . . . and they give us hope and inspiration when we're ill or sad. Yes, like rays of sunshine, flowers make our happy days happier and our sad moments lighter. So, when you're in doubt about a gift . . . say it with flowers from Joy's at 23rd and West End . . . or Joy's at 229 6th Avenue, North.

—Station WLAC, Nashville, Tenn.

Second, the effective commercial must *emphasize detail* soundly. The name, price, character, and other important data of every commercial should be stressed as pleasingly as possible. To gain this emphasis, the writer should aim for easy reading and pleasing repetition of important facts. Note the repetition in the following commercial:

HOWARD MOTORS does it again! HOWARD MOTORS has just made the most tremendous automobile deal in their entire history. Because the new car SELL-A-THON was such a big success last month, HOWARD MOTORS has arranged to take over the entire remaining factory output on brand-new 1957 DeSotos and Plymouths! Now—in September—at a time of the year when other dealers have had their supply of new cars reduced, HOWARD MOTORS has completely replenished their inventory! That means—no waiting. It means *immediate* delivery on *any* brand-new 1957 Plymouth or DeSoto in the entire line. *And*—because HOWARD MOTORS *did* take over the entire remaining factory output of new cars, we can sell them at the same low prices which were featured during the August SELL-A-THON! Stop in and see for yourself—tonite until 10—all day tomorrow, Saturday, or all day Sunday from 9 a.m. until 10 p.m.

—at air-conditioned HOWARD MOTORS, at 5711 S. Western Avenue!

—Station WGN

Third, the effective commercial must *reflect care in the use of the ad-lib*. The fully ad-libbed commercial is questionable because few persons can be both brief and extemporaneous; the written commercial with interpolated ad-libs is questionable because it creates an impression of undue length. The ad-lib is also to be questioned because it frequently smacks of insincerity or its attempted humor falls flat.

Fourth, the effective commercial must be *characterized by originality*. Something about it must make it different from the many other commercials which the listener hears in the course of a normal day. Therefore, vocabulary, stylistic approach, or other qualities that create originality should be developed. Originality is clearly a difficult attribute to gain with many routine products and businesses. Yet, many writers display genuine originality, as an examination of the programs of the best stations reveals.

Fifth, effective commercials are based on a *knowledge* of several minor considerations.

1. If an inconsistency exists between sound and spelling, the name should be pronounced slowly and spelled, as in the following: "Remember the name, Loesser. Spelled L-O-E-S-S-E-R."
2. Words demanding special care in pronunciation should be underlined for the announcer.
3. Unconventional punctuation is often preferable to the accepted practice. Note the following: "Harrison's—that's it—the name you must remember. That is—if you want to take advantage of a real bargain."

319

4. The commercial should be clearly recognizable as such. It should not be "sneaked in" as a bona fide news item or presented in any other such objectionable manner.

5. Inside commercials (commercials within a unit program) should be avoided or kept to an absolute minimum. They annoy listeners as do few other devices.

6. The writer of the commercial must be careful of the use of old jokes and gag lines. These attempts at humor invariably are met with a derision that weakens the message of the commercial.

7. The commercial should not put the announcer "on the spot." It should not expect him to endorse the product personally; it should not be cast in the first person without his consent; and it should not be embarrassing for him to read.

8. The writer of the commercial should not expect the announcer to be a finished actor. Therefore, he should be wary of the commercial that demands histrionic ability. Change of voice, difficult dialects, and emotional reactions (laughing, crying, etc.) must be used with the utmost caution.

9. The writer, whenever possible, should compose his commercial with a particular announcer in mind. The male announcer holding forth on cosmetics, for example, is often incongruous enough to be ineffective, unless the commercial is written impersonally. Then, too, specific announcers often have individual talents which can be capitalized upon.

10. The writer must beware of statistics and highly specialized data which, however important, tend to becloud the commercial for the "average" listener.

PROGRAM CONTINUITIES

The program continuity, as the name implies, is the running dialogue for shows. Music programs, for instance, need introductions, observations, and other writing to carry them along. The writer, therefore, assembles the material needed in the form of a continuity. Consequently, the continuity is actually a collection of several types of writing. Most often it contains an introduction for the program itself, introductions for specific phases of the program, commercials, observations, occasional jokes or other forms of humor, and a sign-off announcement.

The following are typical program continuities:

10 Mary
2 Coughlin

LAWRENCE WELK
DATE: SATURDAY, SEPTEMBER 28, 1957
TIME: 8:05–8:30 P.M.

THEME: BUBBLES IN THE WINE, FIRST 8 SEC. APPROX., FADE UNDER AFTER THE "POP"

WELK: (RECORDED OPENING) (0-103-1) (:11)

THEME: (THEME UP) (AFTER WELK'S GREETINGS) (A FEW BARS & FADE OUT)

ANNCR: Good evening, your host is ———. Our programs to follow feature notable singing and dancing music starring Lawrence Welk and Guy Lombardo! Two more fine bands beautifully styled, offering—on recording, of course—their own distinctive patterns of orchestral melody and romantic song.

321

THEME:	(TO FITTING EMPHASIS AND OUT)
ANNCR:	Pete Fountain on clarinet takes a first Lawrence Welk tempo for a cheerful Saturday promenade around our record sound track! Fact is, tonight's whole program is shared between the Messers Welk and Fountain. So, it's Pete and his clarinet and "Sweethearts on Parade."
MUSIC:	(SWEETHEARTS ON PARADE)
ANNCR:	Lawrence Welk, now! The maestro shoulders his accordion to sketch a couple of portraits in tone color. Feminine subjects, they are. Names are "Diane" and "Charmaine."
MUSIC:	(DIANE — CHARMAINE)
ANNCR:	Pete Fountain, again! This time Pete deals with a problem that's troubled every son of Adam since the Old Gentleman met Miss Eve. Pete puts it in the form of a musical question.
MUSIC:	(SHOULD I)
ANNCR:	Again Lawrence Welk! This time a kind of folksy flavor! Coming off the accordion keyboard two Welk favorites:
MUSIC:	(ONE ROSE — YOU'RE THE ONLY STAR)
ANNCR:	From "Connecticut Yankee," Pete Fountain takes a wistful little ballad for clarinet treatment. Remember "Thou Swell"?
MUSIC:	(THOU SWELL)
ANNCR:	Folks, you are listening to a Lawrence Welk recital; top pop music by the top pop band the country over . . . the maestro this evening sharing the solo spotlight with Pete Fountain and his clarinet. This very instant it's Lawrence Welk on accordion, of course! And on the lead sheet: "Little Sir Echo," followed by "It's a Sin to Tell a Lie."

MUSIC: (LITTLE SIR ECHO — IT'S A SIN TO TELL A LIE)

ANNCR: Lawrence Welk and his champagne music! Here's the swirl and sparkle of "Bubbles in the Wine." One-ah-Two-ah, Lawrence-ah-Welk-ah. . . .

MUSIC: (BUBBLES IN THE WINE)

ANNCR: Ah well, two ballads of true love next, after a round of champagne music. Again the Welk accordion. And the wholesome sentiments set to melody are "Tenderly" and "When Your Hair Has Turned to Silver."

MUSIC: (TENDERLY — WHEN YOUR HAIR HAS TURNED TO SILVER)

ANNCR: Bringing an accordion and clarinet recital to a close, Lawrence Welk recalls an old-time rollicking dance measure. Everybody join in and let the rafters ring to "The Beer Barrel Polka."

MUSIC: (BEER BARREL POLKA)

MUSIC: THEME: PICK UP ON MELODY AFTER "POP" AS IN OPENING TO TIME AND FADE FOR:

WELK: (0-103-15) (:12)

MUSIC: VERY BRIEFLY FOR CLOSE

ANNCR: Thank you, Lawrence Welk. Friends, you're more than welcome to be with us one week from tonight for another transcribed program of champagne music. (MUSIC OUT) Stay tuned now, for a third program of mood and melody by Guy Lombardo from Lombardoland! Remember Wayne King, Lawrence Welk and Guy Lombardo together with a lot more of the best there is, are regularly heard on WGN-Radio, the *Chicago Tribune* station, etc. . . . . .

323

6 Lucy
2 Fran

> LOMBARDOLAND
> DATE: SATURDAY, SEPTEMBER 28, 1957
> TIME: 8:30 P.M.

THEME: AULD LANG SYNE . . . . . ESTAB AND UNDER BRIEFLY FORE

ANNCR: Should Auld Acquaintance be forgot . . . .

MUSIC: THEME: HOLD AND UNDER FOR:

> The Guy Lombardo theme . . . the Guy Lombardo gifts of music and of song bid us welcome, indeed, to a final half hour of melody and romance from Lombardoland. Guy Lombardo! His transcribed theme and treatment re-creating many an unforgettable Auld Lang Syne.

THEME: FULL AND TO CLOSE

ANNCR: A little while back we heard the Pete Fountain clarinet version of "Sweethearts on Parade" as the Lawrence Welk overture . . . let's hear the same tune, same sentiments, now, in the Lombardoland style, Kenny Gardner voicing the lyric by Charles Newman to the music written by Carmen Lombardo. Shall we join—"Sweethearts on Parade." Kenny Gardner . . . .

MUSIC: (SWEETHEARTS ON PARADE)

ANNCR: Tony Craig and the Chorus team up in a sometime motion picture tune by Ira Gershwin and Jerry Kern. The date of publication, 1944. The film was called "COVER GIRL." Yet, the lovely melody comes down the years as appealing as ever: "Long Ago and Far Away."

MUSIC: (LONG AGO AND FAR AWAY)

324

ANNCR: Bill Flanagan next with the Lombardo Trio, a song and story to touch the heart: "EVERYWHERE YOU GO."

MUSIC: (EVERYWHERE YOU GO)

ANNCR: Once more Kenny Gardner! Seems hardly possible this radiant ballad goes back to 1929 . . . But it does! It's the Hoagy Carmichael classic, the one and only "Star Dust." Kenny . . . . . .

MUSIC: (STAR DUST)

ANNCR: Ladies and gentlemen, for a recital of the sweetest music this side of heaven, you are present at a recorded concert in the Royal Canadian manner by Guy Lombardo from Lombardoland. Kenny Gardner carries on, now. Kenny now singing the charming "Coquette."

MUSIC: (COQUETTE)

ANNCR: Bill Flanagan, next —— contagious mood and graceful melody! Bill singing the enchanting story of "La Vie en Rose."

MUSIC: (LA VIE EN ROSE)

ANNCR: Kenny Gardner and the Trio return with cheerful view of life and love. The idea persuasively styled and sung is "Enjoy Yourself."

MUSIC: (ENJOY YOURSELF)

ANNCR: Once more Kenny Gardner. Words and music by Larry Hart and Richard Rodgers! The ballad dates from 1937. And a mildly philosophical inquiry finds expression in "Where or When."

MUSIC: (WHERE OR WHEN)

ANNCR: The Lombardo Quartet offers a reading in three-quarter time! Tune and title, "The Blue Skirt Waltz."

MUSIC: (THE BLUE SKIRT WALTZ)

ANNCR: Bringing a recital of mood and melody to a close, Guy Lombardo himself conducting, the Royal Canadians take leave of us to the measures of Provost's graceful "Intermezzo."

MUSIC: (PROVOST'S INTERMEZZO)

MUSIC: THEME

ANNCR: Guy Lombardo, his soloists, and his ensemble have been our Royal Canadian hosts during a third half-hour of melody and romance presented as a transcribed visit to Lombardoland. Remember to hear Wayne King, Lawrence Welk and Guy Lombardo— all three—these Saturday evenings.

MUSIC THEME TO TIME

ANNCR: —— speaking. Remember, also, this is WGN-Radio, the *Chicago Tribune* station.

THE COMMENTARY

A type of radio and television program that can be highly successful in careful, talented hands is the commentary. The commentary, as the name implies, is a series of observations on a given subject. Although the most popular commentary is that which treats the day's news, many other fields are also covered. Sports, the theater, women's fashions, local feature stories, and a host of other material are the bases for successful commentaries.

The commentary can best be understood by thinking of the commentator as a newspaper columnist broadcasting his material. In fact, many commentators have used the expression "columnist of the air" to name their programs. The role of the commentator is to observe, to interpret, to provide background information, and hence to inform. He is expected to examine his subject authoritatively and tell his listener in

326

a pleasant, unassuming, yet capable manner facts that the listener does not know.

TONE

Aside from respecting the general considerations of writing for radio and television, the writer must exercise care as he decides on the tone of his program. Tone is important because the appeal of the commentary, like the appeal of the newspaper column, is essentially that of a personality. The listener must react favorably to the commentator; or, to state the matter negatively, he must not be repelled by an atmosphere of conceit, condescension, or other offensive quality. As a result, the writer of the commentary must constantly be on guard to create a pleasing tone, one that will attract and hold listeners.

The tone of the commentary, however, naturally varies with the type of material. The commentary on the news, for example, must be dignified and generally serious; the commentary on popular music may be light, even breezy. The commentary on the week's religious news must reflect scientific impartiality; the commentary on the theater may be heavily flavored with personal opinion. The commentary on the world situation must treat up-to-the-minute facts; the commentary on sports can reminisce about events months or years old.

WRITING THE COMMENTARY

Despite differences of subject and tone in commentaries, certain fundamental points are common to all types. A discussion of these points follows.

First, the writer *must always remember the power of his*

medium of expression. Radio and television, like the newspaper, carry tremendous force in influencing public opinion, for many listeners accept without question the statements made. Consequently, the writer of the commentary must realize the impact his material is likely to make and proceed accordingly. Hence, his keynote is responsibility.

Second, the writer *must clearly separate fact from conjecture and opinion.* His writing must leave no doubt in the mind of the listener concerning the line between established and nonestablished fact. Even though the station and the sponsor may protect themselves by such statements as "the opinions of the commentator are his own," the writer should not feel free to offer non-fact as fact. The writer must be especially careful of such statements as "Public opinion is clearly in favor of this proposal" and "There can be no doubt as to the outcome of this issue." Such statements are often easy to make but without basis in fact. Therefore, the writer is, in effect, submitting opinion as fact.

Third, *accuracy must be all-prevailing.* As is the case with the newspaper reporter, the writer must check and recheck his facts. Although statements from the wire services are nearly always accurate, facts from other sources frequently are not. Because imparting inaccuracies is one of the fastest ways to lose prestige, the writer must be extremely careful. He must never relax his vigilance, or mistakes in facts are certain to result.

Fourth, the writer *must not let himself sound like the Oracle at Delphi.* Although he is expected to be authoritative, he must not issue his material as final, unquestioned pronouncements; and he must not let his writing develop a patronizing or condescending ring. Some little devices can be recognized immediately as objectionable. For example, easily seen are the objectionable aspects of the overuse of the first person pronoun; of an excessive overemphasis on personal experience; and of a too obvious attempt to aggrandize one's role in life or as a commentator. Essentially, the writer gains a note of authority without being overbearing by striving throughout for a semblance of humility.

Fifth, the writer *must not let his commentaries become narrow or one-sided*. The writer of the commentary, like most persons, has favorite subjects which reflect his interests. Unless he is careful, these subjects are likely to dominate his program to the exclusion of equally important ones. Therefore, he must attempt to treat every aspect of his subject, to give both sides of every controversial question, and to reflect a general atmosphere of breadth. Prejudice, slanting, and coloring are conditions to be shunned.

SUSTAINING ANNOUNCEMENTS

A type of writing that closely resembles the commercial is the sustaining announcement. This writing covers the announcement made as a public service, the announcement to advertise one of the station's programs, and the announcement made in the public interest.

The announcement made as a public service includes a wide field. Such announcements include "plugs" for the sale of defense bonds, charity drives, clean-up campaigns, medical research, and similar causes. The organizations behind these drives generally have their own publicity staffs who supply releases with instructions for timing and delivery. The station, however, often elects to re-cast the release, and in such instances a writer is so instructed. Also, the writer may have to compose the sustaining announcement to conform to the editorial policy of the station or because he has been given only the basic facts. In such instances, the writer proceeds as if he were writing a commercial.

The announcement to advertise a program is often a short

329

statement between programs. For established programs, it usually consists of a brief announcement such as "Start the day right by listening to . . . . on the Breakfast Hour, every weekday morning beginning at seven o'clock over this station." For new programs, it usually contains some kind of "come on" element.

The announcement made in the public interest is generally prompted by some condition of the moment. Examples cover the following situations: urging citizens to vote—reminding listeners of the deadline for tax returns—urging cautions for driving—stressing accident prevention in the home—reminding listeners of the advent of daylight saving time. This type of announcement is always brief, with an attempt at a slogan or emphasis of a striking fact. Here is a typical announcement: "Voting is a privilege and a duty in a democracy. Exercise your privilege and do your duty!"

MISCELLANEOUS WRITING

Writing for radio and television involves several other types not readily classifiable. One of the most common of such types is the **station-break announcement.**

The station-break announcement may be a simple statement to identify the station, a slogan to advertise the station, or a commercial. The simple announcement to identify the station usually follows this pattern: "This is station WOR, New York." . . . "You are listening to station KYW, Cleveland." . . . "This is station WXZ in the Nation's Capital."

The slogan to advertise the station generally follows this pattern: "This is station WFIL, where the news watch never stops." . . . "You are tuned to station KDKA, where you get news every hour on the hour." . . . "This is station WRVA, the station with programs for all the family."

The station-break announcement used as a commercial follows this pattern: "Station WLMA, where Kahn's, the home of good used cars, brings you the day's news every evening at six." . . . "This is station WTBC, through whose facilities you can hear the Wiley music hour tonight at 9 o'clock." . . . "You are listening to station WBAL, which will broadcast the Burns-Tulsa game tomorrow afternoon at 2 o'clock."

The requirements for the writing of the station-break announcement are clearly apparent. The writer must have a well-developed sense of originality to gain the novelty needed; he must be able to write a clear, crisp sentence; and he must be able to vary the language to suit the message.

Another type of miscellaneous writing is the **announcement and blend-out for the program** staged by an outside agency. If, for example, a church, a civic organization, or a college group is to present a program, the station naturally supplies the announcer to introduce and sign off the program. He, of course, needs prepared material. Here is a typical announcement, followed by the close-out and transitional sentences: "At this time, station WCOJ presents the Choir of the West Chester State Teachers College in a 15-minute program of Christmas carols. The Choir will sing 'O Little Town of Bethlehem,' 'O Holy Night,' 'Silent Night,' and the 'Hallelujah Chorus.' The Choir will perform under the direction of Dr. Arthur E. Jones, Professor of Music. We take you now to the Phillips Memorial Auditorium on the college campus." . . .

"You have been listening to a 15-minute program of Christmas carols, sung for you by the Choir of the West Chester State Teachers College, under the direction of Dr. Arthur E. Jones. The program came to you from the Phillips Memorial Auditorium on the college campus. We take you now to our studios in Coatesville."

331

This program differs from the ordinary continuity in that the station merely broadcasts the program. It presents the program without interruption from the station, thus placing the outside agency or group "on its own" from the time it is given the air until the station retakes the air.

A third type of miscellaneous writing is the **extemporaneous remark**—which obviously is not "extemporaneous." The extemporaneous remark covers such situations as the casual remark of the disc jockey in mid-program that the next record reminds him to complete his Christmas shopping; the observation that summer is drawing closer; the little humorous story; and the reminiscence. The extemporaneous writing is often done by the announcer who uses it, but such is not necessarily the case. Examples of effective extemporaneous remarks are usually found in the network broadcasts where professional gag writers are employed. However, regardless of how small a station may be, someone should prepare extemporaneous remarks, for they are an essential of many programs. They should always be done well in advance, one should note, for when the announcer is permitted to ad-lib, the program often becomes dull.

EXERCISES

1. Select five offensive commercials from your radio listening of the past week and rewrite the commercials to make them both acceptable and effective.
2. Write a continuity for a 15-minute program of popular music.
3. Compose sustaining announcements for any five worthy causes.
4. Write five good station-break announcements.
5. Compose a three-minute off-camera writing to describe a film of a raging department store fire.

6. Write a commentary for the popular music "hit parade" of the past month.
7. Write a newscast for a 10-minute program of local news.
8. Write a commercial for a sale at a local men's clothing store.
9. Evaluate any five sustaining announcements currently used by the major network stations.
10. Write the announcement and the blend-out for a church service.
11. From the sports page of a large metropolitan daily, prepare a five-minute sportcast.
12. Evaluate any three commentaries on news currently broadcast on national hook-ups.
13. Write a commercial for a local restaurant that wants only a "selected clientele."
14. Examine the front-page stories of your local newspaper and choose the stories you would use on a large metropolitan television newscast.
15. Compose a station announcement for a "wake-up" program that is to be aired every morning from six until nine, beginning next week.

Writing for Magazines

A field which attracts many writers, both amateur and professional, is the magazine. The remuneration, the personal satisfaction, and the opportunity for fame lure many to attempt all types of magazine writing, even though the probability of success is frequently small. To understand the field, a grasp of certain basic facts is helpful.

As a starting point, one should note that the expression "magazine" covers a wide area. Actually, the term is so broad that it cannot be defined precisely. There are presently in the United States over 7,000 publications classified as "magazines," but the label designating them is their only similarity.

334

At the one extreme are the excellently done publications such as *Fortune*, containing a collection of high-quality short stories, essays, poems, and illustrative material. At the other extreme are the so-called "pulps," which are usually collections of love stories, westerns, and other thrillers, printed on the cheapest of paper. At the one extreme is the publication leveled at a wide audience—the family magazine, the popular weekly, the Sunday supplement. At the other extreme is the publication leveled at a narrow audience—the professional magazine, the trade journal, the union magazine. At the one extreme is the publication resembling a well-printed book in every detail except for the cover. At the other extreme is the "magazine" such as the Sunday supplement which is nothing more than a section of the newspaper. Between the extremes cited lies every conceivable variation. Therefore, a collection of "magazines" can be a strange assortment, indeed.

A second point to be noted is that the writing found in magazines is as varied as are the publications themselves. Some magazines reflect a highly formal approach with a definitely finished quality of writing. Such a publication is the university quarterly which carries detail-laden articles cast in the heavy, ponderous style of the scholar. Other magazines have an informal approach with a light, bouncy style. Such a magazine is the popular weekly. Some magazines, such as the trade journal, are cast in a specific technical language; others, such as the supermarket magazine, use the language of the newspaper. Some magazines restrict language to conservative usage; others permit colloquialisms, slang, and even vulgar expressions. Thus, in each instance one can see a different pattern of writing.

A third point is that some magazines carry only articles by their staff members. These publications are the province of an editor with a full-time staff. He assigns articles, edits copy, and acts as general director. Such a publication is the "company" magazine—the publication maintained by an industrial or business organization for its employees. Other magazines, however, carry articles written entirely by outside writers for varying fees. Such a publication is the *Atlantic Monthly*. Also, there are the magazines which carry articles by both their own staff and outside writers. Such a publication is the popular weekly.

A fourth point is that writing for magazines is generally a part-time enterprise. Although many magazines employ full-time writers, the majority of writing comes from persons actively engaged in other fields. Among the most common authors are: the authority in a given field (e.g., medicine, law, education) who explains an important or complex point in his field; the newspaperman who does an extensive feature story (e.g., crime in Chicago, an interesting housing development in New York, a political problem in San Francisco); the free-lance writer who does an article of general interest; the individual who recounts an interesting personal experience.

Because writing for magazines is generally a part-time activity, the opportunity for aspiring writers is fairly extensive. They can be relatively certain that, if their material merits publication, they can achieve success—*if* they can get their material into the right hands at the right time.

A fifth important point is that the magazine, like other institutions, is always in a state of change. Editorial policies shift; new trends become discernible; new magazines appear. These changes, of course, must be recognized by anyone interested in writing for magazines. Thus, one must be ever aware of the picture of the moment.

QUALITIES AFFECTING SALABILITY OF MATERIAL

Before one seriously considers writing a magazine article, he frequently asks over and over, "What qualities make a manuscript salable?" Naturally, the answer to this question largely determines one's whole attack on the task. Although no all-inclusive answer can be given, nevertheless certain basic qualities can be cited. The relative strength of these qualities, one should note, varies from one magazine to another.

The first consideration which a magazine recognizes is the *appeal* of a given article for its readers. As already stated, every magazine aims to capture a specific audience; consequently, it chooses its material accordingly. Therefore, the manuscript editor constantly asks himself as he considers material, "Would this interest the readers of our magazine?" If he thinks the material has such appeal, he then proceeds to the other considerations. If not, he rejects the manuscript immediately. The manuscript editor holds his important position because, among other reasons, he is believed to possess a sensitivity to the demands of the magazine's readers.

The second quality which affects the salability of an article is *pertinency*. An article that deals effectively with a timely topic stands a good chance of acceptance by a magazine interested in that field. An article, for example, that deals authoritatively with the benefits of and the ill effects from sunburn certainly will be considered by a health magazine for its June issue. An exhaustive treatment of winter care for boats certainly will be examined carefully by the editor of a boating magazine. Pertinency is an important consideration for the self-evident reason that readers want to read about the subjects which interest them most at the moment.

337

The third consideration is *originality*. An article that possesses an original view, new information, or some other novel quality has a definite count in its favor. A national magazine, for instance, recently carried a highly successful article on juvenile delinquency—a topic worn thin by endless treatments. The article, however, was tremendously popular because of the originality therein. The approach was new, the information was new, the treatment was new. Thus, originality was the keynote of its success.

The fourth consideration is the *identity of the author*. Obviously, some articles are certain of immediate acceptance because of the identity of the author. An article by a presidential cabinet member, for example, will certainly reach print. Similar cases are the writings of well-known authors, established figures in the entertainment world, and well-known personalities. The obscure individual suddenly caught in the spotlight is also certain to have material published. In fact, even if he does not take the initiative, he is sure to be approached. The entire consideration of "identity of the author," one should note, sometimes becomes an almost insurmountable barrier for the unknown author. As a result, many writers have a genuinely difficult struggle before attaining any success.

The fifth consideration is *effectiveness of expression*. If an article is to be published, it must be written clearly, forcefully, and correctly. Because of this consideration, manuscripts otherwise salable are often returned. The editor believes the material to be usable, but the expression is so badly wrought that using the article is impossible. In some instances, the magazine may purchase the article with the thought of editing it, but such is the case only when the material is unusually good or the expression does not need much recasting.

LITERARY FORMS IN MAGAZINE WRITING

To understand the present situation in magazine writing, one must know the principal literary forms employed. The most common forms are the short story, the essay, the personality sketch, the popularizing facts article, the utility article, and poetry. These terms, of course, are broad, and, therefore, several subdivisions exist for each. This fact is significant because many magazines are interested only in highly specialized forms within the major form. For instance, some magazines are interested only in the short expository essay rather than in essays in general. Some magazines will consider the traditional short story but not the other common forms. Other magazines emphasize the utility article at the expense of all other forms. The writer, therefore, must be aware of specialized form demands before he prepares his material.

Also to be noted is the fact that, with each form, there is an appropriate style. The traditional short story, for example, is generally cast in the "literary" style—the style that one associates with the literary masters. The utility article, on the other hand, is often cast in the style employed in the newspaper feature story. Thus, as the writer thinks of form, he should also think of style.

The following discussion treats the major literary forms and the most common subdivisions within each.

1. **The Short Story**—The short story is the form most often attempted by aspiring writers. This form is popular among writers because it is popular among readers. Manuscript editors of the quality magazines estimate that attempts at short stories outnumber all other forms by a ratio of three to one. Naturally, only a small fraction of those attempting the short story ever see their material in print.

339

What are the qualities necessary for writing the short story? The answer is that the writer must have three attributes: (1) inspiration, (2) the ability to perceive, and (3) the ability to portray. The term "inspiration" actually means desire. Unless the writer burns with the desire to compose, he can hope for little success. He must want so earnestly to write short stories that he is willing to undergo all sorts of discipline, study, and concerted effort. He must not be one who is discouraged easily. Rather, he must be prepared to practice and re-practice, to write and re-write, to strive and re-strive. His desire must be so strong that he can withstand the most barbed criticism. As for discouragement, he must remember the time-worn advice of the professional, "Don't feel discouraged about rejection slips until you have enough to paper every room in the house."

The phrase "ability to perceive" means that one must be able to recognize short story material. He must be able first to recognize the story itself, and then to recognize the subtleties, the intricacies, and the little qualities that give depth and appeal. How to develop the ability to perceive can scarcely be reduced to a set of rules—in fact, many writers and teachers of writing believe that this ability is almost completely congenital. Others, however, feel that it can be developed. In either case, there are certainly exercises that will help. The simple practice, for example, of jotting down all the observations of a given week that might be incorporated into a projected novel sharpens one's ability to perceive. So do little discussions among aspiring writers about the dominant qualities in atmospheres which they know (hometown places, football stadia, shopping crowds, etc.). The importance of the ability to perceive can be realized in an analysis of the truly great short stories, for these works invariably reflect an unusual insight into common events and experiences. The short stories, for instance, of Nathaniel Hawthorne, Charles Dickens, and Robert Louis Stevenson illustrate the importance of this ability. Note, for example, Hawthorne's ability to perceive as shown in this passage from "The Ambitious Guest":

One September night a family had gathered round their hearth, and piled it high with the driftwood of mountain streams, the dry cones of the pine, and the splintered ruins of great trees that had come crashing down the precipice. Up the chimney roared the fire, and brightened the room with its broad blaze. The faces of the father and mother had a sober gladness; the children laughed; the eldest daughter was the image of Happiness at seventeen; and the aged grandmother, who sat knitting in the warmest place, was the image of Happiness grown old. They had found the "herb, heart's-ease," in the bleakest spot of all New England. This family were situated in the Notch of the White Hills, where the wind was sharp throughout the year, and pitilessly cold in the winter—giving their cottage all its fresh inclemency before it descended on the valley of the Saco. They dwelt in a cold spot and a dangerous one; for a mountain towered above their heads, so steep that the stones would often rumble down its sides and startle them at midnight.

The ability to portray is the attribute which receives most attention in courses in short story writing. This phrase means simply the ability to find the most effective words, stylistic devices, and structural patterns for relating the story—or, in simpler words, the best way to tell the story. Once again, there can be no set of rules for developing this ability. The writer simply must learn to recognize the most effective manner of telling his story.

The initial step in developing this ability is acquiring a

sound sense of criticism of short stories in general. One must have this sense of criticism in order to pass judgment capably upon his own efforts.

One can proceed by reading a specific story and asking such questions as: What are the qualities which make this writer successful? What are the strengths and the weaknesses of this story? What makes this work unusual, routine, or whatever it may be? When one can answer these questions satisfactorily, he is on his way to developing his sense of criticism.

The next step is to work with one's sentences, paragraphs, and over-all story to obtain the most emphatic expression possible. Only when one is satisfied that his expression cannot be improved should he think of submitting his manuscript to a publisher. The ability to portray is undoubtedly the most difficult of the three attributes to develop. Consequently, many persons can say truthfully, "I could be a great writer, if I could only write!" These are the persons who genuinely want to write, who see many experiences and events to write of, but who are unable to find the words and the general expression.

Types of Short Stories

After recognizing the qualities necessary for writing the short story, the writer should know the three types of short stories for which there is the best market. They are (1) the traditional, (2) the detective, and (3) the slice of life.

The *traditional short story* is the kind most persons know. It is the story which has a structural pattern consisting of five parts—the situation, the generating circumstance, the rising action, the climax, and the denouement. Such a story is Edgar Allan Poe's "Masque of the Red Death." The situation is the

342

backdrop for the action; the generating circumstance is the action or event which starts the action rising; the rising action is the series of acts or thoughts which heighten the basic question or the suspense; the climax is the point at which the action is resolved into a single, inescapable conclusion; and the denouement is the final unraveling of the plot. The traditional has always been the most popular of the short story forms, and hence the kind most often published.

The *detective story* is characterized by what is often termed the "reversed plot" structure. It is the story wherein the author presents a highly complicated situation, which is often the denouement of the story, and then proceeds to unravel it. The detective story makes heavy demands on the writer. He must have great powers of reasoning; he must have a very logical mind; and he must have an extraordinary ability to invent. With these attributes, there must be an ability to present details with clarity and vigor. Let us consider, by way of an example, a common brand of detective story.

A man is found murdered under baffling circumstances. The author presents all the facts, and, if the story is sound, the reader is completely puzzled. The author then proceeds, as does A. Conan Doyle in his famous Sherlock Holmes stories, to heighten the situation with details that seem irrelevant or meaningless. Next he begins to weave his skein of facts together skillfully until suddenly, as the story closes, he solves this baffling murder in a manner that elicits admiration and wonder.

The author of the successful detective story must always demonstrate a clear superiority over the reader. The superiority must be based on imagination, logic, and reasoning; it can never be founded on cheap deception or withholding of facts. Hence, the sound detective story resembles the complicated puzzle to be solved only by a superior mind—one that leaves lesser minds standing by to admire or to envy.

There can be many variations of structure and plot in the detective story, and, for this reason, the writer must analyze carefully the magazine to which he plans to send his story. Some magazines, usually those catering to the masses, want only the standard puzzlers, the "whodunits." They are not interested in the more complex, more finely wrought works. Others, however, want the more delicately done type—the stories in the tradition of the literary masters. Consequently, the detective story market must be analyzed carefully. The most important statement to be made of this market, however, is that there is always a sale to be found for a good detective story. Success, therefore, often lies in finding the right magazine.

The *slice of life short story* is characterized by an absence of structural pattern. It is based on the principle that in life there are many little scenes which, in themselves, are intensely interesting. It, therefore, depicts these scenes only, without thought of beginning, ending, or other structural consideration. The slice of life author is comparable to the operator of a moving picture camera who looks at a mass of people and shoots any scene that appeals to him. He has no special interest in what has preceded or what follows; he is interested purely in the appeal of a given scene. In fact, the appeal is heightened by not knowing what has preceded or what has followed. The slice of life technique has been handled admirably by such famous writers as James Stephens, Katherine Mansfield, and Thomas Wolfe.

The specific market for the various kinds of stories can be determined only by analyzing magazines. Although the discussion on kinds of magazines presented in this chapter is helpful, the writer still can learn his market only through analysis. Therefore, many writers keep a card file of such analyses to guide them in preparing and submitting manuscripts.

2. **The Essay**—Because the essay is the most common type of article found in magazines, special consideration must be given it. The essay is either formal or informal in approach and treatment. Each type, the author soon learns, lends itself to specific materials and approaches better than the other.

The **formal essay,** as the name implies, follows a formal pattern. It is characterized by seriousness, authoritativeness, and a sharply outlined approach. Thus, the formal essay is employed to write of important topics in a serious manner. It is used, for example, by the statesman writing of the international situation, by the educator explaining the school system, and by the general writer expressing a serious viewpoint on a matter of general interest.

The formal essay follows a basic structure of three parts—introduction, body, conclusion. The *introduction,* obviously the first part, has three functions; it sets the over-all structural pattern of the essay, it establishes the atmosphere to characterize the writing, and it attempts to lure the reader to continue reading the work. Notice how the following introduction to a well-known essay [1] by Alexander Hamilton performs this function:

Assuming it as an established truth that in case of disunion the several states, or such combinations of them as might happen to be formed out of the wreck of the general confederacy, would be subject to those vicissitudes of peace and war, of friendship and enmity with each other, which have fallen to the lot of all neighboring nations not united under one government, let us enter into a concise detail of some of the consequences that would attend such a situation.

[1] *On War Between the States of the Union.*

345

Writing for Magazines

The *body* of the formal essay is the part containing the actual message. In the instance of the formal argument, it advances the reason for the stand. In the instance of the expository writing, it carries the actual explanation. In the instance of the descriptive writing, it presents the details. Thus, it is truly the "body" of the essay.

The *conclusion* serves to draw the entire writing together in the form of a summary and to leave a dominant thought with the reader. Notice, for example, the conclusion to Hamilton's essay:

This is an idea not superficial nor futile, but solid and weighty. It deserves the most serious and mature consideration of every prudent and honest man, of whatever party. If such men will make a firm and solemn pause, and meditate dispassionately on its vast importance; if they will contemplate it in all its attitudes, and trace it to all its consequences, they will not hesitate to part with trivial objections to a constitution, the rejection of which would, in all probability, put a final period to the Union. The airy phantoms that now flit before the distempered imaginations of some of its adversaries would then quickly give place to the more substantial prospects of dangers, real, certain, and extremely formidable.

The **informal essay,** in contrast to the formal, does not have a pronounced structural pattern; it is often light and humorous in tone; and it has a genuinely subjective quality about it. The informal essay lends itself especially well to casual observations, humor, and trivia. The informal essay, popular from the time of Charles Lamb, is far more demanding upon a writer's ability than is popularly supposed. It is, many persons soon learn, one of those deceptively difficult tasks to perform. Consequently, most persons have to work hard in learning to write informal essays.

346

At present, the market is strongest for the "reflective essay" —the essay which expresses a viewpoint upon a condition, an event, or a problem. The reflective essay may be formal or informal, according to the author's approach and treatment. Actually, the reflective essay is basically nothing more than the reflective newspaper column extended to magazine writing proportions.

The qualities necessary for handling the reflective essay are writing ability, note of authority, originality, and general appeal. The need for the ability to write clearly, forcefully, and correctly is clearly apparent. Certainly the essay must be written effectively if it is to be acceptable. The second quality, note of authority, is the one which is genuinely important, for the writer must demonstrate clearly that he has a sweep and a grasp of his field. The reflective article that does not reveal keen thinking coupled with wide knowledge rarely impresses many readers. There can be no errors in facts and certainly no flaws in reasoning. The third quality, originality, is important because the reader wants information that he has not met before. He wants something new, something that no other writer has given. Hence, the writer must have originality of thought and approach. The final quality, general appeal, is the most difficult to explain and to attain. It is the general charm that the essay of reminiscences possesses; it is the note of respect that the essay of the revered figure commands as it appears in print; it is the intangible quality of the appealing columnist.

Because of the necessity of the last three qualities, the writer of the reflective essay is usually someone who has demonstrated clearly his right to speak. The well-established figure in politics, professional life, journalism, or similar activities is most often the one to write the reflective essay because of his claim to authority. Consequently, the novice writer can rarely hope to sell a reflective essay unless the appeal of his work offsets his lack of reputation.

The market for the general reflective essay lies primarily in the quality magazines; the market for the specialized reflective essay (business, sports, theater, etc.) lies in magazines dealing exclusively with those particular fields. This statement, however, is no more than a generality. Because of the broad editorial policies of many magazines, reflective essays often appear where least expected. Consequently, the writer should once again analyze magazines to determine potential market.

3. The Personality Sketch—The personality sketch has always been a highly popular type of writing because of the self-evident truth that "interesting personalities are interesting." Almost any newsworthy figure is automatically a possibility for a personality sketch, and the degree of interest involved is the best index of his value as a subject.

There are several difficulties faced in writing the personality sketch, the greatest being that the best subjects have nearly always been covered. One can scarcely rise to a high position in the world of sports, politics, entertainment, or similar field without becoming the subject of an article of this kind. Consequently, the writer must gain a new approach if he is to be successful.

Another difficulty arises because most sketches demand the writer have personal contact with his subject. This situation presents a problem for the unknown writer in gaining an interview. Well-known personalities are reluctant to deal with unknown writers because there is no guarantee that the material will be printed and because there is no foreknowledge of the writer's basic integrity in presenting facts accurately and sympathetically. Why, for example, should a screen star give an interview to an unknown writer when he does not know where, if at all, the article will appear in print and with what unfavorable statements, distortions, or outright untruths?

A final difficulty to be noted is that the interviewing involved is often a genuine problem. The subject of the sketch may be excessively modest, too demanding, or otherwise "hard to handle." Aside from remembering the attributes of the successful interview discussed in Chapter 3, one can do little to remove this difficulty.

The success of the personality sketch stems from the author's ability to create an interesting three-dimensional character. The personality revealed should be one that gives the reader a new insight; an understanding of the subject not otherwise possible; a picture from another angle. Because this result is often difficult to achieve, good personality sketches are not numerous.

Finding a market for the personality sketch is difficult primarily because many magazines employ their own or established writers to do this work. *Time*, for instance, has a staff member do a personality sketch for its cover story for every issue, while *Sport* generally uses its own staff or established sports writers to do its sketches. The reason for this practice is that the basic question of accuracy of facts is answered. As can be readily understood, magazines must be careful of accuracy of facts for the same reasons—potential libel suits and loss of prestige—that newspapers must exercise care. Consequently, the best approach is to use the writers upon whom there is some check or whose accuracy has been demonstrated.

The unknown writer is most likely to sell a personality sketch in the following instances: (1) he has material that has some quality of the scoop; (2) he has found an interesting subject, usually an obscure but important personality, not yet treated; (3) his writing has a distinctly appealing quality (an insight, a charm, an attractive ring).

4. **Popularizing Facts**—A field with a high degree of potential success for writers is that of popularizing facts. To understand this statement, one need only realize that most persons are eager to learn more of subjects which appeal to them. Consequently, a writer can be successful if he submits to the right magazine a well-written article popularizing facts in an interesting field.

A cursory examination of magazines of all kinds over the past decades shows popularizing facts articles on the following: the making of golf balls, the relative cost of automobile license plates from state to state, changes in women's clothing styles, the reaction of theater-goers to certain plays, taxpayers' gripes, the conditions behind the do-it-yourself trend, women *vs*. men drivers, the origin of some common words, the meaning of common surnames, the cost of maintaining the White House, the art of glass making.

In preparing the popularizing facts article, the writer can follow a simple procedure. First, he should select an interesting but unpublicized field. He should then examine the field so thoroughly that he is something of an authority. Next he should compile the facts most likely to interest the readers of the magazine to which he will submit the article, and finally he should begin to write. Naturally, his writing must be slanted toward the particular magazine.

To illustrate the above procedure, a specific instance is helpful. Almost 20 years ago there was little knowledge and less interest concerning the flying squirrel. A graduate student at Cornell University, because of his interest in this little animal, did an exhaustive study for a Ph.D. thesis. The subject of the flying squirrel, however, lay dormant for almost 15 years, when another writer did a popular piece for the *National Geographic Magazine.* This, in turn, caused feature writers throughout the nation to write little essays on the flying squirrel for Sunday supplement magazines.

In this instance, the original writer had accomplished the task of becoming an authority and writing the material. If, however, he had wanted to sell his material to a magazine, he would have had to select the phases most likely to interest the general reader and re-cast it in a simple, easy-to-read style. The second writer and the Sunday supplement writers did this.

A common practice in unearthing popularizing facts material is to make a search of textbooks, scholarly journals, and other publications wherein some interesting subject may be treated in the manner of the specialist. Herein one often finds material that can be refined to the popular level with little effort. Thus, the writer need be nothing more than a selector and a re-writer. The caution to be exercised, however, is to be certain that the material is common property. Facts about astronomy, for example, are common property. The details of a recent experiment are not likely to be usable without specific credits. Thus, the writer must exercise care.

5. The Utility Article—The utility article, as shown in Chapter 4, explains how to develop a skill (e.g., play golf), how to perform a task (e.g., build a house), or how to proceed in any other complex or unfamiliar activity. The difference between the utility article as it appears in the newspaper and in the magazine is usually simply a difference in length. The newspaper article is generally briefer, hence more superficial.

The market for the utility article is a wide one, indeed. Many magazines carry utility articles; consequently, many manuscript editors are receptive to good ones. The probable success of the utility article can be determined by (1) novelty of material and approach, (2) note of authority, and (3) general effectiveness of expression. Because these qualities are discussed in Chapter 4, there is no need to explain them again.

The secret of the successful utility article lies in finding an interesting source of information. An obscure newspaperman, for example, recently sold an article on faking antiques to a national magazine. He obtained his information from an elderly cabinet maker who explained how unscrupulous persons can create highly deceptive replicas of originals. His article sold because of its authoritative ring, its timeliness, and its general appeal.

The unknown writer is handicapped in his search for utility article material in one field; this is the field involving the well-known person. He is handicapped because the well-known person, as has been shown, is generally reluctant to deal with unknown writers. The reason, once again, is the question of the writer's basic integrity and doubts concerning the actual printing.

6. Poetry—Before one can speak of the writing of poetry for magazines, a definition is necessary, for the term "poetry" is too all-inclusive. It may mean anything from the highly serious, complex poems of the magazines devoted to the advancement of poetry to the light, humorous quatrains appearing in the popular magazines. Therefore, two terms should be employed. The term "poetry" should be used as it is in college literature classes—to denote the lofty expression of great literary masters. The term "verse," on the other hand, can mean simply light rhymed material.

The market for poetry is both extremely competitive and highly limited. Professors of literature estimate that nine out of every ten persons who genuinely appreciate poetry attempt to write it. Naturally, many of this group submit their material to the few magazines that print poetry, thus creating a heavy supply for a limited demand. The publication of poetry today is practically limited to the quality magazines, the university quarterlies, and the few magazines such as *Poetry* which devote themselves, against great financial odds, to the publication of poems.

And what of remuneration? The sad fact is that payment is the exception rather than the rule. This fact is true because of the supply and demand factor referred to above. The quality magazines pay, but even their fees are relatively small. Why, they reason, should they pay $100 when the author will be more than willing to surrender his work for considerably less?

The market for verse is both wider and more remunerative than the market for poetry. Genuinely humorous verse always merits a reading by the editor of the popular magazines. Some magazines devote a full page to this kind of writing, and many close out the blank space after articles with little verses. The aspiring writer should note, however, that the market is keenly competitive, the returns are definitely limited, and the opportunity for fame is quite restricted. Such writers as Franklin P. Adams and Ogden Nash have attained reputations through verse, but theirs are exceptional instances.

THE WRITING PROCESS

When a writer believes he has material worthy of publication, he should first think of the literary form to be employed. He should settle upon the short story, the essay, the feature article, or whatever other form best suits his material and his abilities. A writer, for example, may have had the experience of narrowly escaping death in a small fishing craft during a heavy storm. In this instance one of at least three forms can be used—the short story, the reflective essay, or the personal experience. This writer, like all writers, must make this basic decision at the outset. Later planning may alter this first decision, but, nonetheless, it represents the initial step in writing.

THE MARKET

The second step in the writing process is to consider the probable market, or, to state the matter more bluntly, the specific magazines to which the manuscript can be sent with some hope of success.[2] As a cursory examination reveals, all magazines do not carry the same kind of material, and the writer, therefore, should not waste time and postage in sending his manuscript to unreceptive editors.

The question of market is so important that some authorities on magazine writing believe it should precede all other considerations. Consequently, they place it as the first step in the writing process. They argue that, before a writer begins, he should determine the specific magazine to which to submit his work. Then he should "slant" his entire planning and actual writing toward that publication. Selling a manuscript, they argue, demands such slanting. However, whether determining potential market is the first step or the second, it must be considered carefully.

The initial procedure in considering potential market is to try to visualize one's material in various magazines. An article on junior high school sports, for example, would hardly appear in *Field & Stream*, but it would be appropriate to several sports magazines. An article on cooking might be visualized in *Harper's Magazine*, but it would be more suitable to a women's magazine. If the article seems "at home" in a given

[2] Kinds of magazines are discussed on p. 365.

publication, the writer should make a more detailed analysis of the magazine before deciding to submit his manuscript. This analysis involves five steps: (1) analyzing the articles; (2) examining the entire contents; (3) analyzing the style of the contributors; (4) examining the advertisements; and (5) determining the editorial policy.

Analyzing articles is revealing as an indication of the kind of material in which the magazine is interested. A currently popular quality magazine, for example, generally carries 12 to 14 essays, two short stories, and two or three poems. The essays are nearly always written by authorities of a sort; one of the short stories is the work of an established author while the other is the work of an unknown writer published as encouragement to aspiring authors; and the poems are written by both well-known and unknown authors. Further analysis reveals that the essays deal with currently important questions such as politics and education; the short stories are generally of the character delineation type; and the poems are upon conventionally "safe" subjects. This analysis, therefore, shows important aspects of this magazine as a potential market.

Examining the contents of a magazine is revealing as an indication of the areas whereon the emphases are placed. The publication referred to above, for example, emphasizes essays on current questions, good quality fiction, and serious poetry. The reason for these emphases is that this magazine, like all magazines, has a specific type of reader in mind. It aims to capture the intellectually inclined segment of society—those persons interested in the topics and the literature well above the popular level. Therefore, it chooses its material accordingly. Naturally, the writer gains an insight into potential market from studying such emphases.

Analyzing the style of contributors is helpful as an indication of editorial policy regarding general approach. A magazine exclusively for men, for example, is likely to permit considerable latitude in style. The conversational tone, the informality, and the air of relaxation of the men's club are likely to be present. In such a magazine, the highly formal approach of the excessively discreet literary magazine would be inappropriate. Thus, style analysis reveals an important facet of the magazine.

An analysis of advertisements shows much of the age, cultural, and social group at which the magazine is pointed. The magazine for adolescents, for example, can be recognized by its advertisements for young people's clothing, popular records, current fads, and other products likely to interest this age group. An analysis of advertisements, therefore, serves further to reveal a magazine's policy.

Determining editorial policy (largely a matter of considering the foregoing analyses) tells the writer whether his article harmonizes with the tone of the magazine. This tone, as with the newspaper, is established by the magazine in its first issue, and it is changed or retained over the years primarily through selection of material. The article that is consistent with desired tone is likely to be considered sympathetically. Conversely, the article that clashes with this tone stands little chance of even slight consideration.

Planning the Magazine Article

The third step in the writing process is the actual planning. Although planning naturally varies with the form (short story, essay, feature article, etc.), certain common truths must be observed. The first is that planning must be all-inclusive—that is to say, it must treat every facet of the subject thoughtfully and thoroughly. The writer must turn his subject over and over in his mind in order to see every aspect.

This first deliberation, many authors believe, is the most important phase.

After the writer has considered his material exhaustively, he should list all pertinent thoughts, without regard to final outline. *Any* thought, however small, should be listed at random, for when this list is eventually complete it becomes the basis for the final outline. Note, for example, the listing of thoughts, followed by the final outline, for an article on "Who Should Attend College."

List of Thoughts

— colleges are already overcrowded
— population is increasing
— so is number of persons wanting to go to college
— society needs college-trained people
— more than mental ability should be considered
— well-rounded students make best citizens
— any solution must be subjected to periodic study
— every citizen has a democratic right to go to college
— intellectual ability is often only a small part of the reason for success in a given field (e.g., medicine, theology, teaching)
— no plan will satisfy everyone
— colleges can't be expanded rapidly enough to meet demands because of lack of buildings, professors, and funds
— ultimate benefit of college education to both the applicant and society must be considered
— this nation has traditionally upheld the right of the maximum education for all
— applicants for some curricula may have to be given preferential treatment
— a thorough study must be made immediately of every phase of the problem
— any system must be as fair as possible to both the individual applicant and society

— much controversy is likely to result
— every major phase of the problem is enigmatic
— taxpayers' institutions (state colleges and universities) will have to exercise special care in admitting applicants because they are more subject to public pressures

Final Outline

I. Introduction:
   A. Important problem because there are already more applicants than can be admitted.
   B. Already pressing problem growing steadily worse because of increase in population and in proportionate number of applicants.
   C. Colleges cannot be expanded to meet needs in time because of lack of sufficient funds, lack of personnel to teach and administer, and inability to build colleges rapidly enough.
   D. Three conditions must be recognized in evolving answer to problem: (1) democratic right of citizens to college education, (2) ultimate benefit of individual's education to society, (3) equality of opportunity for admission.
II. Body:
   A. Democratic right to a college education:
      1. Nation must continue to recognize principle of "maximum educational opportunity for all."
      2. Problem is of special significance to taxpayers' institutions (state colleges and universities) because they must construct an unassailable system of admissions.
   B. Ultimate benefit of individual's education to society:
      1. Intensive study of society's needs should be made immediately.
      2. Genuinely enigmatic problem to determine which college-trained persons likely to help society most.
      3. Some fields, possibly science and professions, will have

to take precedence over others. Hence, applicants for
these fields must be recognized first.
  C. Equality of opportunity for admission:
    1. System of insuring equality of opportunity for admission must be constructed immediately.
    2. System must recognize the desires and the abilities of the individual and the needs of society.
III. Conclusion:
    1. Solving problem cannot be postponed.
    2. No perfect solution is possible.
    3. System undoubtedly will have to be adjusted periodically.

ROUGH DRAFT

After the final outline has been constructed, the writer
is ready to begin his first draft, or "rough copy," as it is
often termed. This he should be prepared to do slowly,
thoughtfully, and painstakingly. Especially important to
recognize at this time is the truism that no writer, amateur
or professional, works with equal facility at all times. Writers, being artists, experience times when they write easily,
naturally, and effectively. Conversely, they also experience
times when they have the greatest of difficulty in composing
simple material. The right word cannot be found; the sentences come haltingly; and the entire article seems like the
work of one best suited to accounting, plumbing, bricklaying, tree pruning, or any other occupation distantly removed from writing. Obviously, the writer should watch
for the first situation, the one wherein he is "in the mood,"
"on the right track," "in the groove," or whatever else he
may term the condition. This caution is especially important
because writers are always reluctant to discard completely
any product of their efforts. Thus, writers often waste time

attempting to improve a poor paragraph, whereas actually they would gain by beginning anew.

When the rough copy has been completed, the writer should put it aside for a few days, if possible, and then return to improve it. The intervening time gives a perspective which is invaluable. The writer can now come to his work with a calmness, a detachment, and an energy that enable him to rework his thoughts and his sentences more easily. Also of significance is the fact that many writers make several drafts of their original material. They do so because of the freshness of viewpoint gained with each draft.

When the author is thoroughly satisfied with his work, he is ready to make his final copy. This is the last step in the actual writing for some authors. For others, however, there is still another stage—that of seeking the critical judgment of other persons. The usual procedures are to ask a competent friend to evaluate the work, to read it to a small group, or to engage a writer or a teacher of writing to criticize it. If one of these procedures is followed, the writer obviously must make another copy.

Of especial value in seeking the criticism of others is that factual errors may be avoided. The effective article, the author should never forget, must "hold water." Thus, great care must always be exercised. Factual errors, incidentally, are sometimes found in soundly established authors. Two examples of such errors are to be seen in O. Henry's story, "Gift of the Magi," and Willa Cather's story, "Paul's Case." O. Henry opens his story with these sentences:

One dollar and eighty-seven cents. That was all. And sixty cents of it was in pennies.

Certainly one need not be a financier to see the impossibility of this situation.

In the instance of "Paul's Case," which is an otherwise excellent story, Miss Cather has the central characters sipping lemonade on their front porch in Pittsburgh, Pennsylvania, on the last Sunday in November. Because this time of year usually finds winter weather in Pittsburgh, a grave question of accuracy arises.

Another value in seeking critical judgment is that "miscellaneous" pitfalls may be avoided. A second person can often detect unconscious plagiarism, triteness, grammatical errors, misspellings, and misuse of words. Certainly no explanation of the importance of avoiding these pitfalls is necessary.

SELLING MATERIAL

LITERARY AGENTS

Beginning writers with manuscripts for sale often ask the question, "Should I work through a literary agent?" To reach the answer, one should know the three types of literary agencies.

The first is the prominent agency, the one which handles the work of established writers. These writers employ these agencies because of the time saved in contacting magazines directly and because the agencies can often effect a more advantageous agreement. Such agencies generally pride themselves on the quality of their merchandise and the reputation of their clients. Consequently, the aspiring writer experiences great difficulty in gaining acceptance by one of these agencies, but, if successful, he has definite advantages, the strongest being that the agency has an entree into the offices of leading magazines. By virtue of the agency's endorsement, the manuscript often gains a careful reading not obtainable otherwise.

361

The second advantage of working through this type of agency is that it generally has an acute sense of potential market for every kind of manuscript. Whereas the writer may lose much time in sending his manuscript to dozens of magazines, the agency can send it immediately to the editors likely to give serious consideration.

The second type is the lesser known agency. This is the relatively new agency which has not yet gained a business foothold. It has no well-known writers as clients, and thus it is striving to establish itself. This agency generally accepts as clients anyone whose work it believes has merit. Consequently, a capable writer can often effect an agreement with such an agency. The advantages are once again that the agency has an entree into editorial offices and it is likely to have a good sense of potential market. The caution to be sounded, however, is that the agency is often overanxious to sell material. Therefore, the talented writer may find his material sold to relatively unknown magazines for a small fee, thus sacrificing good material to the agency's financial gain. Also, the contract with this kind of agency is generally clearly favorable to the agency. Legally, it may hold the manuscript indefinitely, as it often does, in the hope of eventual sale. Thus, the writer may well see his material go out of date.

The third type of agency is to be avoided at all costs; it is the one which is clearly dishonest. Usually it follows this pattern. Advertisements are placed in the cheap magazines and newspapers to lure aspiring writers. The reader is told that the agency accepts manuscripts, if they are "good," from unknown writers. The reader, full of high hope, sends his manuscript. Shortly thereafter he receives a letter telling him that his work "shows real promise," but that it needs a critical review. The letter explains that for a "fee" the critical review will be provided. The fee is sent, a critical review is returned with the manuscript, and the writer then revises and returns his work to the agency. After several months, the manuscript is again returned to the writer with the suggestion that perhaps it should be rewritten for another market. Once again a suggestion for a critical review is given—for a "fee," of course. This process naturally can go on indefinitely. In short, the agency exists for the primary purpose of capitalizing on the aspirations of naive persons.

Do's and Don't's of Submitting Manuscripts to Magazine

Whether the writer works through an agency or independently, there are certain do's and don't's of preparing and submitting manuscripts that will bear consideration. A listing of the most common follows.

1. Manuscripts should be typed neatly, on one side of the paper only, with each page properly numbered. All material should be double spaced. Ample margins should be left at top, bottom, and sides.
2. Manuscripts should be accompanied by a self-addressed, stamped envelope for their return.
3. Although a letter attempting to "sell" the manuscript is sometimes helpful, most editors prefer to judge the manuscript on its merits. Therefore, a letter should be included only when the author is certain that it will help.
4. If an article, such as a startling personal experience writing, contains material likely to be challenged, it should be accompanied by proof of accuracy or a statement that such proof will be submitted upon demand.

5. If consideration of the manuscript will be increased by the author's identity, he should make certain that his identity is made clear. Sometimes a mere footnote on the title page of the manuscript is sufficient. Other times a letter to the editor may be needed.

6. Authors should always keep a carbon copy of their work against the possibility of loss in transit. If the author wants to know that a manuscript has been received, he may send it by registered mail, "return receipt requested." This procedure, however, may irk an editor or his staff, especially in the instance of the unsolicited manuscript.

7. If a magazine states flatly that it does not consider unsolicited manuscripts, the editor should be queried before the manuscript is sent. This step removes prejudice against the article, and when a magazine holds fast to its policy, it prevents a waste of postage.

8. Editors dislike correspondence about manuscripts, especially unsolicited ones. A delay in receiving word of acceptance or rejection may well indicate favorable consideration. Consequently, a letter of inquiry may do harm rather than good.

9. The writer should keep a card catalog or some other record of his experiences in submitting manuscripts. Such a record frequently becomes an invaluable guide in attempting to place additional articles.

10. The writer should note any special instructions contained in the magazine involved for submitting manuscripts. These instructions often give important details concerning address, responsibility assumed, and general advice for preparation.

KINDS OF MAGAZINES

If a writer is to be successful, he must know the various kinds of magazines. He must have this knowledge because, as already shown, he must have a sense of market. Magazines may be classified in several ways, but the simplest, most logical procedure is to group them according to their basic purpose; that is to say, according to the readers they seek, the material they publish, and the general editorial policy they reflect.

The attempt to classify magazines, however, is not so easy as it may appear. Some magazines, naturally, can be classified readily because their nature and purpose are immediately clear. The professional magazines, for example, have been aimed over the years at specific groups. This fact is also true of the business magazines and the children's magazines. Yet, in other instances, the situation is quite different. To understand better the trends that make classification difficult, some generalities advanced by magazine editors and others interested in the field are worthy of note.

The first significant fact is that, at present, no magazine has an exclusive right to significant material; or, in other words, significant material is likely to be found in a wide variety of magazines. Over the past decade, for example, the following apparent incongruities appeared: a major league baseball player wrote an article on his sport for the *Atlantic Monthly;* the *New Yorker* carried a highly serious article blasting a well-known digest; *Life* devoted an entire issue, at an increased price, to an almost scholarly discussion of religion; the company magazine of a public utility carried an article on Christmas cards. A picture of the wide field presently covered by magazines can be seen by examining the articles condensed for *Reader's Digest*. In a representative sampling one sees articles upon every conceivable subject, directed toward readers of all types.

A second significant fact is that magazines are becoming more and more visual. Whereas a few decades ago a simple illustration or two was the rule of the day, magazines now use large pictures and other illustrative material freely, and they constantly devise new make-ups to gain attractive layouts. This fact is especially true of the popular weekly. Thus, the author can sometimes make the difference between acceptance and rejection of his article by including interesting illustrative material or a pertinent suggestion for a layout.

A third significant fact is that the hurry, the hustle, and the general emphasis upon speed of twentieth-century life have influenced magazine writing. The fast tempo of modern life has placed an emphasis on brevity, sharpness, and incisiveness not known heretofore. As a result, the leisurely approach of earlier times has given way to a more condensed, more pointed treatment. It has affected especially the writing of the popular weeklies, many of which are read in snatches in the subway train, the dentist's waiting room, and the club lounge. The present-day reader, it seems, does not want to study a magazine at length; he wants to read quickly and easily. This situation has given rise also to the popularity of the digests and the pocket-size magazine of capsules and brief articles.

A fourth significant fact is that magazines are coming more and more to deal with the problems of the day. Whereas a few decades ago the magazine was something of a piece of literature, the present-day publication has approached steadily the role of "newspaper of the nation." Now it tends to present and interpret significant topics of the moment rather than merely to reflect on familiar matters. Consequently, articles of general interest now outnumber the short story and other forms of creative writing.

A fifth significant fact is that magazines today, like newspapers, are definitely big business. The capital investment necessary to launch a magazine is higher than ever; circulations, of necessity, are larger; and the whole field has become increasingly competitive. For the writer, this situation means that many magazines pay substantial fees for material, but it also means that competition to sell articles has increased.

The following is a discussion of the prominent types of magazines. The purpose is to give the aspiring writer some idea of the peculiar nature of each type, especially as it concerns opportunities for publication. The writer should remember, however, that the magazine field, as previously stated, is always changing. Consequently, opportunities for writers also change, either favorably or unfavorably.

1. Quality Magazines—The term "quality" is used rather loosely to denote the magazines which deal with the arts, current questions, and intellectual topics in a dignified, fairly exhaustive manner. The quality magazine is pointed squarely at the person interested in the loftier, more complex, and more significant aspects of life. Examples of the quality publications are the *Atlantic Monthly, Harper's Magazine,* and the *Saturday Review.*

The quality magazines, with some few exceptions, have traveled a rough road, and many have risen and attracted a large following, only to die a slow death. *Scribner's* is an example of a genuinely excellent quality magazine that suffered such an eclipse.

The quality magazines are a strong lure for the aspiring writer because of the fame derived. The writer, for example, who places an article in the *Atlantic Monthly* joins a famous fraternity—that of the great figures who have written for

367

that publication since its founding in Boston in 1857. In that fraternity are some of the most famous names in American literature—Emerson, Whittier, Lowell, Holmes, Thoreau, Perry—and such highly important personalities in American political history as Woodrow Wilson, Al Smith, and Wendell Willkie.

The quality magazines represent a potential market for the essay, the short story, the general feature story, and poetry. Also, some quality magazines use squibs, vignettes, shorts, and similar writings.

No general statement concerning the fee paid by the quality magazine can be given. As stated elsewhere, the larger the circulation, the higher the fee is likely to be. Then, too, the quality magazine frequently adjusts the fee according to the prestige of the author.

2. Professional Magazines—The professional magazine, as the name implies, is a publication aimed squarely at the members of a given profession. Examples of professional magazines are the *American Medical Journal*, the *National Education Association Journal*, and the many "law reviews" published throughout the nation. Because the magazine is designed for a specific professional group, its material must bear directly on the activity of that group. Consequently, most articles are written by members of the profession.

The only opportunity for the nonprofessional writer to publish in this magazine lies in one of three situations: he writes of a professional matter from a layman's viewpoint; he writes of an "outside" subject of interest to the professional group; or he ghost-writes an article for a professional person.

An example of a layman writing of a professional matter is to be seen in a recent article in a county medical magazine entitled "The Layman Looks at His Doctor." This article is based on a layman's assembling, evaluation, and presentation of local opinion about the physician and his role in society.

An example of an "outside" subject of interest to a professional group is to be seen in an article on compulsory automobile insurance in a legal journal. In this article an insurance executive cites some obscure ramifications of this type of coverage.

Examples of ghost-writing are, of course, numerous. Often a professional man merely lacks the ability to express himself effectively. Therefore, he tells his story to a writer who outlines the material, writes the article, and then submits it for the approval of the "author." Although the article always appears in the professional magazine under the professional man's by-line, it may appear in the popular weekly with the "as told to" approach.

The professional magazine offers highly limited opportunities for the aspiring writer for two reasons: (1) as shown above, there is a distinctly limited field for the nonprofessional writer, and (2) the professional magazine frequently pays only a token fee or no fee whatever. This latter fact is true because professional men, interested in fame within their profession, are generally more than willing to forego remuneration to reach print. Hence, the magazine does not have to pay to obtain acceptable manuscripts.

3. Business Magazines—Because business in its many forms is the basis of the American economic system, business magazines have become a necessity. Every major field has at least one magazine, and many have magazines for their subdivisions. Consequently, one can find a magazine for literally every product used from "the cradle to the grave."

To understand the nature of the business magazine, one can do no better than examine the definition of an established editor. The following is the definition of W. A. Phair, Editor, *Hardware Age:* "Basically a business magazine is a publication whose contents are devoted exclusively to one industry, one material, or a specific business or profession. The circulation of the magazine is usually restricted to people actually engaged in the business covered by the publication." Although business magazines are pointed toward one area, they nonetheless treat related topics. Many of them tell of economic conditions, stock market predictions, general sales indexes, and every other major phase of the business world. They also present articles and features concerning narrow phases of business life. Some business magazines, such as *Department Store Economist*, contain articles of clearly popular appeal. Hence, they make easy, entertaining reading for persons outside the area treated.

Opportunities for writing for the business magazine, as for similar publications, vary. The large magazines employing a full-time staff present a clearly limited opportunity for the outside writer. His lone chance lies in selling an unusual article on a free-lance basis. The smaller magazines, however, frequently buy articles from outside writers. The writer, therefore, should query the editor when he has material.

The most important attributes for success in writing for the business magazine are significance of material, note of authority, and general effectiveness of expression.

4. Technical Magazines—The technical magazine is a combination of two other magazines: the professional and the business. This fact is true because the technical magazine presents material for the highly trained person—the engineer, the technician, the scientist—and it presents material concerning the general condition of a particular field—aerodynamics, rubber, building construction. Because technical writing is discussed at length in Chapter 14, there is no reason to detail it here.

The opportunities for writing for the technical magazine are essentially similar to those for the professional journal. The magazine, being pointed at a specific group, is successful in proportion to its ability to interest and inform that group. Hence, a writer with material of sufficient value can hope for a favorable reaction to his manuscript. He should note, however, that many technical magazines are in charge of a full-time staff. Consequently, these publications are closed to outside writers in most instances.

Anyone wishing to write for the technical magazines should remember above all else that, because the fields are technical, they are scientific. Therefore, the material and the presentation must be characterized by scientific accuracy, scientific approach, and scientific evaluation.

5. Farm Magazines—A publication almost unknown to the city dweller but very much of a reality in the rural area is the farm magazine. The farm magazine has been a long and popular institution. The first of such publications was the *Genessee Farmer*, founded in 1831, and from that time to this, farm magazines have flourished. At present, there are an estimated 140 farm magazines in the United States, the largest of which, *Farm Journal*, boasts a circulation of over 3,400,000.

The farm magazine, however, should not be pictured as a distinctly individual kind of publication, for actually there are two major differences to be noted. The first is the "general" as opposed to the "specialized" farm magazine. The general farm magazine contains news and material for every member of the family. Thus, it actually resembles the popular weekly, with an emphasis on farm news. For the farmer, there are columns of farm news, prices, and general information; for the women, articles on fashions and the home; for children, little stories and puzzles; for readers of all classes, a host of varied and interesting items. The specialized farm magazine, on the other hand, is aimed at a special farming interest—e.g., dairy, cotton, grain. Thus, it usually contains specialized news, as do the trade journals and the professional magazines.

The second difference to be recognized is that some farm magazines are written for a definite geographical area only. The *Southern Planter*, the *New England Homestead*, and the *Ohio Farmer* are instances of "section" publications. Also to be noted, however, is that the larger general farm magazines have section editions. *Farm Journal*, for example, appears in three section editions—East Central, Western, and Southern. Thus, the larger magazines are actually not completely "general."

There are also certain common tenets to be recognized in the editorial policy of the farm magazines. Above all else, they recognize the importance of farming and everything related to it. The idea of bygone days that the farmer was a "hick," distantly removed from the main questions, thoughts, styles, and other facets of life, has long since disappeared. Instead, the farmer is to be respected for the great contribution he makes, for the detailed knowledge that he must possess, and for the general business acumen that must be his. Another tenet is that the interests of the farmer must be safeguarded. He must receive his share of favorable legislation, and his rights and privileges must be maintained. Still another tenet is that the farm family is a closely knit unit representing one of the mainstays of the American way of life—an anchor of sorts for the upheavals that arise with urban living.

The opportunities for writing for the farm publication are essentially similar to those of the other magazines; that is to say, opportunities vary according to the nature of the specific magazine. The larger general magazines naturally present a wider chance. Almost any article of interest to the farm family is likely to receive favorable consideration. In the instance of the specialized farm magazine, the opportunity is naturally limited to the particular field involved.

The person wishing to write specialized articles for the farm magazine should observe, however, one special caution; his material must always reflect a thorough knowledge of his subject. The farmer is traditionally suspicious of anyone holding forth authoritatively on farming. Consequently, he looks with a suspicious eye on the writings in the farm magazines; he wants to know that the author knows whereof he writes. As a result, anyone submitting specialized material should be very careful of accuracy of detail, for certain rejection faces articles displaying factual errors, fallacious reasoning, or "lunatic fringe" ideas.

6. **Company Magazines**—Most large business and industrial organizations have a company newspaper, a company magazine, or both. The company publication exists primarily to build a sound relationship between employer and employee. Consequently, it chooses its material with a view to publishing an interesting magazine wherein to "sell" the company to the employee.

As stated previously, this publication is nearly always handled by a company-employed editor and staff. Outside writers, however, are sometimes able to place articles when their material has general interest to employees. A random examination of company publications revealed the following instances of articles by outside writers: a social security official had an article in an automobile manufacturing magazine on a recent change in benefits; a sportsman had an article in a steel company magazine on fly casting; a building engineer had an article in a tire company magazine on hints for home construction; a physician had an article in a large business house magazine on protecting one's self against summer heat; a well-known sports writer had an article in a chain-store magazine on predictions for the coming baseball season.

Difficulty in selling articles to the company magazine exists because the company is generally reluctant to pay for outside articles because it employs a full-time staff.

7. Specialty Magazines—The term "specialty" is used to cover those magazines written in a popular vein about such specialized fields as the theater, sports, coin collecting, travel, radio, television, and similar subjects. Some of these magazines, such as *TV Guide*, have circulations that are phenomenal.

The problem, however, of labeling specialty magazines has become difficult because of changes in editorial policy to include other material. *TV Guide*, for instance, contains much material that could be used elsewhere, and such a magazine as *Theatre Arts* includes many feature stories usable in popular weeklies and other publications.

No general statement can be offered regarding placing articles in the specialty magazines because of the many differences in policy. Some have little or no restrictions. They accept any appealing article, whether by amateur or professional. Others, such as *Sport*, carry only articles by their own staff and others whom they know to be qualified. Neither can any general statement be given regarding remuneration. The larger the circulation, the larger is likely to be the remuneration. Also, once again, the prestige of the author often affects the fee to be paid.

8. Popular Magazines—The term "popular" originally meant a distinctly individual kind of magazine. It was used to denote such publications as the *Saturday Evening Post*, which were founded to furnish reading material for the great

middle intellectual class. Some attempt was made to reach the upper groups, but basically the focus was, intellectually speaking, on the "average" citizen. The popular magazine usually contains fiction, essays, feature stories, puzzles, poems, letters to the editor, and any other feature believed capable of increasing circulation.

Recent years have brought sharp challenges and changes to the magazine world, and some popular magazines considered well nigh invincible have fallen. Today, such once famous names as *Liberty* and *Collier's* are only names; the magazines exist no more. Only the *Saturday Evening Post* remains as a truly successful popular weekly.

Several reasons have been advanced for the failure of popular magazines to survive. Television has been blamed, as have rising costs of publication and public apathy. A more commonly accepted explanation, however, is that other publications have taken over the function of the popular magazine. Although the *Saturday Evening Post* has a circulation of over 4,500,000, it still must fight the competition of magazines not classified under the "popular" label. The quality, the Sunday supplement, the women's, and the farm magazine, to name only a few, now contain material formerly considered the province of the popular magazine. Consequently, many magazines can be said to have "popular" appeal.

As a result of the above situation, one should not think of writing for the popular magazines; instead, he should think of writing popular material. This statement simply means that most material submitted to the popular magazines could be considered by many other magazines, also. As a random examination of any issue of a popular magazine will show, much of the material would be "at home" in many other publications. Therefore, the popular magazine should not be considered to have a distinct corner on any type of material.

However, some general characteristics can be cited as guides for writing for popular magazines. The short stories are of the lighter, more rapidly moving type; serious poetry is almost nonexistent; articles are of the superficial, easy-to-follow variety; and feature stories are definitely in the newspaper tradition.

9. **Women's Magazines**—The field of the women's magazine has been important from its beginning in the last century, primarily because of the great circulation possibilities. Certainly few persons are surprised to learn that women are more likely than men to read popular publications. As a result, this type of magazine represents a genuinely good opportunity for anyone who can write effectively upon subjects that interest women.

The appeal of the women's magazine has not changed greatly over the years. When L. A. Godey founded *Godey's Lady's Book* in 1830, that famous publication catered to two of women's primary interests, fashions and the home. The ensuing years have seen this key emphasis continued in women's magazines, but an interest in topics of a wider nature has become discernible as women have become "emancipated." Thus, today the primary appeal of the women's magazine centers about fashions, furniture, decorations, house plans, decorum, and subjects discussed in women's clubs and similar places. Consequently, an interesting treatment of one of these topics will be read carefully by the manuscript editor.

Besides the above topics, women's magazines look for good short stories and appealing poetry. Although the short stories vary from one magazine to another, basically they are stories that appeal to women. This statement, of course, is a broad one, because women read many types of stories. The poetry, generally speaking, should be on the light or humorous side.

The poetry of the modern impressionistic school stands little chance of acceptance by the women's magazines.

10. **Children's and Adolescents' Magazines**—With the so-called "modern" school, there has come an emphasis on the magazines for children and adolescents. These magazines may be distributed through the schools, as are *Jack and Jill* and *Children's Digest,* or they are handled directly by publishing houses as are *Boy's Life* and the *American Girl.*

The essence of successful writing for children's and adolescent's magazines lies in finding appealing material. Although this statement is a self-evident truth, it actually encompasses a wide area, for understanding these age groups is not easy. The interests of small children, for example, have changed sharply with the advent of television. Whereas heretofore the small child was greatly interested in fairy and animal stories, librarians now report that children are more interested in the material seen on television—western stories, space travelers, comic characters, and travelogues. Understanding the interests of adolescents is even more enigmatic. The area of interests for the teen-ager is so wide, so complex, and so changing that one must constantly seek reliable evidence of the true situation.

The actual writing can be handled fairly easily by knowing the average mental and intellectual levels of the group involved. The style of the small child's magazine, for instance, is nothing more than the recorded speech of the primary school teacher. The sentences are short; the vocabulary is simple; and the style is distinctly conversational. The adolescent's magazine is naturally more mature in content, approach, and style.

Just as the first three grades of elementary school are best handled by women teachers, so are the best articles for this

377

age group usually done by women writers. However, with children from nine years of age upward, successful material is written by both men and women.

Because the small child is so keenly interested in narrative writings, these magazines place a heavy emphasis on little stories. However, they do contain little essays and poems, also. The essays are usually about interesting activities, children in other lands, and similar topics of interest to small children. The poems are generally brief and humorous. The magazine for the adolescents generally contains a fairly even balance of stories and articles of general interest. It also places a fairly heavy emphasis on puzzles, contests, quizzes, and other challenging features.

Magazines for children and adolescents, generally speaking, are always receptive to effectively written, interesting material. Therefore, the writer can be fairly certain of a favorable reception for his article.

11. **Sunday Supplement Magazines**—The Sunday supplement magazine is usually nothing more than a collection of extensive newspaper feature stories illustrated by one or more pictures. Consequently, it can be understood best in terms of the material discussed in Chapter 4. The article in the Sunday supplement magazine comes from three sources: (1) staff writers, (2) syndicates, (3) outside (free-lance) writers. Generally, editors strive for a wide variety of material with the thought of attracting as wide a reading public as possible.

Opportunities for writing for the Sunday supplement obviously are limited to selling material directly to the newspaper or to the syndicate. If one is to sell his material directly to the newspaper, he should first have some contact with the editorial office. This contact is necessary in order that the newspaper may be satisfied with the writer's basic integrity.

Thereafter, articles are generally considered on their merits, although naturally other conditions may influence the editor's decision to accept or reject. A personal association, an established reputation in some field related to the writing, or a record of successful writing naturally is helpful.

To sell material to a syndicate, the writer can either send his material directly or work through an agency. Unknown writers often face difficulty in selling their material to syndicates because of the question of basic integrity. Some syndicates, it seems, are reluctant to deal with persons not known to them. Acceptance, however, is by no means impossible, for most syndicates are always receptive to acceptable manuscripts.

12. Free Magazines—The term "free" magazine is self-explanatory. It is the little magazine which one receives without cost through the mail, at the supermarket, at the convention, or at many similar places. It is a publication of either general or specialized interest, prepared with the definite purpose of advertising a given product. As readily can be assumed, the advertising is "sugar coated," but it is there nonetheless. Instances of the free magazine at present are: an oil company distributes a well-written publication slanted toward the rural reader; an automobile company distributes a sports magazine to owners of its cars; a publishing house distributes a magazine of college and university news to professors.

No blanket statement can be given concerning opportunity for publication or remuneration in the instance of the free magazine. Some of these magazines are closed to outside writers; some are not. Some pay for articles; others publish only donated or borrowed material. Some have a definitely limited scope; others are so wide in scope that editorial policy is scarcely discernible. Therefore, the best procedure for the aspiring writer is to query the editor when he has material suitable to a given magazine.

An interesting point in the history of the free magazine is that some have become so successful that they have progressed to the stage of regular magazines. *Woman's Day*, for instance, was once distributed without cost by the Great Atlantic and Pacific Tea Company. However, the demand for the magazine became so great that publishing costs necessitated some financial return. As a result, a price of five cents was established. Later it became seven cents, and presently it is sold for ten cents. Yet the magazine continues to hold a circulation that has approached five million.

EXERCISES

1. Analyze the contents of the following magazines: a quality, a popular weekly, a Sunday supplement.
2. Diagram the structural pattern of any three magazine stories.
3. Discuss analytically the poetry in any five issues of any quality magazine.
4. Discuss the layout of any magazine that uses illustrative material profusely.
5. Analyze the contents of a company magazine in the light of editorial policy.
6. Select five general magazines from a library reading room and explain the type of reader each is pointed toward.
7. Analyze the advertisements in any three magazines intended for the general public. Try to find instances of advertisements which you consider to be in "poor taste."
8. Select five instances of appealing verse, explaining the reasons for your choices.
9. Assume that you are about to establish a magazine for the general public. What material would you include? Give your reasons.

10. Select and compare the following: a personality sketch in a newspaper and one in a magazine; a utility article in a newspaper and one in a magazine; a newspaper column on politics and a magazine essay on politics.

11. Assume that you have just written the following: Nathaniel Hawthorne's short story, "The Minister's Black Veil"; Matthew Arnold's essay, "Culture and Anarchy"; and Charles Lamb's essay, "Old China." In what magazines would you attempt to place them?

12. What are your three favorite magazines? Why?

Pictorial
Communication

Chapter
13

A phase of journalism that has undergone a period of significant development within the past three decades is photography. Although pictures have been used in newspapers for over a century, the development within recent years has influenced journalism more so than at any earlier time. Certainly the influence of pictures has been present from the first crude woodcuts of Matthew B. Brady's photographs of the War Between the States (which appeared in *Harper's Weekly* in 1857); but the improvements in photographic processes, printing, and photoengraving since 1930 have changed the character of the newspaper drastically.

The most pronounced change has been in newspaper content. As late as the early nineteen thirties, most newspapers carried no more than one or two cuts on page 1 and ten to fifteen in the rest of the paper. Excepting the sports page, pictures were generally portraits and posed photographs. Now, however, the number, the size, and the nature of pictures have changed.

The increase in number is observable upon the most casual of examinations. Newspapers now have cuts on practically every page, and most papers devote at least one full page exclusively to photographs. This latter practice may be followed daily, as in the instance of the tabloids, or it may be reserved for a given day (usually Saturday or Sunday), under the label of "News of the Week in Pictures," or some similar title.

The increase in size is also clearly observable. Most newspapers have increased significantly the size of the cuts, especially on the inside pages where they are often three or more columns wide. The size of the photographs naturally varies with departments. Sports, society, theater, and radio and television pages are much more likely to use large cuts than are news and business. Also, size is often varied according to pictorial make-up, especially in full-page layouts. Consequently, pictures are made larger or smaller to blend into the layout of the particular page.

The change in nature of pictures unquestionably has been the most significant. With the perfection of the high-speed cameras in the nineteen thirties, a type of picture not possible heretofore became a reality. Before that time, the genuinely good action shot now seen daily was not possible. The action shots that were used often seemed unnatural or badly clouded.

383

With the faster-moving shutter, finer-grained film, and better-quality lens there came a clearer, more natural picture. Thus, a remarkable clarity of detail was brought into every phase of newspaper photography.

Another change in the nature of pictures was the altering of editorial policy to use shots heretofore banned. Whereas formerly pictures were of the conventionally posed or orthodox action type, more of the element of the candid camera shots now appeared. Also, due in part to the influence of the picture magazines, notably *Life* and *Look*, which blossomed in the late thirties, the picture horizon widened. There were more shots of accidents, arrests, scuffles, and similar scenes which previously had been considered objectionable.

As a result of this increased use and the changing nature of pictures, there has come into being a trend variously termed "visual journalism," "pictorial journalism," and "photojournalism." Stated in its simplest terms, this trend is simply the practice of emphasizing pictures as a means of relating news and other stories. So strong has this trend become that many editors and publishers predict that the newspaper of the future will be 50 per cent pictures.

Photojournalism in its progress has tried many kinds of experiments, several of which have proved successful. None of its practices, however, has been adopted so widely as the "action sequence," or "pictorial sequence" as it is more often termed. This is the simple arrangement of a series of action shots to tell a story. The pictures may be accompanied by a few brief lines above or below, or they may tell their own story. The pictorial sequence is especially suitable to feature story material—as, for instance, a shot of animals at play. It is also effective, however, in the straight news story—as, for instance, a series showing the reaction of a member of the United Nations delegation to a speech.

THE PHOTOGRAPHER

With the changes in newspaper photography, there has also come a change in the role of the photographer. Formerly, the photographer was nothing more than the man who "took pictures" for the paper. He was viewed as something of a lovable but slow-witted individual who would be a reporter or an editor if he were more intelligent and capable. Although this conception was more popular than accurate, the fact is nonetheless true that he was seldom anything more than a capable operator of a camera.

The photographer of the present, however, must possess several qualities. Above all else, he must be primarily an artist. He must bring to his work an imagination, a sensitivity, and a sense of the qualities of the appealing picture. Certainly he shoots most pictures on instructions from the picture editor or some other superior, but still his decisions at the scene are the basic determinant of the actual picture. To appreciate the quality of work done by top-flight photographers, one need only attend an exhibition of their work. Such exhibitions are held annually by press photographers associations and similar groups across the nation, with awards given for excellence in the various fields (sports, action, straight news, etc.). In these exhibitions one sees the basic quality of all art—the reflection of a personality. The photographs are not simply pictures of persons, events, or actions; they are pictures which reveal the esthetic nature of the person who made them.

Many persons skilled in newspaper photography say that this basic attribute of the top-notch photographer can be summed up in a single sentence: he must have a *feeling for pictures*. By this statement they mean that instinctively the photographer must know and recognize the scenes that provide good pictures. Life to the photographer must be one long series of picture possibilities. Every scene, every event, every action must be thought of in the light of the potential picture it presents. The child toddling after his mother, the corner lounger idly blowing smoke skyward, the crowd boarding the subway train—these and every other scene must be viewed in terms of picture possibilities. In each instance, the photographer must think of how to capture the pictorial aspects that best interpret the essence of the scene.

The second quality which the successful photographer must have is the *mechanical ability* to handle his camera, develop pictures, and perform the other skills incumbent upon him. Although the amateur photographer may assume that acquiring this ability is a simple matter, such is far from the case. Schools of journalism give detailed courses in the intricacies of photography because the mechanics of lighting, shutter speed, developing, printing, and general handling of the camera require detailed study. In fact, these skills are sometimes too difficult for some persons to master. The situation, it seems, is comparable to the man who is naturally clumsy with tools as compared with the man who is naturally skillful. The first man can be eager to learn, diligent in practice, and consistent in effort. Yet, even average performance is simply beyond him. The second man, on the other hand, seems to handle tools by second nature and to perform high-quality work by second nature. The would-be photographer, analogous to the first man, can scarcely hope to be successful in the world of journalism.

The third quality needed by the photographer is the *ability to handle people*. Like the reporter, the photographer deals with persons of all sorts and conditions, but generally he faces more difficulty. This fact is true because of the power and the finality of the camera. Whereas the interviewee can talk with the reporter and thus often get into print that which pleases him, he has no such control over the camera. The camera may catch him at an unfavorable angle or at a "bad" time; yet he has no way of knowing this fact until he sees the actual newspaper. Consequently, many persons otherwise co-operative do not want to be photographed.

Generally speaking, persons to be photographed fall into three groups: those who are willing to co-operate, those who are unwilling to co-operate, and those who are unable to co-operate.

The group *willing to co-operate* can be illustrated by three common types: the obscure individual elated at the prospect of seeing his picture in the paper, the screen star desiring publicity, and the person participating in a campaign.

The group *unwilling to co-operate* can be illustrated by the man arrested for crime, the shy person to whom personal publicity is a genuine discomfort, and the individual caught in embarrassing circumstances.

The group *unable to co-operate* can be illustrated by the participant in the midst of a brawl, the bull fighter making his final thrust, and the parachutist making a landing.

Obviously, the photographer has no problem with the group that is willing to co-operate and the group that is unable to co-operate. Therefore, the second group demands his attention. Sometimes he can coax; sometimes he can flatter; sometimes he can cajole the subject into being photographed by explaining that the unposed shot will be more unfavorable. An example of such an instance is the person under arrest who holds a handkerchief over his face. The standard technique is to explain to the individual that such an act is an open admission of guilt. This technique has been highly successful over the years.

387

There are, however, instances wherein the photographer has no opportunity to reason. Such an instance is the courtroom. Probably more so than any other place, there has been a running battle over the last decade between photographers and courtroom officials. Photographers contend that, as working journalists, they have a right to photograph news; judges contend that photographers disrupt judicial procedure. Photographers counter that they will use candid cameras and eliminate any disrupting influence (tripod, case, flashbulbs, etc.); judges answer that the very presence of the photographer is a disrupting influence.

Present evidence, however, indicates that the photographers are winning the battle. Editorial writers have upheld them logically and effectively, and they themselves have used their power. A recent example is to be seen in the instance of a judge who attacked a photographer for making a shot as he left his chambers. The judge had refused the photographer admittance to the courtroom, and so he waited until the judge was leaving for lunch. As the judge attacked, a second photographer shot a sequence which was displayed across page 1. The purpose, of course, was to embarrass the judge and to win public support for the cause. Such tactics as these have been used with marked success.

The fourth quality which the photographer must have is *originality*. This quality has become increasingly important because the public has developed an antipathy to the standard posed photograph. Only the most naive of readers are deceived by the posed shot of the celebrity greeting the public official, the athlete supposedly catching a ball while looking full face into the camera, and the girl seated on the block of ice to escape the July heat. Originality, however, has also become important because of the demands of modern journalism. With more and larger pictures there must be greater variety. The older tintype posing can scarcely meet the demands of the full page of pictures and other phases of photojournalism. Originality has been encouraged and recognized by the prominent use of by-lines for photographers. Some instances of originality seen in prominent newspapers during the past few years follow:

A photograph of a city hall statue of a military figure astride a horse, around the base of which was strewn a pile of grass and weeds. The grass and the weeds had been thrown there from a truck overturned in an accident. The picture was captioned, "Hay, hay! Neigh!"

A photograph of the ruins of a fire in a tailor's dummy manufacturing plant. The shot showed five models of women standing charred. The caption read, "Model Fire. Nobody Hurt."

A photograph of a group of pigeons standing about a city fire hydrant with one pigeon atop. The cut lines explained that the elevated pigeon was rallying the others to protest a city law to control their number by extermination.

A photograph showing the conflicting cultures in New York's Chinatown. An elderly man in complete Oriental garb sat holding his three-year-old grandson who was clutching a Davy Crockett doll.

A photograph showing a bearded Amish farmer waiting in his drab black buggy for a traffic light on a main highway to change. Next to the buggy was a glittering sports car. The caption read, "Time Stands Still and Time Marches On."

A photograph of a basketball player too tall to enter an arch. Above the arch were the words, "Clearance Six Feet." The purpose of the shot was to show the great height of the player.

A photograph of the nine candidates for May queen at a local college were arranged in the form of a question mark. The cut lines explained that the queen would be chosen at the forthcoming prom by secret vote.

A photograph of a 14-year-old boy with a huge apple on his head. The cut lines explained the facts about the prize apple and the power which William Tell would need in his arrow to move the apple.

The fifth quality which the photographer must have is a *knowledge of libel.* He must have this knowledge, as the reporter must, in order to protect his newspaper. Libel, as previously shown, is defamation by visible communication— that is to say, by words, pictures, illustrations, or any other means of visual communication. The newspaper, therefore, must be as careful of its pictures as it is of its words. A significant fact to be noted is that, like libel through the printed word, libel through photography varies from state to state. To understand better the nature of libel, some specific discussion should be helpful.

A businessman in Idaho sued a newspaper whose photographer had taken a surreptitious picture of him through his kitchen window. The suit was settled out of court, probably because the newspaper held little hope of winning its case. A year later, a gangster's lawyer in New York, facing sentence for a criminal act, was photographed surreptitiously from a neighboring fire escape as he prepared breakfast in the apartment of a woman friend where he had spent the night. In the first instance there were sufficient grounds for a libel suit; in the second there were no grounds because a convicted criminal can scarcely be libeled by such circumstances. (Whether the lessee of the apartment would have a cause of action is not covered by this discussion.)

A prominent society woman on the West Coast was photographed on a mid-city street as she recovered from a sneeze.

Because of the peculiarity of her facial expression and the presence of a tap room in the background, the picture suggested that she was inebriated. The victim was satisfied by a printed apology. A year later, a shapely movie actress was the "victim" of a trick photograph which made her appear elephantine from a rear view. She, of course, had co-operated with the photographer, who had told her his purpose. If she were to sue for libel, she would have no grounds because of her willingness to co-operate.

A picture editor refused to run a shot of a 14-year-old boy mischievously drawing a handkerchief from the hip pocket of a middle-aged man intently watching a parade. He felt that the picture was potentially libelous because it could clearly be interpreted as a boy in the act of picking a pocket. Two months later, the same editor ran a two-column cut of a known pickpocket as he moved suspiciously in a circus crowd. The shot had been taken seconds before a policeman, recognizing the pickpocket, had moved in for the arrest.

The usual procedure for the photographer is to shoot the picture and decide afterwards whether it is libelous—if no law is violated in the actual taking. All pictures, of course, must be examined carefully for potential libel because many shots not suspected of being libelous prove so when they emerge from the darkroom. Also to be noted is the fact that the responsibility for running pictures is seldom the photographer's; it is usually the picture editor's or some other superior's.

In addition to the qualities already cited, the photographer must have the *general ability* needed to be a capable journalist. He must be able to work under the same difficult conditions as the good reporter with the same degree of success. He must understand the function of the entire newspaper in order that he may understand his part. He must be able to sense the presence of scoops, to display ingenuity in working under varied circumstances, and to be a good working newspaperman in every other respect. His role can be summarized by stating that the qualities of the good reporter can be translated into the qualities of the good photographer.

PHOTOGRAPHER SPECIALTIES

Because newspaper photography has become a detailed process, the necessity for specialization has arisen. Consequently, photographers, like other journalists, have specialties. They specialize in straight news, sports, entertainment, society, and every other major source of news. His decision to specialize is usually made by the photographer on the basis of his abilities and his interests.

A young photographer, for example, frequently likes to specialize in the dramatic aspects of news and feature stories. Therefore, he is the one to assign the shot of the painters atop the high bridge, the fire in the tenement district, the riot on the waterfront, the athletic contest. An older man is generally more interested in politics, labor relations, feature story personalities, and specialized studies (traffic conditions, shoppers' habits, historical sites, etc.). Therefore, he likes to specialize in these subjects. In all instances, the photographer needs more than a passing interest to do good work. He must be so interested that he builds up a detailed background of knowledge. A photographer with little interest in politics, for instance, can scarcely know the shots to make at the political convention; nor is the photographer with little interest in baseball likely to know the moments of most import to sports readers.

The need for specialties has increased the number of women photographers. Few men are sufficiently interested in society, fashions, women personalities, and similar subjects to do sound work in these fields. Consequently, women photographers have made their appearance. In instances where the newspaper does not employ a woman photographer, it generally sends a woman reporter on the assignment with the photographer to suggest shots and write the cut lines.

ORGANIZATION OF THE PHOTOGRAPHIC PROCESS

Like other departments, photographic work varies with the size and the nature of the particular newspaper. On the very small paper, the reporter is frequently also a photographer—sometimes of questionable ability. He takes along his camera on assignments and performs both tasks. In the case of the proportionately larger paper, one or more photographers are employed. Specific assignments are given by the head photographer who works in conjunction with the various department editors. In the even larger papers, however, the work of the photographic department comes under the jurisdiction of the picture editor, who may have one or more assistants. This editor works co-operatively with the other editors and makes his assignments accordingly.

The picture editor, however, is more than the person who makes assignments to photographers, for he has many exacting duties. His greatest function is to provide the newspaper with the quality of picture that will please readers and hence increase circulation; he is, therefore, primarily a judge of photography. He tells his photographers what he wants in specific instances and he passes judgment on their pictures. If, for example, he is sending a photographer out on a parade assignment, he may tell him to emphasize "stuff for mothers and kids." Thus, the photographer is expected to shoot pictures accordingly. Shots of officials discussing parade routes are to be bypassed, whereas shots of animals, fancy dress, and comics are to be emphasized. The photographer's prints become, of course, a display from which the picture editor, often in conjunction with other editors, makes the choices. In some instances, the picture editor also writes captions and cut lines; in other instances, these lines are the province of the department concerned (news, sports, etc.).

The picture editor often sits in in top editorial conferences because, as has been shown, the visual appeal of the newspaper is becoming increasingly important. Consequently, editors and executives strive to learn reader interests. The significance journalists attach to pictures is strengthened by recent studies which, although in conflict on some points, agree that more persons look at pictures than look at any other single feature. Consequently, the role of the picture editor is an important one.

In addition, the picture editor must supervise the various functions of his department. He must keep records of assignments, order supplies, supervise the use of equipment, and act as general director of his staff. These duties may sound light, but they can be demanding. The handling of supplies, for instance, involves budgetary matters, as does the decision concerning use of equipment. When, for example, should the picture editor assign the use of the machine gun camera (the use of which involves several hundred dollars) for a football game, or when will the ordinary speed graphic or other camera do? Obviously these are important decisions for the newspaper's economy.

FUNCTION OF PHOTOGRAPHS

Most newspaper readers seldom give any deep thought to the reasons for pictures in their favorite publications. They simply look at the pictures for information, pleasure, or general satisfaction of curiosity, often concluding their reading with the thought that "The pictures today are pretty good," or "not so good," or some other evaluation. They realize vaguely that the pictures add interest and life to the paper, but they do not pursue the thought. Actually, however, there are five important reasons for the inclusion of pictures.

The most important function of the photograph is *to communicate news*. In fact, it is often the most important means of news communication in the entire paper. It can show graphically, thoroughly, and frequently with an amazing degree of insight a particular moment in the news. The shot of the President of the United States, caught as he ponders a question, reveals the moment as columns of words cannot. The beauty, the grace, and the swiftness of the high hurdler in action are shown as the best of sports writers cannot describe him. The tense faces of the relatives of the trapped miners as they watch the rescue elevator come to the surface —what words can match the first-rate photograph? The quality photograph does not tell the reader about a given scene; it does not show it to him; it *brings* it to him. Modern photography, with its ability to reveal minute detail, is often superior to seeing the actual incident. How many persons, for example, have the vision and the vantage point to see the aspects revealed by most photographs? The old statement, "A picture is worth a thousand words," is understatement in the light of modern photography.

The second function of the photograph is *to generate interest*. The shot of the baseball player sliding in just ahead of the tag, the picture of the foreign statesman in native garb, the photograph of the sleek destroyer under way, and the many other cuts in a single issue of the newspaper create an interest that could not exist otherwise. The studies that reveal that more persons look at the pictures than at any other single feature come as no surprise to newspapermen. They have long since observed the car riders, the purchasers of the paper at the corner newsstand, and the guests sitting in the hotel lobby as they open their papers. The eye may be temporarily detracted by a banner line or a startling headline, but inevitably it fastens on the pictures. In fact, many readers go through the paper examining the pictures before anything else. Placing photographs on inside pages, especially those containing many small advertisements, is done for good purpose—photographs are eye stoppers. The reader invariably pauses before turning the page.

The third function of the photograph is *to give another dimension* to a newsworthy figure. The person about whom one reads daily invariably raises the question, "What does he look like?" The central figure in a crime, the principals in the court battle, and every other major news personality—all are photographed to satisfy this question. In those instances where the personality cannot be photographed (courtrooms, closed door sessions, etc.), an artist frequently makes a pencil sketch. The reader's desire to know the face of the personality met in the newspaper also accounts for the use of cuts, usually half-column, of columnists and others who write on a day-to-day basis. The reader, newspapers know, wants to see the picture of the person whom he reads just as he likes to see the picture of the radio announcer whom he hears day after day.

The fourth function of photographs is that of using a portrait *to make a brief but important announcement.* If, for example, a company has promoted its sales manager to vice-president, the newspaper can scarcely make a big story of this single fact. In such instances, however, a portrait suddenly becomes an excellent means of making the announcement.

396

The newspaper simply runs a one-column cut with two or three underlines. Newspapers like portraits in such instances for use on their business page. The business page, as can readily be seen, is often a difficult one for which to find pictures.

The fifth function of the photograph is immediately understandable; it is *to make the page attractive*. Effective photography can dress up a page, create a note of genuine attractiveness, and give a quality of readability not possible otherwise. To appreciate this fact, one need only select a newspaper without a single cut on page 1 and compare it with another newspaper's page 1 having an attractive pictorial layout. The comparison will leave nothing to be said; the difference in beauty and over-all appeal will be self-evident.

QUALITIES OF THE EFFECTIVE PHOTOGRAPH

A question often asked by the person interested in photography is, "What makes a newspaper picture good?" Because photography is a creative experience, no set of rules, no list of qualities, no criteria can be established to answer this question. The best anyone can do is to suggest those attributes found in the genuinely effective photograph. One must remember, however, that these attributes represent nothing more than a basis for discussion of photography.

First, every picture must have a *reason for its existence*. It should leave no doubt in the beholder's mind as to the reason for its presence in the newspaper; rather, it should impress itself upon him as something that could not have been omitted. Further, the reader should have the feeling that every picture was chosen as a result of a careful examination of many shots. He must also feel that every picture

397

fills a carefully considered place in the newspaper. He must never have the feeling that pictures are simply space fillers, dropped at random into the various pages.

A second quality looked for in a good picture is technically termed *composition*. Actually, it is simply arrangement of detail. If, for example, a photographer is shooting a picture of a group of four businessmen conferring, he should think first of arrangement. The men should be placed in natural positions, not in stilted poses that create an impression of artificiality. Next, the photographer must make certain that every detail contributes toward the central meaning of the picture—four businessmen discussing a problem. Any detail that detracts from this thought must be avoided. A coat rack behind the table, for instance, should be removed. A sheaf of papers lying idly upon the end of the table should be centralized to create a note of immediacy of use. If a window in the background reveals distracting detail, the table should be moved away. Every detail must say together, "Four businessmen are discussing a problem." This basic idea of stressing the central idea is frequently termed "emphasis."

There are many ways to gain emphasis, but basically it is attained by placement of figures and use of tone or color contrasts. The pattern most often employed to gain effective placement is termed "thirds." The area to be covered by the picture is divided vertically and horizontally into thirds. The photographer then locates the object to be emphasized at any one of the four intersections of the lines as shown by the letters A, B, C, and D in the drawing shown on p. 399. In this manner, the eye of the reader is kept on the object and hence on the picture. Whenever the reader's eye "runs off" the page, the picture is a poor one.

The proper use of tone and color contrasts can be appreciated by a simple translation of experiences outside photog-

raphy. A careful housewife would scarcely have all-red decorations and all-red furniture in a room. She would strive
rather for the color combinations that accentuate attractively.
This same principle holds for photography. A white backdrop

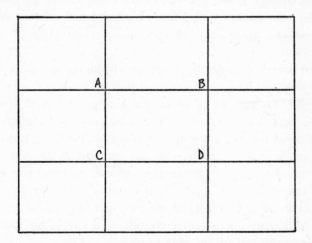

gives little contrast for a man in a light color suit, nor does
a granite wall create sufficient contrast for a gray dog. Therefore, the photographer needs a more effective contrast for
these and similar pictures.

The third quality of the effective photograph is *clarity of
detail*. The photographer must establish every detail so clearly
that no question remains concerning identity. This condition
presents special difficulty when a person must be shown with
some small object such as a piece of jewelry. The retiring
employee given a gold pin, for instance, should not be shown
holding the pin, for obviously its size and color make showing it well nigh impossible. Instead, the shot should show
someone placing the pin in his lapel or some other gesture
related to the presentation. Also, the photographer should

try to avoid pictures which show secondary figures in side face or part face. The group scene, for example, which shows tops of heads on the second row is amateur, not professional, work. To appreciate the difference between top quality and second quality work, one need only compare the pictures in leading newspapers with those of college and other publications where photographers lack either experience or basic abilities.

The fourth quality which the good photograph must have is *accuracy*. The day of artificial posing, staging a scene, or outright "faking" of pictures has disappeared with leading newspapers. Every good picture must possess the unmistakable ring of truth. It must appear as a shot taken without forewarning—a shot caught by the photographer at just the right moment. Accuracy is most often difficult to obtain in those instances where posing "run-of-the-mill" citizens becomes a necessity. For example, an obscure married couple has just won $5,000 in a newspaper contest, and the paper wants a three-column cut of the couple registering their joy. Unless the couple has histrionic ability—and such is rarely the case—the photographer can spend hours without getting a good shot. Consequently, seasoned photographers go out on such assignments wishing it were their day off.

The fifth quality is one which varies with the particular newspaper; it is *compatibility with editorial policy*. This quality places a given picture on page 1 of one newspaper and in the picture files of another. In a recent divorce case, for example, the woman came down the hall of the court building looking straight ahead, apparently to avoid the glance of her husband who was standing in the doorway to the courtroom. However, just as she reached the doorway she stopped, turned, and slapped him viciously across the face. Three photographers got perfect shots, but only one paper, a tabloid, used it. Thus the same picture was "good" for only one paper.

A final statement to be made about the effective picture is broad but important. It is that an effective picture must *attract and hold the reader*. To understand this statement, one should note the two steps in examining a picture—the initial meeting with the picture and the focusing of attention upon it. The initial meeting comes as one sweeps his eyes across the page; the focusing of attention is the stopping to examine. The effective picture, therefore, is one that arrests and holds. Accomplishing this feat often perplexes the best of photographers. Yet, if pictures are to be considered "good," they must have this peculiar ability to stop the reader and interest him in the contents.

REASONS FOR EXAMINING PICTURES

Why does a reader look at pictures? The reader himself is likely to answer the question broadly by saying, "Because they interest me." Such an answer obviously tells little. Consequently, newspapers, students of journalism, and other interested persons have made detailed studies. Their findings, however detailed, can be listed under the groupings discussed below.

FEATURE STORY APPEAL

One of the strongest forces in causing the reader to examine pictures is feature story appeal. Any shot out of the ordinary is likely to stop most readers. For example, a reader coming upon a three-column cut of an old man with a rifle standing grimly in his doorway will certainly pause. Also, the reader seeing a picture of a man holding a baby bear will stop to look and read. The appeal is simply the appeal of the feature story portrayed pictorially.

Gaining feature story appeal for photographs accompanying straight news stories is a real challenge for the photographer; yet he must meet it if he is to be successful. Attempting to gain this appeal for conventional news stories has resulted in some famous pictures. One such instance was that of one of America's most famous financiers who was about to testify before a Congressional investigating committee. As he seated himself, a photographer lifted a woman midget upon his knee. Not knowing what to do, the financier allowed himself to be photographed in this manner. This picture became one of the best-known shots of modern times, causing great embarrassment to the financier and his family but giving to the photographer a real triumph.

FAMILIAR PERSONS

Many readers habitually scan the paper for pictures of persons they know. When they see a familiar face they pause to obtain the answer to "What's he doing now?" This condition is true of the persons whom one knows through direct association and the important figures in public life. Readers pause when they see the picture of a friend or an associate, and they generally pause when they see the familiar face of the President of the United States. In each instance, the reader wants to know the individual's significance with the news of the moment.

FAMILIAR SIGHTS

A reader seeing a picture of a familiar sight pauses as he does for a familiar face; he wants to know why this sight is in the news. A picture of a well-known scene such as the New York skyline, the Golden Gate Bridge, or the Chicago Loop is enough to check the reader in his perusal of the page. His curiosity is aroused, and it must be satisfied.

INFORMATION

As one reads his newspaper, he generally finds a picture of an unusual and interesting subject. A picture of a new-type automobile, a strange attire, or an oddly shaped house makes him pause to look. Then he reads, and often rereads the cut lines, to learn the facts. Thus, he has been attracted to both the picture and the cut lines in his quest for information.

EVENTS SEEN

Just as the man who has seen the football game likes to read the sports writer's account of it, so does the person who has seen the game, an accident, a parade, or any other such event like to see pictures of it. Unlike the reader who merely peruses the newspaper, however, this reader searches diligently for the picture, and, if no picture is to be found, almost certainly he registers his disappointment.

KNOWLEDGE OF THE ACTIVITY

As the newspaper reader turns the pages, he invariably pauses when he comes on a picture of some activity in which he has detailed knowledge. Thus, the nurse pauses to look at pictures of hospitals; the teacher pauses to examine pictures of schools; the construction worker pauses to scan pictures of building operations. In each instance, the reader examines

403

the picture because of his knowledge of the activity. This condition, incidentally, has an interesting sidelight—the reader often examines the picture because of his feeling of professional competence. He looks at the picture critically with the thought of detecting errors.

ATTRACTIVE PHOTOGRAPHY

Even though a given reader may have little knowledge of the qualities of the effective photograph, nonetheless he knows when a picture pleases him. Usually, of course, a picture pleases him when it is well done; that is to say, when it has the attributes already discussed. One of the best means, therefore, of attracting and holding readers, photographically speaking, is to present pictures which mechanically and esthetically meet the highest standards.

SOURCES OF PICTURES

In addition to the photographs taken by staff photographers, newspapers obtain pictures from four other sources. They are picture agencies, publicity agencies, commercial photographers, and amateur photographers.

After staff photographers, agencies provide the greatest number of pictures used by newspapers. Prominent agencies in the United States of America are Associated Press, United Press International Pictures, and World Wide. They supply most newspapers with pictures away from home. Within a few minutes, for instance, after the Associated Press has a picture in its Washington office, the shot is sent by wirephoto throughout the nation. Because of their specialization, the agencies generally do excellent work, and their contributions in photographic research have helped considerably in the advancement of the entire field of photography.

The pictures from commercial photographers are limited almost entirely to portrait work. Many persons who rise in the world of business, industry, education, and similar fields have studio portraits made for distribution upon request. The portraits are generally glossies, so that the paper can have no objection to using them. These persons have the pictures made for the obvious reason that they are thus assured of a pleasing result. Although commercial photographers generally provide nothing more than portraits, sometimes they provide pictures for groups desiring publicity. Small businesses and charitable institutions, for example, often call in commercial photographers to supply pictures to accompany publicity releases. In days gone by, commercial photographers often requested or demanded a credit line, but this practice has tapered off in recent years.

Publicity agencies send pictures routinely with most stories, especially those of a brief nature (promotion of officials, etc.) because they know the value of a picture in the newspaper. These photographs are generally of top quality because such quality increases their chance of being used by the paper. The larger publicity agencies employ their own photographers, most of whom are very capable. The photographs are always accompanied by cut lines so that they are ready for immediate use.

Advertising agencies, like publicity agencies, supply top quality work. The advertising agencies supply pictures for actual advertisements and photographs to be used as regular newspaper material. Thus, advertising agencies are often engaged actively as publicity agencies. The newspapers in one large city, for example, obtain some of their best pictures of

405

the city's major league baseball team, without cost, from the advertising agency having the club as one of its accounts.

Free-lance photographers and agencies provide newspapers with material in those instances where the paper cannot get the shot itself. Free-lance photographers are often highly skilled craftsmen who can earn more by working for themselves or an agency than they can as newspapermen. Free-lance photographers are generally successful because they can reach difficult-to-meet persons, because they can unearth good feature story material, or because of the unusual quality of their work.

Amateur photographers are persons who generally take pictures for sheer pleasure but are more than merely desirous of selling their material. Amateur photographers are most often successful when they get a shot otherwise unobtainable. Among the most common pictures sold by amateur photographers each year are shots of accidents at the time of occurrence or immediately thereafter; interesting feature story material; pictures taken in places inaccessible to photographers (secret conferences, courtrooms, etc.).

In addition to these sources, newspapers gain photographs from many miscellaneous sources. Among the most common are the family and the friends of newsworthy figures; libraries and other repositories of pictures; and files of historical and similar societies.

MOTION PICTURES

One of the most important phases of pictorial journalism is motion pictures. It is important because it is a gigantic industry and because it is unquestionably one of the most influential media of communication. The motion picture industry operates on an annual budget in excess of two billion dollars, and the tremendous force it exerts in molding opinion, influencing moral values, and implanting ideas can never be truly measured. However, only one phase of motion pictures, the newsreel, is journalism, and it, certainly, is a distinctly individual brand.

The selection of material for the newsreel is, in itself, a peculiar process. Usually a variety of scenes is presented. The sequence, as a general practice, consists of a shot of a famous statesman greeting a visiting dignitary; a view of a fire, a flood, or some other disaster; the highlights of a recent sports contest; and something of feature story appeal, such as an unusual marriage, a strange invention, or assorted nonsense. The appeal of the newsreel is aimed at the usual moviegoer who is interested primarily in beauty contests, radio and television personalities, other persons' business, and general trivia.

Because motion picture releases must be aimed at national rather than local audiences, local news is nonexistent. Thus, one sees local news only by accident or coincidence. Also, news is selected primarily for its interest value. Thus, it differs in this regard from the material of the newspaper.

The manner in which journalism operates in the motion picture newsreel is through selection of material, photography, and written and spoken word. The person who selects the material, whether he be cameraman or picture editor, must have a well-developed sense of journalism; the cameraman must display the attributes of the good newspaper photographer; and the script writer for the running comments must be able to handle material journalistically. Consequently, these persons are journalists, even if of a strange kind.

EXERCISES

1. Select from the Sunday edition of any large newspaper the ten best pictures. What are the reasons for your choices?
2. How would you pose a baseball player and his family of eight children for the picture to accompany a feature story?
3. Examine several issues of a tabloid for pictures that are potentially libelous.
4. What characterizes the pictures of your favorite newspaper?
5. Write an account of the difference between the pictures used in any two sharply contrasting newspapers.
6. What newspaper shot seen during the last year is most likely to remain in your memory? Why?
7. Find five instances of poor newspaper photography, stating the reasons for your judgment.
8. In what ways do the pictures in the Sunday supplement magazine differ from those of the news section in a newspaper of your choice?
9. Find three instances of pictures in "poor taste" in nontabloid newspapers. State your reasons.
10. Find five instances of originality in composition. State your reasons.

Technical Writing

With the sudden and powerful rise of industry and business in the last century, a need for a new type of writing arose. This new type was needed to record the activities, to convey the information, and to express the ideas peculiar to these rapidly growing fields. Because this writing was to center about technical phases, it was soon labeled "technical" writing. Actually, however, technical writing was not totally new; it was, rather, an outgrowth of the scientific writing known for centuries. Certainly the philosophers and the scientists from classical antiquity onward engaged in scientific, hence technical, writing. Consequently, like the technical writer of the present, they employed a scientific method of collecting and presenting information.

409

To understand better the individual character of the technical writer and his work, a further explanation is in order. The technical writer is one who gathers, prepares, and writes technical material. His function is to present information and ideas concerned with a technical action, process, or object. Thus, he is expected to present scientifically established facts in a scientific manner. As a result, his writing must be characterized by scientific accuracy, clarity of presentation, exhausive treatment, and impersonal approach.

The task of technical writing has become so widespread that it is now a commonplace. Every business or industrial field is replete with technical writers, and technical writing has developed many subdivisions. For the journalist, technical writing has two major significances: (1) science, business, agriculture, and similar editors must have a clear-cut ability in technical writing, and (2) many journalists make a career of working on technical publications.

At present, technical writers are trying to restrict their work to a more limited function. They protest that they are expected to have an extremely wide knowledge and to perform too many tasks. Their objections concerning knowledge can be readily understood, especially in the instance of the small organization or newspaper. In such instances, the technical writer is often called on for knowledge in every field from ants to ice manufacturing. He is expected to pass judgment on the work of experts or would-be experts in more fields than any mortal can possibly know thoroughly.

Their objections concerning tasks are also well founded, for the technical writer is sometimes expected to be a combination of seven persons—a research expert, a writer, an editor, a supervisor, a layout man, a proofreader, and a printer. Although he can certainly develop proficiency in most of these fields, the task of performing all simultaneously is frequently overtaxing.

As a result of this condition, technical writers ask that their duties be limited to three operations: research, preparing the manuscript, and associated liaison work. The term "research" is not an all-inclusive term; it means simply the investigation necessary to determine the facts in an already familiar field. Thus, it does not mean in any case original research. The expression "preparing the manuscript" is naturally self-explanatory. The term "associated liaison" means only the details closely related to preparing the manuscript for print. It includes maintaining a contact with the printer, the compositor, and the make-up editor to clarify any problem. It does not mean, in any sense, doing the work of these men.

NATURE OF TECHNICAL WRITING

Writing is generally classified under four headings: narration, description, exposition, and argument. *Narration* is writing which has the basic function of telling a story. Thus, a short story is narration. *Description* is writing which has the basic function of describing. Thus, an essay depicting New York harbor is description. *Exposition* is writing which has the basic function of explaining. Thus, an account of metabolism is exposition. *Argument* is writing which has the basic function of advancing and substantiating the reasons for a given stand on a controversial question, prepared with a view to convincing the reader. Thus, an article advocating the lowering of the voting age is argument.

Naturally, there can be no such writing as pure narration, pure description, pure exposition, or pure argument, for each

411

type has elements of the others. Narration, for example, must have elements of both description and exposition, for who can tell a story without describing and explaining? Certainly description has elements of exposition; certainly exposition relies heavily on description; and certainly argument employs the other three forms profusely. Consequently, writing is classified according to its primary purpose.

As readily can be seen, technical writing is almost completely description and exposition. There are frequent touches of argument and narration, but they are the smaller elements. Because technical writing is composed largely of description and exposition, its effectiveness is measured in these terms. If the writer is describing a house, his work is as successful as his ability to make the reader see every detail precisely as it exists. If he is explaining a process, his work is as successful as his ability to enable the reader to follow easily, naturally, and clearly every step.

To understand further the nature of technical writing, one should note its province as compared with that of other types. The province of technical writing is *facts, explanations,* and *theories.* Although other types of writing treat these fields also, frequently they go beyond. Technical writing never does. To see this point, one need only compare technical writing with fiction. Whereas technical writing must always be factual and objective, fiction may be nonfactual and subjective. Consequently, fiction often employs an emotional appeal and other qualities diametrically opposed to scientific accuracy.

The reason that technical writing deals with facts is clearly evident. A technical approach needs facts as its basis. The presence of oxygen in our atmosphere is a fact. The validity of Newton's law is a fact. The necessity of nourishment for survival is a fact. Therefore, technical research and writings are sound when they assume such facts for their basis. The downfall, however, of some technical writers is that they are not sufficiently well informed to separate fact from non-fact. During the past two decades, for example, several writers have been caught badly "off base" in the field of clinical speech. This field has been progressing so rapidly that intensive study has been necessary to keep pace with research. Consequently, by not staying abreast of research developments, these writers made serious errors in facts.

The reason that technical writing deals with explanation is also clearly evident—in fact, the major portion of technical writing is concerned with explaining. Technical writing thus tells of experiments, processes, research, isolated findings, and many other aspects of the technical world. A detailed discussion of the forms employed in exposition is given later in this chapter.

Technical writing deals with theory because in many instances only theory can exist. Thus, the scientist and others in the technical field must employ it. The physical act of seeing, for example, can be explained only by theory. True, much is known about the parts and the function of the eye and related organs, but still only theory can explain the actual process of "seeing." This same situation holds for many functions of the brain. It is also true of many bodily processes, natural phenomena, and actions of animals. The prevalence of theory raises an important caution: theory is to be recognized as theory—it must not be submitted as fact. Also, the writer must recognize the existence of counter-theories. Examples of theories and counter-theories are widespread, for instance, in the fields of psychology and psychiatry.

ATTRIBUTES OF SUCCESSFUL TECHNICAL WRITING

If one is to create effective technical expression, he must understand the attributes of composition of this type. The following discussion treats the qualities most commonly demanded.

1. **Ability to Write Effectively**—Above all else, the technical writer must be able to write effectively. He must be able to express clearly, emphatically, and precisely the object he is describing, the process he is explaining, or any other technical subject he is handling. Consequently, he must study carefully the cautions concerning language sounded in this chapter, for there can be no ambiguity, misunderstanding, or vagueness in technical writing. Also, the technical writer must be able to pass judgment on illustrative material. He must develop competence in appraising pictures, charts, graphs, drawings, and flowsheets (schematic representations, such as a series of drawings to illustrate a process).

A common misconception regarding technical writing is that it is, of necessity, dull and routine. This misconception is without basis in fact, for, excepting the routine report which must be brief and factual, technical writing should strive for interest. In fact, the success of some technical writing demands that it attract and hold the reader. How many persons, for instance, would read thoroughly the little leaflets advertising electrical appliances if they were not written interestingly? Or how many persons would read the technical articles in the popular magazines if they did not attract? Therefore, the technical writer should realize at the outset that, because his work is accurate and factual, it need not be prosaic. Rather, interest should be a definite aim.

The technical writer naturally suffers some limitations in seeking interest. He cannot employ the suspense possible in fiction; he cannot select his details as can the essayist; and he cannot rely on an appeal to emotion as can the feature story writer. Consequently, he must depend on attractive writing and inclusion of interesting detail. A truism to be noted is that enterprising technical writers can create interesting material in practically every situation. Below are listed sentences which have made various pieces of technical writing interesting.

"Our serviceman is as close as your telephone and as fast in getting to your home as speed laws allow."

"The queen bee, in the role of the long-suffering wife, watched approvingly as the workers turned out the drone."

"The baby birds consume so much and grow so fast that they literally eat themselves out of house and home."

"The T-Ford, the faithful 'Tin Lizzie' of the Roaring Twenties, gave its riders many a jolting experience."

"The huge shovel pushed its hungry bucket into the sliding hillside."

"The technician handles his instruments as if they were Stradivarius violins."

"The architect gazed upon his plans as the fond father beams upon his precocious child."

"The open hearth man spat in satisfaction as the glowing ingot passed."

2. Knowledge of Subject—If the technical writer is to be successful, he must demonstrate a thorough knowledge of his subject. This statement is true because technical writing presupposes a mastery of the field involved. There can be no errors in fact and no flaws in reasoning. For this reason, most technical writers try to limit their activities to the one or two fields in which they are specialists.

For the writer attacking an unfamiliar subject, the first step is detailed study of every major phase. This step is often so involved that it consumes the greatest time in a given project. Yet this study is necessary because a weakness in basic knowledge automatically cancels out note of authority; and with it goes any chance to be convincing.

In seeking information, the writer sometimes faces difficulty in recognizing authoritative sources. Generally, the publications of leading figures in the technical field are accurate. Also, the various indexes, guides, and compilations of facts by publishing houses are usually reliable. The writer, however, has no such check to help him as he unearths biographical material. A writer, for example, seeking information about Edgar Allan Poe may well run afoul because of the many misconceptions and unsound biographical treatment involved. Three leading biographies of Poe, for instance, present three sharply different versions of his marriage. Thus, the non-specialist examining any of these biographies is likely to accept it as authoritative. This same difficulty in establishing truth is faced in examining memoirs, letters, and family records of famous persons because of the tendency of relatives to tamper. A good rule-of-thumb is this: wherever the slightest doubt exists, present the fact as a quotation, giving the usual footnote information.

The writer most often guilty of lack of knowledge is the journalist on the small newspaper who attempts too many tasks. Frequently such a writer attempts stories of all kinds—with perhaps a few office duties "on the side." Naturally he cannot have the knowledge to handle all types of stories; thus the mistakes result. A list of some mistakes culled from newspaper and magazines over the past ten years follows:

A writer states that water is "always H_2O." Actually, of course, it can have other chemical formulas.

A writer refers to a whale as the "largest of the fish family." Actually, it is a mammal.

A writer refers to a gesture as being "like waving a red flag in the face of a bull." Although the writer probably realizes that the bull is color-blind, the serious tone of his article raises some doubt.

A writer states flatly that one must learn to post before he can ride any horse. Thus, his article demonstrates ignorance of or failure to mention the "single footer."

A writer speaks of milking a goat from the right side, not realizing that the goat is milked from behind.

A writer uses the expression the "psychological law of association." Because there are several laws of association, this term is inexact. Probably the writer meant the "primary law of association."

A writer confuses badly the terms "misfeasance" and "malfeasance."

3. Ability to Write for Various Readers—An important but difficult ability for the technical writer to develop is that of writing for a variety of readers. If the material is for the trained personnel of a specific field (engineering, agriculture, physics, etc.), the writer obviously must use the nomenclature and the terminology of the field. Such vocabulary is important in order to gain precision of expression and general accuracy of fact. If, however, the material is for popular consumption, then the whole approach and style must be adjusted to that level. The results of a study of contact dermatitis, for example, should be couched in medical terminology for a physician's magazine, but it should be written in much less scientific language for a health magazine.

Notice the writing of the two following passages. Both are from the same issue of *Iron Age*, a weekly magazine for the metal-working industry. The first passage is taken from an article concerning the testing of metals. This article employs the technical language of the industry because the writer knows that it will be immediately meaningful. The second passage, however, is from an article dealing with a subject outside the industry. Consequently, the language of the layman is employed.

Fig. 2 shows the effect on bond strength of increasing pressure for two sets of samples, one reacted at 525°C, the other at 600°C. In both cases, strengths rise, peak and then decline. Specimens reacted at 600°C show strengths considerably lower than those bonded at the lower temperature; a maximum of about 3500 psi for the former and 8000 psi for the latter.

Microscopic examination showed no alloy zone existed for the lower reaction temperature specimens from 4 up to 12 tons per sq. in., where strength was maximum. An increasingly thick alloy zone and rapid decrease in strength developed at pressures from 12 to 20 tons per sq. in. An increase in alloy zone thickness was also noted for samples hot pressed at 600°C.

These two curves are not typical of those in the other three systems; bond strength usually increased with increasing pressure and normally levelled off at some peak value. Occasional slight drops after peaking were attributed to crack formation in the brittle intermetallics which normally developed. . . .

More and more, it's beginning to look like the 1958 session of Congress will vote the biggest-ever peacetime U.S. government. An all-time record budget (not counting war years) is in the making, and next year's election-minded Congress will stamp approval on most of it. The lawmakers may even add a few spending projects of their own.

Tax reduction is out the window, of course; and a return to a red-ink budget is likely if overall government spending continues to rise.

The writer, of course, faces no difficulty when he writes for a professional reader; he does, however, face genuine difficulty when he writes for the nonprofessional reader. At every turn he must strive for a mid-course between leaving his reader in the dark and insulting his intelligence by childish language. In the instance of the contact dermatitis article cited, for example, should the writer for the health magazine speak of the "epidermis" or the "top layer of skin"? Should he speak of a "subcutaneous" infection or an "infection below the skin"?

The secret of writing successfully for a particular group lies in knowing the common ground that exists between writer and reader. The existence of common ground is assured by (1) knowing that the facts stated are comprehensible, (2) arranging a logical pattern of details, and (3) using images, analogies, illustrations, and vocabulary that are immediately clear. Sometimes this common ground is clearly evident, as in the instance of the article for the professional journal. Other times, however, it must be created by definition and explanation, as in the instance of the article for the popular magazine.

4. Verifiability—Good technical writing must be characterized by verifiability. This statement means that the procedure of presenting evidence must enable the reader to check every fact as he proceeds. Thus, reading technical writing is comparable to the auditor's checking an accountant's balance sheet. The auditor first ascertains a few key facts. Then, knowing these facts to be accurate, he checks the accountant's "conclusions." In the instance of the technical writing, the writer is the accountant and the competent reader is the auditor.

Verifiability can be understood further by considering a common form of technical writing, the college physics laboratory experiment. The student first states clearly the purpose of the experiment. Then he tells of the equipment involved,

419

the procedure followed, the results obtained, and hence the accomplishment of purpose. Certainly every step in the entire experiment must be clearly verifiable in the mind of the reader, for, when such is not the case, the writing loses its validity. The same truth holds for the technical writer. He must present or cite all the evidence needed to verify the writing.

In considering verifiability, the writer must be able to distinguish between nonquestionable and questionable fact. To illustrate this difference, a specific example is helpful. The fact that rain falls in Chicago is nonquestionable because it is clearly established. If, however, a writer states that in a specific year Chicago had almost 125 inches of rainfall, the fact is questionable. Hence he should cite some proof to support his statement.

5. Originality—Excepting the workaday forms (routine reports, basic statements, etc.), good technical writing must be characterized by originality. The originality must exist in material and in expression.

Originality of material is gained by giving the reader facts or views not commonly known. Therefore, the writer must have material that is new. However interestingly a piece of writing may be cast, it rarely holds the reader if he already knows the material. Originality of expression is gained through devices already discussed. The quick turn of phrase, the pointed statement, the picturesque figure of speech—these and the many other devices commonly brought to mind when one thinks of originality—must be cultivated. For even though, as already stated, technical writing must be scientific and factual, it should also strive to create a note of interest and general appeal.

BASIC FACTS OF LANGUAGE

Because a study of the basic facts of language is a prerequisite for effective expression, the technical writer must make this effort. A discussion of the most common facts follows.

1. **Language Varies**—Before one progresses far in the study of language, he realizes that it is neither constant nor uniform. Although the changes and the differences within a language are a fascinating study for philologists and others interested in language, they often represent serious problems for writers. The principal ways in which language varies can be grouped under three statements: (1) words vary from time to time for the individual; (2) words vary from person to person; and (3) words vary from group to group.

The variation for the individual is subtle yet important. A specific example should make this truism clear. A person learns today the word "nefarious." However, he understands it in a broad sense only. Later, after meeting the word many times, he uses it in a narrower, hence more precise, sense. As time passes, however, he upgrades or downgrades the word according to its usage in his reading and listening experiences. Thus, the word undergoes a continuous process of change.

The variation from one person to another is apparent upon the most superficial examination. To one person, the word "hypocrite" is a very strong term; to another, it is a routine expression for an even slightly insincere individual. To one person, the word "efficient" is reserved for genuine capability; to another, it is used for any degree above ordinary acceptability. To one person, the word "gorgeous" means something characterized by genuine splendor; to another, it means any sight that is unusually appealing. Thus, words vary from one person to another.

421

The variation from one group to another is also immediately clear. The localisms, corruptions, and colloquialisms of a given group certainly establish this fact. Also of significance are the effects of racial, religious, cultural, and other backgrounds upon the use of words in a given group. Sometimes the variation from group to group is only slight, but at other times it is so serious as to create embarrassments, misunderstandings, and general confusion.

2. Number of Words Changing—The number of words in a given language is always changing because (1) words are constantly being added, (2) words are constantly being lost, and (3) words are constantly shifting in meaning.

The addition of words to our language is of special importance to the technical writer, for most new words come from technical sources. The names of new drugs, new processes, and innovations in the technical world furnish most of the new words. The writer, therefore, must know the new words in his fields. He must also know the general terms that are entering common parlance—such terms as "babysitter," "supermarket," "coffee break," "shopping center," "car pool," for instance.

The fact that words are being lost to our language is not nearly so obvious. Some words, such as "fetch" (bring), "nib" (penpoint), "mudguard" (fender), and "icebox" (refrigerator), are now almost lost or completely lost. A less often recognized loss is that which occurs through change in meaning. For example, the word "let" (which once meant "stop"), the word "prevent" (which once meant "come before"), and the word "box" (which once meant "little case made of boxwood") have been lost in their original meanings. Their change in meaning, therefore, represents a loss as well as a gain.

The fact that words are shifting in meaning presents a problem, for one must determine whether he will be interpreted in the older or the newer usage. An example is to be seen in the word "turnover." This word formerly meant "stock on hand." However, it has been used widely in common parlance to mean "rate of movement of a given item in stock." An item, for instance, that sells well is said to have a "rapid turnover." Because dictionaries now list this usage, technical and other writers have a problem.

3. **Meaning Determined by Context**—As one works with words, he must remember that meaning is not an isolated matter; that is to say, words do not always have one undeviating meaning. Rather, the meaning of many words is determined by the context of the particular sentence. The word "fast," for example, has a different meaning in each of the following sentences:

> They were driving fast.
> We made the bracket fast to the pier.
> The observers fast for the entire day.
> He moves in a fast social circle.

Obviously the difference in meaning can be seen easily in the above sentences. The more subtle differences, however, are not so easy to detect. The word "rapid," for instance, is assumed to mean "at a fast pace." Notice, however, the difference in usage in the following sentences:

> The gas disappeared rapidly. (*A matter of seconds*)
> The digestive system works rapidly. (*A matter of 2 hours*)
> The patient recovered rapidly. (*A matter of 3 months*)

Because meaning of words is determined by context, one must make certain that a word gives the meaning desired. Notice the difficulty in ascertaining meaning in the following instance:

After administering the drug for 3 days, the attending physician noticed that the patient became blue. He then tried another drug.

Does the word "blue" in this instance mean "melancholy" or does it refer to "bodily coloring"? Because of the doubt, the writer should make the meaning clear.

4. **Four Vocabularies**—Every literate person has four vocabularies—speaking, writing, reading, listening. This truism establishes a further significant point: frequently one does not have the same words in all four vocabularies. A child, for example, speaks and recognizes by sound many words that he cannot read or write; and an adult frequently knows and thus recognizes many words that he never speaks or writes.

Knowledge of vocabularies is important for the writer because he must recognize expressions not practical in writing. Many expressions, such as colloquialisms, are effective in spoken but not in written speech. They add color and life to oral speech, but they often cloud meaning in written speech. Hence they must be avoided in writing. Notice, for example, the italicized words in the following sentences. Just what do they mean?

I shall be in your town on Friday night, and I shall have to *put up with* you.
As a result of this situation, you have a right to *carry on*.
The atmosphere of the market was definitely *fishy*.
It was a *bookish* article.
He was a brilliant *fellow* at the university.

Each of these expressions would probably be clear when used in conversation, but, written in isolation, they leave the reader in doubt. If, therefore, a writer wants to use such an expression, he must clarify his meaning either with another sentence or by general implication.

5. Denotation Versus Connotation—Many words have both a denotation and a connotation. Denotation means dictionary definition. Hence, "home" is defined as "the abode of a family group." Connotation means associated meaning. Hence, "home" may have the connotation of "a place where one relaxes," "a place where one is held in affectionate regard," "a place where one most wants to be."

Denotation and connotation present grave difficulty for writers because many words are used almost exclusively in their denotative or connotative sense. A writer, for instance, can be reasonably certain that such words as the following will be interpreted in their denotation: sky, broom, street, chalk, bird, piano. He can be certain because these words rarely have any widespread connotative significance. In other instances, however, many words are most widely known in their connotations: doctor, catholic, episcopal, professor, pregnant, car, trolley, elevator, warden. Each of these words, an examination of meaning reveals, is rarely used in its denotative significance.

The basic problem of denotation versus connotation is, therefore, how should words having both be used? Science answers this question by using words primarily in their denotative sense. The word "circular" means "that which is a circle"; it does not mean merely "round." The word "tolerance" in physics means "allowance"; in psychology it means "ability to withstand mental strain." It is never used in either science as a synonym for "benevolent attitude."

Science, however, is forced to use many words in their connotative sense. The following group of words will illustrate the point: apprentice, learner, pupil, student. Although each of these words means "one who is engaged in the process of learning," each implies a distinct type of learner. The

425

apprentice is one who has stated formally his desire to learn a given trade or craft (carpentry, jewelry making, baking, etc.) and is now "serving his time." The *learner* is simply one who is learning to perform a given act (learning to drive a car, to operate an elevator, to become a sales person). The *pupil* is one who is taking private lessons (a piano pupil, a voice pupil, a dance pupil) or a child enrolled in the elementary grades. The term "student" begins where the term "pupil" ends in the school process. It means every formally enrolled person from the junior high school level upward through graduate school. The scientist, therefore, must use these words accordingly.

6. **Abstract Versus Concrete Words**—All detail is either abstract or concrete. Abstract detail is that for which one can visualize no physical image. This sentence, for example, is abstract: "Virtue is its own reward." Concrete detail is that for which one is able to visualize a physical image. This sentence is concrete: The test tube was filled with a greenish fluid.

Although sometimes the technical writer must use abstractions, he should exercise care. If he is certain that the abstraction will be clear to his readers, he can simply state it. In other instances, however, he must make it clear by translating it into concrete detail. Note the following passage:

Mass hysteria is a deterrent to progress. Because our citizenry is becoming emotional about this crisis, we face additional difficulty in reaching a solution to this problem.

This passage opens with abstract detail, but the next sentence resolves it into a concrete image. Thus, the reader is able to interpret the abstract detail immediately.

7. **Scientific Versus Nonscientific Language**—Language can be classified in many ways. It can be formal or informal,

accepted or not in "good usage," conversational or written, and several other such distinctions. For the technical writer, the important classification is scientific versus nonscientific.

Scientific language is that which has an established, precise meaning admitting of no latitude. It is the language which conveys to every informed person the same thought. If, for instance, someone writes, "The meter registered 4,231 kilo-watt-hours," there can be no latitude of interpretation. By virtue of the phraseology, everyone knowing these words obtains precisely the same meaning. On the other hand, if the same person writes, "It was a fairly pleasant early summer day," there can be no precise meaning. "Fairly," "pleasant," "early," and "summer" are words which can be interpreted broadly; they have a wide variety of meanings. Thus, this language is nonscientific.

One's first thought is that the technical writer should use scientific language exclusively. This would be an ideal situation if it were possible. However, as the writer soon learns, there are two principal reasons why such can never be.

First, there are many situations wherein scientific accuracy is not possible. How, for example, can anyone speak scientifically of the superiority of appearance of one kitchen sink over another? Certainly he can compile statistics to show that on a given day in a given set of circumstances more women preferred one sink to the other, but statistics in this instance would not constitute scientific proof.

The second reason that scientific language cannot be used exclusively is that many broad terms have no synonyms. The term "wall," for instance, is a broad term. A wall may be of brick, plaster, steel, stone, or any other solid. It may be thick or thin, permanent or temporary, transparent or nontransparent. Hence, such a term needs qualifying adjectives to help. Thus, a sentence approaching scientific accuracy would read: "A seven-inch cement wall was erected. The composition was two thirds grade A sand to one third grade A cement."

The technical writer, therefore, should use scientific language wherever possible. When he is unable to do so, he must qualify his words with the precise modifiers that make his meaning clear.

8. **Misused Words**—One of the pitfalls facing writers is the misused word. Every day one can find words misused by persons of all intellectual levels. This situation is dangerous because the misuse of a word tends to increase in geometrical, rather than arithmetical, progression. As a result, there are currently many words which are widely misused.

A few examples will serve to clarify this point. The word "impeach" does not mean to "remove from office"; it means to "bring to trial with a view to removing from office." Hence, one President of the United States (Johnson) has been impeached, but no President has been removed from office. Another such word is "alibi." This term means a formal defense that one was "not at the scene of the crime when the crime was committed"; it does not mean "weak excuse." However, this word has been misused so widely that it is now acceptable colloquially for "weak excuse." Obviously, no careful writer uses it in such a manner. An even more embarrassing usage concerns the word "sadistic." This word, commonly used to signify an interest in gory details, actually means a form of sexual perversion.

The only caution to be given the writer is to check the meaning of every doubtful word, to examine word usage routinely, and to watch for new meanings for familiar words. The new meaning, sad to relate, often serves to inform one that he has been misusing a familiar word.

9. **Unacceptable Words**—In every language there are words which are considered unacceptable. The reasons for re-

jecting these words vary according to the particular form. For instance, vulgarisms are not accepted primarily because there is already an acceptable word to cover the instance; hence, there is no reason to accept a distortion as a synonym. Why, for example, should authorities accept "enthuse" when "enthusiastic" is already sanctioned? Or why should the distortion "complected" be accepted as a synonym for "complexioned"? Slang is not accepted because it generally lacks preciseness, it seldom has any universality of meaning, and it rarely survives for any long period. Most other unacceptable words (localisms, corruptions, etc.) are also rejected by authorities for good reasons.

Writers must be wary of using unacceptable words, even though the temptation is often strong, because (1) a question of the writer's general intellectual level is raised and (2) unacceptable words are often vague, confusing, and otherwise objectionable.

10. **Standards of Usage**—The writer must be aware of standards of usage in order to be understood and to be recognized as one who uses language carefully.

A problem, however, arises from the fact that standards, like language, change, thus necessitating the need for keeping abreast of changes. A few short years ago, for example, ending a sentence with a preposition was unthinkable. Now authorities are in fairly common agreement that such an ending is permissible if one would have an awkward construction otherwise. Also, a short time ago one was expected to use the "as . . . as" construction in positive situations and the "so . . . as" construction in negative situations. (He is *as* tall *as* I. She is not *so* tall *as* I.) Now most authorities permit the "as . . . as" construction in both situations.

To keep abreast of changes, one must make a thorough study of authoritative writings before deciding on usage. The above usages are now almost universally sanctioned. However, only a relatively few authorities permit "It is me," "who is this for," and "he graduated (instead of 'was graduated') from high school."

FORMS IN TECHNICAL WRITING

Before the writer selects a specific structural form for his work, he must be certain of the idea to be expressed. If the idea is at all hazy or loosely formed, he should pause to deliberate. After his deliberation has given a clear concept, he is ready to think of key words and structural form. To illustrate: a writer is considering an article on the "shape" of automobiles. He wants to express his unfavorable reaction to the appearance of this year's cars. As he explores his subject, he realizes that he is thinking of over-all outline, silhouette, symmetry, and general balance. These qualities in the latest models, he finds, are disturbing to his esthetic sensitivity. Next, he is ready to seek for key words. After making notations of key words and phrases, he is ready to think of structural form and outline.

Because the nature of technical writing is exposition, several structural forms can be used. Naturally, each form best suits a given type of material. An explanation of a chemical experiment, for example, would scarcely follow the same pattern as a depiction of the customs of a racial group. Thus, the technical writer must decide upon form in terms of material. A discussion of the most common forms follows. In each case, an attempt is made to relate the form to instances of common use.

1. **Appearance Order**—The appearance order, the most common type of description, is simply the conventional manner of stating what one sees. It is especially suitable for any situation wherein the writer wants to picture a scene. It is

the form used to explain the arrangement of a composing room, the floor plan of a department store, the plotting of a real estate development, and similar scenes.

The appearance order is closely related to the "obvious to hidden" order and the "time" order. The principal difference is that the appearance order enables the writer to select and arrange the details to be described; he is not held to the pronounced structural pattern of the other forms. Consequently, the appearance order lends itself to a more informal approach.

2. **Time Order**—The time order, or the "chronological order" as it is often termed, is a straight recital of steps or events in order of occurrence. An account of the testing of a new submarine, for example, would lend itself well to the time order structure. The account would detail each phase in order of occurrence with a summarizing statement of success or failure in the last paragraph. The time order structure is used effectively for accounts of experiments, tours, operations, processes, and all other situations wherein each step is the logical forerunner of the next.

The great advantages of the time order are that organizing the material and creating a pattern for the reader are accomplished naturally. The writer simply takes the chronological order of the steps or events for his headings, thus gaining an outline for himself and the reader. With this outline, a degree of clarity of presentation and interpretation is assured.

3. **Space Order**—The space order structure is that wherein a subject is treated in terms of its physical area. An account of a geographical region, for example, can be handled most effectively by the space order structure. In fact, some geographical treatments cannot be handled otherwise. A description of the speech patterns of New England, for instance, would be almost impossible to treat otherwise. The space order structure is also most effective for accounts of

431

racial habitat, meteorology, regional distribution of crops, and similar subjects.

4. Deductive Order—The deductive order is that wherein the writer proceeds from the general to the specific. The writer makes a general statement at the outset and then proceeds to specific examples to support the general statement. Examples of the deductive order are common. An instance is to be seen in an article concerning conditions on the nation's highways. The article begins by stating that conditions are "more alarming than is popularly realized." It then proceeds to substantiate this general statement with statistics on automobile accidents, failure to punish violators of speed and other laws, and low level of driver efficiency. The article closes, as this type so often does, by reiterating the general statement.

5. Inductive Order—The inductive order is the opposite of the deductive order. Whereas the deductive order proceeds from the general to the specific, the inductive proceeds from the specific to the general. To make the above treatment of conditions on the nation's highways inductive, the writer would simply state his specific instances one by one, building up to the general, which he would place in his conclusion. Whether to use the inductive or the deductive order is often nothing more than a matter of opinion. Often the inductive order creates a note of suspense as the reader wonders what general statement will be advanced; but, on the other hand, the deductive often has the force of arousing interest at the outset.

6. A *Priori* Order—*A priori* reasoning is that which proceeds from cause to effect. Hence, *a priori* order in writing is simply that which proceeds from cause to effect. It is a type of writing that lends itself well to prognostic material. The economist, the sociologist, and the city planner often use this structural form to predict future conditions. The economist, for example, attempts to predict conditions for the next decade. Consequently, he considers conditions of the present (cause) and predicts conditions of the future (effect).

Because students frequently have difficulty in distinguishing between the deductive order (general to specific) and *a priori* order (cause to effect), some further explanation is needed. In the deductive order the writer deals entirely with facts; he presents facts to establish his general statement. In *a priori* order, however, the writer uses facts primarily as tools for reasoning. Thus, *a priori* writing is more an exercise in reasoning than, like deductive writing, an exercise in arrangement of fact.

If one remembers this distinction, he will be able to distinguish between inductive and *a posteriori* order.

7. **A Posteriori Order**—*A posteriori* reasoning is that which proceeds from effect to cause. Hence, *a posteriori* order in writing is simply that which proceeds from effect to cause. Economists, for example, have been trying to explain the depression of the thirties since it descended with such startling suddenness in the Fall of 1929. The depression, of course, was the effect. The cause is still a subject of dispute. Thus, economists must employ the *a posteriori* method in reasoning and writing of this subject.

The *a posteriori* method is also used by physicians in diagnosing ailments, by pathologists in studying disease, by researchers in finding causes, and by many similar investigators.

8. **Obvious to Hidden Order**—The procedure of explaining from obvious to hidden features is used most often when the reader is not familiar with the object, process, or institution under discussion. This order is used orally by demonstrators in department stores, by real estate salesmen, by lecturers, and by others who are called on to explain something not clearly visible. It is used in written expression to explain

new apparatus, complex equipment, detailed machinery, and similar objects.

When employed by writers, this structure taxes severely the ability to present and explain clearly, accurately, and interestingly. Of necessity, it frequently relies on drawings and other illustrative material.

9. **Relationship Order**—The relationship order is simply an explanation of the parts of a whole with a view to showing their relationship to each other. Thus, it is actually a series of explanations which dovetail into each other. It is especially well adapted to explanations of the functioning of organizations, the correlation of various researches to solve a problem, and the interrelationship of departments of large industries and businesses.

A specific instance of this order can be seen in the explanation of a paper manufacturing plant. The explanation simply considers all major departments, picturing their work and hence their relationship to each other. Thus, the article shows the role of each department in the process of manufacturing and selling the product.

10. **Comparative Importance Order**—The comparative importance order is the procedure of presenting details in order of importance. This form, like each of the others, best suits given instances. It is especially appropriate for advancing arguments for the use of technical processes, defending scientific theory, and advocating consideration of pertinent questions. Thus, it is basically exposition to convince, or, more appropriately perhaps, out-and-out argument.

Examples selected at random from technical journals include the following: a highway engineer advocates a new-type all-weather turnpike; a physician scores the overuse of the "wonder drugs"; a scientist calls for more required science courses in the high school curriculum; a lawyer defends compulsory health insurance as being constitutional; a cardiologist presents a prescription of exercise for persons over 50 years of age.

THE WRITING PROCESS

All facts stated thus far should be considered as essential knowledge for the technical writer. These facts constitute the minimum necessary for handling the three steps in technical writing: (1) defining the problem; (2) performing the necessary research; and (3) writing.

Defining the Problem

The first step in technical writing, definition, actually means defining both the subject and the essential terms. If, for example, one is to attempt a scientific analysis of cultural apathy, he must define at the outset both "cultural" and "apathy." If he were to write of weather conditions, he would have to define carefully each of these terms. Then, as successive terms appear, he must define them. The technical writer should always remember two important reasons for definition: (1) definition is necessary to make clear the premise, purpose, or hypothesis of the writing; (2) definition is necessary throughout to insure scientific procedure, clarity of presentation, and ability to convince.

A problem in language arises because some words fall beyond definition. Consequently, in such instances the writer must clarify his definition by explanation. Assume, for example, that a writer wants to explain that the sales of a car are due to its "pleasing appearance," "highly satisfying performance," and "maneuverability and ease of driving." How can he possibly define these terms in terse, clear, all-encompassing language? Yet terms like these must be used in scientific writing, and consequently they must be explained satisfactorily.

Other problems in definition arise because of conditions of language already cited. Connotation, colloquialisms, misused words, broad terms, and similar situations serve to increase the difficulty of definition. Consequently, they must be recognized as problems in order to be handled.

On the brighter side is the fact that definition, strange though it seems, sometimes gives the writer an opportunity to be original and hence interesting. Some interesting definitions selected from technical writing follow: a college professor terms the light derisive treatment which one student gives another "affectionate abuse"; a sociologist refers to teen-age love as a state of "pleasant stupor"; a zoologist, before giving a serious definition, states that a parasite has been defined as a "man who goes through a revolving door on someone else's push."

Performing the Research

The second step in technical writing—performing the necessary research—includes the gathering, the evaluation, and the application of background and supporting data. This step naturally demands ability in scholarly procedures. Aside from the obvious considerations of accuracy, thoroughness, and care, the writer should observe three other considerations as he compiles and prepares his material for the actual writing—classification, probability, and point of view. These considerations, as an analysis will show, have significant bearing on technical writing.

Classification

Classification, as can be seen, is the grouping of material into categories. If, for example, one were to write a technical paper on automobile driving conditions, he would have to classify logically all types of conditions. He could begin by thinking of "normal" versus "unusual" conditions, but he would soon realize that such terms are inexact and relative. A heavy rainstorm, for instance, that washes out the main highway is certainly "unusual," and, no doubt, the light spring rain that barely dampens the windshield is "normal." But what of the situations between? When specifically does a rainfall move out of one category into the other? Recognizing this fact, the writer then seeks additional categories such as "fairly difficult," "difficult," "very difficult," "hazardous," and "extremely hazardous."

The great value of classification is that it becomes the essence of organization, analysis, argument, and presentation. When the writer classifies his material, he has the basis for his outline; he has the structure for the analysis upon which his conclusions are based; he has his arguments arranged; and he has his method of presentation.

To appreciate further the value of classification, one need only realize its importance in the great writings of all time. Classification is the basis of discussion of trends in literature, schools of thought in society, viewpoints in science, and every type of study. The ability to classify has been a keystone for such famous persons as Newton, Descartes, Franklin, Arnold, Einstein, Toynbee, and many, many others. It is also the basis for refuting many popularly accepted ideas.

A few years ago, for example, a writer deceived the public with an explanation of the low level of reading ability of

437

many American school children. He contended that, if the children were taught to read phonetically, as is done in some other countries, the situation would be greatly improved. Although this book was a best seller, it is based on fallacious reasoning refutable by the simplest of classification. If one groups language according to phonetic qualities, he sees immediately that English is not phonetically sound. Hence, handling English phonetically is impossible. How, for instance, should one pronounce and interpret the word "read" in the following sentence: "I read the newspaper every day"? Instances such as this are, of course, numerous. If those reading that book had been able to classify languages phonetically, they would have detected the fallacy immediately.

Probability

Probability concerns itself with the measure of assurance, confidence, or authoritativeness to be attached to a statement. It means, in the language of the layman, the amount of "stock to be placed" in a given statement.

Sometimes probability is no problem whatever. If, for example, one were to consider the situation of a normally hungry fox catching a rabbit, there can be no question about the rabbit's future. If one falls into water, he certainly gets wet.

In other instances, however, probability is more difficult to measure. Consider this statement: "persons of limited education are unable to grasp the intricacies of investment buying and selling." This statement is obviously true in the vast majority of instances. But in exactly what percentage? Certainly there are persons of limited education who have made a fetish of learning about this subject. Perhaps they have even made fortunes in the stock market. The problem, therefore, is to know how great their number is.

Degree of probability is naturally most difficult to determine in the less scientific fields—the fields wherein many basic factors cannot be measured scientifically. Examples of such fields are sociology, psychology, philosophy, education, and anthropology. How, for example, can one be certain how teen-agers will react to a new movie actor; how women will accept certain new styles; how men will respond to a political figure?

Point of View

In writing, point of view has precisely the same meaning it possesses in common parlance; and, surprising as it may seem, the technical writer must recognize point of view as a serious consideration. This fact is true because, in instances where material is not completely scientific, point of view enters. A consideration of cultural groups, for example, frequently turns on point of view because all facts cannot be measured scientifically. Thus, a writer preparing an article on cultural groups is influenced by his point of view. He has to decide, for example, when to consider people as being of the "lower," "middle," or "upper" classes. Undoubtedly, in such an instance, point of view influences definition. To see the influence of point of view on definition, one need only ask any ten persons of varied background, "How much money makes a man rich?" The answers to this question invariably are sharply different.

One's point of view is influenced most by his experience, his background, and his philosophy. This fact is important because it gives the writer some inkling of the strengths and the weaknesses of his point of view. A newspaperman, for example, has a close contact with the illegal, dramatic, sensational aspects of life. He, therefore, must strive to realize that all of life is not composed of these elements, else his view will become one-sided. Thus, his experience and his background—which of course also influence his philosophy—become the dominant influences on his point of view. The effect of philosophy is apparent, for philosophy gives one the values that establish one's whole outlook on life.

WRITING

As the technical writer turns to his actual composition, he should observe two considerations: (1) the peculiar nature of and requirements for technical writing as discussed in this chapter and (2) the general procedure for writing for magazines as discussed in Chapter 12. These considerations, if carefully observed, will enable him to create effective technical expression.

EXERCISES

1. Write an article of 1,000 words or less in which you explain a camera by the "obvious to hidden" order.
2. Make outlines for explaining a rattlesnake; a beagle; a mustang.
3. What order best suits each of the following: a milking machine; a paint testing site; a tour through an automobile assembling plant; a detachable plastic model of the human head; a tree nursery?
4. Select and evaluate an article from a technical magazine.
5. Evaluate the technical articles in any three newspapers.
6. How important is a knowledge of technical writing to each of the following: a professor of anthropology; a professor

of history; a professor of astronomy; a professor of comparative religion; a professor of biometry?

7. Select five instances of originality in technical writing, stating briefly your reasons for so choosing.
8. What aspects of a study of literature are technical?
9. What aspects of retail selling are nontechnical?
10. Analyze the contents of (1) a magazine of technical material
designed for laymen and (2) a magazine of technical material
designed for specialists in the particular field.

Advertising and Public Relations

Chapter

15

Two phases of journalism frequently considered under the same heading are advertising and public relations. They are so considered because the public relations department is often an integral part of the advertising department. In such cases, the public relations director is either considered a subordinate of the advertising director or he is expected to work in close relationship with him. Actually, however, advertising and public relations are separate operations pointed toward the same goal—advancing the cause of a person, a group, or an

442

organization. This chapter, therefore, will consider advertising and public relations as separate operations.

ADVERTISING

If one were to mention the word "advertising" to a representative cross section of American citizens, a variety of responses would arise within the minds of the hearers. To some, the word would connote the dignified but deceptive efforts of commercial establishments to catch as many victims as painlessly as possible. To others, it would signify a means employed by businesses to sell products. To others, it would mean vaguely certain pages of the newspaper, the displays in magazines, the billboard pictures, and similar ways of telling or coaxing the public to buy a given item. Relatively few persons would think immediately of the great benefits effected in America and other nations by advertising.

Certainly one of the greatest of such benefits is the opportunity given citizens to know that which is available in a great number of fields. Before one decides to buy a television set, for example, he usually learns through advertising the principal features of every leading brand. Thus, he can speak knowingly of price, screen size, tubes, and general performance. Thereafter, as he listens to a salesman extol the advantages of a particular set, he can cross-question and make sound comparisons. Advertising also enables people to learn of advances in many areas. Magazine advertising, for example, provides genuine education to many housewives. Herein they learn the latest developments in kitchen units, washing machines, dryers, and the many other appliances that improve the home. Certainly, therefore, advertisements perform a valuable service in this regard.

A second benefit of advertising, one frequently overlooked,

is its role in raising standards of living. Home lighting; construction material; drug, furniture, and food advertisements—all have played a gigantic part in raising the American standard of living. Surprising though it may seem, many persons have learned much about proper sanitation, well-balanced diets, guides for healthful living, and other important facts related to more comfortable and more profitable living through advertisements. To measure the extent of this genuinely salient influence on American life is impossible, but to know that it has been powerful can easily be realized.

A third important benefit of advertising is that it is the life blood of business; and business is the life blood of the American economy. Through advertising, every business from the largest chain organization to the corner grocery sells its products. If advertising were to be banned from all media for even a very short time, American economy would be paralyzed.

A fourth benefit is that advertising is frequently a protection for the citizen against fraud and deception. Although some advertising is fraudulent or deceiving, most advertising is clearly reliable. The self-respecting newspaper and magazine, for example, run only advertising which they know to be honest and hence completely accurate. The same holds true for most radio and television stations, the major outdoor advertising companies, and reputable printers. As a result, the public is protected against dishonest enterprises. Also, because of codes of ethics, a generally high level of propriety exists in advertising. Consequently, a further protection is afforded against vulgar, indecent, or otherwise offensive material.

A fifth benefit of advertising is that, by virtue of operating on a high plane, it helps to raise the general moral tone of society. The high level of newspaper and magazine advertising, for example, represents a contribution toward a sound moral atmosphere. To appreciate this fact, one need only compare the illustrative material in newspaper and magazine advertising with that of the calendars distributed for an all-male clientele (calendars in barber shops, automobile parts stores, etc.). Many of these calendars could never hang in any home pretending to an acceptable moral standard.

For the person associated with advertising in any of its facets, the foregoing discussion is important. If he takes cognizance, he will realize that he is not a huckster attempting to move second-rate items; he is not a high-pressure salesman striving to unload merchandise at any cost; he is not a spellbinder trying to soften a victim for a sale. Instead, he is an honest craftsman explaining and selling an item that will represent a valuable acquisition. He, therefore, is involved in a constructive service, one that brings daily benefits to many persons—even though most of them never realize this fact.

Basic Attributes of Effective Copy

A discussion follows of the basic attributes for writing effective advertising copy. As is generally the case in such discussions, one can do little more than describe the attribute and its importance. Presenting a formula for its development is impossible because the attribute is often largely a congenital ability.

1. **Knowledge of People**—Although the writer of advertising copy must certainly possess many attributes, above all else he must know people. This statement is not limited to those at whom the advertisement is pointed; it means people in general.

The writer must know people in order to understand the conditions that cause them to favor one product but to shun another; that make them pause to read one advertisement but to pass another; that draw a favorable response (even though they have no interest in the product) to one advertisement but induce an unfavorable reaction in another. In short, he must know people to understand the "psychology of the buyer."

Certainly "knowing people" does not demand highly formal training in psychology, sociology, and similar sciences. Rather, it entails simply a common-sense observation of people in general—their reading habits, buying practices, and other behavior patterns that influence their reading of advertisements. Although scientific studies of the reading of advertisements are available, the writer must rely principally on his own judgment and observation. In fact, if he does not have such judgment and powers of observation, he is not likely to write effective copy.

To illustrate this point, one need only consider the advertisement for automobiles. In this instance, no writer should have to turn to authoritative sources to learn that men usually check mechanical features first and external features thereafter; whereas women generally concentrate on externals, leaving judgment on mechanical aspects to the men. If the writer does not know this much about people at the outset, he can scarcely hope to write copy that sells.

The writer must also know people in general, rather than just a specific type of reader, because he must handle many kinds of copy. He may write about furniture, used cars, paper salvage, and groceries all in the course of his normal work. Thus, his knowledge of people must be as wide as his field of work.

2. **Originality**—Originality, that difficult-to-develop but necessary quality, is one of the basic considerations in hiring and retaining advertising copywriters. In fact, when a writer

has appealing originality, his success is generally assured because other deficiencies can be tolerated. The writer must develop his originality in every phase of advertising—writing, illustration, layout—for triteness is considered intolerable in top-quality work. To chart the way to originality is naturally impossible; yet a few hints can be given.

One of the most helpful is to study originality in others. When one can detect this quality in others, he is more likely to recognize it in himself. Another is to strive for new ways of making old statements. This gives practice in the all-important technique of using effective synonyms. A third way is to place at one's fingertips the various devices (rhyme, inversion, etc.) discussed in this chapter. The most important, however, is to re-evaluate one's own abilities by asking, "What qualities of originality (humor, facility with words, etc.) do I have that I can capitalize upon?"

To appreciate the importance of originality, one need only make a list of the advertisements he remembers from his reading of the past several months. In each instance he will remember because of some quality of originality—some quality which made the advertisement different from others. Especially important in this regard is the fact that slogans, mottoes, or otherwise catchy lines often remain when the other material is forgotten. Consequently, such displays of originality are genuinely important.

3. Command of Language—To write strong advertising copy, one must have a wide command of language. This statement applies to language in general and to language for advertising in particular. A command of language in general is important because the writer must never expose the advertiser to financial loss, ridicule, or damage to prestige. If the writer, for instance, is speaking of a gift of an automatic pencil to purchasers, he must state the important conditions unmistakably: for example, with every purchase of $5.00 or more, one to a customer, on a specific day only, etc. Thus the writer forestalls any accusation of a come-on or other deception. A command of language for advertising in particular is important because many advertisements are aimed at a special group (fishermen, young adults, housewives, etc.). Consequently, the writer must use language that is immediately meaningful, authoritative, and interest-generating. Notice the relative effectiveness of the following advertisements, each designed to convey the same message to workmen:

Do your present shoes tire you during your working day? If so, we suggest you try our new lightweight Toughies. They are strong and durable.

Are your shoes like iron weights? Try our lightweight Toughies! They take a beating but you never feel them!

Knowing the language of particular groups entails the necessity of keeping up to date. Teen-agers, for example, seem always to be acquiring new clothing styles which occasion new terms. The same is true of athletic groups, businesses, and similar interests. Such terms, obviously, must be familiar to the writer of copy leveled at these groups. A further problem is posed because a given term may have several meanings within closely related activities, thus increasing the probability of error in usage. The term "dog," for example, has several meanings within the mechanical world. It may mean a form of driver held to a piece of metal being machined; it may mean the catch at the bottom of a dredging bucket; it may mean the release on the gear-shifting lever of a truck. Consequently, the writer often faces difficulty in using this and similar terms.

4. **Command of Rhetorical Devices**—To be successful, the copywriter must have the common rhetorical devices at his

command. These devices are especially important in the writing of the headline. The most commonly employed devices are rhyme, alliteration, assonance, repetition, parodies, puns, and figures of speech in general.

Rhyme has proved to be highly important because of its known tendency to develop an associative pattern. How many of us, for example, could remember easily the number of days in each month without the familiar "Thirty days hath September"? This same principle tends to make the reader remember the advertisement that rhymes:

"Even in the rain and snow all our trucks are on the go."
"For cars with appeal, just see Greel!"
"Flowers from Fry will satisfy."

Alliteration, the repetition of the initial sound for emphasis, is also quite effective in many instances:

"Ford's out front!"
"When better cars are built, Buick will build them."
"Dodge dependability"
"Pontiac proudly presents"

Assonance is internal similarity of words. Such combinations as the following illustrate assonance: line, kind; ponder, wonder; book, back; rag, rug; sky, ski.

"Car care is important."
"Don't dilly dally!"
"Plan to plunge!"

Repetition, the simple act of repeating for emphasis, is used in a wide variety of situations:

"You, you, and you! We want your car!"
"This car gives you power, power, power!"
"Tell your family, tell your neighbors, tell your friends, tell everybody about our offer!"

The *parody*, which is the imitating of the characteristic style and message of a well-known work, usually in a humorous manner, has long been a popular device:

"The north wind doth blow, and we shall have snow
So prepare now by checking your furnace!"
"Good things come in Thrall packages!" (Thrall is a trade name.)
"Let Forge do it!" (Forge is a trade name.)

The *pun*, which is a play on words, is one of the most appealing devices—when the pun is clever:

"Our tires will never let you down!" (A tubeless tire advertisement)
"We'll clean, we'll press, we'll dye for you!" (A tailor's advertisement)
"A man with sox appeal!" (An advertisement for men's socks)

The term *"figures of speech in general"* is used to cover the figures not already cited, clever twists of phrases, and other phraseology likely to attract attention:

"Safety is no accident!"
"Run, don't walk, to our big sale!"
"Don't get married! At least until you talk to us about our low-cost rental of formal attire."
"Hitch horse sense to horse power."
"Today is yesterday's tomorrow!"
"Make money by spending money."
"Yesterday a dream—today a dream room."
"Less work; more leisure. More leisure; more trouble."

5. Ability to Handle Facts—A final attribute necessary to write effective copy is the ability to handle facts. This attribute involves the ability to recognize, evaluate, and arrange the facts in a given advertisement. A copywriter, for example, may be given a set of details concerning a shoe sale. As he

450

examines the list, he sees such facts as "reductions as much as 50 per cent," "famous name brands," "once-a-year sale," "not all sizes available," "no refunds or exchanges," "store open until 9 o'clock on Wednesday and Friday evenings," "latest styles."

The writer must note immediately that the important details are "sale," "once a year," "reductions as much as 50 per cent," "famous name brands," "latest styles." He must further realize that "no refunds or exchanges" is strong language. Consequently, this idea must be recast to read less aggressively, as, for example, "Because of the special nature of this gigantic event, all sales must be final."

In this initial handling of facts, the writer often gets his headline almost immediately. In the above situation, for example, the writer would probably settle immediately upon "Once-a-Year Sale of Famous Name Brand Shoes."

Although the handling of facts is actually nothing more than good common sense, the writer must guard and check continually to place the emphasis correctly.

Advertising and Editorial Policy

The editorial policy of a particular publication naturally influences (1) the clients to be accepted, (2) the nature of the writing, and (3) the material to be included.

The question of clients to be accepted is generally a clear-cut matter. Most publications immediately reject advertisers whose enterprises they consider to be fraudulent, illegal, deceptive, or offensive. Most publications also announce pointedly their particular taboos. Church publications, for example, do not carry liquor advertising; high school papers generally do not run tobacco advertisements; some newspapers refuse any political advertising whatever. However, every publication is faced with situations which must be decided individually. What, for instance, should a newspaper do regarding an advertisement for a book banned in Boston but nowhere else? What should be done about a book offensive to a small group? What should be done about advertisements for organizations that seem to be "on the wrong track," as for instance, a group with a distinct bias? These questions sometimes become genuinely ticklish, as was the case during World War II when a group of newspapermen sought space in a New York paper to criticize the Federal Government's handling of publicity.

Editorial policy influences the nature of the writing by virtue of announced policies. Generally, any expression considered objectionable is not permitted; any statement that is misleading must be recast; and language in general must conform to the principles of the official stylebook. Naturally, all publications do not have identical policies. The tabloid, for example, will permit screamers and other devices not used in more conservative newspapers. Also, all newspapers do not maintain an equally close check on the language of patent medicine and other advertisements that appeal to the less well-educated segment of the populace. The one unifying force among all publications is the codes of the various advertising associations, such as the Advertising Federation of America, which invoke certain regulations upon their members.

Editorial policy covers material to be included as closely as it does the nature of the writing. Publications, generally speaking, strive to keep illustrative and other material in "good taste." As a result, the scantily dressed young lady seen on some calendars does not make her appearance in the advertisements of self-respecting publications. Neither do the drawings of inebriates, mentally deficient persons, and other questionable depictions often found in comic strips and cartoons.

Client and publication sometimes disagree sharply, usually through the advertising agency acting as middleman, but the publication generally prevails. Recently, for example, a newspaper and a client had a difference of opinion over an advertisement wishing everyone a happy new year. The advertisement featured a baby attired only in a top hat. The newspaper insisted on some clothing about the midriff. Finally, the client agreed to a bowing pose with the baby doffing the hat, thus satisfying the newspaper.

WRITING THE COPY

As the writer prepares his first draft of the actual composition, he must know the general details of layout. He must know the size of the advertisement, the pictorial or other illustrative material to be included, and the general effect to be gained. These details naturally determine the length and the content of his writing. They are also important because they determine type size and over-all arrangement of material. The details of layout are generally evolved in a conference of the head artist, the artist doing the actual work, and the copywriter. Their rough draft is then subject to the approval of the client or his representative.

As the writer works over his rough draft, he should remember the cautions and the guiding principles already cited. He should also note the information contained in the following discussion of commonly accepted principles.

1. **Pattern of the Advertisement**—The writing pattern found successful over the years is built on the premise that advertisements are meant to accomplish four acts: (1) to attract the reader, (2) to interest him, (3) to convince him, and (4) to move him to action.

Attracting the reader is gained most often by one or a combination of the following: an arresting headline, an interesting layout, attractive illustrative material.

Generally one can *interest* the reader by telling him clearly but compellingly why he should be interested in this item. Perhaps it will save him money; perhaps it will improve his health, his home, or some other possession; or perhaps it will give him pleasure or satisfaction. Whatever the appeal, it must be presented interestingly.

Convincing the reader is often correlated with interesting him. Basically, it is substantiating the reason for recommending the item. The writer may rely on statistics ("By actual test, four out of five prefer . . ."); he may rely on testimonial ("So and so, hard-hitting third baseman of the Indians, says, 'I wouldn't think of starting the day without . . .'"); he may rely on self-tests ("Try . . . for one day. If you are not completely satisfied, etc."); or he may rely on any of a wide number of similar devices. Whatever device he uses must convince the reader, or the advertisement fails.

Moving the reader to action is the suggestion or statement concerning procuring the item: ("Twenty-five cents at all leading druggists'," "On sale everywhere in the United States and Canada," "Send today," etc.).

2. The Outline—The importance of a detailed outline for the entire writing cannot be overestimated, for such an outline represents a sound foundation. The outline should contain first the basic purpose of the advertisement. If, for example, one is writing an advertisement for an electric blanket, the purpose naturally is to sell the blanket. Next, the writer should list the ideas to be used in accomplishing this basic purpose. In this instance, the principal ideas are (1) comfort, (2) health benefits, (3) ease of use, and (4) economy. Now that the writer has basic purpose and principal ideas, he is ready

for supporting evidence. Thus, he should list evidence to bolster his four principal ideas.

For comfort, he can list facts to show that the blanket remains at a temperature predetermined by the user, regardless of room temperature.

For health benefits, he can gather evidence to prove the ill effects of changing temperatures.

For ease of use, he can explain the simplicity of the control, the fact that no other top covering is needed, and that making the bed and related matters are thus made easier.

For economy, he can show that no extra cost is involved in dry cleaning and that the initial cost is only a "fraction more than that of ordinary blankets." Therefore, his outline presents the framework for his finished product.

3. The Typical Prospect—Whenever one is preparing copy, he should have in mind a typical prospect in the particular field. For instance, the writer of a music conservatory advertisement seeking children as pupils should think of a typical young mother. From among his circle of friends and acquaintances he should select a "normal" young mother and, picturing himself as a direct salesman, he should ask, "What arguments will convince her? What features in this situation will appeal to her? What will really move her to sign on the dotted line?" The answers to these questions are essentially the ideas to be noted in preparing copy for this situation. Therefore, the visualization of a typical prospect is important.

4. Short Sentences and Paragraphs—Short, clear sentences are more likely to impress and remain than are long, involved constructions. Short sentences are also more appropriate because they make for easier reading. Paragraphs should be short because many readers, seeing a lengthy paragraph, refuse even to scan it. Many of these readers, however, will peruse a short

paragraph or two. If these paragraphs hold their interest, they proceed to the next.

5. Emphasis of Key Words and Thoughts—Key words and thoughts should be emphasized by italics, larger type, or whatever other device is effective, because many readers scan, rather than read, advertisements. They simply look for the principal details and ideas. Consequently, the emphasizing of key words and ideas appeals to these readers. Also, key words and ideas should be emphasized because they stand out for the ordinary reader, thus impressing themselves on his mind.

6. Natural Ring—Advertising copy should have the ease and the naturalness of friendly conversation. Any choice of words that tends to be stilted, any turn of phrase that appears condescending, and any ring of patronage should be avoided. Copy is likely to be most effective when the reader feels that he is being addressed as an equal.

This situation, as in newspaper and similar writing, poses the problem of explaining necessary words not likely to be understood.

7. Assertiveness—A mistake commonly made by the beginning writer is that of building up slowly to the main idea. Instead, he should present the idea at the outset. Thus, the copy should not lead up to the fact that tires are to be sold at the low price of $18.75; the advertisement should begin with the headline, "Tires at the unheard-of price of $18.75!" The copy should then concentrate on this fact by stating something like this: "When have you seen first-quality tires for this price? Yet we have them because we were able to take advantage of a manufacturer's close-out. And we want to pass the savings on to you."

The writer must never forget that newspaper and magazine readers do not read the publication as they would a book—that is to say, they do not read every word. Rather, they skip, skim, and slide through their reading, pausing wherever they are attracted and held. Consequently, few readers examine the material in body type thoroughly unless they are genuinely interested. Therefore, the main facts must be presented first, rather than the lesser details.

8. Brevity—One of the besetting sins of writers in general is verbosity. Because the importance of brevity is clearly established by readers' habits, limitations of space, and general effectiveness of expression, the advertising copywriter must compose as concisely as possible. Then, when his work is complete, he should pare to the absolute minimum. Naturally, he must not eliminate important detail or lose effectiveness of expression, but, if he finds that fewer words express the thought as well, he should trim accordingly.

9. Appearance—Copy, illustrative material, and general layout should have the pleasing appearance of the well-dressed person, the nicely landscaped lawn, or the attractively furnished home. Consequently, every phase must add up to an initially appealing work. To achieve this end, artist and writer must beware of crowded material, lack of a pleasing amount of white space, and any other distracting quality. Although rules can be cited concerning use of type and spacing, they all constitute one thought—that of making the advertisement attractive, readable, and generally pleasing.

10. Clearly Established Proof—Whenever a writer makes a statement, the truth of the fact should be immediately clear or it should be substantiated. For example, if a writer says that a car "gets 21 miles to a gallon" of gasoline, he should cite some proof, such as "by scientific test," "by owners' filed statements," or "in a road test by an impartial agency." Facts can also be substantiated by testimonials, money-back guarantees, free–no obligation trials, and similar devices. Any vague statement is naturally suspected of inaccuracy or actual

457

dishonesty. Examples of vague statements are "housewives tell us," "owners report," and "we know for a fact."

Some statements, of course, do not need substantiation. Examples are "insulation is certain to lower your fuel bill," "good tires are a life insurance policy," and "milk gives the child his greatest source of much-needed calcium."

PUBLIC RELATIONS

Two terms commonly confused are "publicity" and "public relations." The term "publicity" means simply attracting public attention to a product, an institution, or a person. Hence, a cigarette gains publicity when it is mentioned on the radio, a college gains publicity when its football team attains national ranking, a screen star gains publicity when his picture appears in the newspaper. Publicity, naturally, can be favorable or unfavorable. The above instances are favorable. If, however, the cigarette is mentioned in an objectionable sense, the football team is exposed as unsportsmanlike, the screen star is photographed inebriated, the publicity is unfavorable.

Public relations, on the other hand, includes more than mere publicity. It is concerned with everything affecting the public concept of a person or a unit (a business, an industrial plant, a college, etc.). The public relations program of the cigarette company, for example, strives to create a favorable public opinion of everything related to the company. The same is true for the college football team, the screen star, and every other person or group attempting to establish favorable public relations. The scope of the public relations program, therefore, is far broader than mere advertising.

The public relations man and his department exist today

458

as an out-and-out necessity in industry, business, education, and similar fields. This situation is true because many groups are squarely dependent on public reaction. Industrial concerns, charitable organizations, research centers, athletic teams —these, and many more, need a favorable public reaction in order to obtain the support on which they thrive.

Because of the nature of the public relations program, the person in charge performs a variety of activities. Naturally, his most important is that of preparing releases for newspapers and magazines. However, he also discharges other duties not normally realized. He prepares news for radio and television; he addresses clubs, civic groups, and other organizations; he works in close contact with the advertising department; and he performs or is associated with every other activity wherein the person or the unit attempts to reach the public.

The need for preparing releases can readily be understood. The need for addressing outside organizations exists because, in many of these groups, are persons well worth influencing. The local service club, for instance, often enrolls the leaders in business, industry, and the professions. The need to work with the advertising department exists because both programs are pointed toward the same goal. The need to be associated with any activity pointed toward public knowledge exists because such activity is, in reality, public relations.

ESTABLISHING THE PROGRAM

The persons and the units requiring public relations programs naturally vary sharply. With each variation there is an accompanying need for variation within the whole program. Therefore, no single formula for establishing and maintaining

459

a program can be given. However, there are certain common steps found in creating all such programs. A discussion of these steps follows.

Phases To Be Publicized

The first step in any program is to decide the phases to be publicized. Let us assume, for example, that one is to do the public relations work for a charitable agency. The primary purpose of such an assignment is to "sell" the public on the value of the agency's present work, its plans for the future, and the support needed. These are the affirmative phases of the program. Negative phases, however, must also be recognized. In the instance of the charitable organization, the public relations program must recognize the false ideas, the unfounded rumors, and the general "loose talk" which invariably exist. There is always, for example, the rumor that salaries are too high, that administrative costs are excessive, and that undeserving persons receive benefits. The public relations program, therefore, certainly must concern itself with these negative aspects.

When the objectives of the public relations program have been established, they should be recorded in precise, concise phraseology and given to every key person in the organization. By so doing, the public relations director creates a clear picture of the function of his office. Thus, he has taken a firm step toward gaining the co-operation needed. The following is a statement of the objectives of the public relations program of a charitable organization.

1. To make our citizenry think of the Civic Association as an indispensable part of our community.
2. To acquaint our citizenry with our philosophy, our work, and our goals.

3. To inform our citizenry of our actual financial needs.
4. To inform our citizenry of our methods of soliciting funds, operating our office, and distributing our funds.
5. To recognize and combat any false rumors, charges, and implications.

Area of Attention

The second step is to determine the area toward which the program is to be aimed. A national organization, for instance, needs national publicity, whereas a purely local organization usually needs only local publicity. However, there are more than geographical areas to be considered. There are the cultural area, the economic area, the racial area, the religious area, the age area, and many others, according to the person or the unit being publicized. Although these areas are sometimes difficult to locate, they are distinctly important. They are important because public relations efforts must be used as profitably as possible.

A ramification of the problem of area lies in the fact that some areas shift fairly rapidly. A population shift, for example, may readily open or close a market for a given product. Hence, the area for the public relations division of the product changes with the shift.

Media To Be Used

The third step is to determine the media to be used. In most instances, the standard media of newspapers, radio, and television are to be used. In others, however, additional media can be used—magazines, house organs, public advertising, and others. The media to be used naturally change with the person or the unit being publicized. A national furniture manufacturer would probably use every medium already cited, whereas a small organization would use just one or two. A small neighborhood improvement league, for example, would scarcely seek radio and television publicity. Rather, it would concentrate on publicity through the neighborhood press, local organizations, and display advertising in the windows of local merchants. The question of media to be used can be summarized by saying that the key factors are (1) availability of media and (2) effectiveness of available media.

Course of Action

The fourth step is to construct a course of action for the entire program. Before doing so, however, the public relations head must know the manpower hours available; the number of assistants, if any; the amount of secretarial help; and the time needed to perform the duties contemplated. When he has these facts, he can consider them in their relationship to the area of attention and the media to be used. Thus, he can construct his course of action.

Once the course of action is constructed, the public relations man should establish a definite routine for gathering material, writing stories, visiting editors, and every other duty necessary to his position. The importance of a routine is twofold: (1) the organized program is more effective than the unorganized one and (2) others, learning the routine, are more likely to co-operate. The organized program is more effective because of the self-evident benefits of planning. The public relations man who knows when he is to visit, when he is to gather stories, and when he is to write his material can thus develop the pattern that best suits his situation. Conversely, the public relations man who does not organize is usually the victim of piled-up work and a generally less thor-

462

ough job. The importance of acquainting others with one's routine lies in the fact that they also can plan more effectively. If, for example, the traffic division head knows that the public relations man visits every Tuesday at 10, he will try to have some material ready at that time. If, however, he never knows the day or the hour, a less desirable situation is certain to exist.

Evaluating the Program

The fifth step is to construct a plan of checking, testing, and hence evaluating the public relations program. This step is especially important because organizations often learn months after establishing a program that they are on the wrong track. A large steel company, for instance, recently learned that its public relations program was weak because it was built on newspaper releases. It found in its particular area that radio was a more effective means. It also learned that its best course lay in sponsoring the weather forecast. Consequently, it purchased this time and thus scored an important gain in good public relations. Basically, evaluating a public relations program is similar to testing an advertising campaign.

Certainly there are many intangibles that make evaluating a program difficult, but the shrewd public relations man, like the good newspaperman, has an uncanny ability to sense the effectiveness of his work.

GENERAL BACKGROUND POINTS

Because of the basic similarity of all public relations programs, certain fundamental background points are worth noting.

463

1. **Releases for Newspapers**—As the public relations man prepares material for release to newspapers, he should remember that his best chance of getting his material printed is determined by four conditions: (1) the newsworthy quality of the release, (2) the quality of the writing, (3) the strength of the contact with the editor, (4) the amount of news the paper has at the moment.

The importance of the *newsworthy quality of the release* can be seen immediately. Newspapers naturally are always interested in a good story. Therefore, the public relations man who can unearth such a story is certain of success.

The *quality of the writing* is a far stronger consideration than is often known. Many times, for example, an editor glancing at a well-written story immediately accepts it because he needs material. If, however, the story needs rewriting, it may well go on his filler spike or into the wastebasket. Generally, the publicity man should try to write the story as if he were working for the newspaper; that is to say, his story should be written in the light of the qualities of the good news story. Any obvious "plug" should be omitted or toned down, and every attempt should be made to erase any vestige of the publicity release.

The importance of the *contact with the editor* is also clearly evident. There should be no need to explain that an editor frequently uses material simply because of his friendship with the publicity man.

The *amount of news* on hand at the moment is, of course, unpredictable, because the public relations man cannot always know when the paper will be tight. He can, however, prepare for this eventuality by writing material that can be held for several days, if necessary. Also, he can have some general idea of certain days that are always tight or light.

464

Election day and the day thereafter, for example, are always tight; Saturdays, on the other hand, are usually light.

2. **Magazine Publicity**—The best way to gain publicity through magazines is to place a news or a feature story therein. An industry, for example, that has a new process of interest to a particular group automatically provides the public relations man with a story for the magazine leveled at that group. Trade and business magazines, for instance, are always seeking informative articles of interest to their readers. Also, the public relations man can frequently submit squibs and miscellaneous items to magazine columnists. Naturally, unearthing such material is a challenge to the ingenuity and the originality of the public relations man, but it is also a reliable indication of ability.

3. **Radio and Television Publicity**—Opportunities for publicity through radio and television lie primarily in submitting material for newscasts. This material, which is often the material released to newspapers and magazines, obviously must be written in the style of the newscast. Also, there is an opportunity to place company officials on interview programs; to associate a company official with some community activity being aired; or to obtain some other favorable mention.

4. **Timing and Releasing Information**—If a public relations program is to be effective, every aspect must be co-ordinated and timed. This co-ordination and timing are naturally the functions of the public relations director. Consequently, all releases to the press and other media of communication should be made through his office.

Although this fact is simply common sense, the public relations director must exercise great care in this regard. This situation exists because many persons within a business or other unit frequently develop a tendency to do their own public relations work, thus endangering the entire program.

5. Sources of Material—Although persons <u>outside</u> public relations work often assume that the source of material is <u>highly limited</u>, such is actually not the case. The fact is true that news centers about the main activity of the person or the unit, but much other news often exists as well. This "secondary" news takes many forms. One of the most common and most effective is the mention of <u>company personnel</u> in <u>outside activities</u>. Notice the public relations value of the following:

> Richard K. Lute, Western Steel Co. executive serving as chairman of the United Fund Drive, announced today that the campaign is nearing a successful completion.

Releases such as this are frequently pushed by two public relations men: the industry's and the outside activity's.

Another source of material lies in potential <u>feature</u> stories. Among the newspaper feature stories from a representative selection, <u>all mentioning the place of employment</u>, are the following: a story of a woman who collects odd hats, a story of an amateur philatelist with an amazing collection, a story of a man who raises pet skunks, a story of a salesgirl who collects autographs, a story of a steel worker who knits. In many instances, newspapers locate these stories through tips from public relations men.

6. Authenticity—Newspapers and other publications must obviously know that everything printed is true. Therefore, when they receive material from public relations men unknown to them, they look for <u>official proof</u> before considering the material.

Because of this situation, the public relations man should place his releases on official stationery and cover it with a signed letter. The letterhead should contain a telephone number or other information telling where the public relations man can be located readily. This practice should be followed because questions sometimes arise or the newspaper may want more information.

7. **Membership in Organizations**—Because of the nature of the public relations man's work, he must have extensive and varied personal contacts. To make these contacts may sometimes be difficult, but one easy way lies in joining organizations. Especially helpful, of course, are the newspapermen's organizations. Also helpful, however, are service clubs, civic groups, and similar organizations.

EXERCISES

1. Evaluate the advertisements in any issue of a conservative daily.
2. Compare the advertisements in a men's magazine with those of a women's magazine.
3. Cite and explain your objections to any three advertisements you consider to be in "bad taste."
4. Cite five examples of unusually effective advertisements. Explain the reasons for your choices.
5. List and explain briefly 10 illustrations of originality in advertisements.
6. Find three advertisements which you consider to be misleading. Explain briefly the misleading aspects.
7. Evaluate the advertisements in any issue of a tabloid.
8. Evaluate a full-page advertisement in a local newspaper.
9. Write a half-page advertisement to be placed in a local newspaper. You may choose your subject and details.
10. How would you develop a public relations program for a local men's clothing manufacturer?
11. Evaluate any public relations program with which you are familiar.
12. Write your description of the ideal public relations man.

Glossary

The following list represents the basic newspaper terminology in use today. The student of journalism should view this list as a "must" to be learned if he is to move about freely and successfully in the newspaper world.

Ad. Shortened form of "advertisement." Although the term usually denotes classified ads, it is used to cover any advertisement in the paper.

Ad copy. Copy for an advertisement. It consists of all matter to be printed, with appropriate directions for setting and arranging.

Add. Additional parts of a story. When the first page of a story is sent to the composing room, it is marked "number 1" or "page 1." The next page is marked "add 1" or "page 2," according to the system used by the particular newspaper. The term "add" is employed similarly by the wire services to identify the consecutive parts of the stories filed.

Advance. Story not to be released until a specified time or until a definite order has been issued. In this category are wire service stories released in advance and advance copies of speeches.

Agate. 5½ point type. (See p. 171.) This is the smallest type used by most newspapers.

Glossary

Alley. Aisle in the composing room. Hence, there are the ad alley, the linotype alley, the proofreader alley, etc.

All in hand. Denoting the fact that all copy has been given to the linotype operators.

All up. Term used as a synonym for the sentence, "The copy has all been set in type." It is also used by the various departments of the newspaper to indicate that their work has been completed.

Angle. Viewpoint or premise from which a story is to be written or the slant taken. Hence, the angle may be humorous, serious, etc. (See p. 206.)

A. P. Associated Press.

Art. Pictures used in a newspaper.

Assignment. News-gathering task assigned to a reporter or a picture-taking task assigned to a photographer.

Assignment book. Editor's record of assignments. The record usually bears the name of the story and the reporter to whom it has been assigned.

Astonisher. (1) Name applied by some newspapers to a banner line; (2) name applied by some newspapers to a startling lead; (3) newspaper slang for an exclamation point.

Axe-grinder. (1) Editorial that purports to be news; (2) person who has a personal motive (usually publicity for a cause) in supplying news to a paper.

Bad break. Term used to denote any situation wherein the type causes an unpleasant appearance; as, for instance, a short line at the opening of a second column.

Bank. (1) Lines under the headline that enlarge upon or add to the ideas in the headline (see p. 176); (2) slanting table on which type is kept in the composing room.

Banner. Line that crosses the entire page or the greater part of the page. Also known variously as a "streamer," a "banner line," and a "screamer."

Bastard type. Type that does not conform to the standard system of "one point equals $\frac{1}{72}$ inch."

Beat. (1) Story printed by one newspaper before its rivals have been able to obtain it; (2) story that is the exclusive property of one newspaper; (3) district or special news source (courts, city hall, etc.) assigned to a reporter. In the first two uses listed, the term "beat" is synonymous with the terms "scoop" or "exclusive."

Bleeding cut. Cut that touches the outside edges of either of the outside columns. Once viewed as a serious error, the bleeding (or bleed) cut is now used widely in the newspaper and book world.

Blind interview. One wherein the person interviewed is quoted but not named. Examples are "a White House spokesman," "a high government authority," "an unimpeachable source."

Body type. Type used in the body of the story. Newspaper body type is generally 7 or 8 point.

Break. (1) Actual occurrence of events that are newsworthy (thus, a story "breaks" when it happens); (2) release of facts for a story (thus, a story is given reporters with the understanding that they will "break" it at a specified time); (3) point at which printed matter "breaks" to be continued in another column.

Bromide. Overused expression such as "hall of fame," "quick as a deer," "fleecy clouds," etc. Also termed a "cliché," a "trite expression," a "stereotype."

Bug. (1) Ornament used in a headline; (2) sending apparatus used by a telegrapher.

Bulldog. (1) Name given to the first edition of a newspaper; (2) name sometimes given to a specially printed edition.

Bullpup. First mail edition of a Sunday newspaper.

By-line. Reporter's name placed over the story. Thus we read, "By Joseph K. Preston."

Cablese. Abbreviated or coded copy sent by cable.

Canned copy. Copy provided by publicity agents and others desiring publicity. (See p. 62.)

Caps. Abbreviation for capital letters.

Caption. (1) Heading; (2) heading over a picture.

Case. (1) Cabinet at which the printer works; (2) terminology used for capital and small letters. Thus, a printer speaks of "upper case" and "lower case" letters.

Catchline. Guideline or slugline used to identify a story before the type is set in page form. Thus, a story slugged "kill" will bear that catchline at the top of the type until the type is set in the page.

Challenge. Term used to denote a situation wherein the copyreader reports his doubts of a story's authenticity to the slotman.

Chase. Frame in which all the metal (type, cuts, etc.) for a given page is placed. In large print shops, the stereotype mat is cut from the chase; in small print shops, the chase is used on the press.

Cheesecake. Slang used within and without the newspaper world to denote pictures of shapely women, especially emphasizing their legs.

C.l.c. Abbreviation used for capital and lower case letters.

Clear. Term used to indicate completed action. Thus, a story "clears" the copy desk when it leaves for the composing room. When a department completes its work, it is said to be "all clear." Thus, the city room is "all clear" when all stories for an edition have been written and sent to the copy desk.

Circus make-up. Make-up wherein many headlines of various kinds and sizes are used. The idea is to have each story act as a circus barker to attract attention. (See p. 198.)

City editor. Editor in charge of local news. On very large papers, this editor may have so many reporters and rewrite men working for him that a separate room is required. This room is appropriately termed the "city room."

Clean. Term used to denote copy or proof which needs few corrections.

Clipsheet. Sheet of stories supplied by a publicity agent or agency. Because the sheet has printing on only one side, it may be clipped as desired.

Col. Abbreviation for "column."

Condensed type. Narrow, hence "condensed," type. (See p. 173.)

Copy. (1) Material to be set in type, as news copy, ad copy, etc.; (2) person about whom a story is to be written. Colorful public figures, for instance, sometimes are referred to as "good copy."

Copyboy. Boy who carries copy from one department or person to another. He also does errands and performs other minor duties in the news room. Frequently, he is termed an "office boy."

Copycutter. Composing room employee who assigns copy to linotype operators. His name arises from the fact that he frequently cuts copy apart, especially on long stories, to speed the copy into print.

Correspondent. (1) Person who submits news from his home town or area, usually on a space basis, to a newspaper; (2) reporter assigned by his newspaper to a distant news source. Most large newspapers in the United States, for instance, maintain correspondents in their own state capitals and in Washington, D.C.

Cover. To handle an assignment. Hence, a reporter "covers" a story by getting the facts and a photographer "covers" the story by getting the pictures.

Credit line. Line that credits a source. Examples of the credit line are the wire service credits at the opening of the story and the line beneath a photograph crediting a photographer or an agency.

Crossline. Single-line headline. (See p. 176.)

Cub. Beginning reporter.

Cut. (1) Metal plate bearing a picture or illustrative material; (2) copyreader's term for eliminating material from a story.

Cut line. Term used synonymously with "caption for a cut." Sometimes called "underline." The term "cut lines" usually means the lines under the cut, but it may also include the lines over a cut.

Cutoff. Rule placed across one or more columns in order to make a solid line.

Dagger. Reference mark.

Dateline. (1) Line at the beginning of a story giving the point and/or the date of origin; (2) lines across the top of the page giving the date and the name of the newspaper.

Dead. (1) Part of the newspaper already in type in which no further changes will be made (the classified ad section, for instance, is "dead" several hours before the presses begin); (2) metal page already used that will not be used again. Generally, a pressroom employee strikes the type page with a hammer to deface it and then returns it to the stereotype department for remelting. (*Note*—the terms "killed" and "dead" must not be confused.)

Deadline. Time at which all the work of a given department must be completed. Thus, there are deadlines for the news department, the copy desk, and the various departments of the composing room and the pressroom.

Deck. Part of a head that adds to or enlarges upon the main lines. Also termed a "bank." (See p. 176.)

Desk. (1) Copy desk; (2) place of authority. Hence, a reporter calls the "desk" (the city editor or his assistant).

Devil. Term used to denote a "printer's apprentice."

District man. Reporter assigned to cover a definite section of the city. He maintains a vigilance over hospitals, police stations, morgues, and other places likely to be news sources. He is known also as a "legman."

Dog watch. Period after all regular issues have gone to press, but some personnel stay on duty to watch for material for replates or extra editions. Also known as the "lobster trick."

Dope. Slang term for advance news story material, background material for a story, actual facts of a story.

Double leading. Placing of two, rather than just one, metal strips between lines of type to fill out space as the page is set in metal form.

Double struck. Two-page layout made up as a single unit. The double struck is often used in department store advertising.

Doublet. Word or material set twice by mistake and repeated in the same issue. A synonymous term is "dupe."

Down style. Style of writing wherein the use of capitals is reduced to a minimum. Its opposite is, of course, the "up" style.

Glossary

Drop lines. Lines of a slanted headline.

Dummy. Diagram showing the position of stories, features, cuts, ads, etc., that are to appear on a given page.

Dupe. Same as "doublet."

Ears. Little boxes placed on either side of the nameplate on the first page of the various sections of the paper. The ears usually give circulation figures, a slogan, the name of the edition, or some similar statement.

Editor. Name given loosely to an editorial department employee who is in charge of a department. Thus, one finds the sports editor, the city editor, the radio editor, etc. The simple title, "editor," is usually given the highest-ranking person on the newspaper, excepting the publisher.

Editorialize. Expression of opinion in a news story or a headline that supposedly is nonopinionated.

Em. Square of a particular size of type. The name is derived from the fact that originally it was the square of the letter "M." The lines separating the parts of a headline (banks, crossline, etc.) are said to be so many ems wide.

En. One half of an em.

Exclusive. Story that is the property of one newspaper exclusively.

Fake. Falsified story.

Fat head. Headline too crowded for the space it occupies. Thus, it is difficult to read.

Feature. (1) Act of giving prominence to a story; (2) feature story (see p. 110); (3) comics, cartoons, drawings, and similar material used in the paper.

File. (1) Sending of a story, usually by telegraph; (2) filing of material, as in the business world.

Filler. Material that can be placed almost anywhere in the

476

paper to fill out blank space. Filler is most often very short stories or simple statements that are almost dateless.

Fingernails. Printer's terminology for "parentheses."

Five W's. "Who, what, when, where, why." With the interrogative "how," they represent the questions to be answered in the conventional lead. (See p. 64.)

Flag. (1) Piece of lead placed in a projecting position in a column of type to warn the printer that a change is to be made; (2) name plate of the newspaper; (3) editorial heading.

Flag waver. Newspaper that emphasizes patriotism excessively.

Flash. Wire service terminology for the first capsule statement of an important news break. This term has come to cover similar statements sent by telephone or radio.

Flimsy. Carbon copy on onionskin or similarly thin paper.

Flush head. Headline with all lines beginning flush at the left side of the column but leaving uneven blank spaces at the far right. (See p. 175.)

Folio. (1) Page; (2) page number.

Follow. (1) Further developments in a story that has already been in print (hence, big stories almost always have a "follow"); (2) smaller story accompanying a bigger story. This latter story is frequently termed a "supplementary story."

Font. Complete set of type of one size and family.

Form. Metal square (chase) into which the type to be used on a particular page is placed.

Foto. Newspaper photograph.

Future. Notation placed in the "futures" file to remind the particular editor that a story will develop on that day.

Galley. Metal tray on which is kept type that has been set.

Glossy. Photograph with a shiny finish. The glossy is preferred because it provides better detail when used for a cut.

Goodnight. Expression used to denote that one's work is finished and he may leave.

Grapevine. Copy not limited by time. Hence, it may be copyread and saved until material for print is needed.

Green proof. First proof pulled after type has been set. Consequently, this proof must be read carefully for typographical errors.

Guideline. Name given to a story to identify it. This term is synonymous with "catchline" or "slug." Thus, a story slugged "theft" would bear that guideline above it for purposes of identification. Obviously, guidelines are removed before the page is printed.

Hairline. Border rule that prints a very fine line. Used for fine cutoff work.

Half stick. Material set in half column.

Handout. "Canned" copy distributed by a press agent or a publicity office.

Hanging indent. Headline having the top line flush to the left and the lower line or lines indented. (See p. 175.)

Head. Term used synonymously with "headline."

Headlines. Main lines over a story. (See p. 164.)

Hellbox. Box in the composing room wherein discarded type and other lead to be remelted may be thrown.

High lines. Lines cast unevenly by the linotype machine so that, when printed, they appear unusually black.

Hold for release. Line appearing as titular matter on copy not to be printed until a given date (stated on copy) or until a release order has been given.

H. T. C. Abbreviation for the expression "hed to cum."

This expression is used by the copyreader or the editor to state that the story is to be set before the head is decided on.

Human interest angle. Appeal of the personal element, apart from the straight facts, of a given story. (See p. 111.)

I. N. S. International News Service.

Insert. Term used to cover material to be placed in the body of type already set.

Ital. Abbreviation for "italics."

Jump. Part of a story continued on another page. The lines telling where the jump is located are called the "jump lines" (e.g., "Continued on page 7, column 5"); and the headline over the continued part is called the "jump head."

Kill. (1) To decide not to use (hence to kill) a given story; (2) to discard type already in galley or page form; (3) to deface by striking with a hammer a type page so that it may not be used. The last situation occurs in the pressroom as pages are taken from the presses after a printing.

Label head. Head that lacks life or originality. So called because it presents the appearance of having been seen, like a label, many times before.

Layout. Same as "spread."

L. C. Abbreviation for "lower case" letters.

Lead. Introductory sentences of a story. (See p. 64.)

Leaders. Row of dots.

Legman. District man. (See p. 60.)

Library. Newspaper repository for cuts, clippings, editions, reference material, etc., commonly needed. Also known as the "morgue."

Glossary

Lobster trick. Same as "dog watch."
Local. (1) Sometimes a synonym for "city," as "local room"; (2) a local story.
Localize. To emphasize the local angle of a story.

Make-up. Self-explanatory term covering the arrangement of material on a given page. (See pp. 190–203.) The representative of the editorial departments in the composing room is the "make-up editor"; the composing room employee who assembles and arranges the type is the "make-up man."
Masthead. Information in every issue of every paper listing the place of publication, the top officials, and other pertinent facts about the newspaper. Usually on the editorial page.
Mat. Abbreviation for "matrix."
Matrix. (1) Brass mold used for type casting; (2) papier-mâché or fiber impression of a photoengraving or a page used in casting lead.
M. E. Abbreviation for "managing editor."
Mill-line rate. Advertising rate per agate line per million copies circulated.
More. Term written and encircled at the bottom of news sheets when copy extends over two or more pages. At the bottom of the last sheet, the writer uses one of the conventional signs (30, etc.) to indicate that copy has been completed.
Morgue. Term synonymous with "library."
Must. (1) Story which an executive decrees must be used; (2) employee whose rise is assured.

Name plate. Large heading on page 1 which gives the paper's name.

News summary. (1) Index or summary of the day's news; (2) wire service round-up of the day's or the week's news.

Night side. Term used to cover employees working the night shift.

Nonpareil. (1) 6-point type; (2) unit of measurement for type widths.

Obituary. Biography of a dead person, usually run at the time of the death. Also known as an "obit." Obituaries of well-known people are generally written in advance so that, in case of sudden death, they are ready for use.

Overline. Term used to denote "caption over a cut."

Overmatter. Synonymous with "overset."

Overset. Material set in type that cannot be used because the allotted space is already full. Synonymous terms are "overmatter" and "overs."

Pad. To make a story longer by padding it out.

Page proof. Proof of the entire page. Such a proof is rarely taken of news pages but is frequently pulled on feature material pages of the Sunday edition.

Photojournalism. Emphasis on pictures as a means of relating news.

Pi. Term used to denote type so badly jumbled as to be beyond use. Also spelled "pie."

Pic. Picture.

Pica. 12-point type. (See p. 171.)

Pick-up. Self-explanatory term used at close of newly set material to indicate that such material is to precede material already set. Thus, a new lead may read: "Pick up 'At the time the judge, etc.'" Abbreviated, P.U.

Pictorial journalism. Relating a story through a sequence of pictures.

Picture editor. The editor in charge of pictures. His duty

---

may be simply to write the lines for all pictures used in the paper, or he may have further duties extending to being in full charge of a corps of photographers.

Pig iron. (1) Heavy, serious material; (2) material that allows no opportunity for light treatment.

Pix. Pictures.

Plane. Wooden block used by the printer to make certain that the type surface of the page is smooth. The printer slides the block over the type, tapping the block lightly with a mallet.

Plate. Metal page made by the stereotype department to be placed on the presses.

Play up. To emphasize an angle of a story or to emphasize any material that is being placed in print.

P. M. Paper that appears in the afternoon.

Police blotter. Record kept in police stations of arrests. The district man checks the police blotter for information.

Pork. (1) Material that can be saved from one edition to another; (2) material that can be prepared and saved for use at almost any time.

Precede. Material that precedes a story. Examples of precedes are late bulletins placed before stories already set in type, editors' notes, and explanations.

Q-A. Question and answer material. This kind of material is used in stories telling of extensive questioning. Examples are court proceedings, congressional investigation hearings, and lengthy interviews.

Quad. Blank type character or space which presents a printed square because its width equals its height.

Query. (1) Question sent by telegraph to a newspaper by a correspondent asking whether a given story is wanted and the desired length; (2) question sent to a newspaper

482

by one of its regular reporters about a story; (3) question received by mail from a reader and answered in print.

Quotes. (1) Synonym for "quotation marks"; (2) synonym for "direct quotations."

Rack. Cabinet used for the storage of type.

Read-in. Printed material, two or more columns wide, that reads into one column to the right.

Read-out. Printed material, two or more columns wide, that reads into one column to the left.

Release copy. Copy received by the newspaper to be held until a specified date. Examples of release copy are speeches of well-known people, wire service feature stories, and important statements. The purpose of release copy is to enable the newspaper to have the material in type at the time of release.

Replate. Page of type that has been recast. The page is usually replated because a very important story or new development has been received after the page has been cast.

Revise. (1) To change a written account; (2) a second proof to check changes necessitated by errors shown in the first proof.

Rewrite. See p. 76 for a complete discussion.

Rim. Copy desk. (See p. 137.)

Ring. Synonym for "encircle." (See p. 157.)

Ring machine. Linotype machine used for making corrections.

Ring man. Linotype operator who makes corrections.

Roto. Abbreviation for "rotogravure."

Run. Synonym for "use." Hence, to "run" a story is to use a story.

Run flat. Synonym for "use as is." Therefore, copy that is to be "run flat" is copy which is not to be changed.

Running story. Story sent to the composing room in parts. Hence, the story is "running" until all parts have been received.

Rush copy. Copy that is to take precedence in being set.

Sacred cow. Persons, groups, or institutions given special favorable treatment by a newspaper.

Schedule. List of stories. Every editor keeps a schedule for his department, and the slotman keeps a schedule for the copy desk. (See p. 137.)

Scoop. Story that is exclusively the property of one paper. This term is synonymous with "beat" and "exclusive."

Screamer. Large, bold headline covering all or nearly all of a page. This term is synonymous with "streamer" and "banner."

See copy. Self-explanatory direction placed on proof when an error is detected.

Sheet. Slang for "newspaper."

Short. Very brief story.

Shout. Printer's slang for "exclamation point."

Sked. Abbreviation for "schedule."

Skeletonize. To omit from wire copy words not necessary for understanding. Wire copy is skeletonized to save time and expense in transmission.

Slant. Angle or perspective taken on a story. Also, the practice of preparing magazine articles or other material with the purpose of submitting it to a specific publication. Hence, the material is slanted toward the particular publication. (See p. 354.)

Slot. Section cut inward on the copy desk in which the head copyreader or "slotman" sits. (See p. 137.)

Slug. (1) Guideline or catchline name by which a story is

484

known; (2) strip of metal used between lines of type to fill out a story.

Soc. Abbreviation for material for the "society" page.

Spike. To decide not to use a story. This term arises from the fact that usually the story is placed on the editor's spindle file.

Spot news. News which gives little or no forewarning of its occurrence. Examples of spot news are accidents, fires, and altercations. (See pp. 50–54.)

Spread. Arrangement of material over two or more columns. Hence, a picture and a story over three columns are said to be a "three-column spread." This term frequently is used synonymously with "layout."

Squib. Very short news item; frequently used as a filler.

Standard type. Type of standard width.

Standing. Material kept in type because it is used frequently. Boxes are kept standing for such material as baseball statistics; some heads, such as the box head over the columnist's writings, are kept standing because they are used daily; many ads are kept standing because there is frequently little or no change.

Step lines. Term synonymous with "drop lines." (See p. 174.)

Stereotype. See "bromide."

Stet. Editor's or copyreader's order to the printer to "let it stand." If a correction is made and the editor or the copyreader decides to let the original material stand, he simply writes "stet" in the appropriate place. (See p. 158.)

Stick. Unit of measurement denoting about 2 inches of type.

Stone. Flat surface upon which the printer makes up the page.

Streamer. Same as "screamer" or "banner."

Supplementary story. Same as "follow."
Syndicate. Organization that sells feature material to the newspaper. Syndicates generally handle comics, columns, and other features.

Table. Term covering any tabular material printed.
Take. Small part of any story. Hence, a small part of the news story sent to the composing room is referred to as a "take."
Telephoto. Photograph sent by wire.
Thirty. The end. This term is written numerically. (See p. 159.)
Tie-back. Part of a story that ties the story back to something already printed.
Tight. More news than is needed for a particular issue. Hence, on days when newsworthy events are plentiful, a paper is said to be "tight."
Time copy. Copy set in type to be held for future use. Hence, time copy is not limited severely by time.
Tombstone. Term used to cover a situation when identical heads appear side by side. The heads are said to "tombstone" each other.
Tr. Abbreviation used in proofreading for "transpose."
Trim. To reduce the length of a given story. (See p. 138.)
Turn. A story "turns" when it runs from the bottom of one column to a logical place in the next; or when it runs from the bottom of the last column on one page to the top of the first column on the next.
Type book. Book showing all the variations of type used by a given newspaper.

Underlines. Lines used beneath a cut. Synonymous with "cut lines."

U. P.   United Press.

Up style.   Style wherein the use of capitals is emphasized. Its opposite, the "down" style, naturally reduces the use of capitals to a minimum.

Verse style.   Style wherein copy is set in the manner of poetry.

Wooden head.   Dull, lifeless head.

Wrong face, wrong font.   Type used is not of the kind (family, size, etc.) specified.

Yellow journalism.   Journalism which emphasizes the obscene, the risqué, the gory, the sensational. (See p. 30.)

Basic Reference Library
for the Journalist

The journalist should have the following publications at his fingertips for general reference. Since it is obviously impossible to list all authoritative publications in the various fields, this list represents an absolute minimum from which to choose.

In addition to the titles listed, the journalist should also have available those reference works which pertain to his local situation—school and college catalogs, city directories, local almanacs, etc.

Atlases:
Alsberg's American Guide
American Guide Series
Rand, McNally Commercial Atlas and Marketing Guide
Rand, McNally Standard World Atlas

Biographical Sources:
Authors Today and Yesterday
Current Biography
Dictionary of American Biography
Dictionary of National Biography (English)
Living Authors
Who's Who

488

Who's Who in America
World Biography

Dictionaries:

American College Dictionary (Harper & Brothers)
Dictionary of American History (James Truslow Adams,
   Editor; Scribner)
New English Dictionary on Historical Principles (Murray)
Webster's Collegiate Dictionary (G. & C. Merriam)
Webster's New International Dictionary of the English
   Language

Directories:

Agricultural Index
Annual Magazine Subject Index
Broadcasting and Telecasting Yearbook
Editor & Publisher Yearbook
Engineering Index
Industrial Arts Index
New York Times Index
N. W. Ayer & Son's Directory of Newspapers and
   Periodicals
Reader's Guide to Periodical Literature

Encyclopedias:

Columbia Encyclopedia
Encyclopædia Britannica
Encyclopedia Americana
New International Encyclopedia

English Usage:

American Dialect Dictionary
Dictionary of American English (Fowler)
Dictionary of Modern English Usage (Fowler)
Thesaurus of English Words and Phrases (Roget)
   (In addition, any of the acceptable handbooks of usage.)

Basic Reference Library for the Journalist

Facts:
Facts on File
Information Please Almanac
National Association of Radio and Television Broadcasters
  Code
Standard Dictionary of Facts
The World Almanac and Book of Facts

Proverbs and Quotations:
Bartlett's Familiar Quotations
Benet's Readers' Encyclopedia
Everyman's Dictionary of Quotations and Proverbs
Stevenson's Home Book of Proverbs

Yearbooks:
American Yearbook
Americana Annual
Economic Almanac
New International Year Book
Statistical Abstract

490

Index

491

Index

492

Index

495

Index

Macfadden, Bernarr, 44
McKinley, William, 47
McRae, Milton A., 42
Madison, James, 13
Magazines, adolescents', 377
  articles for, analysis of, 355
  business, 369
  children's, 377
  company, 373
  farm, 371
  free, 379
  kinds of, 365
  selling to, 337
  writing for, 334
    literary forms in, 339
Make-up, 190
  balanced, 193
  brace, 196
  broken column, 197
  circus, 199
  of inside pages, 202
  inverted pyramid, 195
  kinds of, 193
  panel, 200
  principles of, 192
  unbalanced, 198
  variation throughout newspaper, 202
Make-up editor, duties of, 191
Mansfield, Katherine, 344
Manuscripts, do's and don't's of submitting to magazines, 363
  symbols used in marking, 155
Market, for magazine writing, 354
Marks, copyreader's, 155–163
  proofreader's, 182–185
Maryland Gazette, 9
Massachusetts Spy, 12
Mechanical advances, significance of, in 19th century, 24
  in 20th century, 34
Mencken, H. L., 38, 40
Mercantile Journal, 21
Mercury, American Weekly, 6
Mergenthaler, Ottmar, 32
Merit system, in school paper, 280
Monitor, Christian Science, 54
Monthly, Atlantic, 365, 367
Morning Herald, London, 22
Morning Journal, New York, 29, 30
Morning Post, Boston, 21
Morning Post, New York, 21
Motion pictures, 406

Musical organizations, as news source for school paper, 287

Names, checking, by reporter, 57
  getting in the paper, 59
Narration, 411
Nast, Thomas, 47
National Education Association Journal, 368
National Gazette, 14
National Industrial Recovery Act, 36
New-England Courant, 4
New England Homestead, 372
New-England Weekly Journal, 4
New York *Daily Graphic,* 44
New York *Daily Mirror,* 44
New York *Daily News,* 54
New York *Evening World,* 29
New-York Gazette, 7
New York Herald, 22, 25, 32
New York Herald Tribune, 63, 213
New York *Illustrated Daily News,* 43
New York *Ledger,* 25
New-York Loyal Gazette, 11
New York *Morning Journal,* 29, 30
New York *Morning Post,* 21
New York *Sun,* 22, 28
New York Times, 23, 31, 39, 63, 179, 213, 223
New York Tribune, 23, 25, 27, 32, 39
New-York Weekly Journal, 7
New York World, 29, 36, 223
New Yorker, 365
News, characteristic qualities of, 52
  coloring, 78
  definition of, 50
  finding, 54
    for radio and television, 304
  interviewing for, 101
  school paper and, 270
  slanting, 78
  sources of, 54, 60
    in early American papers, 8
    knowledge of, 57
    in school paper, 284, 288, 290
  structure of, in writing news story, 64
    in writing for radio and television, 307
  treatment of, 78
  unsolicited, 62
  values of, in make-up, 202
  writing of, 64
    for radio and television, 302–306

Index

Politics, writing for radio and television, 310
Polls, in school paper, 294
Popular magazines, 374
Popularizing facts, as feature story, 123
  in magazine, 350
Porcupine's Gazette, 14
Position of stories, in make-up, 201
Post, Cincinnati, 42, 43
Post, Kentucky, 43
Post office and censorship in World War I, 41
Post-Revolutionary period, 13
Postoffice Act of 1792, 16
Prepositional lead, 126
Press, Cleveland, 43
Press, Penny, 42, 43
Press, "Copperhead," 27
  releases to, 62
  responsibilities of, 208, 209, 211, 212
Printing, beginning of, 1
  mechanical advances in, 24
Probability, in technical writing, 438
Problems, personnel, of school paper, 274
Professional magazines, 368
Program continuities, 321
Promises, respecting, by reporter, 58
Proof, in writing advertising, 457
Proofreading, 182
  marks used in, 182–185
Proverbs, list of books of, 490
Public Ledger, Philadelphia, 23
Public relations, 442, 458
  background points concerning, 463
  establishing program of, 459
  evaluating program of, 463
  vs. publicity, 458
Publicity, agencies for, 404, 405
  magazine, 465
  in public relations program, 460, 465
  in radio and television, 465
  vs. public relations, 458
Publick Occurrences Both Forreign and Domestick, 2
Publisher, influence of, on editorial policy, 223
Pulitzer, Joseph, 29, 36
Pulitzer chain, 43
"Pull out," to determine reader interest, 214

Pun, 450
Pun lead, 126
Punctuation marks, general, 143
  individual, 154
Pyle, Ernie, 42, 250, 253
Pyramid, inverted, in heads, 174
  in make-up, 195
  in news story, 67
Pyramid method of writing, 67

Quality magazines, 367
Question and answer style, 262
Question lead, 124
Question mark, use of, 149
Questions, asking reader's, in interview, 99
Quotation(s), direct, by reporter, 59
  list of books of, 490
Quotation lead, 125
Quotation marks, use of, 149

Racial groups, influence of, on editorial policy, 218
Radio, announcements in, 329, 331
  audience demands in, 311
  publicity on, 465
  writing for, 297, 310
Ramsey, David, 22
Readability, copyreading for, 138
  in heads, 168, 201
  in make-up, 201
  in news story, 201
Reader demands, effect of, on editorial policy, 214
Reader's Digest, 366
Register, Albany, 20
Relationship order, in technical writing, 434
Releases, press, 62
  in public relations program, 464, 465
Religion, influence of, on editorial policy, 217
Repetition, 449
Reporter, attributes of successful, 55
  roving, 61
Research, in technical writing, 436
Respect, professional, as attribute of reporter, 60
Responsibilities of newspaper, to government, 211
  to individuals, 209
  to society, 208

498

Index